ISSUES IN MEDICAL LAW AND ETHICS

Cavendish
Publishing
Limited

London • Sydney

ISSUES IN MEDICAL LAW AND ETHICS

Derek Morgan
Reader in Health Care Law and Jurisprudence
Cardiff Law School

Cavendish
Publishing
Limited

London • Sydney

First published in Great Britain 2001 by Cavendish Publishing Limited, The Glass House, Wharton Street, London WC1X 9PX, United Kingdom

Telephone: + 44 (0)20 7278 8000   Facsimile:+ 44 (0)20 7278 8080

Email: info@cavendishpublishing.com

Website: www.cavendishpublishing.com

British Library Cataloguing in Publication Data

Morgan, Derek, 1954–
Issues in medical law and ethics
1 Medical laws and legislation – Great Britain 2 Medical ethics
I Title
344.4'1'041

ISBN 1 85941 591 1

Printed and bound in Great Britain
Cover illustration © Daniel Pudles 2001

PREFACE

> If you think that such questions require nothing but answers, you are
> deceived. We reply with actions, just as with actions we ask questions.
>
> José Saramago, *The Year of the Death of Ricardo Reis*,
> 1994, London: Harvill, p 74

My former, and sadly late, sociology tutor Steve Box once wrote that it is to
the Preface that readers turn to learn something of their author. Here, then, is
some biography. The essays collected together in this book have been written,
and rewritten, over the past 10 years, usually either as a conference or seminar
paper or at the invitation of a colleague to contribute a legal perspective on
some particular issue or theme in modern medical practice or science. I hope
that the intellectual debts I owe to the materials out of which I forged my own
offerings are clear; but there are other professional and personal
acknowledgments that I have to recognise and I am delighted to be able to do
so here.

Six of these essays appear in print for the first time, although the ideas
with which they work have been fashioned in a number of different ways and
places. Material that now appears as Chapters 1, 2 and 3 formed the basis of
papers that were delivered at the Fourth World Congress of Bioethics in
Tokyo in 1998, the Third World Congress of the American Society of Law and
Medicine in Toronto in 1992, and the 10th International Meeting for Medical
and Pharmaceutical Research and Technology, Montpellier, France, in 1994.
Formulations of these essays were also delivered as seminar papers at
Faculties of Law at Uppsala University, Sweden, the University of
Copenhagen, the Australian National University, Canberra, Griffith
University, Brisbane and University College, London. Chapter 6, also
originally drafted as a conference paper, was delivered in an abbreviated form
at the Tokyo Bioethics Congress. Chapters 11 and 12 contain work that was
presented at seminars at the Law Faculties of Bond University, Queensland,
the University of the Northern Territory, Darwin, the University of Tasmania,
Hobart, Sydney University, the University of Western Australia, Perth, and at
the Multidisciplinary Conference on Medical, Ethical and Legal Aspects of
Palliative Care, Department of Philosophy, Warsaw University. Chapter 10
was prepared for and delivered as a public lecture at the Murdoch Institute of
the Royal Children's Hospital, University of Melbourne, and was defended
again at a seminar at the Centre for Life at the University of Newcastle upon
Tyne.

The purpose of recalling the incarnations of these papers is not only to
display one of the undoubted benefits of academic life. Rather it is to be able
to introduce my thanks to all those colleagues who have listened patiently –
and those who have not – and commented perceptively on what has emerged.
I have learnt something each time I have presented one of these papers. I am
especially grateful to my friend Linda Nielsen of the University of
Copenhagen for her generous hospitality on a variety of occasions, and to

Loane Skene, of the University of Melbourne, and Secretary of the Australian Institute of Health Law and Ethics. It was an invitation from the AIHLE while I was a Visiting Professor at Griffith University in Brisbane in 1999 to undertake a seminar tour for the Institute that enabled me to gather disparate thoughts together in a coherent form. Judy Allen in Perth, Ros Atherton and Belinda Bennett in Sydney, Don Chalmers and Margaret Otlowski in Hobart, John Dewar in Brisbane, and Steve Parker and Loane Skene in Melbourne were delightful and accommodating hosts.

Six of these papers have previously appeared in print in one form or another, although I have (to a greater or lesser extent) updated and amended them for this collection. In each case I am grateful to both the editors of the journals or collections of essays and to the copyright holders for permission to reprint my work here. They are listed separately in the Acknowledgments.

What little of medical ethics and philosophy I know has come from two sources. I worked from 1989 for five years in the Centre for Philosophy and Health Care at University College Swansea. Although I learned from all my colleagues and the postgraduate students that we taught there, I benefited intellectually most from conversations with and criticism from Martyn Evans, now the Director of that Centre, and from Zbignew Swarski. Secondly, I have gained an inestimable amount as a member since 1995 of the British Medical Association's Medical Ethics Committee. Under the chairmanship first of Stuart Horner and later of Michael Wilks, I have taken from the debates and discussions with colleagues from departments of clinical practice, nursing, ethics and law, a better understanding of and insight into the ethical dilemmas of modern medical practice. Its incomparable secretariat, now headed by Vivienne Nathanson with Ann Sommerville and Veronica English, have, in a real sense, aided my understanding.

Awen Edwards, Emma Hitchings, Alison Loynd, Chantal Omer and Helen Wright at various times did background research work funded by the Cardiff Law School Research Committee and I am grateful to them and the Committee for that assistance. The Research Committee's support also enabled me to travel to Griffith University in 1999 as part of a research leave, without which this and a number of other projects would not have come to fruition. The staff of the Cardiff University Law Library and the Legal Resource Unit, directed, first, by Peter Clinch and, now, Duncan Montgomery, answer inquiries and chase references with extraordinary speed and accuracy. My present secretary Helen Calvert – and before her, Dawn Morgan – helps to plan schedules and make academic arrangements which open opportunities for thinking and writing that would probably not otherwise exist. Alison Fryer-Jones offered patient assistance in reading a proof copy of this collection. I am especially indebted to my editor at Cavendish, Ruth Massey, whose autopsy of my manuscript first rendered it into publishable form. She then, patiently and persistently, persuaded me to flesh out skeletal references and excise as many inaccuracies and inconsistencies from the body of the text as she could find.

This book would have been written and produced much more quickly if it were not for four people; Allan Hutchinson, Bob Lee, Katherine O'Donovan and Celia Wells. Then again, it is probably also true that it would not have been produced at all without them. Each read, and occasionally re-read, drafts of what are now Chapters 1–6, in which I have begun to sketch out what I think a serious critical reflection on modern medical law should consist in. These chapters have, in truth, been very difficult chapters to write, containing, as they do, ideas with which I have been struggling for at least the past 10 years or, as in the case of Guido Calabresi's book, *Tragic Choices*, since it was first published in 1978. Allan, Bob, Katherine and Celia insisted that I edit and explain, clarify, correct and conclude. They have been both good friends and fierce intellectual mentors and critics who have between them sustained me intellectually and emotionally for the better part of 25 years. Each of them has contributed academic and editorial suggestions that have strengthened this statement. Each is exempt from responsibility for the form that it now takes and its substance. That I owe more to one of them than the others is entirely for personal rather than professional reasons.

I have been particularly fortunate that my closest counsellor and friend over the past 20 years has also been an unfailingly supportive colleague and critical observer of my work who also enjoys a genetic relationship with my stepson Joe and my daughters Alice and Lydia. Together, this crew, who each knows something of the discipline and demands, the sacrifices and the selfishness of writing, have enriched and enlivened my life and in no small way given added value and values to my work. In large part, I understand *what* I do, and to a small degree *why* I do it, through them. If there is any feeling of mutuality or reciprocity then I may even feel that it is not all without purpose. Thank you each. But especially thank you Celia.

Stonesfield, Abergavenny
February 2001

ACKNOWLEDGMENTS

Chapter 4 was published in McLean, S (ed), *Contemporary Issues in Medicine*, 1995, Aldershot: Dartmouth; Chapter 5 in Sheldon, S and Thompson, M (eds), *Feminist Perspectives on Health Care Law*, 1998, London: Cavendish Publishing; Chapter 7 in Barron, L and Roberts, DF (eds), *Issues in Fetal Medicine: Proceedings of the 1992 Galton Symposium*, 1995, London: Macmillan (copyright of the Galton Institute); Chapter 8 in Cusine, D and Templeton, A (eds), *Reproductive Medicine and Law*, 1990, Edinburgh: Churchill Livingstone; Chapter 9 in Marteau, T and Richards, M (eds), *The Troubled Helix: The Benefits and Hazards of the New Human Genetics*, 1996, Cambridge: CUP; and Chapter 12 in (1994) 14 Legal Studies, where I am grateful to the editors for permission to republish.

Grateful acknowledgment is made to Daniel Pudles for permission to reproduce the illustration which appears on the cover.

CONTENTS

Preface   *v*

Acknowledgments   *ix*

Table of Cases   *xv*

Table of Legislation   *xix*

PART I
MEDICAL LAW, TRAGIC CHOICES
AND THE RISK SOCIETY

1 **WHAT IS MEDICAL LAW?**   3

   MEDICAL LAW: UNPLUGGED   3

   THE VOCABULARY OF MEDICAL JURISPRUDENCE   7
     'Treat me gentle'   7
     Constituting medical law   9

2 **MEDICAL LAW AND THE LAND OF**
   METAMORPHOSES   13

   METAMORPHOSIS 1: SCIENTIFIC MEDICINE   13

   METAMORPHOSIS 2: EPISTEMOLOGY AND ETHICS   18

   METAMORPHOSIS 3: THE NATURE OF THE PATIENT   20

   METAMORPHOSIS 4: THE CHANGING CONSTITUTION   24
     The knowledge economy and the social investment State 25
     Holistic government and problem solving   26
     The Europeanisation of constitutional law and
       globalisation of law   27
     Globalisation   29

   METAMORPHOSIS 5: THE NATURE OF LAW'S RESPONSES   32

3 **BIOMEDICAL DIPLOMACY: TRAGIC CHOICES**
   AND THE RISK SOCIETY   37

PART II
SOME LANGUAGE QUESTIONS

4 **HEALTH RIGHTS, ETHICS AND JUSTICE:**
   THE OPPORTUNITY COSTS OF RHETORIC   47

   ALLOCATION   48

   RIGHTS   50

RIGHTS TO HEALTH CARE?   53

RIGHTS TO HEALTH CARE AND THE OPPORTUNITY
    COSTS OF RHETORIC   54

OF MARKETS AND MORALS   60

5   **FEMINISMS' ACCOUNTS OF
REPRODUCTIVE TECHNOLOGY**   **63**

THE CONCERNS OF REPRODUCTION   63

FEMINISMS' RESPONSES TO REPRODUCTION
    AND REGULATION   68

THE BIOMEDICAL MODEL   69
    The critics   70
    The Contextualists: '... no daughters to comfort her and
      no sons to support her'   71

REPRODUCTIVE 'CHOICE'   75

METAMORPHOSES: ETHICS, HEALTH AND FAMILY   76

6   **WHERE DO I OWN MY BODY? (AND WHY?)**   **83**

INTRODUCTION   83

OWNERSHIP AND AUTONOMY   83
    Ownership   84
    On autonomy   87
    Who owns?   90

ENGLISH COMMON LAW   92

BODY SHOPPING   97
    Why do these questions appear now?   97

CONCLUDING REMARKS: SHOPPING THE BODY   103

**PART III
INTROS: ENTRANCES AND ARRIVALS**

7   **THE LEGAL STATUS OF THE EMBRYO AND THE FETUS**   **107**

EARLY ATTITUDES TO THE FETUS   107
    Legal conundrums and philosophical excursus   109
    The classical common law position   114

THE HUMAN FERTILISATION AND EMBRYOLOGY
    ACT 1990   118
    General prohibitions   119
    Human embryo research   120

THE CONSENT REQUIREMENTS OF THE ACT   121
   Posthumous treatments   123
CIVIL LIABILITY: CONGENITAL DISABILITY   124
CONCLUSION   126

**8 LEGAL AND ETHICAL DILEMMAS OF FETAL SEX
    IDENTIFICATION AND GENDER SELECTION   129**
DIAGNOSTIC ISSUES   129
HOW CAN SEX BE DETERMINED?   131
   What might selection be used for?   133
PRENATAL SCREENING, PRENATAL DIAGNOSIS
   AND GENETIC INFORMATION   134
   Screening for congenital malformations   134
   Screening for chromosomal abnormalities   135
   Screening for inherited diseases   135
   The search for the perfect baby?   136
FETAL SEX IDENTIFICATION, ABORTION AND THE LAW   144
   How prevalent is sex selection?   144
   The mania for sons   146
   What is the ambit of the Abortion Act 1967?   147
REPRODUCTIVE ETHICS: THE SEARCH FOR
   THE PERFECT SOCIETY?   149

**PART IV
ATTEMPTS AND FAILURES IN MEDICAL LAW:
THE CASE OF GENETICS AND RISK SOCIETY**

**9 THE TROUBLED HELIX: LEGAL ASPECTS OF
    THE NEW GENETICS   155**
EPISTEMOLOGY, ETHICS AND GENETICS   155
GENETIC INFORMATION AND PRIVACY   159
   Medical confidentiality and the public interest   166
   Genetics and existence: the abortion section   168
   Children and consent   173
CONCLUSION   177

10 AFTER GENETICS   **179**

   GENETICS: THE REGULATORY QUADRILLE   180

     (a) Identity issues: the strange case of nucleus substitution   187

     (b) The legality of taking and storing ovarian tissue
       and gametes   194

   LAW, SCIENCE AND PUBLIC POLICY   199

**PART V
OUTROS: EXITS AND DEPARTURES**

**11 TRAGIC CHOICES AND MODERN DEATH:
SOME *BLAND* REFLECTIONS**   **203**

   ON RITES   203

   ON RIGHTS   209

   LAST RIGHTS   210

   THE CASE OF TONY BLAND   217

   NEGOTIATING DEATH AND TRAGIC CHOICES   219

**12 ODYSSEUS AND THE BINDING DIRECTIVE:
ONLY A CAUTIONARY TALE?**   **223**

   ODYSSEUS AND AUTONOMY   223

   THE EXPERIENCE OF DYING AND THE
     'VULGARISATION OF SURGERY'   225

   TERMINAL CONSIDERATIONS   228

   A LONG EXPERIENCE OF DYING AND THE
     DEVELOPMENT OF LIVING WILLS   231

     (a) The US   231

     (b) Advance directives and English law   234

   A FRAIL REFLECTION?   248

     Competent choices   249

     The identity question   251

     Identity and interpretation   253

     Directing what; advancing where?   254

   WHO WANTS TO DIE FOREVER?   256

BIBLIOGRAPHY   **259**

Index   275

TABLE OF CASES

A (Children) (Conjoined Twins) [2000] 4 All ER 961 .4, 40, 86, 216
AK, Re (2001) 58 BMLR 1 20
Allen v Bloomsbury HA [1993] 1 All ER 651 157
Airedale NHS Trust v Bland [1993] AC 789;
    [1993] 1 All ER 821; [1993] 2 WLR 316 . . . . .4, 40, 84, 89, 217, 218, 219, 220,
                                     221, 222, 224, 229, 231, 238,
                                  240, 241, 242, 248, 249, 258
Associated Provincial Picture Houses Ltd v
    Wednesbury Corp [1947] 1 KB 233   4, 59
AG v Guardian Newspapers (No 2) [1988] 3 All ER 545 .166, 167
AG's Reference (No 3 of 1994) [1997] 3 All ER 936 . . . . .101, 118
Auckland Hospital v AG (1993) 1 NZLR 235 . . . . .214, 215

B, Re [1981] 1 WLR 1421 . . . . .137, 138, 139, 141, 171
B, Re [1987] 2 All ER 206 4
Belle Bonfils Memorial Blood Bank v Hansen
    579 P 2d 1158 (Colo 1978) 99
Bliss v South East Thames RHA [1987] ICR 700 195
Bolam v Friern HMC [1957] 2 All ER 118 . . . . .231, 247
Bolitho v City and Hackney HA [1997] 4 All ER 771 84
Burton v Islington HA [1992] 3 All ER 820 . . . . .116, 117, 118

C, Re (A Minor) (Wardship: Medical Treatment)
    [1989] 2 All ER 782 . . . . .137, 138, 139, 141, 171
C, Re [1994] 1 All ER 819 . . . . .20, 84, 215, 242
C, Re [1998] 1 FLR 384 216
C v S [1988] 1 QB 135 115
Caparo Industries v Dickman [1990] 1 All ER 568 168
Chatterton v Gerson [1981] 1 All ER 257 242
Compassion in Dying v State of Washington 79 F 3d 790 (1996) 211, 212
Coventry Waste Disposal v Solihull BC [1999] 1 WLR 2093 .193
Cruzan v Director, Missouri Department of Health
    497 US 261 (1990) 210, 211, 222, 224, 229, 231,
                                       232, 233, 240, 249
Cunningham v MacNeal Memorial Hospital
    266 NE 2d 897 (Ill 1970) 99

Davis v Davis 842 SW 2d 588 (1992) 100, 110, 112, 113, 123

de Martell v Merton and Sutton HA [1992] 3 All ER 820 ....116, 117, 118

Del Zio v Presbyterian Hospital 74 Civ 3588 (SD NY 1976) 100

Dobson v North Tyneside HA [1996] 4 All ER 464 ....94, 95, 195

Doe, Guardianship of Jane 411 Mass 512 (1992) 249

Doodeward v Spence (1908) 6 CLR 406 ....93, 94, 95, 96

E, Re [1991] 1 FLR 386 174

Elliot v Joicey 1935 SC 57 116

F, Re (Mental Patient: Sterilisation) [1990] 2 AC 1 ....4, 215, 216, 257

F, Re (In Utero) [1988] 2 All ER 193 115

Fleming v Reid (1991) 82 DLR (4th) 298 239

Frenchay Healthcare NHS Trust v S [1994] 2 All ER 403 219

G, Re [1995] 2 FCR 46 ....218, 219

George & The Richard, The [1871] LR 3 A&E 466 114

Gillick v West Norfolk & Wisbech AHA
    [1985] 3 All ER 402 ....4, 40, 84, 174, 195, 197, 198

Guardianship of Jane Doe 411 Mass 512 (1992) 249

HM Advocate v Dewar 1945 SC 5 93

Hamilton v Fife 1993 SC 369 116

Hayes v Dodd [1990] 2 All ER 815 195

Haynes' Case (1614) 12 Co Rep 113; (1614) 77 ER 1389 93

Holgate v Lancashire Mental Hospitals Board [1937] 4 All ER 19 168

J, Re (A Minor) (Wardship: Medical Treatment) [1990] 3 All ER 930 ....169, 170,
                                                                        171, 176

J, Re (A Minor) (Medical Treatment) [1992] 4 All ER 614 ....55, 229, 230, 258

Jobes, In the Matter of 529 A 2d, 434 (NJ 1987) 217

Langside v Kerr [1991] 1 All ER 418 166

Latham v Stevens [1913] Macq Cop Cas 83 166

Law Hospital v Lord Advocate 1996 SLT 848 ....215, 218

Lee v State of Oregon 891 F Supp 1429 (1995)..................................211

MB, Re [1997] 2 FLR 3 ....84, 215, 216
McKay v Essex AHA [1982] QB 1166 142
McWilliams v Ministry of Defence 1992 SC 220 116
Malette v Shulman (1990) 67 DLR (4th) 231 239
Moore v Regents of the University of California
    793 P 2d 479 (1990) 101, 102
Mount Isa Mines v Pusey (1970) 125 CLR 383 ....31, 208

Nancy B v Hotel Dieu de Quebec (1992) 86 DLR (4th) 385 214

Parpalaix v CECOS (1984) Trib Gr Inst De Créteil,
    1 August, Gaz Pal 1984.II.560 ....110, 122
Paton v BPAS [1979] 1 QB 276 115

Quill v Vacco 80 F 3d 716 (1996) 211, 212, 213, 219, 222

R, Re (Wardship: Consent to Treatment) [1992] Fam 11;
    [1991] 4 All ER 177 ....174, 216, 242
R, Re (Adult) (Medical Treatment) [1996] 2 FLR 821 216
R v Arthur (1981) 12 BMLR 1 169
R v Brown [1993] 2 All ER 75 (HL) 85
R v Cambridgeshire HA ex p B (A Minor) (1995) 23 BMLR 1;
    (1995) 25 BMLR 5 ....4, 8, 20, 56, 57, 58, 59
R v Central Birmingham HA ex p Collier
    (1988) unreported, 6 January 8, 55, 229
R v Secretary of State for Social Services ex p Walker
    (1993) 2 BMLR 32 ....8, 55, 229
R v Cox (1993) 12 BMLR 38 238
R v Crozier [1991] Crim LR 138 167
R v HFEA ex p Blood [1997] 60 All ER 687;
    (1997) 35 BMLR 1 ....15, 40, 65, 122, 198, 220, 221, 222
R v Kelly [1998] 3 All ER 741 ....94, 96, 97, 101
R v Lord Saville of Newdigate ex p A [1999] 4 All ER 860 57
R v North West Lancashire HA ex p A, D and G
    [1999] Lloyd's Rep Med 399 ....59, 60
R v Rothery [1976] RTR 550 ....94, 98
R v Secretary of State for Social Services ex p Hincks
    (1992) 1 BMLR 93 ....54, 229
R v Tait [1989] 3 All ER 613 101

R v Welsh [1974] RTR 478 . . . . .94, 98

Rance v Mid Downs HA [1991] 1 All ER 801 124

Rivers v Katz 67 NY 2d 485 (1986) 212

Rodriguez v British Columbia (1993) 107 DLR (4th) 342 .214, 219

S, Re [1992] 4 All ER 671 258

S, Re [1993] Fam 123 216

S, Re [1995] Fam 26 . . . . .4, 40

S v S [1972] AC 24 102

St George's NHS Trust v S [1998] 3 WLR 673 . . . . .84, 89

St George's NHS Trust v S (No 2) [1998] 3 WLR 936 . . . . .215, 216

Schloendorff v Society of New York Hospital
    211 NY 125 (1914) 232

Secretary, Department of Health and Community Services
    v JWB and SMB (1992) 106 ALR 385 . . . . .89, 90

Sidaway v Board of Governors of the Bethlem Royal
    Hospital and the Maudsley Hospital [1985] AC 871 . . . . .88, 102

Skinner v Oklahoma ex rel Williamson 316 US 535 (1942) 232

Storar, Re; Re Eichner 52 NY 2d 363 (1981) 240

Swindon and Marlborough NHS Trust v S [1995] 3 Med LR 84 219

T, Re [1992] 3 WLR 782; [1992] 4 All ER 649;
    (1992) 9 BMLR 46 . . . . .84, 88, 168, 208, 215, 230,
                                            238, 239, 243, 244, 248, 251, 258

T, Re [1997] 1 All ER 906 216

Tarasoff v Regents of California 551 P 2d 334 (1976) 167

Thompson v County of Alabama 614 P 2d 728 (1980) 168

W, Re [1992] 4 All ER 627; (1992) 9 BMLR 22 . . . . .174, 216, 242

W v Egdell [1990] 1 All ER 835 . . . . .166, 167

Washington v Glucksberg 138 L Ed 772 (1998) 211, 213, 222

Watt v Rama [1972] VR 353 117

Webster v Reproductive Health Services 492 US 490 (1989) 112

X v Y [1982] 2 All ER 648 166

York v Jones 717 F Supp 2d 421 (Va 1989) 100, 110

TABLE OF LEGISLATION

UK legislation

Abortion Act 1967 . . . . .114, 139,
146–49, 166, 169
s 1 . . . . .137, 145, 147, 169
s 1(1)(a) .147, 148
s 1(1)(d) 138–40, 148, 171, 172
s 1(2) 147, 148
Administration of Estates
Act 1925—
s 55(2) 114
Anatomy Act 1984 92

Children Act 1989 . . . . .80, 175
s 3 195
s 43(7) 174
s 44(7) 174
Congenital Disabilities
(Civil Liability) Act 1976 . . . . .114, 116,
119, 124–26
s 1 126
s 1A 124
s 1(4) 125, 126
s 1(5) 125
s 4(2) 124
s 4(4) 126
s 30 125
s 44(1)(a)(2)–(4) 125
Consumer Protection Act 1987 98

Damages (Scotland) Act 1976—
s 1 116
s 1(1) 116

Family Law Reform Act 1969 174
s 8 . . . . .174, 194
s 8(3) 174, 175

Human Fertilisation and
Embryology Act 1990 . . . . . .52, 92, 98,
108–10, 115,
118, 120, 121,
123, 126, 129, 141,
187–93, 196–99
s 1 . . . . .120, 191–93
s 1(1) 120
s 1(1)(a) 120, 187, 192
s 1(1)(b) 120, 187
s 1(1)(d) 120
s 1(2) 187
s 1(4) 194
s 2(2) 194, 198
s 3 . . . . .119, 140
s 3(1) 190, 191, 193
s 3(1)(a) 187
s 3(3)(a) 119, 193
s 3(3)(b), (c) 120
s 3(3)(d) 120, 187, 190
s 3(4) 120, 193
s 4 120
s 4(1) 194
s 4(1)(a) 120
s 4(1)(b) 123
s 4(1)(c) 120
ss 12, 14 194
s 14(1)(b) 123
s 17(1)(c) 121
ss 27–29 126
s 27(1) 126
s 27(4)(b) 122
s 28(6) 126
s 30 126
s 35(1) 126
s 37 . . . . .137, 169
s 41(2) 193
s 44 124
Sched 2 120
Sched 2 para 2(1) 122

Human Fertilisation and
    Embryology Act 1990 (Contd)—
    Sched 2 para 2(2)(b) 123
    Sched 2 para 3(2) 121
    Sched 2 para 3(3) 122
    Sched 2 para 3(6), (7), (9) 121
    Sched 3 .109, 121,
                                    194, 197, 198
    Sched 3 para 2(2) 196
    Sched 3 para 4(1) 121
    Sched 3 para 7(1) 123
    Sched 3 para 8(1) 194
    Sched 3 para 8(2), (3) 123
Human Organs Transplant
    Act 1989 . . . . .52, 92, 99, 100
Human Rights Act 1998 . . . . . . .23, 24, 198
Human Tissue Act 1961 . . . . . .92, 196, 236
    s 1 196

Infant Life (Preservation)
    Act 1929 .114, 170

Medicines Act 1983 52

National Health Service
    Act 1977 . . . . .52, 55
    ss 1(1), 3 54

Offences Against the
    Person Act 1861 . . . . .101, 114

Public Health
    (Infectious Diseases)
        Act 1984 .166

Rules of the Supreme Court—
    Ord 24 95
    Ord 24 r 7A .95

Supreme Court Act 1981—
    s 34 95

Surrogacy Arrangements
    Act 1985 52

European legislation

Council of Europe
    Convention on
        Biomedicine and
            Human Rights 31

European Convention on the
    Protection of Human Rights
    and Fundamental
        Freedoms 1950 . . . . .4, 57, 63
    Arts 8, 12 198

Embryo Protection Act 1990
    (Germany) 191
    s 6 191

French Law No 94–654 1994 199

Treaty Establishing the
    European Communities
        1957 (EC Treaty) 198
    Arts 30–36 100
    Arts 30, 59, 60 198

Treaty on European Union 1992
    (Maastricht Treaty) 54
    Art 129 54

International legislation

Bill of Rights Act (New Zealand)—
    s 11 215

Charter of Rights and
    Fundamental Freedoms
        (Canada) .214

Consent to Medical
Treatment Act 1992 (Canada) 245
s 12 245

Human Genome Privacy
Act 1990 (US) 162

Human Genome
Privacy Amendment
Act (US)—
ss 2(b), 101(2) 162

Omnibus Reconciliation
Act 1990 (US) 231
Oregon Death with Dignity
Act 1994 (US) 211

Patient Self-Determination
Act 1990 (US) 210, 231

Rights of the Terminally
Ill 1995 (Northern
Territory, Australia) 40
Rights of the Terminally
Ill 1996 (Northern
Territory, Australia) 40

US Constitution
14th Amendment 211, 212

World Health Organization
Draft Declaration on the
Rights of Patients 1990 53

PART I

MEDICAL LAW, TRAGIC CHOICES
AND THE RISK SOCIETY

CHAPTER 1

WHAT IS MEDICAL LAW?

I have, for the past 10 years, been perhaps more interested in ethical or philosophical aspects of health care and medical practice than in legal ones. My colleagues and students will tell you that this constantly shows; philosophers and ethicists will say that it does not. I have, in that time, been interested in thinking about what we might call 'uses of the body', particularly in its reproductive and affective aspects, but also more generally. The body is now recognised as an immensely complex index of social attitudes and ambivalence, cultural expressions and expectations, public representations and regulation.[1] There have been changes in or challenges to what we might call 'knowledge of the body' and the 'body of knowledge'. Much of what I want to do in this collection involves reflecting on these changes. But I have some preliminary questions that I want to address.

MEDICAL LAW: UNPLUGGED

The question 'what is medical law?' is sometimes posed in a form that appears to assert that 'medical law is not a subject'. I agree in part. Medical law is indeed not *just* a subject; it is also a responsibility. Whether medical law is a legal category in itself is beside the point.[2] The framing of responses properly lying within medical law is part of an intellectual responsibility that lies at the heart of the academic obligation which, as John Fleming has otherwise observed, is to be 'sensitive to movement and direction ... [being] concerned with whence, whither and most important, with why'.[3] To argue that there is no such subject as medical law, that it is no more than an amalgam of traditional categories of tort, contract and criminal law, also misses a number of points. It misses the *dynamic* as well as the *context* of medical law, in

---

1   Considered, eg, in collected volumes such as Komesaroff, PA (ed), *Troubled Bodies: Critical Perspectives on Postmodernism, Medical Ethics and the Body*, 1995, Melbourne: Melbourne UP; Naffine, N and Owens, RJ (eds), *Sexing the Subject of Law*, 1997, North Ryde, NSW: LBC; Hyde, A, *Bodies of Law*, 1997, New Jersey: Princeton UP; Radin, MJ, *Contested Commodities: The Trouble with Trade in Sex, Children, Body Parts and Other Things*, 1996, Cambridge, Mass: Harvard UP; Cheah, P, Fraser, D and Grbich, J (eds), *Thinking Through the Body of Law*, 1996, New York: New York UP; and Dickenson, D, *Property, Women and Politics: Subjects or Objects?*, 1997, Cambridge: Polity.

2   Perhaps, indeed, this is just as well, as Margot Brazier has just identified the conditions for the disappearance of 'medical law'. See her essay with Nicola Glover, 'Does medical law have a future?', in Birks, P (ed), *Law's Future(s)*, 2000, Oxford: Hart.

3   *The Law of Torts*, 1992, Sydney: LBC, p 8.

addition to failing properly to describe the very subject. Medical law, if it is an amalgam, encompasses in addition to contract, tort and criminal law, at least administrative law, procedural law, trusts, conflicts of law, labour law, and, it is now becoming clearer, aspects of personal and intellectual property law too.

Secondly, to describe medical law as nothing more than an amalgam of legal categories shaved away by Salmond, Chitty and Anson from the body of case and assumpsit, fails to appreciate the necessarily interdisciplinary approach which the subject properly demands and which most of its university teachers and students trade in. In the same way that Raanon Gillon has observed that 'philosophy on its own is not sufficient to understand critically health care provision',[4] neither is law itself sufficient for an understanding and appreciation of either health care or health care law, whether critical or not.

Thirdly, the *dynamic* is illustrated by the way in which issues involving aspects of medicine and doctors have impacted upon and, to some extent, transformed those 'traditional' areas: *Gillick*,[5] *Bland*[6] and *Re A (Children: Conjoined Twins)*[7] upon criminal law; the declaratory jurisdiction of the High Court, revived and enlivened by *Re F*,[8] *Re B*,[9] *Bland*,[10] and *Re S*;[11] and in *R v Cambridgeshire HA ex p B*[12] (at least at first instance) the court has addressed both the proportionality test and at last raised doubts about the continued vitality of the *Wednesbury*[13] concept of reasonableness in the modern State, and has broached the jurisprudence of the European Convention on Human Rights in English law.

The *context* is illustrated by the failure of the traditional approach to recognise either the scope or the terrain of medical law or its intellectual parameters. Medical law is in large part a process of *naming, blaming, claiming* and *declaiming*. Each of these questions has important ethical and philosophical dimensions. Naming – is this person ill, unwell, chronic, acute etc; blaming – exploring the role of caring for oneself and one's responsibilities for health care, particularly whether we are responsible for our own health, but also the State's responsibility for provision of health care and our

---

4   Gillon, R, *Principles of Health Care Ethics*, 1994, Chichester: John Wiley, p xxii.
5   *Gillick v West Norfolk & Wisbech AHA* [1985] 3 All ER 402.
6   *Airedale NHS Trust v Bland* [1993] AC 789.
7   [2000] 4 All ER 961.
8   [1990] 2 AC 1.
9   [1987] 2 All ER 206.
10   *Airedale NHS Trust v Bland* [1993] AC 789.
11   [1995] Fam 26.
12   (1995) 23 BMLR 1.
13   [1947] 2 All ER 680.

collective responsibility for other nations' health;[14] claiming – what are our entitlements to health care, of access to services?; and declaiming – about saying who we are and who we want to become, giving a moral and symbolic emphasis to law.[15] This concerns our efforts to define and delineate the sort of society that we say we are and that we want to become; whether we want to sterilise women with intellectual difference, permit surrogacy arrangements, sanction the recovery of sperm from neo-morts for use by their widows or former partners, permit patients to exercise rights of quasi-ownership over their medical records, assert claims to assistance in or with dying, control their fertility by termination of pregnancy without the intervention of the criminal law, determine the sex of the children to which they will give birth, and so on. Each of these questions has important philosophical, ethical, sociological and political dimensions, as well as legal ones, and I explore some, but not necessarily all, of them in this collection.

Martyn Evans has argued that the practice of medicine is driven by a *range* of human values (the relief of suffering prominent among them).[16] This recognition, he argues, should replace an exclusive focus on ethics (hitherto highly dominant in normative analyses of medicine) because the range of human values is more than ethics alone: medicine presupposes moral, aesthetic, socio-political, intellectual and epistemic values which together construct what medicine is, what it does and what it aims at. Ethics refers to the first and most obvious category of values, but in time it might come to be seen as merely a special case of a more general concern. Individuals' illnesses are a fusion of biological processes and biographical experiences; this is true to some extent of all illnesses, but is especially true of chronic illnesses.[17] The treatment of chronic illnesses in particular requires a fusion of biological and biographical understanding. Illnesses are 'episodes in a narrative from conception to corruption';[18] the provision of medical care is a response to narrative episodes, and of course constitutes further such episodes.

When we come to speak of health and illness, then, we are of necessity required to address at least a package of *conceptual* questions;[19] *political* questions – the role and responsibility of the State in securing, promoting or

---

14 The contemporary political validity of this characterisation is amply borne out by the continuing controversy concerning the disbursement of *compulsory* health insurance payments between former West and former East German citizens.

15 Clearly, this draws from and builds on Felstiner, W, Abel, R and Sarat, A, 'The emergence and transformation of disputes: naming, blaming and claiming' (1980–81) 15 Law and Society Rev 631.

16 Evans, M, 'Philosophy and the medical humanities', in Evans, HM and Finlay, IG (eds), *Medical Humanities*, 2001 (forthcoming), London: BMJ, p 150.

17 *Ibid*. I explore this below, Chapter 12.

18 *Ibid*, Evans.

19 Boorse, C, 'On the distinction between health and disease' [1975] Philosophy and Public Affairs 5; Nordenfelt, C, 'On the relevance and importance of the notion of disease' (1993) 14 Theoretical Medicine 15.

damaging the health of its citizens and those whom it affects directly and indirectly, intentionally and accidentally, through the extraterritorial effects of its behaviour;[20] and those of *gender, race and ethnicity*.[21] If our understanding of medicine's task is to be driven by our understanding of the human values at stake, the question 'what is medical (or health care) law?' admits of at least a descriptive and a conceptual answer. And while neither may be easy to articulate, and the boundary between the two may sometimes shade at the margins, to *do* medical law, then, is to do medical ethics, is to trade upon philosophy,[22] whether properly called the philosophy of medicine or medical philosophy or not. To ask, then, 'what is medical law?' (which is rather different from the question, 'what is medical law for?')[23] *is* to ask a philosophical question. Margot Brazier has expressed one voice of concern in precisely this regard: '... unless the law can settle upon some coherent and defensible definition of illness, the elasticity of the concepts of illness may snap,'[24] and the concept of medical law with it.

The simple point here can be summed up from one of Isaiah Berlin's essays, 'Concepts and categories',[25] in which, writing of the purpose of philosophy, he captures one of the essentials of modern *medical* jurisprudence, and perhaps its most acute dilemma:

> Men's views of one another will differ profoundly as a very consequence of their general conception of the world: the notions of cause and purpose, good and evil, freedom and slavery, things and persons, rights, duties, laws, justice, truth, falsehood, to take some central ideas completely at random, depend directly upon the general framework within which they form, as it were, nodal points.

In other words, philosophy counts and it counts centrally in medical law and jurisprudence.

---

20 Townsend, P and Davidson, N (eds), *Inequalities in Health* (the Black Report), 1982, Harmondsworth: Penguin; Williams, B, 'The idea of equality', in Laslett, P and Runciman, WG (eds), *Philosophy, Politics and Society*, 1962, Oxford: Basil Blackwell, pp 110–31; Nozick, R, *Anarchy, State and Utopia*, 1974, Oxford: Basil Blackwell, p 233.

21 I try to substantiate this claim below, Chapter 5. See, importantly, Doyal, L, *What Makes Women Sick: Gender and the Political Economy of Health*, 1995, New Brunswick, NJ: Rutgers UP; Oakley, A, *Essays on Women, Medicine and Health*, 1993, Edinburgh: Edinburgh UP. I have less to say about race and ethnicity here than perhaps I should, for they are important forces in these debates; see, eg, Wolf, SM, 'Erasing difference: race, ethnicity and gender in bioethics', Chapter 4 in *Feminism and Bioethics*, 1996, New York: OUP.

22 See, eg, Maclean, A, *The Elimination of Morality*, p 187ff, esp p 192.

23 Which carries the same sorts of objection as the question 'what is there in horse racing?', carefully considered in the essay of that name by John Wisdom, in Hanfling, O (ed), *Life and Meaning: A Reader*, 1987, Oxford: Basil Blackwell, p 74.

24 Brazier, M and Glover, N, 'Does medical law have a future?' in *op cit*, Birks, fn 2.

25 In *Four Essays on Liberty*, 1969, Oxford: OUP.

THE VOCABULARY OF MEDICAL JURISPRUDENCE

'Treat me gentle'[26]

It is now common to read of and to study courses in criminal justice and, perhaps less frequently, of civil justice. Justice is, of course, a protean notion,[27] and the focusing of debates around such a concept has become an important manner of characterising intellectual inquiry. In the same way as we have, over the past 20 years, seen the rediscovery or revitalised emergence of medical ethics,[28] nursing ethics,[29] environmental ethics,[30] business ethics,[31] scientific ethics,[32] engineering ethics,[33] architectural ethics,[34] archaeological ethics,[35] latterly legal ethics,[36] and so on, a similar energy can be justified to engage debates around, say, gender justice,[37] intergenerational justice,[38] species justice,[39] environmental justice,[40] commercial law and social justice,[41] and, for my present concern more immediately, medical or health care justice and its associated jurisprudence. The architecture of medical jurisprudence is

26 Cf Kennedy, I, *Treat Me Right: Essays in Medical Law and Ethics*, 1988, Oxford: OUP.

27 There is a good introduction to this in the essays by le Grand, J, Flew, A, Skillen, A, Hollis, M and Tur, R, in Almond, B and Hill, D (eds), *Applied Philosophy: Morals and Metaphysics in Contemporary Debate*, 1991, London: Routledge, pp 183–244.

28 The leading British exponents of various positions are probably Harris, J, *The Value of Life: An Introduction to Medical Ethics*, 1985, London: Routledge; Maclean, A, *The Elimination of Morality*, 1993, London: Routledge; Gillon, R (ed), *Principles of Health Care Ethics*, 1994, Chichester: Wiley.

29 A brief introduction is Rowson, R, *An Introduction to Ethics for Nurses*, 1990, Harrow: Scutari.

30 Stone, C, *Earth and Other Ethics*, 1987, New York: Harper & Row.

31 See, eg, Velasquez, M, *Business Ethics*, 1982, Englewood Cliffs, NJ: Prentice Hall.

32 Unger, S, *Controlling Technology: Ethics and the Responsible Engineer*, 1994, Chichester: John Wiley.

33 See, eg, http://lowery.tamu.edu/ethics.

34 Watkin, D, *Morality and Architecture*, 1977, Chicago: Chicago UP.

35 Vitelli, KD (ed), *Archaeological Ethics*, 1996, London: Alta Mira.

36 Boon, A and Levin, J, *The Ethics and Conduct of Lawyers in England and Wales*, 1999, Oxford: Hart.

37 Kirp, D, Yudof, M and Strong Franks, M, *Gender Justice*, 1986, Chicago: Chicago UP; Gilligan, C, *In a Different Voice: Psychological Theory and Women's Development*, 1982, Cambridge, Mass: Harvard UP, comprehensively criticised by O'Neill, O (with commentary by Nussbaum, M), 'Justice, gender and international boundaries', in Nussbaum, M and Sen, A (eds), *The Quality of Life*, 1993, Oxford: Clarendon, pp 303–35.

38 Marmor, TR, Smeeding, TM and Greene, V, *Economic Security and Intergenerational Justice*, 1994, Chicago: Urban Institute.

39 Singer, P and Cavalieri, P, *The Great Ape Project*, 1995, London: St Martin's.

40 Stone, C, 'Do trees have standing?' (1972) So Cal L Rev 450.

41 Braithwaite, J and Drahos, P, *Global Business Regulation*, 2000, Cambridge: CUP; Donson, F, *Legal Intimidations*, 2000, Free Association Press.

determined in large part by its algebra.[42] It is in this sense that medical jurisprudence is concerned both with series of relationships and similarities, while recognising that the coherence, the permanence or the transitoriness of the designs that are offered depend largely on factors quite external to the traditional concerns of law and lawyers.

Perhaps until recently, most authors who came to the study of medical law came from the background of another sub-discipline of law. Accordingly, their interest in questions of medical law is shaped by the way in which that fits into or illustrates a tangential development or a new vector of the subject matter in question. Few of us have come from jurisprudence and fewer still have a real understanding of the practice of medicine; certainly I do not. The drawback with this is that it can lead to a rather formalistic, formulaic, decontextualised understanding of the difficulties and limitations, the intellectual and emotional demands of medical practice. Still less is there much fruitful discussion of what medicine *is*; whether it is an art, a science, a philosophy, an emotion, or a combination – an amalgam – of each of these. It is perhaps not surprising, then, that such a fragmented, fractional approach may encourage some lawyers to fall back on to the uncritical acceptance of familiar values, which may lead to a potentially distorting and limiting, perhaps an *excessive* concentration on, and concern with, rights.

Rights arguments, especially when developed in a sophisticated, calibrated fashion, have an important, influential rhetorical force and value in defining what may be achieved, and they carry that value in a way that is hard to deny.[43] But, an exclusive concern with rights as opposed to other ethical values, for example, care[44] or virtue,[45] produces an atomised, anomised, autonomised individual rather than the community of interest in which modern medical practice is, in my view, best delivered and understood. I want to commend a perhaps unfashionable view of medical law in which rights are necessarily seen as imposing duties of a generally negative kind (treat me gentle, do not treat me against my will, or negligently) rather than of a positive nature (you must treat me;[46] you must treat me a particular way;[47] I am entitled to this care or treatment). Rights of this latter type give rise to what I later call the opportunity cost of rhetoric; the rhetoric of rights in a positive sense has very direct costs which a socialised system of health care is poorly equipped to mediate or even calibrate.

The importance of distinguishing such general questions of distributive justice from the concentration on rights is aptly demonstrated by Michael Freeden. He puts it this way:

---

42 'Al-jebra': the putting together of the broken pieces.
43 See *op cit*, Kennedy, fn 26.
44 *Op cit*, Gilligan, fn 37; Noddings, N, *Caring: A Feminine Approach to Ethics and Education*, 1978, Berkley, Cal: California UP; *op cit*, Wolf, fn 21.
45 Eg, MacIntyre, A, *After Virtue: A Study in Moral Theory*, 1985, London: Duckworth.
46 *Ex p B* (1995) 23 BMLR 1.
47 *Ex p Walker* (1993) 2 BMLR 32; *Ex p Collier* (1988) unreported, 6 January.

> The existence of scarce goods necessitates important decisions on distribution, whereas the insistence on the right to a good ensures that some of it will be available to any rights bearer.[48]

Rights need to be approached with due caution. A misunderstanding of the economics of health care has bedevilled much of the public health system of the past 60 years;[49] we do not need a similar misunderstanding or unsympathetic misapplication of rights talk to add to those problems.

Constituting medical law

There are, however, different sets of questions that we can ask: questions which are predicated upon a different understanding of the role and contribution of law. Here, law is seen not (just) as an autonomous body of knowledge, but as a factor which contributes to, which in part translates and facilitates, the so called 'public understanding of science'; and which also operates in a similar way in contributing to the less well developed inquiry of the 'scientific understanding of the public'.[50] This may vary according to a number of discrete variables and modes of analysis; whether law is seen as only an instrumental response to medical practices, or whether there is an ideological, a symbolic element to it as well, or instead. Hence, my earlier suggestion that we can see medical law as concerned with naming, blaming, claiming and declaiming. And the emergence, although it is better thought of as the construction of medical law, has hardly occurred in a vacuum, either intellectual, cultural, scientific or jurisprudential.

This *construction* of medical law has indeed been paralleled by and has helped to produce a number of remarkable metamorphoses which have left, or are leaving, a deep imprint on modern medicine and its reflection in, reception and regulation by law. I want to turn later to explore this 'land of metamorphoses' where, a bit like Gregor Samsa, we can almost no longer be sure what we might wake up to find in the morning.[51] The late 20th century saw an inversion of the mood that Orlando Figes has described as that of the immediate post revolutionary period in Russia. He has characterised that as an 'age of optimism in the potential of science to change human life and, paradoxically, at the same time, an age of profound doubt and uncertainty about the value of human life itself in the wake of the destruction of the First

---

48 Freeden, M, *Rights*, 1991, Buckingham: Open UP, p 92.

49 Lee, RG, 'Legal control of health care allocation', in Ockelton, M (ed), *Medicine, Ethics and Law*, 1987, Stuttgart: ARSP, pp 94–96; and see below, Chapter 4.

50 Wells, C, 'I blame the parents', in Brownsword, R, Cornish, WR and Llewelyn, M, *Law and Human Genetics: Regulating a Revolution*, 1998, Oxford: Hart, p 135.

51 Kafka, F, *Metamorphosis and Other Stories*, Muir, W and Muir, E (trans), 1999, London: Vintage.

World War'.[52] The late 20th century, in contrast, came to view scientific 'progress' with profound scepticism – at least as to the human and economic costs entailed – while setting in place of uncertainty as to the value of human life a reaffirmation of its individual sanctity or sacredness.[53] Yet, Eric Hobsbawm has called the last half century the 'crisis decades'. He has argued that even more obvious than the uncertainties of world economics and world politics was the social and moral crisis, reflecting post-1950 upheavals in human life, which also found widespread, if confused, expression. These decades have witnessed a crisis of the beliefs and assumptions on which modern society had been founded, as deep as any since the Moderns won their famous battle against the Ancients in the early 18th century. 'This is a crisis of the rationalist and humanist assumptions, shared by liberal capitalism and communism ...'[54]

Why is this? I suggest that it has to do with what I here try to show is the *discovery* of difference, the exploration of different values and the value of difference in the 'risk society'.[55] One of the most remarkable metamorphoses of the 20th century is that from what nature could do to us, to what we can do to nature. According to Anthony Giddens,[56] this transition marks one of the major points of entry in 'risk society'.[57]

'Risk societies' are societies that live 'after nature'. Allied with this is the 'end of tradition'; what ethics (and law) is, what it consists in, how it is applied and to whom and in what ways it is no longer 'uncontested'. To live after the end of tradition, says Giddens, is to be in a world where life is no longer lived as fate. Almost any news story, and much modern medical litigation, turns on this very discovery, as claims of entitlement to posthumous

---

52 Figes, O, *A People's Tragedy: The Russian Revolution 1891–1924*, 1996, London: Pimlico, pp 733, 857n. Figes recalls that Lenin is reported to have said to Pavlov, in one of their discussions, 'man can be changed'. He further observes that 'Thus, one of the pioneers of the eugenics movements of Nazi Germany suggested that "it could almost seem as if we have witnessed a change in the concept of humanity ... we were forced by the terrible exigencies of war to ascribe a different value to the life of the individual than was the case before"'. See, also, Yevgeny Zamyatin's satire on the mechanised State created in such utopias in *We*, 1972, Harmondsworth: Penguin, the intellectual inspiration for Orwell's *1984*.

53 At least in individualised, Westernised societies, and in respect at least of individual, Westernised lives. This is not necessarily to imply that such concerns are exclusive to Westernised societies; see, eg, Williams, N, *The Right to Life in Japan*, 1997, London: Routledge, esp pp 5–15, 85–100; Jakobovits, I (Sir), 'The Jewish contribution to medical ethics', in Byrne, P (ed), *Rights and Wrongs in Medicine*, 1986, London: King Edward's Hospital Fund for London, pp 115–26, and the papers variously collected in Fujiki, N and Macer, DRJ (eds), *Bioethics in Asia*, 1998, Tskuba Science City: Eubios Ethics Institute.

54 Hobsbawm, E, *Age of Extremes: The Short History of the Twentieth Century 1914–1991*, 1994, London: Michael Joseph, p 11.

55 Beck, U, *Risk Society: Towards a New Modernity*, Ritter, M (trans), 1992, London: Sage, originally published as *Risikogellschaft. Auf dem Weg in eine andere Moderne*, 1986, Frankfurt: Suhrkamp Verlag.

56 Giddens, A, 'Risk and responsibility' (1999) 62 MLR 1.

57 A concept I explore again in Chapter 3.

use of sperm, whole body cryopreservation and judgments about conjoined twins serve easily to illustrate. The advent of 'risk society' presumes a new politics because it presumes a re-orientation of values and the strategies relevant to pursuing them. For Giddens, this leads to the so called 'third way' in politics. More generally, this is what gives rise to Hobsbawm's 'general concern with ethics'. Ethics, in the limited sense of a concern with *different values*, has become the paradigm form of social inclusion in the risk society. Ethical debate, perhaps more than politics, is becoming the paradigm form of participation.

The contexts within which the construction of medical law has taken place take the form of a number of different 'metamorphoses'. I suggest that this has five facets: what I have called 'scientific medicine'; 'epistemology and ethics'; 'the changing nature of the patient'; 'constitutional changes and changes in the constitution', and 'the nature of law's response'.

CHAPTER 2

MEDICAL LAW AND THE LAND OF METAMORPHOSES

In Chapter 1, I asked what medical law might be and suggested that the answer engaged a whole range of values, including philosophical, ethical, legal and sociological ones, with the art or practice of medicine; that medical law was a necessarily interdisciplinary study; and that the answer to my question involved both a descriptive and a conceptual limb. I concluded by suggesting that this construction of medical law – at least in the past 50 years – has taken place in the context of a number of significant scientific and social changes. In this chapter, I turn to an introduction to those changes: to view the development of medical law in the 'land of metamorphoses'.

METAMORPHOSIS 1: SCIENTIFIC MEDICINE[1]

The 20th century has seen unparalleled changes in the nature of the scientific basis of medicine, and as 'medicine became imbued with science, so the limits of its endeavour have changed',[2] moving from what Jonathon Glover once called *Causing Deaths and Saving Lives*,[3] to what might be seen as 'saving death and causing lives'. Perhaps in medicine and science this is nowhere more aptly illustrated than in the decoding of the structure of the double helix; the discovery by James Watson and Francis Crick of the molecular structure of the very foundations of life. And with this has come, for medical jurisprudence, a metamorphosis every much as startling as the scientific and technological changes themselves. Radical scientific changes in what can be achieved, whether through cloning or genetic testing, recovery, storage and use (sometimes posthumously) of gametes, have seen what I call the reconstitution of the body. Whether this comes about as a result of a conspiracy of the scientific and medical professions against the laity to push professional dominance into domains traditionally outside medicine's province, or whether we are witnessing the destabilisation of the boundaries of lay and professional competence in an age of democracy, as Roy Porter has recently argued, with the medical and nursing professionals driven to break

---

1   This is a different, less sophisticated conception than that engaged by Joe Jacob in his book, *Doctors and Rules: A Sociology of Professional Values*, 1988, London: Routledge.

2   *Ibid*, p 22.

3   Glover, J, *Causing Deaths and Saving Lives*, 1977, Harmondsworth: Penguin.

out from the iron cages which professional strategies have built for them,[4] falls to be discussed elsewhere.

The expansion of the capacity to act 'has not been accompanied by a comparable expansion of the capacity to predict, and as a result the prediction of the consequences of scientific action are necessarily less than the action itself'.[5] Of course, I do want to deny, whatever others may hold, that many of the advancements in science, medicine and surgery are real and true contributions to human well being; the development of micro-surgery is an obvious example and there are many others. But that is quite a different point from the present. Science has acquired the power 'to define situations beyond what it knows about them',[6] in large part because the interesting and difficult consequential questions are not scientific ones, but social and ethical ones. Selective examples may help further to illustrate this specific point. They disclose that we may be overwhelmed by the belated suspicion that it is life, more than death, that has no limits.[7]

It would formerly have been the case that death, as Mr Orange, Mr Pink, Mr Blue, Mr Blonde, Mr Brown and Mr White discovered,[8] is not negotiable in the way of other facts of life.[9] But we may begin to wonder at the sense in which we use these very words; there is a sense in which we might begin to ask, 'are birth and death important?'.

Let me give some suggestive examples:

- Newspapers in the UK have reported the suggestion that a deceased woman should be allowed to give evidence in a criminal trial recorded on videotape before her death.[10]

- A man has recorded on videotape his wish that his frozen sperm should be used after his death to impregnate his former wife in order that she might bear a child genetically related to both of them. Similar instances have been noted in the UK of such wishes being made.[11]

- Under the headline 'Dead men can still have children',[12] it was reported that a urologist at a New York Hospital extracted sperm from Anthony Baez – a man killed in a fight – at the request of his widow, so that she

4   See his monumental *The Greatest Benefit to Mankind: A Medical History of Humanity from Antiquity to the Present*, 1997, London: HarperCollins, p 702.

5   *Ibid*, p 9.

6   de Sousa Santos, B, *Toward a New Common Sense: Law, Science and Politics in the Paradigmatic Transition*, 1995, London: Routledge, p 47.

7   Garcia Marquez, G, *Love in the Time of Cholera*, 1988, Harmondsworth: Penguin, p 10.

8   Tarantino, Q, *Reservoir Dogs*, 1994, London: Faber & Faber.

9   Ramsey, 'Death's pedagogy' (1974) 20 Commonwealth 497.

10   See, eg, (1992) *The Guardian*, 15 June.

11   Eg, (1985) *The Guardian*, 25 September, p 19.

12   (1995) *The Guardian*, 21 January.

could have the children which they had dreamed of having together. Shortly after, *The Independent*[13] reported that a similar operation had been performed on a man killed in a car accident. These were just the first, earliest examples of a procedure which, if not common, is no longer so closely related to the realms of fiction.[14]

• In October 2000, it was widely reported that a child had been conceived by parents in America so that he could become a donor in a life saving operation needed by his sister, and a Scottish couple in Dundee petitioned the Human Fertilisation and Embryology Authority to allow them to choose the sex of an embryo using IVF treatment following the woman's sterilisation so that they could ensure the birth of a daughter to 'replace' their three year old infant Nicole, killed the previous year in a domestic accident.[15]

• An Italian surrogacy story clearly demonstrates some of the contemporary complexities.[16] This tells of the birth of a baby girl from the egg of a woman who had died in a car accident two years earlier. At the time of the woman's death, four fertilised eggs remained in IVF storage. The baby's mother, a 'surrogate' mother, was the dead woman's husband's married sister, who is also, therefore, the baby's aunt. Dr Pasquale Bilotta is quoted as having said to Italian newspapers that 'It was strange and very sweet to see two men suffering as they waited the birth of the same daughter ... This isn't a case of incest, but of a child adopted by one of its relations ... The baby is not an orphan, but, if you like, a child with a bigger family than normal'.

• Finally, Marion Ploch was 'killed' in a road accident. She was pronounced 'brain stem dead' at the hospital in Erlangen, Germany, on arrival. The fetus with which she was pregnant was at 19 weeks gestation, the lowest fetal age case of which I am aware that the following procedure has been attempted. Ploch was put on a life support machine for six weeks in the hope that her fetus would be brought to sufficient maturity to enable it to be born alive. She had died and the fetus died. As Ann Oakley controversially commented after another such attempt, in Middlesbrough, England: '... you don't need a brain to have a baby.'[17]

---

13 (1995) *The Independent*, 26 January, p 10.

14 See Morgan, D and Lee, RG, 'In the name of the father: *ex parte Blood*' (1997) 60 MLR 840, discussing *R v HFEA ex p Blood* [1997] 2 All ER 687 (CA); (1997) 35 BMLR 1 (HC, CA).

15 (2000) *The Daily Telegraph*, 18 October, (2000) *The Guardian*, 17 October, further discussed in (2000) *The Independent on Sunday*, 22 October, p 22.

16 (1995) *The Guardian*, 12 January, p 11. I have traced further examples of this sort with Robert Lee in Lee, RG and Morgan, D, *Human Fertilisation and Embryology: Regulating the Reproduction Revolution*, 2001, London: Blackstone.

17 Conference presentation, British Association for the Advancement of Science, Bristol, September 1990.

The Italian birth to which I have just referred, Cardinal Ersilio Tonini condemned because 'we have reached the point of producing human beings as if they were boxes'. These terms of endearment remind me of Lady Bracknell's admonishment to Mr Worthing in Oscar Wilde's incomparable play, *The Importance of Being Earnest*.[18]

Other developments at the ending of life illustrate this perhaps just as clearly as do reproductive technologies.[19] Death and dying, withholding and withdrawing treatment, euthanasia and assisted suicide provoke an endless debate. This negotiation is brilliantly captured by David Watkin: '... the most radical change in our modern cosmos has come about through our changed conception of death and immortality; for us, death is an episode in life's renewal ... Instead of being oriented toward death and fixity, we are oriented toward life and change.'[20]

A second type of scientific change comes from developments in and consequent upon genetics and pharmacology. Adverse drug reaction is the fourth largest cause of death in the UK. Two million Americans are thought to suffer an adverse drug reaction each year, of which over 100,000 result in death.[21] The development of pharmacogenetics, addressing the role of genetic variation in an individual's response to drugs, illustrates the general point.[22]

---

18 *The Plays of Oscar Wilde*, 1948, London: Collins, Act 1, pp 462–63. Recall that Jack Worthing, whom Lady Bracknell is interrogating about his suitability and standing for engagement to her daughter Gwendoline, has just revealed that he was abandoned at birth by his parents and found in a handbag in the cloakroom at Victoria Station on the Brighton line. Lady Bracknell fulminates: 'The line is immaterial Mr Worthing. I confess I feel somewhat bewildered by what you have just told me. To be born, or at any rate bred, in a handbag, whether it has handles or not, seems to me to display a contempt for the ordinary decencies of family life that reminds one of the worst excesses of the French Revolution. And I presume you know what that unfortunate movement led to ... I would strongly advise you, Mr Worthing, to try to acquire some relations as soon as possible, and to make a definite effort to produce at any rate one parent of either sex, before the season is quite over ... You can hardly imagine that I and Lord Bracknell would dream of allowing our only daughter – a girl brought up with the utmost care – to marry into a cloakroom, and form an alliance with a parcel?'

19 I return to look at this in more detail in Chapter 11.

20 In *Morality and Architecture*, 1977, Chicago, Ill: Chicago UP, p 47, discussing what he calls Lewis Mumford's 'hymn of praise dedicated to the new man of the 20th century, the godless, liberated humanist'.

21 [1998] J American Medical Association, 15 April.

22 Drugs are currently designed for and prescribed for a *general* patient population. Efficacy is tested by 'trial and error' and doctors' 'best guess' treatments based on a generalised picture of the efficacy and safety of a drug. The process is time consuming and hence expensive, and the doctor may make ineffective choices, thus adding inefficiency to the process.

It aims to find means by which to control the factors that influence drug response when a drug is tested and prescribed.[23]

Pharmacogenetics researches the consequences of genetic variation[24] and is, in some ways, the forerunner of genetic profiling. The potential impact that this may have on health care provision includes prognosis before diagnosis (a form of predictive medicine); targeted therapies for a more rational system of tailored health care and an increase in so called 'mini-buster' rather than 'blockbuster' drugs.[25] And, as well as illustrating the extraordinary changes in medicine itself, pharmacogenetics is a part of the metamorphosis of the patient from what might be called the 'generic' to the 'genetic', which I shall discuss shortly.

The implications of these developments in 'scientific medicine' for health care and for our analysis of science and technical societies more generally are important, far reaching and challenging. John Gray expounds some of the normative or evaluative criticisms in his book, *Beyond the New Right*.[26] Arguing, with critics such as Ivan Illich, that it must be accepted that there are limits to health care, Gray's first concern is with the over-medicalisation of life and death, which, writ large, we may incorporate as a plea against the over-sophistication of the technological controls and stresses of life. Similarly, Ulrich Beck suggests that, in its most advanced stage, 'medicine produces pathological conditions it defines as (for the time being or permanently) incurable, which represent totally new conditions of life and danger and cross the existing system of social inequalities'.[27]

Secondly, and this is related, Gray complains that modern medical care and treatment cannot be shown to have provided benefits proportionate to the claims made for it, or indeed proportionate to the costs lavished on it. As Thomas McKeown has shown, improvements in health care have arisen much more from developments in sanitation, environment and personal lifestyle than they have from individual 'medical' breakthroughs.[28] So, whereas, at the outset of the 20th century, 40 out of 100 patients died of acute illness, in 1980, only one out of 100 did so; in the same period, deaths from chronic illness rose from 46 to 80 out of 100, often preceded by a long period of illness.

---

23 A patient's response to a drug is dependent on a number of environmental and genetic factors.

24 With tools available from genomics research, some of it involving the study of single nucleotide polymorphisms (SNPs), the sites where variability occurs.

25 McCarthy, A, *Social, Ethical and Public Policy Implications of Advances in the Biomedical Sciences*, October 1999, London: Wellcome Trust, Pharmacogenetics Workshop.

26 Gray, J, *Beyond the New Right*, 1993, London: Routledge, p 162ff.

27 Beck, U, *Risk Society: Towards a New Modernity*, Ritter, M (trans), 1992, London: Sage, p 208.

28 McKeown, T, *The Role of Medicine*, 1979, Oxford: Basil Blackwell.

Thirdly, much of what has been incorporated within modern medical care lies, argues Gray in distinction to Porter, outside the medical domain, 'and can be performed safely and intelligently by trained lay people'.[29] This has come about as a result of what Beck calls the 'noiseless social and cultural revolution' in which the logic of progress has come to incorporate 'the possibilities for thoughtless and unplanned exceeding of limits'.[30] Genetics is, in many ways, the paradigm of Beck's notion of 'unplanned excess', not in the sense of planned excess where limits are exceeded by design or deception, but one which is, in large part, due to the very different methodologies of science and law and science and ethics.

METAMORPHOSIS 2:
EPISTEMOLOGY AND ETHICS

The philosophy of medicine (as distinct from *ethical* questions which medical treatments and interventions might be thought to raise) might treat medicine, by intervening in our bodies, as an intervention in what it is to *be* human. It suggests that there is something particular about *medical* interventions which affects us in ways which are distinct (not different but distinct) from non-medical interventions, such as our employment or our houses. A phenomenological tradition (more commonly encountered in continental philosophy) is more deeply schooled than the Anglo-American tradition, in seeing questions only of humans as humans; as with broad idealist traditions, it is more interested in points of view or perspectives. In the Anglo-American tradition, there is less interest in abnormal psychology, the pathology of the mind, the notion of illness and the experience of disease. Of course, one does not need to adopt an existentialist or phenomenological approach to realise that a visit to the doctor's surgery or clinic raises questions *about oneself*. For those in the analytic tradition, there is perhaps a desire to confine such questions to such situationally specific instances; in the phenomenological tradition, such sites are merely places where questions about oneself are most explicitly available. It is not only at the doctors that the question 'what does this mean for me?' arise; it is part of the constant process of asking 'what is it to be human?'

The question of what relation medicine has to the notion of humans as human, what it is to talk of the self, introduces the philosophy of mind. So, while the philosophy of medicine might include questions of ethics, it cannot suggest that ethics stand alone as a discipline in their own right; it includes an examination of ethical questions in so far as they contribute to the

---

29   *Op cit*, Gray, fn 26, p 168.
30   *Op cit*, Beck, fn 27, pp 204, 209.

examination of perspectives on what it means to be human. Medicine is, then, by definition, intimately bound up with the question, or questions, of identity. Questions of identity are bound up, sometimes more than we might want to say, with our corporeal self. Our body is part of what it is to be me (short, tall, thin, bald, 46), but also my self. These are one kind of epistemological question which recently provoked serious study, and they have important implications for our understanding of medicine and people.[31]

But, it has also been claimed that there are important changes in the ways in which moral decision making in medicine has developed, which have no less significant implications for a study of medical law. Boaventura de Sousa Santos has argued that we are living in a state of epistemological turbulence:

> It is as though Durkheim's motto has been reversed. Rather than studying social phenomena as if they were natural phenomena, scientists now study natural phenomena as if they were social phenomena.[32]

There are indeed suggestions that the very basis of ethical inquiry and the knowledge available to us have changed radically,[33] although Gillian Rose once roundly denounced this analysis as evidencing 'despairing rationalism without reason'.[34] Thus, Bruce Jennings has observed that moral decision making within medicine[35] is becoming increasingly institutionalised and subject to formalised procedures and constraints. Across a broad range in the landscape of contemporary medicine, such as human subjects research, organ procurement and transplantation, assisted reproduction, the rationing of health care and the forgoing of life sustaining treatment:

> ... ethical choice and agency are now embedded as never before in a network of explicit rules and formal procedures and processes for making decisions. These rules stipulate (within certain limits) what types of decision may be made, how they may be made, by whom, and with the assistance of what resources.[36]

Thus, science and medicine are increasingly drawn and driven into ethical debate which raises the clash between scientific method (small, step by step approaches and trial and error and answering small questions) and

---

31   Evans, M, 'Philosophy and medical humanities', in Evans, HM and Finlay, IG (eds), *Medical Humanities*, 2001 (forthcoming), London: BMJ, p 150.

32   *Op cit*, de Sousa Santos, fn 6, p 34.

33   Nietzsche, F, eg, *Beyond Good and Evil*, Hollingdale, RJ (trans), 1973, Harmondsworth: Penguin, section 32; Gilligan, C, *In a Different Voice: Psychological Theory and Women's Development*, 1982, Cambridge, Mass: Harvard UP, comprehensively criticised by O'Neill, O (with commentary by Nussbaum, M), 'Justice, gender and international boundaries', in Nussbaum, M and Sen, A (eds), *The Quality of Life*, 1993, Oxford: Clarendon, pp 303–35; Lyotard, J-F, *The Post-Modern Condition: A Report on Knowledge*, 1979, Manchester: Manchester UP.

34   Rose, G in her final book, *Mourning Becomes the Law: Philosophy and Representation*, 1996, Cambridge: CUP.

35   As, incidentally, in other professional and public organisational settings.

36   Jennings, B, 'Possibilities of consensus: towards democratic moral discourse' (1991) 16 J Medicine and Philosophy 447.

philosophical, metaphysical and ethical questions. And, such rules are increasingly institutionalised; they are embedded in statutes, regulations, directives, court opinions, administrative mandates and institutional protocols. In decisions regarding terminal care, for example, these rules inform counselling and educational mechanisms, encouraging individual patients and their families to engage in treatment discussions[37] and to give prior statements about wanted and unwanted treatment.[38]

This 'embedded' quality has important relationships with the kinds of ethical concerns and the way in which they are expressed. Jennings argues that there has been an important recent shift away from epistemological questions about the relationship between a rational, knowing subject and a rationally knowable, objective morality as the primary focus of ethical theory, towards an approach which aims to understand morality 'as a socially embedded practice'. These transformations have important consequences for the ways in which we conceptualise and even describe the setting of a legal framework and the establishment of ethical standards for regulating scientific and technical societies.

METAMORPHOSIS 3:
THE NATURE OF THE PATIENT

The nature of the patient has changed. I do not mean this *just* in the usual fashion which attends that assertion; that people have become more rights oriented, more consumerist about health care and the deliverers of health care. I mean also that *the patient has disappeared*, if by 'the patient' we are understood to mean some generic, stand all patient. I shall explain this idea further in a moment.

But, we probably could defend the thesis that patients have become more rights oriented. One of the reasons for it is shown in one of the very metamorphoses that I have already identified:[39]

> In so far as there has been a shift from power based in medicine as an art to power based in the objectives of science, medicine has changed the doctor from encompassing the uniqueness of the disease carrier in front of him to the generalizations of science. This shift to impersonal medicine has caused patients to look for their own objectivity in the relationship by the assertion of claims to self-determination. In turn, this is reinforced by modern ideas of the paramountcy of the consumer.[40]

---

37 See the discussion of Laws J at first instance in *R v Cambridge HA ex p B (A Minor)* (1995) 23 BMLR 1, p 16.
38 See, eg, *Re AK* (2001) 58 BMLR 1; *Re C* [1994] 1 WLR 290, discussed below, Chapter 12.
39 As Margot Brazier has argued in respect of assisted conception services.
40 *Op cit*, Jacob, fn 1, p 2.

Jacob then goes on to wonder how far it is possible to be consensual 'when need on one side and expertise on the other is presupposed?'.[41] Does the doctor's desire to treat the patient and exercise professional authority, on the one side, and the patient's need to seek help, on the other, 'create incommensurable objectives for its parties?'.[42]

Over time, this has helped to transform the experience of patients who believe that they have not received optimal care from the lachrymose to the litigious, from naming through blaming to claiming. The 'procreative tourist'[43] surfing the waves of information is merely in the vanguard of the information activists' more settled development of the surgery, the theatre and the clinic. A preliminary study on the impact of the information revolution, recently published by Benita Cox, reported that 40% of obstetricians interviewed said that use of the internet 'could *damage* the traditional doctor patient relationship'.[44] This, Cox observes, poses a threat to the 'institutionalised doctor-patient power relationship'.[45] 'Empowered' patients are challenging the professional's medical advice and choices of treatment, sometimes by finding alternative sources or providers of treatment on the internet.[46]

It is possible to identify two characteristics of a model of the doctor-patient relationship in the bio-information age to which this analysis gives rise. They are what I call the 'shopping' and the 'cynical' traits. Both, in my view, have dangerous limitations and pose particular challenges to the doctor-patient relationship, at least as it has until recently been conceived. The 'cynical' trait, of course, is that which, following Oscar Wilde, people display when they believe that they know the price of everything and yet the value of nothing. Such cynicism is like credit to the 'shoppers' of the new bio-information age; it ignores even the possibility that health itself may be of value and one which it is not possible to price: '... nobody knows how much health care will be worth to him in terms of money and pain.'[47]

Margot Brazier and Nicola Glover have cautioned of the way in which technology is threatening to circumvent any 'gate-keeping' role for health

---

41   *Op cit*, Jacob, fn 1, p 168.

42   *Op cit*, Jacob, fn 1.

43   Knoppers, B and le Bris, S, 'Recent advances in medically assisted conception: legal, ethical and social issues' (1991) 17 Am J Law and Medicine 329, p 333. And see Brazier, M, 'Regulating the reproduction business?' (1999) 7 Med L Rev 166 for specific examples of the use of the internet.

44   Cox, A, *The Impact of the Internet on the Doctor-Patient Relationship*, 2000, London: Imperial College Management School.

45   One of the best studies of the asymmetry between doctor and patient remains *op cit*, Jacob, fn 1, esp pp 168–69.

46   For a particular example, see various issues of *The Guardian*, *The Telegraph* and *The Daily Telegraph*, week beginning 9 October 2000.

47   Illich, I, *Limits to Medicine*, 1976, London: Penguin, p 235.

professionals; whether or not this is a good thing depends, centrally, on the role and function that is ascribed to the doctor or the nurse. If, however, we believe, as I do, in concert with Brazier and Glover, that a case can be made that, in large part 'the medical role is to protect the patient',[48] then the 'shopping' trait harbours distinct threats. Surrendering concepts of illness and according legitimacy to desire alone means, according to Brazier and Glover, that consumer protection laws could (in theory) 'offer sufficient guarantee of the quality of the goods supplied and standards of service provision'.[49] Such a future, where medical law is subsumed into consumer law, may be seen as a logical development of regarding medical law as a sub-set of human rights. 'Expanding definitions of illness coupled with the present tendency to prioritise self-determination as *the* basic human right in medical law, assume that health is essentially a personal concern.'[50]

How are doctors to respond; what is to be their role? The *potential* for danger, confirmed by Cox's early research, was highlighted some time ago and beautifully illustrated by Franz Inkelfinger, the former editor of the *New England Journal of Medicine*, as he lay dying of cancer:

> I do not want to be in the position of the shopper at the Casbah who negotiates and haggles with the physician about what is best. I want to believe that my physician is acting under a higher moral principle than a used car dealer. I'll go further than that. A physician who merely spreads an array of vendibles in front of his patient and then says 'Go ahead, you choose, it's your life' is guilty of shirking his duty, if not malpractice.[51]

This informs my more general thesis that medicine and, hence, medical law is not *just* for treating people right, but for treating them gentle *too*. I see this not as in opposition to Kennedy's claim that medical law properly understood is but a sub-set of human rights, but as complementary to it. It is an argument that medical law as a species of human rights law is valuable and significant if seen as and limited to a protection against harm (howsoever defined) and abuse, but limited in use and in scope if seen in the form of a claim right.[52]

And, there is a form of equity argument here too. In a later essay on advance directives I argue that 'going off well' must not be reserved for the well off. The point can be generalised. The current ascendancy of autonomy and rights 'ignores the fact that disease and disorder fail to recognise such rights'.[53] The consumerist model presupposes rational market actors and resources which, while shopping for medicine and health care on the internet

---

48 Brazier, M and Glover, N, 'Does medical law have a future?', in Birks, P, *Law's Future(s)*, 2000, Oxford: Hart.

49 *Ibid.*

50 *Ibid.*

51 Inkelfinger, FG, 'Arrogance' (1980) 304 New England J Medicine 1507.

52 In the classic Hohfeldian conception; see his *Fundamental Conceptions*, 1923, New Haven, Ct: Yale UP.

53 *Ibid*, Brazier and Glover, p 3.

and elsewhere, may offer 'recreation for the "worried well"'[54] but may also fail to meet the needs of the sick and the destitute. Individual rights claims have an insidious history of gravitating towards those who are articulate and affluent enhancing *their* access to medical technologies of their choice,[55] while remaindering others to the margins of the resource arithmetic. A picture of patients staggering home with copies of the Human Rights Act, the Patients' Charter and the Bar List bulging in their Louis Vuitton, Gucci and Dolce & Gabbana shopping bags will fail to see, let alone meet, the needs of the poor, the illiterate and the sick.

But in addition to these sorts of changes in the 'nature of the patient', what I also mean is that *the patient has disappeared*, if by 'the patient' we are understood to mean some generic, stand all patient. Not only has burgeoning feminist and race-sensitive work rendered suspect any bioethical approach geared to the generic 'patient', methodological engagements urge a return to cases rather than principles, to narratives rather than norms.[56] This shift is being mirrored or shadowed in new paradigms in health law.[57] In the place of the generic patient, we have what might be called the 'genetic' patient; patients who have gender, class, race, ethnicity, age and individual identity and biography; we have, as Susan Wolf has proposed, a theatre teeming with peoples all of different voices:[58]

> The erasure of difference in bioethics was not simply an artefact of the field's early embrace of principlism ... it is a legacy of the field's commitment to a liberal individualism born of the work of Kant and Mill. Bioethics strained for universals, ignoring the significance of groups and the importance of context. It rushed to generalise about 'the patient', 'the subject', 'the doctor', and 'the researcher'. It claimed to find basic truths about the doctor-patient encounter.[59]

Several of the essays that follow take up all or parts of this theme. But the importance of this point should not be overlooked. While it may be axiomatic that bioethics as much as medical law has not been about the doctor and patient who have everything in common, see treatment decisions the same way and meet as equals (indeed, the patient 'hardly needs autonomy ... when the physician already agrees'),[60] the importance of difference has been, at best, understated.

---

54 *Op cit*, Brazier and Glover, fn 48, p 15.

55 *Op cit*, Brazier and Glover, fn 48, p 15.

56 See Wolf, SM (1994) 20(4) Am J Law and Medicine 395 for a comprehensive review, and Fairbairn, G and Fairbairn, S (eds), *Ethical Issues in Caring*, 1988, Aldershot: Avebury.

57 *Ibid*, Wolf.

58 See Wolf, SM, 'Erasing difference: race, ethnicity and gender in bioethics', Chapter 4 in *Feminism and Bioethics*, 1996, New York: OUP.

59 *Ibid*, p 70.

60 *Ibid*, p 68.

... the only person who might claim that race is of no significance in the United States is a person of the dominant race, asserting the privilege to ignore it ... the damage done by a bioethics that erases difference occurs on a number of levels. Individual cases are wrongly construed, entire patterns of profound harm are left unchallenged, bioethics itself becomes complicit in those harms, and the field devolves into a bioethics by and for those who least need it – the already dominant.[61]

It is very difficult to know whether we can simply say, *mutatis mutandi* medical law in England and Wales, but I am tempted to believe that we can. As Margot Brazier and Nicola Glover have adequately demonstrated, in the new era of human rights, one of the core challenges for the next generation of medical law and lawyers will be to ensure a just distribution of the claimed benefits.

METAMORPHOSIS 4: THE CHANGING CONSTITUTION

The fourth challenge is presented by wider political forces, not unique to, but highly germane to both the practice of modern medicine and the principles of contemporary science. 'Changing constitutions and constitutional change' reflects the changing constitution of political society. In the same way that, as Jacob has shown, a study of doctoring and medicine is a necessarily political study, a study of the constitution,[62] studying aspects of the changing constitution provides an important context for studying medical law. This is given an added dimension by the introduction of the Human Rights Act 1998, which will soon transform some questions of medical law into constitutional challenges. But, for the present, I want to focus on three pivotal constitutional changes which affect medical law. These are the relationships between:

• the knowledge economy and the social investment State;

• holistic government and problem solving; and

• the Europeanisation and globalisation of law.

Let me briefly explore each relationship.

---

61 *Op cit*, Wolf, fn 58, p 71.

62 *Op cit*, Jacob, fn 1, p 1. He quotes the American sociologist Everet Hughes to substantiate this point: 'The power of an occupation to protect its licence and maintain its mandate, the circumstances in which they are attacked, lost or changed; all these are ... [the] study of politics in the very fundamental sense of studying constitutions.' Hughes, E, *Men and Their Work*, 1958, Chicago, Ill: Free Press of Glencoe, p 85.

The knowledge economy and the social investment State[63]

The profound forces of globalisation have sharply altered the operating environment for government. Barriers to the exchange of money, ideas and entertainment can no longer easily be sustained. Economies are more difficult to insulate from global business cycles and autonomous defence strategies are disappearing. The challenge is how to balance prosperity with social inclusion, capitalism with community, and how to modernise welfare systems, public services and labour markets. There are very specific challenges, such as how to manage the transition to an economy based on intensive application and development of knowledge; how to manage the breakdown of the old structures of the life cycle on which 20th century education and welfare were founded; reversing trends towards inequality and social exclusion; protecting the environment and planning long term sustainability; and, for our present purposes, ensuring that science and new technology enhance our lives rather than bringing unacceptable risks.

For medicine, this is most profoundly seen when considering the impact of growing commercialisation. Issues such as intellectual property and patent regimes for biotechnology, the funding of the national science base and the imperatives for research have important impacts on the doctor-patient relationship. This is felt in diverse ways, ranging from the whole design of health care delivery, the very definitions of illness and health themselves, which medical services are provided and to whom and on what basis, through to more 'micro' level concerns, such as confidentiality, access to records and the use of health care information for non-health purposes, such as insurance. One of the central tasks for governments of the 21st century will be to provide the economic constitution for the new 'knowledge economy'.[64] As the asset base of the economy shifts, the traditional assets of Adam Smith's economies – land, labour, raw materials and machinery – are becoming less critical to competitive advantage. Intangible assets, know-how, creativity and brands are becoming increasingly critical.[65] The reasons for this include the production of unprecedented amounts of scientific knowledge, which is especially characteristic of biotechnology, while such research has been made hugely more productive by bio-informatics – computer based methods of searching for new gene strings and compounds. The consequences for economic policy and government legislation and regulation are profound. Probably the two

---

63   This, and the immediate analysis that follows, is based on Hargreaves, I and Christie, I (eds), *Tomorrow's Politics: The Third Way and Beyond*, 1998, London: Demos, esp pp 1–39, the essays by Charles Leadbetter and Anthony Giddens.

64   *Ibid.*

65   *Ibid*, Leadbetter, p 12.

most important are the problem of *regulatory lag*, especially in the biotechnology industry, with legislation and regulation often lagging several years behind the fastest moving industries,[66] and significant issues of *ownership*. It is predicted that the 'knowledge economy' will open a range of ownership questions. Thus, just as the legitimacy of the publicly owned private company had been established as the natural dominant organisation, as human capital becomes the most valuable asset in modern economies, the most successful companies will be those based on hybrid models blending ownership based on human and financial capital. Secondly, as the knowledge base for future industries is largely publicly funded and owned, a further hybrid of public-private ownership will be needed to share and exploit this knowledge. Thirdly, the rise of industries based on biology already pose troubling ethical questions about who should own the knowledge on which they are based, such as genetics and patenting:

> ... markets are often a poor way to organise the distribution of know-how; networks and other collaborative arrangements become more important ... that in turn means that traditional, market clearing models of pricing and value are not relevant ... the new knowledge economy will require us to develop new measures of value and economic performance.[67]

Holistic government and problem solving[68]

Governments in all Western countries have become caught between the public's resistance to paying more tax, leading to the abandonment of an interventionist role and the 'hollowing out' of the State, and their continuing demand to provide high quality health, welfare infra-structures and social order.[69] Rising demands include those for health and long term care, that governments are searching to achieve more with less. Perri 6 has suggested that the core of the problem of modern government stems from the 19th century model of organisation around which it is structured. This is one that looks to functions and services rather than solving problems. 'Government needs to be more holistic, achieving greater integration across the public sector. It also needs to become more preventive, shifting the balance away from curing problems ... towards preventing them.'[70]

The next generation of government will need to focus on 'horizontal integration and thinking between fields and functions'. Holistic government will be preventive, culture-changing and outcome oriented. In practice, this

---

66 *Op cit*, Leadbetter, fn 63, p 19.

67 *Op cit*, Leadbetter, fn 63, p 22.

68 This, and the immediate analysis that follows, is based on Perri 6, *Holistic Government*, 1997, London: Demos.

69 See below, Chapter 4, for a discussion of aspects of this debate.

70 *Ibid*, Perri 6.

will mean inter-departmentalism, collaboration across functions, central co-ordinating mechanisms across networks, fewer agencies with broader responsibilities, agencies with restricted abilities to pass on costs, joint production of services, case managers, information management and customer interface integration, and holistic budgeting and purchasing.[71] The elision of the formerly separate categories of social care and health care is probably only the first, clearest example of this philosophy and strategy in action. This will produce at a more fundamental level a re-examination of questions such as illness, disease, health and well being, and, in consequence, may have profound implications not just for service delivery and liability, but for the very shape and meaning of 'medical' responsibility, hence medical law, altogether. If Margot Brazier and Nicola Glover are correct that, by 2050, much medical law will have been subsumed into consumer law, it may be that environmental and environmental health law will have accommodated much of the rest – including those aspects of genetics that have not been appropriated by the market.[72]

The Europeanisation of constitutional law and globalisation of law

'Europeanisation', following John Bell,[73] connotes a common experience, common principles, a locus of comparison and the originator (through the institutions of the European Union) of constitutional problems. The idea that the British Constitution is idiosyncratic or simply part of the common law is too basic. As an established constitutional system in the 18th century, the 'common law' provided the inspiration for reform of jury trials in press cases in Sweden to constitutional monarchy in Belgium. And, it has been influenced throughout its development by ideas from elsewhere; such as reform of suffrage in the 19th century to the Ombudsman system in the 20th.[74] The common law is not an island, and its traditions and practice owe much to, as well as contribute much to, an evolving European legal order. As Patrick Glenn has recently written:

> For most of its history the common law was in the *process* of becoming a common law, and its history is above all one of relations with other laws, themselves also common in considerable measure, both in England and Europe.[75]

---

71 *Op cit*, Perri 6, fn 68.

72 Of which by far the most important will be what Lee Silver has called Reprogenetics Types I and II; see Silver, L, *Remaking Eden: Cloning, Genetic Engineering and the Future of Humankind?*, 1998, London: Weidenfeld & Nicolson, pp 86–87.

73 Bell, J, 'The Europeanisation of law', in Watkin, T (ed), *The Europeanisation of Law*, 1998, London: UKNCCL, p 75.

74 *Ibid*.

75 Glenn, HP, *Legal Traditions of the World*, 2000, Oxford: OUP, p 235.

The common law is not, then, an island, and these relationships make it more desirable to speak of 'common laws' rather than just 'the common law'. And, a contemporary 'common law tradition' must today be highly flexible and accommodating if it is to continue to provide some measure of commonality to the diverse legal orders which have been associated with it; 'since a common law tradition has diversified internally, *its relations with other legal traditions have also intensified*'.[76]

The potential benefits of a Europeanised comparative and constitutional agenda might be greater insights into shared problems, greater articulation and formality of principles and greater willingness to make use of the rules and law (assuming that that is held to be a common good). These features have important lessons for the shape, scope and parameters of health care as much as for any other central feature of the responsibilities of modern government. Of course, ethical relativism, cultural heterogeneity and legal specificity are jealously guarded ideals. Yet, in each country of Europe, including Eastern Europe, similar questions arise with respect to law, medicine and bioethics. But, there are differences of a philosophical, economic, social, political and even geographical nature which are not easily (even if desirably) bridged. Against this background, Albin Eser has argued that legal initiatives in bioethics and medical law may be required for one or more of four reasons:[77] *a symbolic function of law;*[78] *a protective function;*[79] *a regulative or declarative function;*[80] and *a technical function.*[81]

Of course, we might ask whether it matters whether and how we regulate given that 'procreative tourism'[82] – the forerunner of a more generalised medical tourism which is the corollary of an enhanced shopping market for

---

76 *Op cit*, Glenn, fn 75, p 228, emphasis added.

77 *Legal Aspects of Bioethics in Europe* and *Bioethics, Proceedings of the 1st Symposium of the Council of Europe on Bioethics*, 1989, Strasbourg: Council of Europe, pp 41, 42.

78 Declaring certain values and interests as worth protection against any infringement (of which prohibitions on altering the structure of the nucleus of an embryo and protecting the life of the unborn fetus are commonly given as paradigm examples).

79 Providing sanctions for abuses within the bioethical field, and for minimising risks to patients and significant others affected by the application of biotechnology – such as potential children who might be born following assisted conception.

80 Because there is probably no legal system with a comprehensive biomedical law, the legal status of many bioethical practices is unclear in the absence of parliamentary intervention, which is seen or appealed to as securing clarity and certainty in handling controversial areas of bioethics. Again, regulation of the permissible extent of embryo research is a particularly clear example.

81 For stabilising confidence between physician and patient by providing reliable rules for their relationship. One example of this might be ground rules relating to access to lawful abortion facilities, another dealing with aspects of confidentiality in respect of genetic knowledge obtained during the course of pre-natal or ante-natal screening.

82 A term coined by Bartha Knoppers and Sonia le Bris in *op cit*, fn 43, p 333.

health – makes anything and everything available somewhere,[83] whether there is even any point in continuing to engage in debate about what we will permit within a given jurisdiction. Identifying and addressing the tension between the sovereign realm of private choice and commons of a medical republic will be a crucial component in moving towards a reflective position that informs our regulatory instincts. At its heart are not simply questions of public morality, but the health and welfare of society in many senses. This negotiation between jurisdictions, the search for some common, basic *mores* and possibly norms, moves towards harmonisation or approximation of law, and the countervailing instincts of subsidiarity and 'margins of appreciation' are part of the very concept and process of *'biomedical diplomacy'* that I introduce in Chapter 3.

Globalisation

Contemporary theorists and political ideas are read in many languages and dialects; the intellectual globalisation of liberal political issues,[84] increasing interconnection of international business and finance, rapid communications, and the challenges of centralised and localised decision making structures and balances are faced across the world.[85] Some argue that this leads to a universality of problems and calls for universal solutions; much as traditional natural law theorists have proclaimed for at least 2,500 years. Yet, John Bell has correctly cautioned that 'there are no uniquely right answers in the design of constitutional systems', and that specific traditions of history and culture of individual countries may lead them to make choices of governmental structure which mark them out from others.[86] Legal transnationalisation is, however, not a monolithic phenomenon; rather, it is diverse and combines uniformity with local differentiation, top-down imposition with bottom-up creation, formal declaration with interstitial emergence and boundary maintenance with boundary transcendence.[87] These constitutional questions have a deep impact on the design of responses to globalisation, or for that matter Europeanisation. Nonetheless, there are significant features of what Jacob has suggested we might properly regard as another sort of constitutionality issue, the role and regulation of medicine and medical practice,[88] that invite generalised reflection.

---

83   We might even see the emergence and development of specialist package tour companies for specific health demands, such as Lung Poly, Eye Tours, Queasy Jet, Virgin Births and Xeno Air. For an example of life imitating art, see www.bodrumdialysis.com (Turkish hotel with 24 hour kidney dialysis centre. Note the irony: a Turkish hotel).

84   Audaciously proclaimed by Frances Fukyama as *The End of History*, 1993, Harmondsworth: Penguin.

85   *Op cit*, Bell, fn 73, p 73. See, also, Beck, U, *What is Globalisation?*, 2000, Cambridge: Polity.

86   *Op cit*, Bell, fn 73, p 75.

87   *Op cit*, Bell, fn 73, p 252.

88   *Op cit*, Jacob, fn 1, p 1.

But, it is the power of transnational corporate actors, enhanced by their ability to conduct business across State boundaries, an ability facilitated by the crumbling of those barriers as individual regimes themselves undergo seismic political changes,[89] that dominates the globalisation literature and agendas. In the last quarter of the 20th century, transnational interactions intensified, from the globalisation of production systems and financial transfers, 'to the world wide dissemination of information and images through the mass media and communication technologies, and through the mass translocation of people either as tourists, migrant workers or refugees'.[90] An overview of the studies on globalisation discloses a 'multifaceted phenomenon with economic, social, political, cultural, religious and legal dimensions intertwined in the most complex ways'.[91] The 'globalisation process' has, according to de Sousa Santos, three main components: a new international division of labour, changes in the inter-State system (the political form of the modern world) and the debate over whether or not there has emerged a global culture.[92]

While 'globalisation' has been used in recent years to analyse the dramatic intensification of a variety of transnational, international trends and interactions, de Sousa Santos has cautioned us to remember that, while tempting, it would not be entirely appropriate to see 'globalisation of the legal field' as a radically new phenomenon without historical antecedents. While some of this undoubtedly represents a qualitatively new development, 'the modern world system, within which the globalisation of social interaction occurs, has been in place since the 16th century' and the roots of the most recent legal, as well as cultural, social, political and economic transformations 'are to be located in this historical development'.[93] Indeed, a transnational legal culture can be illustrated in the reception of Roman law in the 12th century and beyond. National sovereignty is not an insuperable obstacle to the creation of transnational regimes, as States can, and do, subordinate their domestic legal regimes to international standards when it suits them to do so, in what de Sousa Santos calls 'sovereignty pooling'.[94] Thus, they sign and respect international treaties, amend laws to conform to international commitments and expectations, harmonise regulatory practices and policies with trading partners to facilitate trade, and permit the development and expansion of private legal regimes to accommodate needs of transnational

---

89 For an introduction to some of this literature from a legal perspective, see Arthurs, H, 'Globalization of the mind: Canadian elites and the restructuring of legal fields' (1997) 12 Canadian J Law and Society 219.

90 *Op cit*, de Sousa Santos, fn 6, p 252.

91 *Op cit*, de Sousa Santos, fn 6, p 253.

92 *Op cit*, de Sousa Santos, fn 6, pp 253–58.

93 *Op cit*, de Sousa Santos, fn 6, p 251.

94 *Op cit*, de Sousa Santos, fn 6, p 254.

corporate movements,[95] leading two commentators to speak of a new *lex mercatoria*[96] and another of a the appearance of a new *jus humanitatus*.[97]

In relation to biomedicine, this is part of the concept of '*biomedical diplomacy*'. The study of globalisation in relation to health and medical care has hardly surfaced; the closest yet is perhaps the World Health Organization's series of studies on Health Futures, *Health Futures in Support of Health for All*,[98] and the *Health Futures Handbook*.[99] Some further specific examples may be drawn from intellectual property rights and regimes, pharmaceutical licensing and development, and the Council of Europe Convention on Biomedicine and Human Rights. Current aspects of transplantation practice will extend further if xeno-transplantation ever becomes a practical reality, as will the trade, whether legal or not, in body parts, body tissues and organs. In more traditional public health terms, globalisation studies will encompass the re-emergence of infectious diseases and the impact of genetic technologies.[100] And, in re-conceptualising an international concern with health care, globalisation will require focusing on issues such as gender,[101] race and ethnicity,[102] the health effects of global environmental change and the primary infrastructures necessary for health,[103] the growth and potentials of telemedicine,[104] and medical and health care tourism. It may yet grow, without ever developing into a *lex medicalus*.

A global *scientific* order is today taken as axiomatic; maybe it has been for many years. Legal responses to this economic and scientific globalisation have reinforced the belief that the 'inevitable role of law', as Windeyer J once memorably put it, is marching with medicine (and I might add science), 'but in the rear and limping a little'.[105] But, there is a change under way. If, for example, we are concerned to essay a chronological history of biomedical diplomacy, the date of 11 October 1997 might feature significantly. That was

---

95 *Op cit*, Arthurs, fn 89.

96 Dezalay, Y and Sugarman, D, *Professional Competition and Professional Power: Lawyers, Accountants and the Social Construction of Markets*, 1995, London: Routledge, p 8.

97 *Op cit*, de Sousa Santos, fn 6, pp 365–73.

98 See Sapirie, S and Orzeszyna, S, *Health Futures: The Results and Follow-Up of the 1993 Consultation*, 1995, Geneva: WHO.

99 Garrett, M, *Health Futures Handbook*, 1995, Geneva: WHO.

100 Bennett, B, 'A right to health? Health rights, human rights and the law' (unpublished: I am grateful to Dr Bennett for permission to cite from this draft).

101 See Doyal, L, *What Makes Women Sick? Gender and the Political Economy of Health*, 1995, New Brunswick, NJ: Rutgers UP.

102 *Op cit*, Wolf, fn 58.

103 *Ibid*, Bennett.

104 Bauer, JC and Ringel, MA, *Telemedicine and the Reinvention of Healthcare*, 1999, New York: McGraw Hill.

105 *Mount Isa Mines v Pusey* (1970) 125 CLR 383.

the one when French President Jacques Chirac called for a global Code of Scientific Ethics, of which the first emanation might be thought to be the call for a prohibition on the cloning of human beings. This is something for which former US President Clinton called, albeit in the form of a moratorium rather than an outright ban.

Reflection on the existence of 'procreative tourism' suggests a starting point for understanding the tasks that 'biomedical diplomacy' may have ahead. Bartha Knoppers and Sonia le Bris[106] have identified a range of emergent assumptions about the necessary forms of limitation and prohibition of assisted conception, and a narrower area in which disagreement or national difference is more pronounced. They identify areas of general consensus and those on which there is less or no agreement. They suggest that the possibility of a comprehensive policy, or of legislation encompassing all of these new technologies, may never be forthcoming and may not even be desirable given these fundamental differences. And, furthermore, even if internal domestic regulation could be harmonised or approximated, today's modern 'global village', which both encourages and facilitates 'procreative tourism' to allow individuals to exercise their personal reproductive choices in other less restrictive States,[107] poses the most significant obstacle to limiting or addressing market solutions for those who are able to afford them. I shall return to this point in Chapter 3.

METAMORPHOSIS 5:
THE NATURE OF LAW'S RESPONSES

We have come a long way since Patrick Devlin's

> ... pleasant tribute to the medical profession that by and large it has been able to manage its relations with its patients on the basis of such an understanding [that conduct be regulated by a general understanding of how decent people ought to behave] without the aid of lawyers and law makers.[108]

We may even, I venture, have moved an appreciable degree from Windeyer J's assessment, quoted earlier.[109] Practices and procedures attendant upon death, no less than birth, are an example of these metamorphoses. Whether or not that is a good thing is, as Gregor Samsa found,[110] another question. Put

---

106 *Op cit*, Knoppers and le Bris, fn 43, p 329. Although now somewhat dated, the fundamentals of the approach which they adopt are still illuminating.

107 *Op cit*, Knoppers and le Bris, fn 43, p 344.

108 Devlin, P, 'Samples of lawmaking', in *Medicine and Law*, 1962, Oxford: Clarendon, pp 83, 103.

109 *Mount Isa Mines v Pusey* (1970) 125 CLR 383.

110 Kafka, F, 'Metamorphosis', in *Metamorphosis and Other Stories*, 1999, London: Vintage.

simply, however, there is, as the construction of medical law itself discloses, more law, more types of law and more sites on which it operates. Gunther Teubner has identified this as part of the 'juridification' of social spheres,[111] Marc Galanter has claimed that it is evidence of 'law abounding',[112] and Richard Susskind has described it as 'hyper-regulation'.[113] The nature of law in the 'risk society' has changed. I mean that not in the sense proposed earlier by Eser, that law may have different functions: the instrumental, the symbolic, the protective and the declaratory. Nor, although this is important, in the senses suggested by John Griffith, identifying the gap between intended, unintended, foreseen and unforeseen consequences of law making.[114] Rather, I mean that following the 'noiseless social and cultural revolution' which Beck has identified as a characteristic of medicine in the risk society, the nature of law is different in that, as more areas of social life become 'legalised', it thereby disqualifies other versions of truth.[115] Biotechnology and biomedicine are a highly topical illustration of this.[116]

The 'risk society' is one which creates *manufactured risk*; 'science and technology create as many uncertainties and they dispel – and the uncertainties cannot be 'solved' in any simple way by scientific evidence'. As I have already suggested, Beck argues that these scientific changes have brought about a 'noiseless social and cultural revolution' of the 'lay public's social living conditions without its consent'.[117] Beck's thesis is that progress in scientific medicine *necessarily* implies unplanned excess, the harmful effects of which are unintentional.[118] Thus, social costs, while statistically quantifiable as risks, become difficult to guard against, anticipate or even calculate. How does medical law respond, given the stories that we want to tell and the people whom we say that we want to be? Whether law does or even can keep pace with the demands produced by the metamorphosis in scientific medicine, is one type of question. How it does or might do that provokes an equally important and challenging question: has law itself become the subject of a metamorphosis?

---

111 Teubner, G, 'Juridification: concepts, aspects, limits, solutions', in Teubner, G (ed), *Juridification of Social Spheres*, 1987, Berlin and New York: Walter de Gruyter.

112 Galanter, M, 'Law abounding: legislation around the North Atlantic' (1992) 55 MLR 1.

113 Susskind, R, *The Future of Law*, 1998, Oxford: OUP.

114 See 'Is law important?' (1979) 56 New York UL Rev 339.

115 See, in a different context, Smart, C, *Feminism and the Power of Law*, 1989, London: Routledge, p 23, and Davies, M, *Asking the Law Question*, 1994, North Ryde, NSW: LBC, p 253.

116 Parker, S and Bottomley, S, *Law in Context*, 1997, Sydney: Federation, p 66.

117 *Op cit*, Beck, fn 27, p 206. See, also, Jonas, H, *Philosophical Essays: From Ancient Creed to Technological Man*, 1974, Englewood Cliffs, NJ: Prentice Hall; Jonas, H, *The Imperative of Responsibility: In Search of an Ethics for the Technological Age*, 1984, Chicago, Ill: Chicago UP; National Science Foundation, 'Biology and law: challenges of adjudicating competing claims in a democracy', 1997, Washington DC.

118 *Op cit*, Beck, fn 27, p 209.

Marc Galanter has suggested that this hyper-regulated world is characterised by more laws, more lawyers, more claims and more players of the law game. Societies spend more on laws and lawyers. Legal institutions including courts and firms increasingly operate in rational, businesslike manners and lawyers and judges are more entrepreneurial and innovative. Law, as Jennings has also suggested,[119] is plural, decentralised and issuing from more sources; more rules are being applied by more actors to more varied circumstances. More law, more pervasive law, and more information about law, also means that law is less autonomous, less self-contained and more open textured, responsive to methods and data from other disciplines. Legal outcomes are more contingent and changing. Outcomes are increasingly negotiated rather than decreed,[120] such that, perhaps paradigmatically in medicine, law increasingly operates through indirect symbolic controls rather than through imposing coercion.[121] And, as it becomes more contingent, flexible and technically sophisticated, it becomes more costly and is priced out of use by many people.[122]

Paralleling Hobsbawm's 'crisis decades' and Beck's description of this period as a 'secret farewell to an epoch of human history', Galanter has observed in strikingly similar fashion that:

> Law itself is being transformed ... As the law expands and penetrates the world, it changes in the process. Its institutions flourish but lose their autonomous, self-contained quality. On every front, we can observe the boundaries of the legal world becoming more blurred and indefinite.[123]

Thus, law firms become more businesslike; courts become more like other governmental bodies and their judgments increasingly resemble legal scholarship. And, as Jennings has also recognised, the traffic is not one-directional. As law becomes less autonomous, so other institutions and discourses, such as the family and the hospital, absorb legal ideas and simulate legal forms.

Hence, not only does medical law become more like consumer law, civil law and common laws exhibit similar features and methodologies, ethical choice becomes embedded and institutionalised, and courts become more and more sensitised to moral argumentation and maybe even decision making takes on an overtly or covertly moral dimension. If politics, medicine, ethics,

---

119 *Op cit*, Jennings, fn 36.

120 There is an excellent illustration and application of the meaning of this part of Galanter's argument in Black, J, 'Regulation as facilitation; negotiating the genetic revolution', in Brownsword, R, Cornish, WR and Llewelyn, M, *Law and Human Genetics: Regulating a Revolution*, 1998, Oxford: Hart, pp 29–68.

121 That this is hardly a novel phenomenon, nor one newly observed, can be gathered from, eg, Kai Ericson's elegant study, *Wayward Puritans*, 1966, Boston: Allyn and Bacon, *passim*.

122 *Op cit*, Galanter, fn 112, p 24.

123 *Op cit*, Galanter, fn 112, pp 17–18.

law and patients have all changed, is the world (however we judge this?) a better place? What job does medical law *do* in this world, a new utopia or a pale shadow of some elysian field?[124]

There are various ways in which we might characterise the nature of law's responses to changes in medicine, ethics and the risk society. I believe that medical law and medical laws are typically constructed around one, or more, of what might be called the *colloquial*, the *contractual*, the *chaotic* or the *constitutive* canons. These responses are not, I think, mutually exclusive and may, indeed, in cases be sequential. The *colloquial* response is, however, the most pervasive of law's responses to these other metamorphoses as it is the stigmata of biomedical diplomacy itself in the risk society, and I introduce it more fully below. Biomedical diplomacy is part of determining an appropriate legal response from others, such as the contractual, the chaotic and the constitutive. The colloquial response is, itself, part of the process of mediating naming, blaming, claiming and declaiming and not just a response in itself. *Contractual* responses (by which I do not mean formal, legal contracts, but those that might also be described as 'compactual') are evidenced in the nature of the doctor-patient relationship, in the negotiation of death, and in collusive actions between doctors and patients, as seen in some of the scarce resource allocation litigation.

One sense in which we might identify *chaotic* responses, used in the sense identified by Ulrich Beck and Elisabeth Gernsheim-Beck,[125] is to imply a sense of disorder or lack of system, at the level of the legal text. As Dewar has suggested of family law, however, this concept of chaos is a *normal* one, in that medical law engages (much as family law) with areas of social life, feeling, emotion, pain and identity, that are themselves riven with contradiction and paradox. Thus, there are no agreed responses, as to the role of law or the appropriate type of law if it is to be invoked, either domestically or internationally, to contested areas of modern medical developments, such as genetics, assisted conception and surrogacy, and physician assisted suicide, to take just three examples. Finally, we may say of a *constitutive* response that it recalls that law is not something that is separate from other social structures and practices, but is a part, indeed a constitutive part, of them.[126] Law regulates social behaviour not just as a set of rules imposed from 'outside', but by being internalised in that behaviour. Law, as Clare Dalton has memorably written:

---

124 See, also, Yevgeny Zamyatin's satire on the mechanised State created in such utopias in *We*, 1972, Harmondsworth: Penguin.

125 See their *The Normal Chaos of Love*, 1995, Cambridge: Polity. For an attempt to apply the 'normal chaos' argument to another site of law, see Dewar, J, 'The normal chaos of family law' (1998) 61 MLR 467.

126 Sarat, A and Felstiner, WF, *Divorce Lawyers and their Clients*, 1995, New York: OUP.

... like every other cultural institution, is a place where we tell one another stories about our relationships with ourselves, one another, and authority ... When we tell one another stories, we use languages and themes that different pieces of the culture make available to us, and that limit the stories we can tell. Since our stories influence how we can imagine, as well as how we describe, our relationships, our stories also limit who we can be.[127]

Medical law is, then, on this account, where we write prescriptions about who we will be and who we might become. This engages the core meaning of biomedical diplomacy, making and taking tragic choices in the risk society, which I now explore.

---

127 Dalton, C, 'An essay in the deconstruction of contract doctrine' [1985] Yale LJ 999, citing Lopez, A, 'Lay lawyering' (1984) UCLA L Rev 1.

CHAPTER 3

BIOMEDICAL DIPLOMACY: TRAGIC CHOICES AND THE RISK SOCIETY

With these different metamorphoses, this general concern with ethics to supervise or regulate scientific development, the rediscovery of the value of the sacredness or sanctity of human life and the celebration of difference and different values, why, it might be asked, did the century not end in a mood of unparalleled celebration and marvel at the progress and achievements of scientific medicine and modern biomedicine? Why, if Hobsbawm is indeed correct, did it end with a rejection by substantial bodies of public opinion of the only claims which the era had to have benefited humanity, claims resting on 'the enormous triumphs of a material progress based on science and technology?'.[1] The answer lies in part in the very processes which I have identified in Chapter 2; process is critical, choices are challenging, paradigmatic shifts are troublesome and the relationship between law and ethics and science, at best an uneasy accommodation, is strained when it is believed, whether real or not (for myths are important), that law has become the alter ego of science rather than its conscience.[2]

The unprecedented speed of change in medical practices has *produced* new, radical uncertainty and hence anxiety: '... when people face what nothing in their past has prepared them for they grope for words to name the unknown, even when they can neither define nor understand it.'[3] Antoine de Saint-Exupéry memorably captured this of an earlier transformation:

> ... we lack a perspective for judgments that go so deep ... Everything around us is new and different – our concerns, our working habits, our relations with one another. Our very psychology has been shaken to its foundations, to its most secret recesses ... To grasp the meaning of the world of today, we use a language created to express the world of yesterday.[4]

The result of this in scientific medicine, in biomedical ethics and medical law is that we run the risk of adopting what might be called the Red Queen defence: forever rushing to stay in one place.[5] The price of pragmatic

---

1   Hobsbawm, E, *Age of Extremes: The Short History of the Twentieth Century 1914–1991*, 1994, London: Michael Joseph, pp 11–13.

2   de Sousa Santos, B, *Towards a New Common Sense*, 1995, London: Routledge, p 4.

3   *Ibid*, Hobsbawm, p 287.

4   de Saint-Exupéry, A, *Wind, Sand and Stars*, 1975, London: Pan, pp 39–40.

5   'You see, it takes all the running you can do, to keep in the same place. If you want to go somewhere else, you must run at least twice as fast as that.' Carroll, L, 'Alice through the looking-glass', in Gardner, M (ed), *The Annotated Alice*, 1960, Harmondsworth: Penguin, p 210. The metaphor is adapted from Ridley, M, *The Red Queen: Sex and the Evolution of Human Nature*, 1994, Harmondsworth: Penguin.

consensus, indicative certainly of the current British approach to these questions, especially in the balance between individual rights and public policy is that 'again and again, as new medical developments emerge, we debate the same issues in different guises'.[6] In place of this we need a 'lengthened foresight'[7] in order to help us avoid replicating and amplifying mistaken approaches and solutions, or applying methods and outcomes suitable for the resolution of one set of issues to others which will not bear them.

We need, in short, to develop and apply a theory of *biomedical diplomacy*. Such a theory would have four tasks:

(a) to chart the intellectual history and identify responses to and possible fora to respond to demands for supra-national regulation of biomedicine;

(b) to identify shifts in philosophical practices and epistemologies;

(c) to identify increasing regulatory sites and practices of biomedicine in the 'hyper-regulated society', the practices of juridification; and

(d) to identify and show how societies might negotiate the 'tragic choices' of the 'risk society'.

And, to be comprehensive, such a theory would need to be explored and explicated on at least three levels: a descriptive level, an evaluative or normative level, and a conceptual level. Each level would engage a different task or set of tasks. These would include:

(a) at the *descriptive level*, an examination of who does what in biomedicine; how scientists, philosophers, ethicists, sociologists, lawyers and lay people come to work within or at international, governmental and other agencies in the field widely called 'bioethics'. This demands what might be called an ethnography of 'biomedical diplomacy'; an intimate investigation into the living and working habits, the intellectual and political conversations and compromises, the ethical trades and philosophical passes that shape and form modern biomedical discourse. The focus would here be on mode and form and not to whom they are done;[8]

(b) at the *evaluative* or *normative level*, as an exercise in comparative public policy making, examining how both the individual State and the international community recognise and regulate the boundaries of risk, technology and power. This suggests an examination of biomedicine, medical ethics and law within different epistemological, theological, ethical and legal regimes and cultures. And, as I have attempted to show, it requires this at a time of enormous upheaval: pluralism is replacing old

---

6   Brazier, M, 'Regulating the reproduction business?' (1999) 7 Med L Rev 166, p 167.

7   Jonas, H, *The Imperative of Responsibility*, 1984, Chicago, Ill: Chicago UP, pp 25–50.

8   For an alternative formulation, see Jacob, J, *Doctors and Rules*, 1988, London: Routledge, p 25.

certainties;[9] the generic 'patient' is disappearing;[10] and we have passed from the era of 'pleasant tributes' to the medical profession to hyper-regulation and juridification. This exercise in comparative public policy making and formulation and the responses to the forces of globalisation requires an examination of laws, regulations, codes of practice or *non-intervention* or *non-regulation*. In this, biomedical diplomacy focuses on the movement from bioethics to biolaw, on how and why issues are promoted and others not;

(c) at the *conceptual level*, where the theory examines how 'risk societies' attempt to identify and negotiate, conceal and evade the 'tragic choices'[11] that modern biomedicine requires. *Biomedical diplomacy*, negotiating the tragic choices, is in part about ensuring that we may enjoy some of the benefits of Hans Jonas' call for 'lengthened foresight'.

Tragic choices are the tragedies of cultures. They disclose the values accepted by a society as fundamental and they concern those choices that a society finds intolerable.[12] Tragedy is a cultural phenomenon; societies differ as to what is tragic and what are deemed appropriate ameliorative methods.[13] How tragic choices are made, how they can be made, is necessarily governed, in some measure, by earlier attempts at resolution.[14] According to Calabresi, 'tragic choices' arise from scarcity of goods, where there is a conflict between the societal values implicit in the distribution of those goods and humanistic moral values. Two continual 'moving progressions' are inevitable in tragic choices; the first is concerned with making the initial tragic choice, determining both how much of a good should be produced and, thereafter, how this determination should be distributed, and to whom. Health care is a clear and obvious example of this, although it has some unusual connotations, such as how illness is defined, what counts as illness and how doctors are implicated in this.[15]

Secondly, there is a progression which lies beyond these allocation questions; it is the dimension which might called a legitimation question: '... composed of the succession of decision, rationalization, and violence as

---

9   Bauman, Z, *Postmodern Ethics*, 1993, Oxford: Blackwell; Bauman, Z, *A Life in Fragments*, 1995, Oxford: Blackwell; *op cit*, de Sousa Santos, fn 2.

10   Wolf, SM, 'The rise of the new pragmatism' (1994) 20 Am J Law and Medicine; Williams, P, *The Alchemy of Race and Rights*, 1991, Cambridge, Mass: Harvard UP; Doyal, L, *What Makes Women Sick?*, 1995, New Brunswick, NJ: Rutgers UP.

11   Calabresi, G with Bobbitt, P, *Tragic Choices*, 1978, New York: WW Norton.

12   *Ibid*, pp 17–18.

13   *Ibid*, p 167.

14   *Ibid*, p 158.

15   See, eg, Kennedy, I, *The Unmasking of Medicine*, 1988, London: Allen & Unwin, pp 26–50; Brazier, M and Glover, N, 'Does medical law have a future?', in Birks, P (ed), *Law's Future(s)*, 2000, Oxford: Hart.

quiet replaces anxiety and is replaced by it when society evades, confronts and remakes the tragic choice.'[16] This latter progression is one in which society legitimates, challenges and reassesses the initial choice, leading to its eventual replacement with another choice or a reconfirmation of the initial decision. There is a paradox involved in determining first order sufficiency; a first order determination operates as a second order decision at a higher level of generality: '... no matter how sufficient the first order determination appears, it necessarily diverts resources from other tragic situations.'[17] There is evidence of a number of contemporary transitions and translations in modern medical law, including that from paternalism to a potentially dangerous or damaging form of autonomy;[18] from the therapeutic alliance[19] between patients and doctors to one based on cynicism, markets and forum shopping.[20]

It is characteristic of tragic choices that the allocative decisions necessary in the first and second order determinations are made separately:

> This allows for the more complex mixtures of allocation approaches which are brought to bear on the tragic choice, and it permits a society to cleave to a different mixture of values at each order. Indeed, when the first order determination of a tragic choice appears to be no more than a dependent function of the second order, it will usually be the case that the connection is illusory, serving to obscure the fact of tragic scarcity and – while the illusion lasts – evading the tragic choice.[21]

The 'opportunity costs of rhetoric'[22] are designed to obscure just such scarcity and just such choices. The court, when saying that it will not, indeed cannot, intervene in health care budgets is making explicit choices, to condone existing patterns of distribution, establishing the constitutional membrane in such cases. And, in cases such as *Gillick, Bland, Blood,* and possibly *Re A (Children) (Conjoined Twins)*, the court could, equally, have said that they involved choices that were reserved for parliamentary authority.[23]

---

16 *Op cit,* Calabresi, fn 11, p 19.

17 *Op cit,* Calabresi, fn 11, p 134.

18 As I try to show in Chapter 6.

19 Teff, H, 'Consent to medical procedures' (1985) 101 LQR 432.

20 If it can be done somewhere it should be available to me, and I should be able to access it, whether here or there. Some random examples suffice: *Ex p Blood* [1997] 2 All ER 687; a 59 year old British woman travelling to Italy to access infertility treatment services refused her in England, and a number of patients travelling interstate to the Northern Territory in Australia to avail themselves of the temporary legality of assistance in dying under the Territory's Rights of the Terminally Ill Acts 1995 and 1996; European and transatlantic travel to effect surrogacy agreements; 'transport IVF' throughout Europe; *Re S* [1996] Fam 26 (litigation over the right to care for a dying Norwegian between his wife and his lover); the establishment of Clonaid (see below, Chapter 10); and *Re A (Children) (Conjoined Twins)* [2000] 4 All ER 961.

21 *Op cit,* Calabresi, fn 11, p 20.

22 Which I explore in Chapter 4.

23 Indeed, one objection that Robert Lee and I point out in a commentary on Blood is that Parliament had already expressed itself on the very point in issue; see 'In the Name of the Father: *Ex parte Blood*' (1997) 60 MLR 840.

The metamorphoses that I have identified are an example of the making and remaking of tragic choices that define each culture. In the responses of law to the forces of globalisation, we are examining the role of law in Beck's 'risk society'. This concept has been distilled by one of Beck's interlocutors in a way that may be more accessible for a legal audience. Thus, Anthony Giddens has cautioned that the idea of 'risk society' might suggest a world which has become more hazardous, but this is not necessarily so. Rather, it is a society increasingly preoccupied with the future (and also with safety), a world 'which we are both exploring and seeking to normalise and control'.[24] In this understanding, 'risk society' suggests a society which increasingly lives on a 'high technological frontier' that no one completely understands: this generates a 'diversity of possible futures'.[25] The origins of the risk society can be traced to two fundamental transformations, *the end of nature* and *the end of tradition*.[26] Each is connected to the increasing influence of science and technology, although not wholly determined by them.

The principles of 'reflexive modernisation' within medicine are such that progress necessarily implies unplanned excess, the harmful effects of which are unintentional:[27] '... nothing succeeds like success, nothing also entraps like success.'[28] As a professional power, medicine has secured and expanded for itself a fundamental advantage against political and public attempts at consultation and intervention.[29] Recall the importance of this observation: if the costs of progress are unintentional, they are equally unforeseeable. Beck's thesis is that there has been 'a revolution of the lay public's social living conditions without its consent'.[30] The divergence of diagnosis and therapy in the current development of medicine results in a dramatic increase of so called chronic illness:

> ... illnesses that can be diagnosed thanks to the more acute medical and technical sensory system, without the presence or even prospect of any effective measures to treat them.[31]

These developments of modern technology have set in motion processes which undermine the 'idea of democracy from inside'. Central issues of public policy affecting the future of society, formerly the subject of public debate to shape the political resolve, are *of necessity* bypassed by developments that cannot be foreseen because they are unintended. Technology and medicine

---

24 Giddens, A, 'Risk and responsibility' (1999) 62 MLR 1.

25 *Ibid*, p 3.

26 *Ibid*.

27 Beck, U, *Risk Society: Towards a New Modernity*, Ritter, M (trans), 1992, London: Sage, esp p 209.

28 Jonas, H, *The Imperative of Responsibility*, 1984, Chicago, Ill: Chicago UP, p 9.

29 *Ibid*, Beck, p 210.

30 *Ibid*, Beck, p 206. See, also, *ibid*, Jonas, pp 18–19.

31 *Ibid*, Beck, p 204.

are, thus, becoming the instruments of an uncontrolled 'sub-politics' of medicine, where there is neither parliament nor executive to examine the possible consequences of decisions *before they are taken*.[32]

Thus, the importance of German philosopher Hans Jonas' different, but compelling analysis. Jonas has argued that modern technology, which has produced an ever deeper penetration of nature and is propelled by the forces of market and politics, has enhanced human power 'beyond anything known or even dreamed of before'.[33] Accordingly, the enormously enhanced power which modern science and technology has helped to bring to human beings and their dominion of the world brings with it a change in *responsibility*; responsibility that is a 'correlate of power and must be commensurate with the latter's scope and that of its exercise'.[34] In his analysis, this means that we need to construct and identify a metaphysically based theory of responsibility – of humankind to itself, to distant posterity and to all terrestrial life.

The imperative requiring that we identify this theory of responsibility is to enable us 'to discriminate between legitimate and illegitimate goal settings to our Promethean power'.[35] The enlarged nature of human action – enlarged in magnitude, reach and novelty – raises moral issues beyond interpersonal ethics and requires reflection; responsibility is centre stage and calls for lengthened foresight – what Jonas calls a 'scientific futurology'.[36] This responsibility should be informed by fear, a 'heuristics of fear' – which will help to disclose what is possibly at stake, what values and traditions we may pass up, what approaches and opportunities we ought in all conscience to deny ourselves: '... what we must avoid at all cost is determined by what we must preserve at all cost.'[37]

Easy dependence upon the professional sense of responsibility will become ever more elusive as a new breed of providers of medical technologies emerges. Previous structures of co-operative and corporatist workings may fall under the competitive pressures of a global market. Regulation within the domestic market will become more problematic as the providers of services can operate from a chosen base in an increasingly global market. Access to technology will become easier than ever as the treatment finds the internet.[38] Increasingly, developments will be funded, findings unveiled, possibilities

---

32 *Op cit*, Beck, fn 27, p 210; *op cit*, Jonas, fn 28, p 21 illustrates how the 'most ambitious dreams of homo faber ... show most vividly how far our powers to act are pushing us beyond the terms of all former ethics' and 'demand an answer before *we embark*' (emphasis added).

33 *Op cit*, Jonas, fn 28, p ix.

34 *Op cit*, Jonas, fn 28, p x.

35 *Op cit*, Jonas, fn 28.

36 *Op cit*, Jonas, fn 28.

37 *Op cit*, Jonas, fn 28.

38 For two of the many examples, see www.eggdonorfertilitybank.com; and www.thespermbankofac.org.

mooted, results replicated and then, and only then, regulatory responses sought.

Justice Michael Kirby has made this observation about the dangers of the law failing to keep up with science:

> Science and technology are advancing rapidly. If democracy is to be more than a myth and a shibboleth in the age of mature science and technology and more than a tri-annual visit to a polling booth, we need a new institutional response. Otherwise, we must simply resign ourselves to being taken where the scientists and the technologists' imagination leads. That path may involve nothing less than the demise of the rule of law as we know it. It is for our society to decide whether there is an alternative or whether the dilemmas posed by modern science and technology, particularly in the field of bioethics, are just too painful, technical, complicated, sensitive and controversial for our institutions of government.[39]

The role of law is affected by pragmatic considerations. In cases where control is difficult or impossible, such considerations may lead to accepting technologies despite their ethical drawbacks. The danger – no more yet – is ignoring or deflecting Jonas' plea to identify 'what we must avoid at all cost', which is determined by 'what we must preserve at all cost'.[40] That is the first and, perhaps, most central task for biomedical diplomacy. It is one to which the study of medical law, as a part of a humane reflection on science, must both urgently attend and be dedicated.

---

39 Kirby, M, *Reform the Law*, 1983, Oxford: OUP, pp 238–39.
40 *Op cit*, Jonas, fn 28.

PART II

SOME LANGUAGE QUESTIONS

HEALTH RIGHTS, ETHICS AND JUSTICE: THE OPPORTUNITY COSTS OF RHETORIC

Nobody knows how much health care will be worth to him in terms of money and pain. In addition, nobody knows if the most advantageous form of health care is obtained from medical producers, from a travel agent, or by renouncing work on the night shift ... The economics of health is a curious discipline, somewhat reminiscent of the theology of indulgences that flourished before Luther ... You can count what the friars collect, you can look at the temples they build, you can take part in the liturgies they indulge in, but you can only guess what the traffic in remission from purgatory does to the soul after death. Models developed to account for the willingness of taxpayers to foot the rising medical bills constitute similar scholastic guesswork about the new world-spanning church of medicine.[1]

The right to health has long been advocated as a basic human right, but obviously not everyone can be assured of perfect health; much depends upon genetic factors, natural and social environments, individual lifestyle and bad luck.[2] Yet, health is a vital aspect of modern social life, personal identity and civic participation. It might, then, even be thought to be an important task of modern government that it secure the means by which people can preserve or restore their health. The choices that governments make about health are, as I have suggested in the opening chapter, part of the very fabric of the 'tragic choices' debate. Jonathon Montgomery has even suggested that it may be thought that, like rights to life and to liberty, the right to health care could be regarded as one of a group of basic rights which make active citizenship possible; as with all basic rights, the State would be required to take specific steps to recognise health rights.[3] While it may, in fact, be more accurate and more limited to speak of a right to health care, rather than health care rights, the potential importance of the argument and its language is undeniable. As Michael Freeden puts it, 'the existence of scarce goods necessitates important decisions on distribution, whereas the insistence on the right to a good ensures that some of it will be available to any rights bearer'.[4] But, as I shall show in

---

1   Illich, I, *Limits to Medicine*, 1976, Harmondsworth; Penguin, p 235.
2   Swarski, Z, 'Do I own my body?', unpublished seminar paper, June 1994, Swansea University.
3   This draws on Montgomery, J, 'Rights to health and health care', in Coote, A (ed), *The Welfare of Citizens: Developing New Social Rights*, 1992, London: IPPR, p 82. Standard arguments about health rights are contained, *inter alia*, in Bole, TJ and Bondeson, WB (eds), *Rights to Health Care*, 1991, Dordrecht: Kluwer, and in Chapman, A (ed), *Health Care Reform: A Human Rights Approach*, 1994, Washington DC: Georgetown UP, esp Pt 2, pp 85–164.
4   Freeden, M, *Rights*, 1991, Buckingham: Open UP, p 92.

this chapter, the State's responsibility for providing a health care service is actually a hotly contested philosophical idea, almost as much as the very concept of health itself.[5] This chapter addresses two preliminary questions. First, what, if anything, is the responsibility of the State in securing the proper grounds of distribution of such health care as exists? Secondly, what role, if any, is there within this for arguments based on rights and, specifically, legally enforceable rights? Is there anything here more than rhetoric?

ALLOCATION

The examples upon which I am going to draw and the arguments I am going to deploy are set against the background of the UK health care system, a system apparently in continual transition.[6] It provides an example of the turbulence to which change gives rise and illustrates some of the problems necessarily involved in the distribution of what now seems universally to be acknowledged as a scarce good – health or, more precisely, health costs. Within this context, the proper grounds of allocation of the scarce good that health care has become assume particular significance. One possible approach is that health care should be given to those who, in some way, judged against some sort of criterion, deserve it; that a just system of health care allocation should be backward looking, asking what the individual has done in the past to safeguard, preserve or damage their own health such that the State should reward (or discipline) them in its response. In this sense, State policy would be delivered through its gatekeepers, the medical, nursing and other social welfare professions. An alternative model would be a needs-based model, a forward looking model, in which treatments might still be denied, or prioritised, according to need.

Other possible grounds of distribution exist, but I want to take just two examples of the directly competing notions of what might be entailed in the State's responsibility and obligations for health care and compare the libertarian position offered by Bernard Williams with that of the leading conservative Robert Nozick. Williams argues:

> Leaving aside preventive medicine, the proper ground of distribution of medical care is ill health: this is a necessary truth. Now in very many societies, while ill health may work as a necessary condition of receiving treatment, it does not work as a sufficient condition, since such treatment costs money, and not all who are ill have the money; hence the possession of sufficient money

---

5   For an introduction to this vast literature see, eg, Currer, C and Stacey, M, *Concepts of Health and Disease: A Comparative Perspective*, 1986, Leamington Spa: Berg.

6   For an introduction to the background of the National Health Service, see Klein, R, *The Politics of the National Health Service*, 1983, London: Longman; for a brief survey of the recent changes set within that background, see Holliday, I, *The NHS Transformed*, 1992, Manchester: Baseline.

becomes in fact an additional necessary condition of actually receiving treatment.[7]

Nozick urges that 'it cannot be assumed that equality must be built into any theory of justice'.[8] He says of the passage quoted from Williams that he seems to be arguing that if, among the different descriptions applying to an activity, there is one that contains an 'internal goal' of the activity, then 'the only proper grounds for the performance of the activity, or its allocation if it is scarce, are connected with the effective achievement of the internal goal'. Thus, according to Nozick's reading of Williams, 'the only proper criterion for the distribution of medical care is medical need'. To this, Nozick objects.

Does it follow, he asks, that the internal goal of an activity should take precedence over, for example, a person's particular purpose in performing the activity? If someone becomes a barber because he or she likes talking to a variety of different people, is it unjust of them to allocate services to those to whom they most like to talk? Or, if they work as a barber in order to pay tuition at school, may they not cut the hair of only those who tip well? Nozick ponders why the doctor's skills and activities should be allocated differently, via the internal goal of medical care. When the layers of Williams' argument are peeled away, he writes:

> ... what we arrive at is the claim that society (that is, each of us acting together in some organised fashion) should make provision for the important needs of all its members ... Despite appearances, Williams presents no argument for it. Like others, Williams looks only to questions of allocation. He ignores the question of where things or actions to be allocated and distributed come from. Consequently, he does not consider whether they come already tied to people who have entitlements over them (surely the case for service activities, which are people's actions), people who therefore may decide for themselves to whom they will give the thing and on what grounds.[9]

Nozick's argument has, of course, been criticised. Len Doyal and Ian Gough reject it as incorporating a Lockean view of ownership, an essentially individualistic view in which I and only I am entitled to decide what to do with the fruits of my labour. For them, this is flawed in its descriptive nature of production. Production, they write, is 'a social process in which many mix their labour [and] any rights associated with ownership can no longer be focused exclusively on the individual'.[10] A further important recent criticism

7   Williams, B, 'The idea of equality', in Laslett, P and Runciman, WG (eds), *Philosophy, Politics and Society*, 2nd series, 1962, Oxford: Clarendon, pp 110–31.

8   Nozick, R, *Anarchy, State and Utopia*, 1974, Oxford: Basil Blackwell, p 233.

9   *Ibid*, pp 234–35. I learned of this debate and began to understand its subtleties from lectures given by John Day, of the University of Leicester. His own interpretation of it, and his response, are now recorded in his essay, 'Justice and utility in health care', in Allison, L (ed), *The Utilitarian Response: The Contemporary Viability of Utilitarian Political Philosophy*, 1993, London: Sage, p 30.

10 Doyal, L and Gough, I, *A Theory of Human Need*, 1991, London: Macmillan, pp 137–38.

has come from within the conservative tradition to which Nozick appeals. John Gray has objected that the night-watchman State of the kind advocated by Nozick is incompatible with what he calls 'limited government', of which conservative government is the embodiment:

> A limited government has tasks that go well beyond keeping the peace ... It has also a responsibility to tend fragile and precious traditions, to protect and shelter the vulnerable and defenceless, to enhance and enlarge opportunities for the disadvantaged, to promote the conservation and renewal of the natural and human environment and to assist in the renewal of civil society and the reproduction of the common culture without which pluralism and diversity become enmity and division.[11]

The implications of this argument for health care are important, far reaching and challenging. Gray expounds these normative or evaluative criticisms in the concluding chapter of his book. Arguing, with critics such as Ivan Illich, that it must be accepted that there are limits to health care, Gray's first concern is with the over-medicalisation of life and death. Secondly, and this is related, he complains that modern medical care and treatment cannot be shown to have provided benefits proportionate to the claims made for it or indeed proportionate to the costs lavished on it. As Thomas McKeown has shown, improvements in health care have arisen much more from developments in sanitation, environment and personal lifestyle than they have from individual 'medical' breakthroughs.[12] Thirdly, much of what has been incorporated within modern medical care lies, in truth, outside the medical domain 'and can be performed safely and intelligently by trained lay people'.[13]

If Gray is correct in his analysis, it may be that insistence on rights is completely misplaced, unless those rights are rights to be left alone, rights to refuse invasive or unlooked for medical interventions, whether at birth or in death, rather than to insist upon the provision of certain types of high quality, but also high technology and unproven health care interventions.[14] That is an important caveat to the arguments which now ensue about what I have called conceptual limitations in respect of rights arguments in respect of health. I then illustrate a range of questions with which we are faced when considering the question of allocation.

RIGHTS

The idea that patients have rights sits uncomfortably within the general shape of UK health care law. Issues such as informed consent are couched within

---

11 Gray, J, *Beyond the New Right*, 1993, London: Routledge, p 50.
12 McKeown, T, *The Role of Medicine*, 1979, Oxford: Basil Blackwell.
13 *Ibid*, Gray, p 168.
14 *Ibid*, Gray, esp pp 166–72.

ordinary malpractice principles, confidentiality is justified by reference to the public good and not by individual privacy rights and rights to health care under national legislation are, for practical purposes, unenforceable.[15] But, as Paul Craig has reminded us:

> One may reach the conclusion that a particular interest is incapable of being framed as a justiciable legal right, but still believe that it generates a constitutional obligation which the legislature is bound to advance. Such an obligation is of importance in itself, and may, moreover, have indirect implications for the interpretation of other legal doctrines.[16]

In other words, even if a legal right cannot be spelled out from a particular series of premises, it does not follow that some general (moral) obligation or expectation cannot properly be laid at the door of the State. To discuss fully that contention would require an extended dissertation on the relationship between moral and legal claims to rights and the role of the State, of which I give only a brief résumé here. We might hold that rights sum up our moral conclusions (that is, they are a useful way of speaking about the work that we have done elsewhere); they are a way of putting forward a moral case.[17] Of course, to assert that human beings have rights is not identical to asserting that they have human rights: 'The latter complex term has developed this century into a key phrase, denoting a pre-eminent notion of rights.'[18]

Human rights provide the criteria for making value judgments, reflecting normative judgments as to what it is permissible for free and responsible people, acting either individually or through their governments, to do. Human rights, then, can be used to evaluate the laws of States by deciding whether the standards inherent in such rights are reflected in positive law. They also provide justifications for conduct and arguments for changes to existing laws to give effect to them. Legal rights we may more usually understand to be those rights recognised in the law of individual States or at international law, where law refers to a body of binding rules, institutions and procedures regulating relationships and orderly change and protecting interests of men and women living together in a political society. Legal rights

---

15 *Op cit*, Montgomery, fn 3.

16 Craig, P, *Public Law and Democracy in the United Kingdom and the United States*, 1990, Oxford: Clarendon, p 7.

17 This sort of argument underlies the work of writers such as Finnis, J, *Natural Law and Natural Rights*, 1985, Oxford: Clarendon. Others, such as Raz, J, in *The Morality of Freedom*, 1986, Oxford: Clarendon, and Dworkin, R, in *Taking Rights Seriously*, 1977, London: Duckworth, have sensitised us to the place of morality with respect to law, and have argued that morality (Raz) or principles (Dworkin) can be used as safety nets onto which judges may fall back and rely when gaps appear in the law. They do not explicitly address the questions of whose views, and what morality, but they fall within the mainstream of modern liberal thought on questions of the relationship between law and morality.

18 *Op cit*, Freeden, fn 4, p 6; see, also, Kennedy, I, 'Agenda for health ethics and law' (1991) 70 Bull Medical Ethics 16.

entitle the right holder to insist on their observance and various remedies, judicial and otherwise, are available.[19]

Law and legal rights are pervasive at all levels of social life; there are legal rights governing family relationships, education, working conditions, property (including wealth and resources) and State relationships with individuals. Many legal rights are the positive legal counterpart of human rights as moral rights and, therefore, reflect those values as well as protecting particular interests. Of particular interest here, however, is the relationship between law, rights and health care: the scope, boundaries and content of what we may call health care law. We might identify at least three levels of health care policy and practice which might be and are differently affected by law, or affected by different types of control exercised by the State. These three levels might be identified as the macro level – the form of the health care delivery system; the meso level – identifying the boundaries of that system; and the micro level – at which the specific patient-health carer relationship is defined.[20]

At the macro level, there is little formal legal regulation, but there is, in addition, a great deal of administrative regulation. The main legislative provisions are contained in the National Health Service Act 1977 as variously amended and the Medicines Act 1983. In this context, and recalling the discussion of allocation, it should be remembered that the role of primary care (90%) vastly outstrips that of hospital care (10%); and, while the present cost structure is in inverse proportion to that, this itself is in the process of change.

The meso level, which identifies the legal boundaries of health care, suggests what may permissibly be done in the name of health care. Here, three examples of legislative intervention are the Human Organs Transplant Act 1989 (forbidding the commercial sale and purchase of human organs), the Surrogacy Arrangements Act 1985 (forbidding commercial involvement in the establishment and management of surrogacy arrangements) and the Human Fertilisation and Embryology Act 1990, but there are many others. The micro level, which establishes the legal relationship between individual patients and doctors and other health care workers, is now replete with examples, drawn from various areas such as consent, confidentiality, negligence, non-resuscitation decisions, and many others. In these last two categories, the meso and the micro levels, in the sense suggested by Devlin, the relationship between doctors and their patients is no longer one which is immune from legal regulation, control and direction. The important question which arises for present purposes is whether these functions have moral dimensions. Clearly, they *can* have moral dimensions, but the enforcement of morality is not itself necessarily numbered among them. However, I want to suggest that

19 For a more comprehensive review of these notions, from which this outline is derived, see Palley, C, *The United Kingdom and Human Rights*, 1991, London: Stevens.

20 Following Dickens, B, 'Ethics', FIGO Symposium, *Ethics in Reproduction*, 1994, Paris.

there *are* areas of medical law where the goal comes closer to the enforcement of moral notions *as such* than perhaps in other cognate areas of the law, such as family law, or social welfare law. Examples of this, which are not incontestable, include those where the law is used to give shape to moral aspirations. Here, we might consider abortion, sterilisation, assisted conception, embryo research, female circumcision, organ transplantation, the treatment of certain groups of patients, such as the severely handicapped newborn, those in persistent vegetative state, or those living in coma, to take just selected examples. Notice, however, that very few of these examples are drawn from, or rely upon, what could be characterised as any positive programme of rights to health care.

RIGHTS TO HEALTH CARE?[21]

Before a detailed programme for implementation of health rights could be drawn up, there are a series of preliminary issues to be addressed. Conceptual difficulties exist in relation to the idea of health and the causes of ill-health. The former needs consideration to establish the content of health rights and the latter in order to address the strategies appropriate to realise them. A careful analysis of the types of rights and duties which are claimed by citizens is also needed. For example, individual entitlements which are claimed by citizens from relevant agencies will be suitable for some areas, whereas in others, collective or group rights of some sort will be more effective.

As I have suggested before, similar questions arise with respect to law, medicine and bioethics in many, especially Western, countries. There are, of course, many differences of a philosophical, economic, social and geographical nature that are not easily reconciled, and it is also true that, throughout the European Union and the Member States of the Council of Europe, moral and legal pluralism reflecting these variations is evident. Yet, it is sometimes overlooked that that pluralism typically operates at the margins of what might be called the ethical stationery. The depth and breadth of agreement far outweigh and outpace moral disagreement, whether the supporting reasoning is of a broadly consequentialist or of a deontological kind. Recognising this, the World Health Organization Draft Declaration on the Rights of Patients (1 March 1990, revised August 1990) suggests that shared social, economic, cultural, ethical and political considerations have given rise to a movement throughout Europe towards a fuller elaboration and fulfilment of the rights of patients. Throughout Europe, it is clear that there are

---

21 This draws particularly on the valuable analysis and distinctions introduced by Montgomery; see, esp *op cit*, fn 3, pp 87–90 for a discussion of individual and groups rights, and important distinctions between and considerations within these categories.

shared principles which are being adopted in many countries and which seem to be independent of system characteristics. More recently, in the Treaty of Maastricht, the European Union has declared that:

> The Community shall contribute towards ensuring a high level of human health protection by encouraging co-operation between the Member States and, if necessary, lending support to their action. Community action shall be directed towards the prevention of diseases, in particular the major health scourges, including drug dependence, by promoting research into their causes and their transmissions, as well as health information and education.[22]

But, differences of an economic and political character serve only to underscore the problems of cultural comparisons when we move from the high levels of abstractions at which international documents pitch these aspirations to more concrete attempts to implement these 'rights'. What does it mean to give operational scope to these ideals, how do health 'rights' arguments actually fare when it comes to trying, say, to enforce what look like clear expressions of rights in individual cases? It is to that question that I now turn.

RIGHTS TO HEALTH CARE AND THE OPPORTUNITY COSTS OF RHETORIC

Four particular examples will serve to illustrate the arguments which I want to pursue here. Section 1(1) of the National Health Service Act 1977 provides:

> It is the Secretary of State's duty to continue the promotion in England and Wales of a comprehensive health service designed to secure improvement: (a) in the physical and mental health of the people of those countries; and (b) in the prevention, diagnosis and treatment of illness.

And s 3 provides:

> It is the Secretary of State's duty to provide throughout England and Wales, to such extent as he considers necessary to meet all reasonable requirements: (a) hospital accommodation; (b) other accommodation for the purpose of any service provided under this Act; (c) medical, dental, nursing and ambulance services.

In *R v Secretary of State for Social Services ex p Hincks*,[23] several patients who had been waiting for up to three years for pain relieving operations, much longer than was medically advised, sued the Health Secretary. The delay arose in part from a shortage of orthopaedic beds in the Birmingham area, a wait caused in part by a decision not to build a new block in the hospital on grounds of cost. The Court of Appeal held that there was no right to bring the

---

22 Treaty on European Union 1992, Art 129.
23 (1992) 1 BMLR 93.

action. Lord Denning said that the Health Secretary could be considered to have failed in the discharge of the statutory duty only if his exercise of it was so thoroughly unreasonable as to be one that no reasonable Secretary could have made. The Act did not create, according to the court, an absolute duty to provide services irrespective of economic decisions taken at a national level. According to Lord Denning, the provision had to be read subject to the qualification that the Secretary of State's duty is to meet 'all reasonable requirements such as can be provided within the resources available'.[24] Bridge LJ gave perhaps a more convincing judgment when he rejected the plaintiffs' argument that, since the statute did not place any limits on the extent of the Secretary's duty based on longer term financial planning, none could be envisaged unless the statute expressly so provided. He held that, if no limits in respect of longer term financial planning were to be read into public statutory duties such as that apparently under consideration, then the Secretary would be faced with a bottomless (or, at least, ever-deepening) pit. The argument put forward on the plaintiffs' behalf was even more difficult to accept as a realistic claim when it was realised, he said, that the further that medical and technological advances go in the direction of even more comprehensive patient care, the greater would be the financial burden placed on the Secretary if he were to avoid a dereliction of his duty under the National Health Service Act 1977.[25]

A similar line of reasoning has been adopted in three cases which have sought to fashion a similar sort of challenge, *R v Secretary of State for Social Services ex p Walker*,[26] *R v Central Birmingham HA ex p Collier*,[27] and *Re J (A Minor) (Medical Treatment)*.[28] Here, I only want to consider in any depth *Re J*, which is of particular interest because the patient tried to establish a right to a certain *kind* of treatment. A 16 month old boy who had been injured in a fall suffered cerebral palsy and the court was asked by his natural parents to determine whether, if a life threatening event arose, J should be given artificial ventilation and other life saving measures whether the clinicians in charge of his care believed this was in his best interests or not. They indeed had argued that there was no medical evidence favouring ventilation. The issue was whether the court should ever require a medical practitioner to adopt a course of treatment which he or she did not believe to be in the best interests of the patient. Lord Donaldson rejected any such argument and added in response to a moral claim to treatment (a right imposing on someone else a duty to give treatment) that: 'The sad fact of life is that health authorities may on occasion find that they have too few resources, either human or material or both, to

---

24 (1992) 1 BMLR 93.
25 *Ibid*.
26 (1993) 3 BMLR 32.
27 (1988) unreported, 6 January.
28 [1992] 4 All ER 614.

treat all the patients whom they would like to treat in the way in which they would like to treat them. It is their duty to make choices.'[29] Balcombe LJ said:

> I find it difficult to conceive of a situation where it would be a proper exercise of the jurisdiction to make an order positively requiring a doctor to adopt a particular course of treatment in relation to a child, unless the doctor himself or herself was asking the court to make such an order.[30]

He stressed 'the absolute undesirability of the court making an order which may have the effect of compelling a doctor or health authority to make available scarce resources (both human and material) to a particular child, without knowing whether or not there are other patients to whom those resources might more advantageously be devoted'.[31]

Thirdly, consider the case of *R v Cambridgeshire HA ex p B (A Minor)*,[32] a case which involved the fight by a father to obtain health care for his dying daughter. It is also the clearest indication that we have of the viability with which rights arguments are regarded by the English courts. B had been treated for a lymphoma to which she had responded, but had then been diagnosed with leukaemia that was clearly progressing rapidly. She had had a bone marrow transplant from her younger sister, but, following a further relapse, it was apparent that the cancer was moving towards its terminal stages. Her doctors advised that further treatment was contra-indicated, a decision which her father sought to challenge, first clinically and then legally.[33] A second opinion he obtained put B's chances of survival somewhat higher than she had originally been given, and with this opinion he approached the health authority to fund a second bone marrow transplant. Taking account of the clinical judgment, the nature of the treatment and the estimated chances of success, the health authority declined to fund the treatment. He sought judicial review of that decision.

At first instance, Laws J framed the relevant question in a straightforward manner, clearly indicative of the wider importance of the approach to the case:

> Of all human rights, most people would accord the most precious place to the right to life itself. Sometimes public authorities, who are subject to the jurisdiction of this court, have the power of life and death – or at least to decide, as I find is the case here, whether a person otherwise facing certain

---

29 [1992] 4 All ER 614, p 623.

30 *Ibid*, p 625.

31 *Ibid*, p 625.

32 (1995) 23 BMLR 1 (CA); (1995) 25 BMLR 5 (HC).

33 Lest it be thought that I am critical of the father here, let me make it clear that, if such a case concerned any of my children, I should have fought just as vigorously as B's father for treatment that stood a reasonable chance of success to be given. For what it is worth, I would consider myself *as one of their parents* to be under a moral obligation to them to do that, at least up to the point where they said, 'Derek, enough'.

death should, by means of all resources at the public body's disposal, be given the chance of life.[34]

This is an echo of Lord Woolf's judgment in *R v Lord Saville of Newdigate ex p A*,[35] where the Master of the Rolls said that 'where a fundamental right such as the right to life is engaged, the options open to a reasonable decision maker are curtailed'. He argued that they are curtailed because it is 'unreasonable to reach a decision which contravenes or could contravene human rights unless there are sufficiently significant countervailing considerations'.[36] For Laws J, in *ex p B*, certain rights, broadly those occupying a central place in the European Convention on Human Rights, including the right to life, are 'not to be perceived merely as moral or political aspirations nor as enjoying a legal status only upon the international plane of this country's Convention obligations'. Rather, he said, they are to be 'vindicated as sharing with other principles the substance of the English common law'. What that meant in concrete terms was that:

> ... the law requires that where a public body enjoys a discretion whose exercise may infringe such a right, it is not to be permitted to perpetrate any such infringement unless it can show a substantial objective justification on public interest grounds.[37]

In relation to a fundamental right, such as the right to life, Laws J argued that there was no room to draw a distinction, as the health authority had sought to do, between acts and omissions of a public body which might lead to death. While that position might be tenable in criminal law, the authority's decision about the allocation of public funds, while not a positive act that threatened B's life, was nonetheless one about resources without which B would certainly die. That decision had, to the health authority's knowledge, materially affected for the worse B's chances of life. He concluded that her right to life had been 'assaulted' by the decision and, accordingly, that it could only be justified by showing 'substantial public interest grounds'.[38] It was then necessary to turn to see whether such grounds existed. One might have expected, following the earlier line of cases already discussed, that Laws J would have concluded that, in making these second order 'tragic choice' decisions,[39] a health authority balancing competing demands on limited resources would not be required to balance one person's rights against another, even when, as in this case, a right to life is concerned. Much modern medical care, as I argue in Chapter 11, is about just such issues. The courts cannot write the waiting lists of the country's hospitals or surgeries.

---

34   (1995) 23 BMLR 1, p 6.
35   [1999] 4 All ER 860.
36   *Ibid*, p 872.
37   (1995) 25 BMLR 5, p 12.
38   *Ibid*, p 14.
39   See above, Chapter 3, for discussion of these principles.

Laws J found, however, that it was evident that, in reaching the authority's decision here, it had taken into account in reaching a conclusion as to B's interests only *medical* facts; it had paid no attention to her family's views as to whether the proposed treatment should be provided or withheld. The importance of requiring these to be taken into account, he said, was evident:

> The doctor's obligation is to ascertain and explain all the medical facts, and in the light of them articulate the choice that must be faced. Their expert views on the medical issues, however, do not constitute the premises of a syllogism from which an inevitable conclusion as to what is the best interests of the patient may be deduced. It is not at all a matter of deduction from the medical facts. It is a personal question which the patient, if he is of full age and capacity, will decide in the light of medical advice. In the case of a little child, others must decide it – not the experts, but those having, legally and morally, the overall care of the patient.[40]

More significantly for this present argument, Laws J also castigated the authority's approach to the need for transparency in taking resource allocation decisions. Accepting that funds available for health care are not limitless, and that courts must not proceed to make orders with consequences for the Health Service budgets in ignorance of the knock-on effects on other patients, nonetheless, he said:

> ... where the question is whether the life of a 10 year old child might be saved, by more than a slim chance, the responsible authority must in my judgment do more than toll the bell of tight resources. They must explain the priorities that have led them to decline to fund the treatment.[41]

It is very important to appreciate precisely what Laws J is proposing and to understand how *circumscribed* he saw the role for the court even when called upon to vindicate a claim which was to be given 'the most precious place' in the roll of rights. Even here, he said, '*however* agonising the circumstances, if [the] decision was taken within the legal limits of the respondents' statutory functions, this court will have *no place* to interfere'.[42] That, I would venture, is a sentiment which even the most vehement and ardent critic of rights, let alone rights to health care, could agree. Thus, and I do necessarily underestimate this, the right to health care becomes in fact a *right to transparency* about the tragic choices that are being negotiated. The importance of such a requirement and entitlement is that it goes to the heart of the patient's relationship with the health care system at all levels, from departments of State and officials, through health authorities and administrators, to individual doctors, nurses, paramedics and assistants. It is, if you like, a component, and a rather ignored one at that, of the person's *right*

---

40 (1995) 25 BMLR 5, p 16.

41 *Ibid*, p 17.

42 *Ibid*, p 11, emphasis added.

to know. It engages important political and civic values as much as philosophical and ethical principles.

But, what happened to these arguments when the case came on in the Court of Appeal? Sir Thomas Bingham, the Master of the Rolls, dismissed Laws J's finding as to the involvement of the family in the decision making process peremptorily, saying that it 'entirely fails to recognise the realities of the situation'.[43] More tellingly, he criticised the judge's approach to the whole question of resources, saying that 'in a perfect world any treatment which a patient, or a patient's family, sought would be provided if the doctors were willing to give it, no matter how much it cost, particularly when a life was potentially at stake'.[44] In a stinging rejection of Laws J's review of the resourcing question, he questioned the whole involvement of judicial craft in fashioning acceptable outcomes:

> I feel bound to regard this as an attempt, wholly understandable but nonetheless misguided, to involve the court in a field of activity where it is not fitted to make any decision favourable to the patient.[45]

While difficult and agonising judgments have to be made as to how a limited budget is best allocated to the maximum advantage of the maximum number of patients, 'that is not a judgment which the court can make' and 'it is not something that a health authority ... can be fairly criticised for not advancing before the court'.[46]

Since *ex p B*, the Court of Appeal has, if anything, driven the dagger of utilitarianism deeper into the back of rights and resources arguments, although it singularly resisted giving it a final twist. The dagger may be bloodied, but the corpus of rights has yet to give up the ghost. In *R v North West Lancashire HA ex p A, D and G*,[47] Auld, Buxton and May LJJ, while roundly condemning 'unfocused resort to the European Convention on Human Rights' as cluttering up its consideration of adequate and more precise domestic principles and authorities, nonetheless *dismissed* a health authority's appeal against an order quashing certain of its 'policies' as having improperly evaluated a particular illness (in this case, transsexualism). But, they not only confirmed that a health authority is entitled to make choices between various claims and that those choices will be open only to the limited review of *Wednesbury* principles,[48] the court further held that the precise allocation and weighting of priorities was a matter for each authority, allowing for exceptions from that policy in 'exceptional circumstances'.

---

43 (1995) 23 BMLR 1, p 8.
44 *Ibid*, p 9.
45 *Ibid*, p 10.
46 *Ibid*, p 9.
47 [1999] Lloyd's Med Rep 399.
48 *Associated Picture Houses Ltd v Wednesbury Corp* [1947] 1 KB 233.

Indeed, it was lawful for an authority to leave those circumstances undefined, wreathed in a thick film of opacity.

The authority *was* obliged (a) accurately to assess the nature and seriousness of each type of illness, (b) to determine the effectiveness of various forms of treatment for it, and (c) to give proper effect to that assessment and determination in the formulation and individual application of the policy. On the facts, Auld LJ found that, although the authority recognised transsexualism as an illness, 'its recognition of it was at best oblique and lacked conviction'.[49] Buxton LJ advised that a health authority can decide that it will not fund certain types of treatment at all, 'even a condition medically recognised as an illness requiring intervention categorised as medical and curative, rather than merely cosmetic or a matter of convenience'.[50] However, in explaining the role of the court in reviewing resourcing questions, he cautioned that the court would subject decisions which affected 'fundamental interests' (such as health) falling short of 'fundamental rights' (such as life) to 'careful scrutiny':

> The more important the interest of the citizen that the decision affects, the greater will be the degree of consideration that is required of the decision maker. A decision that ... seriously affects the citizen's health will require substantial consideration, and be subject to careful scrutiny by the court as to its rationality. That will be the case in respect of decisions which involve the refusing of any, or any significant, treatment in respect of an identified and substantial medical condition.[51]

The relationship between transparency and opacity, between rationing and rationality, reveals an entirely formalistic, procedural role for health care law, a limitation which mirrors and is derived from the economic limitations which lie at the root of the UK health service. Improvements will always be possible, and the demand for health care consumption will remain, in the economist's terms, elastic. And this, of course, is one of the foundational problems which have bedevilled health service planning since the inception of the National Health Service.

OF MARKETS AND MORALS

The National Health Service sought the promotion of a comprehensive health service to secure improvement in the physical and mental health of the nation, and also to secure the prevention, diagnosis and treatment of illness through the provision of effective services. Such services were to be provided free. This

---

49   [1999] Lloyd's Med Rep 399, p 408.
50   *Ibid*, p 411.
51   *Ibid*, p 412, *per* Buxton LJ.

was to be made possible by the State ownership and control of resources. These were to be allocated, at zero price, at the point of consumption, thereby ensuring freely available health care. It was assumed that the population would thereby grow healthier, and thus the costs would cease to rise and perhaps even begin to fall. As Lee points out,[52] the economic flaws in this argument are now obvious, and indeed, should have been obvious at the time. Neoclassical writers such as Pigou as early as the 1920s had shown themselves well aware of the price elasticity of individual demand in relation to public services.[53] Notions of price elasticity dictate that an attempt to supply services at zero prices will be met by significant increases in demand above what would be demanded at prices set by marginal cost.

Against this background, the attempt to establish a workable notion of rights to health care as a way of resolving or even responding to questions of just allocation of health benefits may seem to be a rhetorical nightmare. The territory of theory and the politics of practice illustrate how attempts to make expectations realities through the language of rights are doomed to disappointment or failure: broken on the wheel of fortune, or, more frequently, its absence. Health care lawyers can swim up to the bar at the pool of resources, but only to check that the attendant has mixed the cocktails correctly – certainly not to say what should and should not be served, nor in what order. Neither shaken nor stirred, the responsibility for allocation decisions in health care rests firmly in control of professional administrators and clinicians.

---

52 See Lee, RG, 'Legal control of health care allocation', in Ockelton, M (ed), *Medicine, Ethics and Law*, 1987, Stuttgart: ARSP, pp 94–96.

53 See Pigou, A, *A Study in Public Finance*, 1928, London: Macmillan.

CHAPTER 5

FEMINISMS' ACCOUNTS OF REPRODUCTIVE TECHNOLOGY[1]

THE CONCERNS OF REPRODUCTION

Reflecting on reproduction, one quickly realises the enormity of the field that law's engagement might cover. It might address prevention (contraception, sterilisation); negotiation (or what Hilary Homans has identified as a 'contraceptive career',[2] which might include family 'planning'); assistance (reproductive technologies, surrogacy); alternatives (childlessness – chosen or otherwise, adoption); consequences (termination of pregnancy,[3] fetal therapies, maternal management, parenthood, parenting, suitability, child rearing, child support); images and ideologies (of motherhood, fatherhood and parenthood); responsibility; regulation, and so on. Each of these has drawn forward feminisms' analyses, critiques, evaluations, constructions. I decided to look, albeit cursorily, at different sorts of responses that feminisms' jurisprudences have offered to reproductive technologies, although, in fact, I shall say little about *specific* technologies. My concern in this essay has been to

---

1   In writing of 'feminisms', I do so in the sense implied by Margaret Davies in her illuminating analysis, *Asking the Law Question*, 1994, Sydney: LBC, p 172ff. Throughout this essay I have followed my customary practice of referring to and citing from only materials which I have to hand in my study when I write. Each reference in support of a proposition should, then, be regarded only as representative or emblematic of literature which could have been cited. Glaring omissions from my citations might charitably be understood in this light; more likely, in fact, they are based on ignorance. The usual suspects have not read this essay; therefore, the usual caveat is omitted.

2   Homans, H, 'The medical construction of a contraceptive career', in Homans, H (ed), *The Sexual Politics of Reproduction*, 1985, Aldershot: Gower, pp 45–63.

3   Equal access to abortion across Europe as being guaranteed under the European Convention on Human Rights was voted on by the Parliamentary Assembly of the Council of Europe 74:56 (see (1993) 341 *The Lancet* 1271–72), but failing to secure the necessary two-thirds majority for acceptance requiring individual Member States to consider new legislation. Catherine Lalumière had hoped by this measure not only to increase women's rights but also to *reduce* abortion tourism.

read a number of signposts which feminisms' scholars have left[4] and to offer a translation of what I read on those posts.[5]

I decided to look at reproductive technologies for four reasons. First, perhaps better than any other area of reproduction, technological assistance in conception is the most emblematic of *different* feminisms' approaches to reproduction (notice that I do not, here, say 'differences between'). The development of assisted reproduction programmes and the medicalisation of infertility 'raise some of the most difficult questions for feminist theory and practice.'[6] The techniques and trappings of assisted conception – AI, IVF, GIFT, cryopreservation of gametes, eggs and embryos, gamete and embryo donation, and surrogacy – also challenge traditional views of procreation and parenthood, a challenge that has legal as well as ethical implications. According to Lene Koch, 'One of the most difficult problems that have confronted feminist critics of *in vitro* fertilization (IVF) and the other new reproductive technologies, is the great enthusiasm for IVF among involuntarily childless women'.[7] Carol Smart has even doubted that there can be a satisfactory feminist response to reproductive technology; to argue that they contribute to and reinforce (male) dominant ideologies of motherhood and womanhood is to deny individual women's experiences and announced intentions, and may be to suggest that individual women are not able – autonomously – to choose for themselves, to weigh and balance the consequences of infertility treatments and the possible opportunity costs of the treatments and the very real costs of disappointment and 'failure' in conception. On the other hand, to argue that they contribute to and liberate women from the burdens of unlooked for consequences of infertility in them or their presently chosen partner is to suggest an uncomfortably determinist approach to mental and physical well being and notions of personhood.[8]

The second reason why I wanted to focus on reproductive technology is that concern with, and demand for, reproductive medicine has become a

---

4   Any number of books or articles detail particular aspects of reproductive technology; for a valuable bibliographical source, see McHale, J and Fox, M with Murphy, J, *Health Care Law: Text and Materials*, 1997, London: Sweet & Maxwell, pp 695, 751 and 812, and for an accessible, introductory review of a 'feminist approach to ethics', see pp 119–28.

5   This notion of translation bears a specific meaning, and is far from uncontroversial. I mean by 'translation' the process of augmenting and modifying the original which involves neither objectification and appropriation nor annihilation of the texts in question: 'I will have to change the text as I am reading it, but this does not mean that I am destroying it to further my own interests ... It is not a compromise, but a reconciliation, a closing of the distance between the translator and the other's text, between one language and another. And, as Jacques Derrida suggests, a translation considered in this way ensures the survival of a text, enabling it to live on and grow after its publication.' *Op cit*, Davies, fn 1, p 178 (citations omitted).

6   Anleu, SR, 'Reproductive autonomy: infertility, deviance and conceptive technology', in Peterson, K (ed), *Law and Medicine*, 1994, Melbourne: La Trobe UP, p 36.

7   Koch, L, 'IVF – an irrational choice?' (1990) 3(3) Issues in Reproductive and Genetic Engineering 235.

8   Smart, C, *Feminism and the Power of Law*, 1990, London: Routledge, pp 223–24.

global matter. The existence of a few specialist clinics has revealed a global market for assisted conception services. And, with the facilitation of travel and the phenomenon of speed, the ability to avail oneself of the services available at the reproductive tourist office make the franking of the stamp on the ethical envelope more interesting. Where technological development results in the blurring of national boundaries, the increasingly difficult task of one country insulating itself from events elsewhere in the world has given rise to the possibility of what has been called 'procreative tourism' and 'ethical dumping'.[9]

One small example will suffice. Following the birth of twins to a 59 year old English woman in an Italian clinic because of doubts about the desirability of any UK clinic offering treatment to a post menopausal woman, then Health Secretary Virginia Bottomley lamented that 'We cannot stop people going to any country in the world for treatment, but maybe we'll renew our efforts to have discussions with other countries as to the examples we set and how they can establish ethical controls over some of the dramatic achievements in modern medicine'.[10] Almost immediately following this, the French junior Health Minister Philippe Douste-Blazy announced its government's intention to introduce legislation to prohibit *in vitro* fertilisation of post menopausal women,[11] and the Italian Health Minister Mariapia Garavaglia was quoted as saying that 'desires are not rights, and babies are not consumer goods', announcing the imminent establishment of a commission to establish 'controls over the treatment of sterile and post menopausal women'.[12]

The third reason for focusing on reproductive technologies is their complexity. Anne Maclean has suggested of surrogacy that it is complex and difficult because it raises not one issue, but a cluster of issues, and issues of different sorts at that. 'It is easy to confuse considerations relevant to one of these issues with considerations relevant to another, or to misunderstand the character of a particular claim or a particular objection.'[13]

There is no single moral issue called surrogacy, and in much the same way, this is true of reproductive technologies generally. People's (moral) worries about surrogacy arrangements will vary greatly depending on the type of

---

9   Knoppers, B and le Bris, S, 'Recent advances' (1991) 17 Am J Law and Medicine 329. For a critical analysis of one particular 'case' of globalisation and the effect of that on a national regulatory scheme, see Morgan, D and Lee, RG, 'In the name of the father? *Ex parte Blood*' (1997) 60 MLR 840.

10   See (1993) *The Independent*, 28 December, p 1; (1993) *The Guardian*, 28 December, p 2, reporting an interview on the BBC's *Today* programme, 27 December 1993.

11   (1994) *The Guardian*, 5 January, p 9, although this was followed immediately by protests from various parts of the political spectrum and different interest groups: *ibid*.

12   (1994) *The Guardian*, 6 January, p 10. For a careful consideration of some of the possible consequences of treating reproduction and issue as if they *were* items of the consumer market, see Radin, MJ, *Contested Commodities: The Trouble with Trade in Sex, Children, Body Parts, and Other Things*, 1996, Cambridge, Mass: Harvard UP.

13   Maclean, A, *The Elimination of Morality*, 1993, London: Routledge, p 202.

surrogacy in question, the relationships of the parties involved to one another, whether it is a commercial transaction and in what circumstances and so on. And this moral concern will engage a variety of wider concerns too; not just about the family and parenthood but about one's whole attitude to what life brings. It seems to me that this is also an important observation about reproductive technologies more generally. The sorts of worries, or objections, the 'issues of different sorts' as Maclean puts it, will carry different force in different circumstances. Thus, worries about resource implications (which can, of course, involve ethical concern), are very different sorts of worries from those deep, inarticulate (speech of the heart) worries about the basic legitimacy of an action or of a general attitude exemplified in an action.

Concerns with surrogacy, then, like reproductive technologies more generally, cluster around commerce, commodity, consumerism and community. In the early 21st century the belief is rife, if not reasonable (and perhaps not so novel), that anything can be bought; that money can buy not only love (or at least its counterfeit), but also anything else (or at least its counterfeit). But, as Margaret Radin points out, the double bind is that 'both commodification and non-commodification may be harmful'[14] and 'it should be clear that there are coherent feminist arguments on both sides of the general issue of baby-selling (commissioned adoption)', as on reproductive technologies more generally.[15]

Finally, reproductive technologies, in their recent manifestations of the past 30 years at least,[16] and the legal accommodations and responses to them, allow us to witness the architectural and engineering dimensions of the *constitutive* aspect of law, rather than, which is often the case, its archaeological and anthropological sitings. The importance of this interpretative dimension is that it proposes that law (like other social institutions) shapes how individuals conceive of themselves and their relations with others. 'The underlying assumption is that social institutions are actualized through a set of assumptions, categories, concepts, values and vocabularies that we have internalized so that we are not consciously aware of how they have affected our ideas and behavior.'[17]

Set against these backgrounds, feminisms' analyses of reproductive technology, laws and regulation have drawn from feminisms' analysis of law and feminisms' analysis of reproductive technology. As Anne Bottomley has suggested: '... authors do not hold in common an agreed formula for what

---

14 *Op cit*, Radin, fn 12, p 127.

15 *Op cit*, Radin, fn 12, p 149.

16 Klein, RD, 'What's new about the "new" reproductive technologies?', in Corea, G *et al*, *Man-Made Women; How new Reproductive Technologies Affect Women*, 1985, London: Hutchinson, pp 64–73.

17 Sarat, A and Felstiner, W, *Divorce Lawyers and their Clients: Power and Meaning in the Legal Process*, 1995, New York and Oxford: OUP, p 13. I am grateful to Katherine O'Donovan for originally drawing this to my attention.

feminism is about other than a shared commitment to the exploration of gender relations.'[18] Feminisms have enjoyed a number of central themes, which Bottomley summates as 'narratives of the feminine, as constitutive of law-in-modernity by exclusion, by difference and by denial'.[19] Reproductive technologies have, I think, brought forward a variant on that analysis, one in which the narrative has been characterised not so much by exclusion, difference and denial, but by the possibilities and problems of *place* and *priority*. It is important to recall that infertility – like fertility – will affect different women and different men in different ways, and in ways that will differ dramatically according to culture, age, class, status and wealth. 'The handicap imposed by reproductive impairment will be at its most severe for an uneducated woman living in a small community where few options other than motherhood are culturally sanctioned.'[20]

Legal responses to reproductive technologies may not, of course, prioritise feminisms' concerns, they may instead exhibit or acquiesce in or constitute societal, theological, patriarchal, technological concerns, some or all of which may be antithetical to those of some or all women, and some or all of which may at least be taken into account if not prioritised. And it is here that one of the sites for feminisms' analyses and critiques of reproductive technologies has been at its most active. In prioritising these other concerns or sites, real damage may be done to the interests of all and to individual women. Cautioning against the tyranny of classifications, Margaret Davies reviews some standard 'categories of feminism', recalling that the tyranny is especially critical unless the temporality and provisional nature of the classifications is carefully attended to. The identity of groups is not fixed or constant, and assigning membership *to* a group is often an act of domination in itself: '... the fixing of such identities by a dominant ideology has always been one of the ways in which oppression is institutionalised.'[21] Reviewing arguments from liberal feminism, radical feminism, intersectionist jurisprudence,[22] feminism and postmodernism, Davies illustrates how supposed complementarity of interests and concerns can be radically reordered through metamorphoses of method and representation.

What links many of feminisms' responses to reproductive technologies, as feminisms' responses to law's regulation of them, Davies argues, is a

---

18 Bottomley, A (ed), *Feminist Perspectives on the Foundational Subjects of Law*, 1996, London: Cavendish Publishing, p vi.

19 *Ibid*, p 1.

20 Doyal, L, *What Makes Women Sick: Gender and the Political Economy of Health*, 1995, New Brunswick, NJ: Rutgers UP, p 147.

21 *Op cit*, Davies, fn 1, p 175.

22 'One of the assumptions made by some writers is that taking women as a group is a sufficient basis for feminist thought, without being sensitive to other systems of oppression which are not co-extensive with, but do "intersect" with gender oppression.' *Op cit*, Davies, fn 1, p 202.

commitment to a project not only directed at substantive 'women's issues', such as rape, abortion, discrimination, and pornography, but one which 'poses a challenge to the fundamental structure of law itself'.[23] It is a challenge to the substantive law, to the ordering concepts of law,[24] to law's (liberal) ideology and to its conceptual self-image, much as to the image of knowledge itself.[25] Feminisms constitute transformative theories as well as transformative politics; the *aim* of feminisms is always transformation, and as a process, feminisms are always in transition as a dynamic. It is in identifying and achieving that transformation that there are different emphases within feminisms, and these are reflected both in the analyses of law and its limitations or possibilities, as well in the specific site of reproductive technologies.

FEMINISMS' RESPONSES TO REPRODUCTION AND REGULATION

I think it is possible to identify three main sorts of analysis of reproductive technologies, which I shall call the 'critical', the 'contextual' and the 'choice' models. Neither form is meant to suggest an exclusive boundary, each displays some unifying themes and each serves to expose 'perhaps the greatest philosophical achievement of feminism over the past 20 years' which is that 'in the practice of moral and political philosophy ... the long absence of women's generic interests from the agenda of these subjects could not be innocently explained'.[26] Each shares a number of organising themes and is clustered around an identifiable core of concerns; these are, principally, concerns with procreation, parenthood, the nature of the family and personal identity. Of course, there are the wider concerns of feminisms, such as patriarchy, as the backdrop against which these particular concerns are framed.

Feminisms' responses to reproductive technologies share a number of salient characteristics. First, there is a general scepticism or rejection of the biomedical model of medicine. Secondly, and possibly, but not necessarily, flowing from this is a belief that whether reproductive technologies are the wrong sets of responses to the wrong sets of problems, or whether at best they promise a limited set of successful outcomes for a very limited set of questions for a limited set of people, there is, nonetheless, something to be understood

---

23 *Op cit*, Davies, fn 1, p 172.

24 For an example of a recharacterisation of such a project, see Dahl, TS, *Women's Law: An Introduction to Feminist Jurisprudence*, Craig, RL (trans), 1987, Oslo: Norwegian UP.

25 *Op cit*, Davies, fn 1, pp 172–79.

26 Frazer, L, Hornsby, J and Lovibond, S, *Ethics: A Feminist Reader*, 1994, Oxford: Basil Blackwell, p 4.

about the appeal that they have. Thirdly, there is a belief in most perspectives of feminism that, where reproductive technologies do properly have a place in early 21st century Westernised societies' responses to the consequences of infertility, they should be free from explicit manipulation by the State to secure other, underlying policy goals which exist for the benefit of the State rather than for the benefit of the individual users of reproductive technologies. Let me address, first, the scepticism with the biomedical model of medicine before turning to review the main tenets of what, crudely, I have called the 'critical', the 'contextual' and 'choice' analyses of reproductive technologies.

THE BIOMEDICAL MODEL

Based on the notion of Cartesian dualism,[27] this model holds that health and disease can be explained through an engineering metaphor in which the body comprises a series of separate but interdependent systems. Ill health is the mechanical failure of some part of one or more of the components of this engine, and the medical task is to repair the damage. The mind is separated from the body and the individual is separated from the social and cultural contexts of their lives. 'Illness' is an objective, positivistic fact, a descriptive, not an evaluative term. Such a model has, in fact, as many feminist scholars acknowledge, led to enormous successes in understanding different types of disease and exploring treatment, and it is mistaken to reject the powerful investigative force which the medical model suggests. However, what has followed from this as well has been a neglect of prevention, now thought to be a major factor in the incidence of infertility, and an overreliance on a curative model in explaining the causes of disease and the different ways in which illness might be experienced.[28] Medical and legal concern with issues of

---

27 Descartes, R, 'Meditations on the first philosophy in which the existence of God and the distinction between mind and body are demonstrated', in Haldane, E and Ross, G (eds and trans), *The Philosophical Works of Descartes*, 1967, Cambridge: CUP, pp 144–99. Descartes argued that the physical body, in line with emergent anatomical science, should be understood as a machine, but that there were other parts of the person which could not be accommodated within this vehicle. The expression 'mind' he used to identify aspects of human consciousness, which in almost all respects differed from the opposite characteristics possessed and exhibited by the body.

28 The best short introduction to this subject of which I am aware remains Doyal, L and Doyal, L, 'Western scientific medicine: a philosophical and political prognosis', in Birke, L and Silvertown, J, *More Than the Parts: Biology and Politics*, 1984, London: Pluto, pp 82–109. Other accessible accounts are in Kennedy, I, 'The rhetoric of medicine', in his *The Unmasking of Medicine*, 1988, London: Allen & Unwin, pp 1–25. The importance of the *philosophical* enterprise on which Kennedy has engaged himself – the exposure of a philosophical misconception at the centre of modern medicine – and the problems which may be encountered in the ethical enterprise are carefully and cogently explored in *op cit*, Maclean, fn 13, pp 187–201; especially important in the present context is her elaboration of how all contemporary medical education and practice '*dehumanises* and *diminishes* the people with whose health and well being they are charged' (p 199).

reproductive technology have generally strayed little beyond this biomedical model. And, it is in the concentration of reproductive technologies with physical aspects of women's health that the biomedical model has had its greatest and potentially most harmful impacts. The Foucauldian identification of a new kind of power relationship, in which 'authorities who understand our bodies have gained the right to make and enforce rules about morality',[29] flows directly from this model. The most thoroughgoing critics of the biomedical model are also those most critical of the whole project of reproductive technologies.

The critics

Four central points of criticism have emerged from the early life cycle of reproductive technologies, and they have remained unanswered as far as those opposed to any use of such technologies are concerned. First, originally developed to address one specific cause of infertility in women, blocked fallopian tubes, IVF moved rapidly from the experimental to the clinical. It is in this step that those who see some advantages to the development of treatment services to address the consequences of infertility are prepared to tolerate the availability of choice for individual women while remaining critical of the overall project of medically assisted conception. More explicitly, the critics charge that reproductive technologies generally and IVF specifically are techniques which augment medical control over procreation generally, and over women's choices and preferences in procreation specifically. Social screening and medical assessment have become part of a new ability to license parenthood to those deemed by the medical profession fit for the burdens and responsibilities. Compared with embryonic matter, such as gametes and embryos, women's physical health has been neglected. Rita Arditti and Gena Corea in the US, Renate Duelli Klein and Patricia Spallone in Australia and the UK focused at an early stage on what was being overlooked or left out of the context of reproductive technology. Thus, in her interview programme with women who had *left* an IVF programme without a child, Duelli Klein recounts recurrent sentiments of abuse, misinformation and malpractice, resulting in their lives being 'wrecked by the trauma of being living laboratories'.[30] Seeing IVF as a 'cure' for infertility ignores the iatrogenic causes of women's fertility problems, such as the IUD and excessive abdominal surgery, and the compromises to which reproductive health is subjected by poor health care, nutrition and other environmental factors.

29 Foucault, M, *The History of Sexuality*, Hurley, R (trans), 1978, Harmondsworth: Penguin, p 146.
30 Klein, D, *The Exploitation of Desire: Women's Experiences with In Vitro Fertilisation*, 1989, Victoria, Aus: Deakin UP, p 7; Corea, G and Ince, S, 'Report of a survey of IVF clinics in the USA', in Spallone, P and Steinberg, D (eds), *Made to Order: The Myth of Reproductive and Genetic Progress*, 1987, London: Pergamon.

Secondly, the critics allege that IVF was also seen as an example of manipulating the female body to serve patriarchal needs. Whether in facilitating the surgical removal of ova from healthy women to help in overcoming the consequences of a partner's low sperm count or motility, or in encouraging infertile women to go to extraordinary lengths to satisfy a partner's desire for a child, 'IVF was viewed as another example of putting all the risk and responsibility for reproductive failure on the shoulders of the woman'.[31]

Thirdly, the fiscal and emotional costs of IVF, compared with the likelihood of failure to conceive and deliver a child, would not be seen as a reasonable choice in a world in which childbearing was regarded as only one option in complex lifestyles. The existence of the demand for reproductive technologies evidences Western society's attachment to perceiving women as unfulfilled without children. The belief in chosen childlessness is disvalued or dismissed, or characterised as the choice of the sexual or relational deviant. Doubts have been expressed by many commentators, such as Christine Crowe, arguing that IVF does not, in any event, represent a proper choice, since other options, like chosen childlessness or adoption are not open or available to all women.[32]

Fourthly, IVF has revealed a profound attachment to genetic lineage which cannot be shared equally between the sexes. Women gestate and deliver, men could only stand by and admire their own physical characteristics as reflected in their children. Attachment to genetic lineage, especially by and for men, has had a distorting effect on women's stated desires to circumvent the consequences of infertility.

The Contextualists: '... no daughters to comfort her and no sons to support her'[33]

It might be thought that, for any contextual account of reproductive technologies to be given, this *necessarily* implies a commitment to a liberal, contingent, in parts rights-based model. I want here to show why I believe that that would be mistaken, although it is undoubtedly *one* of the contexts which is available:

> To view infertility as a medical construction and the desire to have a biologically related child as a social product does not deny the consequences of

---

31   Alto Charo, R, 'The interaction between family planning and the introduction of new reproductive technologies', in *op cit*, Peterson, fn 6, pp 65–66, on which this paragraph draws.

32   'Women want it: IVF and women's motivations for participation', in *op cit*, Spallone and Steinberg, fn 30, and 'Mind over whose matter? Women, in vitro fertilisation and the development of scientific knowledge', in McNeil, M, Varcoe, I and Yearley, S (eds), *The New Reproductive Technologies*, 1990, Basingstoke: Macmillan, pp 27–57.

33   *Op cit*, Doyal, fn 20, p 147.

such definitions. While it is essential to critique the process of medicalisation and to be continually wary of the development of technologies and interventions that aim to alleviate infertility these 'treatments' do not determine totally the capacity of individuals to make choices. That the available options are limited, restrictive and may involve medical intervention does not deny some scope for negotiation, bargaining and resistance.[34]

Without good health, a person's ability to act upon at least some of the choices they make or would wish to make is curtailed. Providing the means by which citizens may preserve and restore or secure their health may be thought to be a fundamental task of any modern State. So, when we come to speak of health, we are of necessity required to address at least a package of *conceptual* questions;[35] *political* questions – the role and responsibility of the State in securing, promoting or damaging the health of its citizens and those whom it affects directly and indirectly intentionally and accidentally through the extraterritorial effects of its behaviour,[36] and those of *gender*. As Lesley Doyal has recently reminded us, many women's lives *are* severely constrained because they are denied the opportunity to make real choices about procreation. This inability to influence one of the most fundamental aspects of biological functioning can have profound effects on both physical and mental health.[37]

This has two aspects; first is the prevention of unwanted pregnancy and responding sympathetically and appropriately to the consequences of contraceptive failure. The second is the circumvention of unlooked for childlessness and responding sympathetically and appropriately to the sequelae which may ensue. This does not necessarily entail that the functional equivalent of access to services for the termination of pregnancy must be mirrored in the provision of reproductive technology programmes. The equivalent of access to abortion services does not necessarily mean that there must be a corresponding 'right' to or access to infertility treatment services, much less that there must be or is a 'right' to have a child. Both are connected, however, to the basic notion of reproductive self-determination; 'infertility can be a major disability and its treatment should be seen as a basic element in

---

34 *Op cit*, Anleu, fn 6, p 36.

35 Boorse, C, 'On the distinction between health and disease' [1975] Philosophy and Public Affairs 5; *op cit*, Doyal, fn 20; Oakley, A, *Essays on Women, Medicine and Health*, 1993, Edinburgh: Edinburgh UP; Nordenfelt, C, 'On the relevance and importance of the notion of disease' (1993) 14 Theoretical Medicine 15.

36 Townsend, P and Davidson, N (eds), *Inequalities in Health* (the Black Report), 1982, Harmondsworth: Penguin; Williams, B, 'The idea of equality', in Laslett, P and Runciman, WG (eds), *Philosophy, Politics and Society*, 2nd series, 1962, Oxford: Basil Blackwell, pp 110–31; Nozick, R, *Anarchy, State and Utopia*, 1974, Oxford: Basil Blackwell, p 233.

37 *Op cit*, Doyal, fn 20, p 93. Are there two problems with this: (a) the effects of environment and diet in men's reproductive health, and (b) recent (contested) changes in the legal regulation of the consequences of failing to control one's fertility?

reproductive self-determination, along with abortion, contraception and maternity care'.[38]

I do not want to be thought to imply that each or any of these different types of question – the conceptual question, the political question and the gendered question – can or does stand independently of any one other or of all. There are cross-cutting intersections and intermixtures of all of them, and the points of intersection and interlayering will often be complex, but interesting and important ones. Feminisms' accounts of reproductive technologies are part of feminisms' accounts of science and the reason, logic and technological certainty and neutrality which it celebrates.[39]

Lene Koch has centrally captured the difficulties which reproductive technologies cause for many critical feminist commentators: '... there is no doubt that IVF is a powerful transformer of women's reproductive consciousness and an irresistible technology that few women can refuse.'[40] The role of the family, and conceptions of personal identity and human nature, are underlined in many ways by programmes of assisted conception, especially in the way in which rational women will use and pursue infertility programmes even when they know that the success rates are low. Koch, in interviews with a sample of women entering and participating in an IVF programme in Copenhagen, observed that although, in a number of cases, women felt deprived of accurate or realistic information, this did not seem to matter: '... it did not seem to have influenced these women's decisions, neither to start IVF in the first place, nor to continue after one or more failed attempts.' She argues that to want a child and try to have it 'is an exercise of the reproductive freedom that the feminist movement has argued for since its very beginning'.[41] This wish to have a child – this authentic wish of the women concerned – 'does not become less strong because it is socially constructed'. Given the information which is available about the success rates of IVF programmes, why do these 'infertile' women appear to persist with irrational hopes and beliefs in the outcome of their project? Her conclusion is an important one: '... as each new reproductive technology enters the market, the definition of infertility changes.' Infertile women are only allowed access to their infertility – it can only become an established fact – once they have followed *all* the acceptable rites of passage, including the latest treatment service, no matter how experimental. If these are seen only as a choice for a child, then they may indeed be regarded as irrational, given the paucity of the established rates at which women leave IVF programmes with a child.

---

38 *Op cit*, Doyal, fn 20, p 147.

39 A good introduction to feminisms' accounts of science is Rosser, S, *Teaching Science and Health from a Feminist Perspective*, 1986, New York: Pergamon; especially useful in the immediate contexts are pp 3–22, 38–61 and 77–89.

40 *Op cit*, Koch, fn 7, p 236.

41 *Op cit*, Koch, fn 7, p 237.

However, if it is acknowledged that 'human identity is closely affected by parental status and *childlessness is an identity which is hard to obtain* and must be fought for in a pronatalist society, since no doubt must exist as to the certainty of the condition',[42] a rational understanding of reproductive technologies is revealed.

What Koch here describes is what might be called the problem of *access to infertility*; whereas infertility used to be considered to be a matter of fate, 'it is nowadays turning into a deliberate decision, at least in a certain sense. Those who give up without having tried the very latest methods (an endless series) have to take the blame. After all, they could have kept trying'.[43] The social role of fertility will always, in some sense, be seen as chosen,[44] part of the 'noiseless social and cultural revolution' in which the exponential development of science and technology, while supposedly serving health, has in fact 'created entirely new situations, has changed the relationship of humankind to itself, to disease, illness and death, indeed, it has changed the world'.[45]

Thus, judged only against the likelihood of producing a baby, a woman's initial introduction to and continued participation in an IVF programme might, to outsiders, lack rationality; it is transformed, however, when it is seen as 'a new element in the procedure by which the woman establishes her future identity'. The decision or the desire to try IVF becomes independent of the efficiency of the technology, because it is 'judged by the yardstick of another rationality'.[46] Koch is no proponent of IVF programmes, far from it; indeed, IVF is a dangerous and expensive technology, which changes motherhood in detrimental ways and it is a high risk, low efficiency technology whose costs foreclose the development and application of preventive cheap low technology solutions that every woman can afford to choose. IVF programmes deleteriously affect the priorities of the health services, but that does not mean that they are not pursued by rational women.

Lesley Doyal offers a similar analysis of the contexts of reproductive technology, in which some of the millions of infertile women are drawn by their desire for a child into the 'epicentre of high technology gynaecology and obstetrics'.[47] She is more concerned with the cultural contexts of fertility, in which the status of mother is still a 'central' one for many women and for whom 'an inability to become a biological parent may have a profound effect

42 *Op cit*, Koch, fn 7, p 241.

43 Beck, U and Gernsheim-Beck, E, *The Normal Chaos of Love*, 1995, Oxford: Polity, esp pp 102–39.

44 Rothman, BK, *The Tentative Pregnancy: Prenatal Diagnosis and the Future of Motherhood*, 1986, New York: Viking, p 29.

45 Beck, U, *Risk Society: Towards a New Modernity*, Ritter, M (trans), 1992, London: Sage, p 204.

46 *Op cit*, Koch, fn 7, p 241.

47 *Op cit*, Doyal, fn 20, p 145.

on women's sense of themselves and their well-being', in which they may suffer a major life crisis, may indeed be 'disabled'.[48] Reproductive technology may, then, be seen not just as a response to infertility, but, more profoundly, as a (bio)technological response to a total life and social crisis *to the person as a whole*. In other words, infertility treatments might, on this view, be recontextualised as something other than a 'medical model' response to particular cellular dysfunction in the reproductive system; rather, it is a response to a life threatening position. The cruel irony, then, is that while reproductive technologies 'have recently been hailed as the miracle solution for all those who cannot conceive within their own bodies', the reality is that 'they are suitable for only a small percentage of infertile women and only a few of these can afford them'.[49] In an arresting phrase which recalls the culturally differentiated experiences of women, to which feminisms particularly have become more attentive, Doyal examines the severe handicaps of a woman unable to have children and who may have 'no daughters to comfort her and no sons to support her'.[50]

REPRODUCTIVE 'CHOICE'

Rosalind Petchesky has observed that the critical issue for feminists is not so much the *content* of women's choices, or even the 'right to choose', as the social and material conditions under which choices are made. 'The fact that individuals themselves do not determine the social framework in which they act does not nullify their choices nor their moral capacity to make them.'[51] The most visible complaint is that, where access to reproductive technologies is permitted, the State should not discriminate against certain individual women because of their sexual orientation, status preference, their race or social status. And yet, almost universally, where legislation has addressed these questions, judgments about 'fitness to parent' are explicitly or implicitly made by the State on grounds which characterise some women as unfit to mother or to parent.

Reproductive technologies have provided some people who are 'infertile' with the hope and chance of having a child and have opened up the possibility of new and exciting opportunities for the formation of families with the separation of genetic, gestational and social parenthood in ways that previously belonged to the realm of science fiction.[52] Even those enthusiastic

---

48   *Op cit*, Doyal, fn 20, p 146.

49   *Op cit*, Doyal, fn 20, p 145.

50   *Op cit*, Doyal, fn 20, p 147.

51   'Reproductive freedom: beyond "a woman's right to choose"' (1980) J Women in Culture and Society 675.

52   Bennett, B, 'Gamete donation, reproductive technology and the law', in *op cit*, Peterson, fn 6, p 41.

about their advent remain conscious of the challenge to 'respect the reproductive rights of infertile people to have access to reproductive technology, while critically evaluating and seeking to transcend the narrow confines of the definition of 'family' within which reproductive technology operates'.[53] And yet, it remains the case that, for most women, infertility is a life sentence; new technologies are characterised by their exclusivity, for the relatively more wealthy, 'suitable couple', who are eternal optimists – Koch's new rationalists as we might call them. And the problem, with their high cost and low 'success' rates and abysmal side effects, is that the very existence of technological solutions to circumventing infertility may be diverting resources away from broader strategies for responding to and preventing 'reproductive impairment'.[54]

METAMORPHOSES: ETHICS, HEALTH AND FAMILY

Reproductive technologies understood in their widest sense have arrived at a time of what Boaventura de Sousa Santos describes as a 'state of epistemological turbulence'.[55] He suggests that, after the 19th century scientist euphoria and the concomitant aversion to philosophical speculation, epitomised by positivism, we were, at the end of the 20th century, seized by the near desperate desire to complement our knowledge of things with our knowledge of our knowledge of things – in other words, with knowledge of ourselves, *independent of any surrounding moral values*.[56] The emergence of the concern with women's interests and health has occurred at a time of other changes which have taken deep root in the practice of ethical and legal thought, some of which are reflected in feminisms' works, some of which have occurred as a *direct or indirect result* of the placing of women as the central concern in inquiry. Within that is the imperative of recognising and acting upon the realisation that, while they share a gender identity and a common biology, 'women are differentiated by factors such as age, sexual preference, race, class and, very importantly, geopolitical status – the wealth or poverty of the country in which they live'.[57] This caution is particularly necessary in the era of emergent globalisation; social, economic and cultural circumstances shape reproductive experiences in such a way that it is as inappropriate to speak then of 'the infertile' as it has become to speak of 'women'. Thus, for some women, 'infertility can be a major disability and its treatment should be

---

53   *Op cit*, Bennett, fn 52.

54   *Op cit*, Doyal, fn 20, p 149.

55   de Sousa Santos, B, *Toward a New Common Sense: Law, Science and Politics in the Paradigmatic Transition*, 1995, London: Routledge, p 34.

56   *Ibid*, p 20, emphasis added. A remarkably similar point is being made in Foucault's *History of Sexuality*, esp pp 135–45.

57   *Op cit*, Doyal, fn 20, p 2.

seen as a basic element in reproductive self-determination, along with abortion, contraception and maternity care'.[58]

In dialogues and constructions of health care law and ethics, Susan Wolf has identified what she has called the rise of a 'new pragmatism' that challenges old paradigms in bioethics, especially those of the so called principle-based approaches. The goal of this new, emergent, pragmatic paradigm is to change the nature of ethical colloquy about access – in this case – to health care. Feminist and race sensitive scholarship, in particular, has rendered suspect any bioethical approach geared to the generic 'patient'.[59]

The hegemony of Western modes of thought, which have much dominated Western political, social and moral philosophy for the last 200 years or so, has been under new assail. Feminisms' and postmodernism's accounts of ethical practices propose a shift towards the understanding of morality as a socially embedded practice, a shift which identifies moral decision making in medicine (as in other professional and public organisational settings) as increasingly subject to formalised procedures and constraints. Across a broad range in the landscape of contemporary medicine 'ethical choice and agency are now embedded as never before in a network of explicit rules and formal procedures and processes for making decisions'.[60]

The shift thus identified is part of a rethinking of the very nature of ethical theory itself; its relationship to the human subjectivity and the cultural context that produces it, the kind of knowledge it can be expected to provide and the force and authority of its claims and its relationship to practice are part of the reconstruction under way. This kind of postmodern philosophical orientation of moral philosophy fundamentally affects our grasp of the relationship between theory and practice. It purports to expose the extent to which classical ethical theories 'rest on assumptions about the transcendental character of reason and a "philosophy of the subject" ... that are no longer tenable'.[61] In other words, it is being claimed that ethical conclusions are being produced and constructed rather than found from contemplation. The older questions are being displaced by a postmodern approach which aims to examine the ways in which meanings and legitimacy of moral notions are established, reinterpreted and transformed over time.

Or, so at first it might appear. Critics of this approach come from at least two directions. First, there is a strand of feminisms which reject a so called

---

58 *Op cit*, Doyal, fn 20, p 147.

59 Wolf, SM, 'The rise of the new pragmatism' (1994) 20(4) Am J Law and Medicine 415, and see Gillon, R and Lloyd, A (eds), *Principles of Health Care Ethics*, 1994, Chichester: Wiley.

60 Jennings, B, 'Possibilities of consensus: towards democratic moral discourse' (1991) 16 J Medicine and Philosophy 447, p 450.

61 *Ibid*, p 448.

'justice of multiplicities',[62] claiming that it ignores common interests which emerge from grand theoretical narratives. One potential consequence is that 'by refusing to lump women's interests together, modern feminist writing may appear to be abdicating itself from the legal arena'.[63] In another area, Patricia Williams has indicated the problem of rights discourse which could be implied here: '... the problem with rights discourse is not that the discourse is itself constricting, but that it exists in a constricted referential universe.'[64] The conferring of rights on the 'historically disempowered' is 'symbolic' of parts of the human condition which has been left out: '... rights imply a respect that places one in the referential range of self and others, that elevates one's status from human being to social being.'[65] Far from classical ethical theories resting on assumptions about the transcendental character of reason and an untenable philosophy of the subject, this approach suggests that rights-based approaches are one example of beginning to take some of those excluded claims seriously.

The second type of critical reception which has been offered despairs the apparent impasse of postmodernism and the incoherence of the 'new ethics' which it appears to suggest. A brilliantly succinct example of this argument is made by Gillian Rose in her final book, *Mourning Becomes the Law: Philosophy and Representation*.[66] Deploring the 'despairing rationalism without reason',[67] she castigates libertarian extensions of the rights of individuals as amounting to an extension, not an attenuation of coercion, and claims that communitarian empowerment of ethnic and gender pluralities as presupposing and fixing a 'given distribution of "identities" in a radically dynamic society'.[68]

---

62   Fraser, L and Nicholson, A, 'Social criticism without philosophy: an encounter between feminism and postmodernism', in Ross, A (ed), *Universal Abandon? The Politics of Postmodernism*, 1988, Minnesota: Minnesota UP.

63   Jackson, E, 'Contradictions and coherence in feminist responses to law' (1993) 20 JLS 399.

64   Williams, P, *The Alchemy of Race and Rights*, 1991, Cambridge, Mass: Harvard UP, p 159.

65   *Ibid*, p 153.

66   1996, Cambridge: CUP.

67   *Ibid*, p 7.

68   *Ibid*, p 5.

There is, I think, a sense, properly understood within postmodernism itself,[69] that what is needed here, what is happening, is not in fact the discovery of new philosophical approaches to knowledge and understanding, but more importantly, the *rediscovery*, certainly within the practice of modern medicine dominated by the 'medical model' or the 'biomedical approach', of something which has been lost; *the person as a whole*.

What is entailed here is not the metaphysical entity of modern bioethics in speaking of the person, not the generic 'patient' which Wolf has sought to banish, what is envisaged is the recovery of the person in the ordinary sense – the individual human being, together with the environment, physical and social, of which she or he is a part. As Maclean explores and explains, the major loss engendered by the medical model of illness and health is medicine itself and those it subjects to its treatments. This is a major sickness of medicine itself, which will be resolved ('the healing of medicine itself') only when there has been a recovery of what overly science-dependent medicine has lost – human beings. In place of the patient, we need to recover the person:

> The point that must now be made is this: the recovery of the human being is the recovery, at the same time, of the values which form the framework of his life as a moral being, or a member of a moral community ... structural features of our everyday moral life ... not principles of which one could be *ignorant* unless one were ignorant of moral considerations as such.[70]

What Maclean believes is needed is the equivalent of Wolf's broad path teeming with people, accommodating 'multiple proposals and critiques as to method, full with attention to feminist, race-attentive and other contributions'. While the precise contours and geography of this space will need careful mapping and landscaping, it is the functional equivalent of de Sousa Santos' plea for a move away from our 'near desperate desire' to be filled with 'knowledge of ourselves ... independent of any surrounding moral values',[71]

---

69 In the sense suggested by Lyotard, J-F, *The Post-Modern Condition: A Report on Knowledge*, 1979, Manchester, Manchester UP, 1992 edn, p 28: 'Postmodernism thus understood is not modernism at its end but in the nascent state, and this state is constant.' The relationship between postmodernism and feminism has been a problematic one, but to that extent no different from other sites of challenge; for an introduction, see Nicholson, LJ (ed), *Feminism/Postmodernism*, 1990, London: Routledge, especially in the present context the essays by Benhabib, S, Haraway, D and Butler, J. The projects identified by Wolf, Jennings and Maclean are, it seems to me, examples of the postmodern move away from large theoretical explanations in favour of a localised discourse but, as Rose demands, *with attention to wide or grand strategy and not as a substitute for them*.

70 *Op cit*, Maclean, fn 13, p 199.

71 *Op cit*, de Sousa Santos, fn 55, p 20.

to supplement a 'culture preoccupied with self'[72] with one sensitive to and sensitised by principles of moral community.

There is a third change which needs to be remarked, and that is in the nature of the form which family came to take in the latter decades of the 20th century. Even without the advent of reproductive technologies, family forms in the late 20th century became more varied than in the 18th, 19th and even the early to mid-20th century. Where it exists, parenthood is certainly no longer, if it ever was, a straightforward matter; it can now be broken into three distinguishable elements: biological parenthood, legal parenthood, and the holding of parental responsibility, in such a way that 'the resulting structure of parenthood in English law is one in which a medieval land lawyer would have taken pride'.[73] The consequences of this we have hardly begun to hazard at. Marilyn Strathern has suggested that the new reproductive technologies and the legislative and other actions to which they have given rise seek to assist natural process on the one hand and the social definition of kinship on the other. But:

> ... this double assistance creates new uncertainties. For the present cultural explicitness is revolutionising former combinations of ideas and concepts. The more we give legal certainty to social parenthood, the more we cut from under our feet assumptions about the intrinsic nature of relationships themselves. The more facilitation is given to the biological reproduction of human persons, the harder it is to think of a domain of natural facts independent of social intervention. Whether or not all this is a good thing is uncertain. What is certain is that it will not be without consequence for the way people think about one another.[74]

The deployment of reproductive technologies is affecting assumptions which we bring to understandings not only of family life but to the very understanding of family itself and cultural practice:[75] '... the way in which the choices that assisted conception affords are formulated, will affect thinking about kinship. And the way people think about kinship will affect other ideas about relatedness between human beings.'[76] And, I would add, the way in which we think about relatedness between human beings will affect the way

---

72 Porter, R, *The Greatest Benefit to Mankind*, 1997, London: HarperCollins, p 7.

73 Eekelaar, J, 'Parenthood, social engineering and rights', in Morgan, D and Douglas, G (eds), *Constituting Families: A Study in Governance*, 1994, Stuttgart: Franz Steiner Verlag, p 87, citing the Children Act 1989 for the introduction of the third component, parental responsibility.

74 Strathern, M, 'The meaning of assisted kinship', in Stacey, M (ed), *Changing Human Reproduction*, 1992, London: Sage, pp 167–68. This essay is a succinct introduction to cultural and linguistic concepts deployed in arguments about the family, demonstrating, in her use of examples, the way in which what are taken as natural facts are themselves social and cultural constructs.

75 Strathern, M, *Reproducing the Future: Anthropology, Kinship and the New Reproductive Technologies*, 1993, Manchester: Manchester UP.

76 *Ibid*, p 149, n 95.

in which we think about the relationship between individuals, groups and the State.

Writing of reproductive technologies becomes part of an exercise in exploring intellectual history – in which here we can only be concerned or competent to chart the origins of that history – technology, rationality and society. Reproductive technology may have brought us to the customs house of human history, where we have to declare what we are taking with us, decide which of the imposts we will pay, and what we will abandon. We are crossing a Rubicon for which there is no return ticket, in which, indeed, there is no duty free zone. Legal responses to and regulation of technology illustrate the way in which we might examine the challenges raised by reproduction itself. Feminisms' analyses propose a challenge to the fundamental structure of law itself,[77] and how an understanding of reproductive technologies may challenge the fundamental structure of identity and knowledge themselves. Surveying some frameworks for feminisms' analyses of reproductive technologies, reviewing responses to the 'noiseless social and cultural revolution' which Ulrich Beck suggests they represent,[78] and establishing their intellectual history[79] is an important part of the project to ensure that they do not come to be thought of as having occurred in what Christopher Hill has ironically observed, of the other English revolution, as a 'fit of absence of mind'.[80]

---

77 *Op cit*, Davies, fn 1, p 172.

78 *Op cit*, Beck, fn 45, p 204.

79 For a template within which this might be forged, see *op cit*, de Sousa Santos, fn 55, pp 1, 40ff.

80 Hill, C, *The Intellectual Origins of the English Revolution*, 1965, Oxford: Clarendon, p 1.

CHAPTER 6

WHERE DO I OWN MY BODY? (AND WHY?)

INTRODUCTION

The idea that I might 'own' my body while yet being prevented from doing some things with it has been an important organising principle in arguments about, *inter alia*, the development of modern medical law. Similarly, much recent academic literature proceeds in part on the basis that *because* an individual is an 'autonomous' being, it is not the proper role of the State to interfere in what is done consensually to that person, certainly if there is no harm to others. Where is the basis for the arguments that I own my body? What purpose or purposes are or might be served by recognition that my body is *my* body?

This paper subjects these questions to critical examination. In the first part, it adopts and uses arguments showing both limitations and misunderstandings of Lockean concepts of ownership of property and Kantian notions of autonomy to suggest that, in a fundamental sense, my body may be mine to use and enjoy, but not to 'own'. It uses Naffine's more recent jurisprudence to suggest that, far from being a universal notion, ownership of the body, at least in its conjugal sense, raises deep issues of gender which render suspect easy ethical accommodation of commerce and commodity in the body.

The second part of the paper is quite distinct. It is a more conventional analysis of the rules of the common law as they apply to the question of property or proprietary rights in and about the body. The later part of that section takes five examples of arguments about ownership to suggest *why* contemporary medical law and ethics have been engaged here, and then, in a concluding section, the paper offers some cautionary remarks on the nature of the 'ownership' debate.

OWNERSHIP AND AUTONOMY

Together, the changes that I discussed above, changes that I called the body of knowledge and knowledge of the body, have resulted in two senses in what we might call 'the individuation of the body'. First, to arguments as to whether I 'own' 'my' body;[1] and whether, in consequence or otherwise, I might do what I want with 'my' body. This individuation of the body with its emphasis on individual autonomy and the market, suggests that 'the West has evolved a culture preoccupied with the self, with the individual and his or her identity, and this quest has come to be equated with (or reduced to) the individual body and the embodied personality'.[2] This, in turn, has resulted in changes of views on 'autonomy' and legal control with respect to medical care which have been sanctioned or permitted by the courts; thus, in only the last 10 years, we have seen significant changes through cases such as *Re MB* and *St George's NHS Trust v S*;[3] *Bland*,[4] *Re C*[5] and *Re T*;[6] *Gillick*;[7] and *Bolitho*.[8]

Secondly, although not uncontroversially, the nature of the patient has changed.[9] I do not mean this in the usual fashion which attends the assertion that people have become more rights-oriented, more consumerist about health care and the deliverers of health care, although I believe that those theses could be defended.[10] What I mean, additionally, is that the patient has disappeared, if by 'the patient' we are understood to mean some generic, stand-all representative. In place, we have patients who have gender, class, race, ethnicity, age and identity; we have a theatre teeming with peoples, all of different constitutions and complexions.[11]

Ownership

Where is the basis for the arguments that I own my body? What purpose or purposes are, or might be, served by a recognition that my body is *my* body?

---

1   Locke, J, 'An essay concerning the true original extent and end of civil government' (2nd treatise, para 27, 1690), in Laslett, P (ed), *Two Treatises of Government*, 1960, Cambridge: CUP, p 287; Kass, L, 'Is there a right to die?' (1993) 23(1) Hastings Center Report 34, showing the context in which Locke's famous remark on 'body ownership' occurs; and Hyde, A, *Bodies of Law*, 1997, Princeton, NJ: Princeton UP, pp 54–57, discussing the misunderstanding of Locke's 'unsophisticated pun' which has given rise to the confusing claim that I might 'own' my own body. See below.

2   Porter, R, *The Greatest Benefit to Mankind*, 1997, London: HarperCollins, p 7.

3   *Re MB* (1997) 38 BMLR 175; *St George's NHS Trust v S* [1998] 3 All ER 673.

4   *Airedale NHS Trust v Bland* [1993] 1 All ER 821.

5   *Re C* [1994] 1 All ER 819.

6   *Re T* [1992] 4 All ER 649.

7   *Gillick v West Norfolk and Wisbech AHA* [1985] 3 All ER 402.

8   *Bolitho v City and Hackney HA* [1997] 4 All ER 771.

9   I attempt to sketch out this change as part of a wider range of metamorphoses in Chapter 2, above.

10 Perhaps the modern *locus classicus* in this vein is Kennedy, I, *Treat Me Right: Essays in Medical Law and Ethics*, 1988, Oxford: OUP. For an essay specifically focusing on the possible contribution of human rights to women's health, see Cook, RJ, *Women's Health and Human Rights*, 1994, Philadelphia: Philadelphia and Pennsylvania Press.

11 Wolf, SM, 'New pragmatism' (1994) 20(4) Am J Law and Medicine 395.

As I have suggested, the idea that I might 'own' my body yet be prevented from doing some things with it has occupied much recent academic literature proceeding in part on the basis that, *because* an individual is an 'autonomous' being, it is not the proper role of the State to interfere in what is done consensually to that person, certainly if there is no harm to others.[12] It follows – in this view – that the Millian principle of harm (to others) is well established – it is *only* harm to others which can properly be the subject of the criminal law or other prohibition by the State.[13]

Lockean concepts of ownership of property and Kantian notions of autonomy are prayed in aid and to suggest that my body may be my own to use and enjoy as I please; that it is my own to 'own'. This has wide ranging consequences for debates in genetics, euthanasia and physician-assisted suicide, sale or other use of tissue,[14] surrogacy,[15] bodily alteration, and so on.

The analogy of the body to property is a familiar one; the derivation of the word property is from the Latin *proprius* (one's own) and is close to the French *propre* (close or near, one's own, proper, clean). There are two different philosophical traditions, either or both of which have been appealed to in the body/property argument.[16] The claim usually arises in law as deciding the just or proper limits of the domination of one person by another. Thus, the body may be property in order to *justify or explain human domination*; a human may be dominated because its body is *just* property. Aristotle derives a

---

12   The premise which lies behind these arguments, which informs much of the literature critical of the House of Lords' decision in *R v Brown* [1993] 2 All ER 75 (HL), for example, is similar to the notion, if indeed it is not the same notion, of self-ownership: that I can do what I want with my body because it is mine.

13   Thus, a traditional starting point for lawyers and political philosophers has been the statement by the 19th century thinker JS Mill that 'the only purpose for which power can be rightfully exercised over any member of a civilised community against his will is to prevent harm to others. His own good, either physical or moral, is not a sufficient warrant' (*On Liberty*).

   We do not want to dwell here on the difficulties to which this *dictum* has given rise: What is harm? Who counts as others? Must force be used to prevent harm to others, or is this merely a necessary condition? What is wrong with the parentalist intervention of others to prevent one causing harm to oneself? In other words, is Mill correct that the State must always misconceive the individual's interests, or be untimely in its intervention? But, the responses to the Wolfenden Report, which recalls Mill's harm principle, illustrate some of the fundamental differences in contemporary thought about the relationship between law and morals.

14   See, Radin, MJ, *Contested Commodities: The Trouble with Trade in Sex, Children, Body Parts, and Other Things*, 1996, Cambridge, Mass: Harvard UP, and Posner, R, *Sex and Reason*, 1992, Cambridge, Mass: Harvard UP for two opposing views.

15   For opposing arguments see, eg, *ibid*, Radin, and Shalev, C, *Birth Power: The Case for Surrogacy*, 1989, New Haven, Ct: Yale UP. The Report of the Brazier Committee, *Surrogacy: Review for Health Ministers of Current Arrangements for Payment and Regulation*, Cm 4068, 1998 offers as one of its immediate objections to the payment of more than nominal expenses to women who act as 'surrogate mothers' that '[p]ayments contravene the social norms of our society that, just as bodily parts cannot be sold, nor can such intimate services' (para 4, p i).

16   *Op cit*, Hyde, fn 1, pp 54–56, on which, quite clearly, this draws.

justification for the government of some over others from the domination of the slave by the master.[17] Leibniz justifies domination over animals by analogising them to machines; thus, if people are property, or machines, they may be dominated too.

A second tradition, one that is generally appealed to in English law, as we shall see, constitutes the body as property in order to *emphasise* autonomy. Thus, John Locke moves from the claim that 'every Man has a Property in his own person' to a general theory of the institution of private property.[18] Locke was, of course, a physician and may have meant this claim quite literally. But there is nothing inevitable about Locke's association of the owned, body as property, with any claim of autonomy and freedom in the self that owns that body. Nevertheless, the hold that this notion has taken on contemporary medical law is illustrated in the Court of Appeal's recent judgment in *Re A (Children) (Conjoined Twins)*, where Brooke LJ is to be found averring that: 'John Locke's assertion that "every Man has a Property in his own person. This no Body has any Right to but himself" *which underpins much of the moral dialogue in this area* is difficult to apply in the case of conjoined twins.'[19]

It is argued that Locke's teaching on property rests on a principle of self-ownership; since I own my body, it is argued, I can decide what to do with it. Locke's argument appears at first to lend support to these conclusions:

> Though the earth and all inferior creatures be common to all men, yet every man has a property in his own person; this nobody has the right to but himself. The labour of his body and the work of his hands we may say are properly his.

At first sight, it seems relatively straightforward. But the context defines and constricts the claim. Unlike the property rights in the fruits of one's labour, the property a person has in his or her own person is inalienable; a person cannot transfer title to him or herself by selling him or herself into slavery. The 'property in his own person' is less a metaphysical statement declaring self-ownership, more a political statement denying ownership by another. This right removes each and every human being from the commons available to all human beings for appropriation and use. My body and my life are my property *in the limited sense* that they are *not yours*. They are different from my alienable property – my house, my car, my shoes – as differently removed from alienability as my children. My body and my life, while mine to use, are not mine to dispose of. In the deepest sense, my body is nobody's body, not even mine.[20] The same sort of conclusion had appealed to Kant:

> Man cannot dispose over himself because he is not a thing; he is not his own property; to say that he is would be self-contradictory; for in so far as he is a

---

17   *Politics*, in *The Complete Works of Aristotle*, 1984, Princeton, NJ: Princeton UP, para 2.

18   *Op cit*, Locke, fn 1, para 27, p 287.

19   [2000] 4 All ER 961.

20   *Op cit*, Kass, fn 1.

person he is a subject in whom the ownership of things can be vested, and if he were his own property, he would be a thing over which he could have ownership. But a person cannot be property and so cannot be a thing which can be owned, for it is impossible to be a person and a thing, the proprietor and the property.[21]

On autonomy[22]

While we are disputing this point, it is probably worthwhile just disposing of another shibboleth which affects this debate and which is frequently and carelessly left lying around by autonomy mongers in modern medical law. It concerns the moral notion – oft appealed to in these sorts of debate – of autonomy itself. For this appeal is made to Kantian ethics, Kant having been the author of the very notion of autonomy now invoked. The use of the word autonomy was first applied to States that were 'self-ruling'. While working with this core concept of autonomy, philosophers and others have taken up and deployed different conceptions of it in seeking to locate various interests and rights of individuals. Most would agree that an autonomous person is one who rules her or his own life, but disagree as to what properly counts as being in such control.

Kant's concern with autonomy was in examining one of the most important features of a human being – which is that he or she has a will. In so far as a person is able to decide what he or she ought to do, he or she is responsible for his or her actions. Any action of moral worth must emanate from a motive of duty rather than inclination. For Kant, autonomy, which literally means self-regulation, requires acting in accordance with one's true self – that is, one's rational will determined by a universalisable, that is, rational maxim. Being autonomous means not being a slave to instinct, or whim or caprice, but rather *doing as one ought as a rational being*. Reason is the faculty which enables one to act from one rather than the other; enables one to choose, for example, what is right. There is, on the surface, little difference here between reason and autonomy, between rationality and autonomy. But, as reason is housed in a body with emotions, rationality is only a necessary condition for autonomy and not a sufficient one. In carrying out an autonomous act, a person must not only act upon the rational assessment of alternatives, but also be able to carry out a decision with authenticity and strength of will. These latter two concepts may be understood to mean that first, there must be some feature of a course of conduct which the individual

---

21 Kant, I, 'Lectures on ethics', in Paton, HJ (ed), 'Groundwork of the metaphysics of morals', 1953, London: Hutchinson, p 165.

22 This section draws from Leon Kass and what I have found to be his influential essay, *op cit*, fn 1.

regards as important, and which constitutes a non-articial reason for pursuing it as distinct from extrinsic reasons provided by praise and blame, reward and punishment, and so on, which are artificially created by the demands of others; that is, a person must perform the action for the right reasons.[23] The final aspect of autonomy involves the executive side of a person's character; a person must be able to carry out her or his decision that may involve courage, integrity and determination.

Various reformulations of this are given as an autonomous person possessing three traits: self-control (not just acting on any desires, but only on those which carry the most weight); procedural independence (free from the domination of others, in which judgments are not founded on fashion, custom or the opinion of others); and competence (that a person can achieve her or his goals).[24] But, autonomy has now come to mean something such as 'doing as you please', compatible with self-indulgence as much as with self-control.[25]

This has infected the legal process. In *Re T*,[26] Lord Donaldson MR argued:

> An adult patient who, like Miss T, suffers from no mental incapacity, has an absolute right to choose whether to consent to medical treatment, to refuse it or to choose one rather than another of the treatments being offered ... This right of choice is not limited to decisions which others might regard as sensible. It exists notwithstanding that the reasons for making the choice are rational, *irrational*, unknown or *even non-existent* ... The fact that, 'emergency cases' apart, no medical treatment of an adult patient of full capacity can be undertaken without his consent, creates a situation in which the absence of consent has much the same effect as refusal.[27]

---

23 For this point, see Peters, RS, *Education, Philosophy, Ethics*, 1996, London: Allen & Unwin. TS Eliot, in his play *Murder in the Cathedral*, provides a classic examination of right actions and wrong reasons; cf the discomfiture of Lord Mustill and Lord Browne-Wilkinson in *Bland*. Lord Goff had said that 'the sanctity of life must yield to the principle of self-determination'; Lord Keith that 'a person is completely at liberty to decline to undergo treatment even if the result of his doing so is that he will die'. Despite the inability of the patient Bland to consent to this, the hospital and physicians responsible for treating and attending upon him might lawfully discontinue all life sustaining treatment and medical support measures designed to keep him alive in PVS including the termination of ventilation, hydration and nutrition by artificial means. Lord Browne-Wilkinson observed that: 'The conclusion I have reached will appear to some to be almost irrational. How can it be lawful to allow a patient to die slowly though painlessly, over a period of weeks from lack of food, but unlawful to produce his immediate death by a lethal injection, thereby saving his family from yet another ordeal ...? I find it difficult to find a moral answer to that question. But it is undoubtedly the law.' Lord Mustill contended that: '... the foundations of the courts' unanimous decision is morally and intellectually misshapen.'

24 Howarth, L, *Autonomy, A Study in Philosophical Psychology and Ethics*, 1986, New Haven, Ct: Yale UP.

25 Such a formulation is, in fact, much closer to a Nietzschean notion of autonomy than a Kantian one; for an examination see, eg, *The Genealogy of Morals*, 1967, New York: Random House.

26 [1992] 3 WLR 782.

27 Citing *Sidaway v Board of Governors of the Bethlem Royal Hospital and the Maudsley Hospital* [1985] AC 871, pp 904F–05A, emphasis added.

And, in the leading House of Lords case of *Airedale NHS Trust v Bland*,[28] Lord Goff observes that 'it is established that the principle of self-determination requires that respect must be given to the wishes of the patient, so that, if an adult patient of sound mind refuses, *however unreasonably*, to consent to treatment or care by which his life would or might be prolonged, the doctors responsible for his care must give effect to his wishes' (emphasis added). This passage was most recently quoted with approval by Judge LJ in *St George's NHS Trust v S*,[29] in a section headed 'Autonomy'.

That there can be different formulations of the same sorts of conclusion based upon different reasoning is amply illustrated by the judgments of the High Court of Australia in the case of *Secretary, Department of Health and Community Services v JWB and SMB* (*Marion's* case).[30] According to McHugh J:

> It is the central thesis of the common law doctrine of trespass to the person that the voluntary choices and decisions of an adult person of sound mind concerning what is or is not done to his or her body must be respected and accepted, irrespective of what others, including doctors, may think is in the interests of that particular person. To this general thesis there is an exception: a person cannot consent to the infliction of grievous bodily harm without 'good reason' ... But save in this exceptional case, the common law respects and preserves the autonomy of adult persons of sound mind with respect to their bodies. By doing so, the common law accepts that a person has rights of control and self-determination in respect of her or his body that other persons must respect. Those rights can only be altered with the consent of the person concerned. Thus the legal requirement of consent to bodily interference protects the autonomy and dignity of the individual and limits the power of others to interfere with that person's body.[31]

He concluded:

> Although the law's respect for the unique dignity of every person is the same, the protection of the physical integrity which is required to preserve the dignity of one person may change from time to time and it may differ from the protection of physical integrity required to preserve the dignity of another. Differing measures of protection are required according to the physical and mental capabilities of individuals at particular times; the baby whose dignity is respected by being carried and cared for by his or her parents grows into a man or woman whose dignity would be offended by such treatment; a donation of blood by a person of full age and understanding may enhance dignity, while the extraction of blood from a person who is incapable of consenting is an invasion of that person's physical integrity. Human dignity requires the whole personality to be respected: the right to physical integrity is a condition of human dignity but the gravity of any invasion of physical

---

28 [1993] AC 789, p 864.
29 [1998] 3 All ER 673, p 685.
30 (1992) 106 ALR 385.
31 *Ibid*, pp 451–52, *per* McHugh J.

integrity depends on its effect not only on the body but also on the mind and on the self-perception.[32]

Before turning to a brief examination of the classical position of the common law, I want to advert to a third type of inquiry, recently offered by Ngaire Naffine, which is central to this question: *'Where* do I own my body?' As I have shown, attempting to locate that question in traditional philosophical territory is difficult, if not doomed. Naffine has offered an even more troubling analysis for those who seek an easy accommodation for the 'owned body', and has sought to disclose that the 'concept of the person as a self-proprietor' which is thought to have such a secure place in modern jurisprudence is an essentially gendered concept.[33]

Who owns?

The self-possessed individual is male and male alone:

> ... can [the] concept of self-ownership withstand close inspection? What can it possibly mean to say that we own ourselves? Who owns what, and in relation to whom? As soon as the concept of self-ownership is subjected to scrutiny, interesting questions arise about the legal relations just implied, about their scope and about their supposed universal application.[34]

Naffine explains that, given the force and vigour of the political and legal rhetoric of self-ownership, there have been surprisingly few 'systematic efforts to expound the legal meaning of the concept in all its legal contexts, to examine its internal logic and then its applications to both men and women within the two major spheres of human relations'.[35] She questions whether the Lockean concept which I have discussed cursorily, above, makes any sense when applied to women as well as to men, at least in its modern application, and at least in what she calls 'the sphere of conjugal relations'. There, she concludes, the universalisability that would be necessary to ground a Lockean conception of general self-ownership evaporates.

> When we consider the person as self-proprietor within the realm of the conjugal, the realm where persons are still explicitly and compulsorily sexed by law, then we are necessarily obliged to consider whether modern men and women can both be self-proprietors when they have intimate relations with one another.[36]

---

32 (1992) 106 ALR 385, pp 417–18, *per* McHugh J.
33 Naffine, N, 'The legal structure of self-ownership: or the self-possessed man and the woman possessed' (1998) 25 JLS 193.
34 *Ibid.*
35 *Ibid*, p 195.
36 *Ibid*, p 194.

She argues that they cannot. Her first task, then, becomes to illuminate the identity of the 'mysterious owner' of self-ownership, which, she shows, is dependent on the recognition of 'the divided self', 'an internal structure in which the incarnate mind is divided from the carnal self', resting ultimately on a Cartesian dualism,[37] which, as I show elsewhere,[38] is a necessary component of much modern understanding of medical law. To quote Naffine at length on this important point:

> Relying on the etymology of the word, we can see that the body is being thought of as 'proper to' or belonging to its subject mind. It is a defining attribute of the subject self (defined as mind), a limiting condition which individualises and distinguishes person from person. This is my body, not your body; it is proper to (and so defines) me not you. The body is not the subject person – because that is the mind – but rather it is an object which belongs to that subject. The body is therefore alienated and fetishized. The body is not literally exterior to the person, in the manner of other objects of property (the other sense of property), and yet it is regarded as a form of external housing for the immaterial mind.[39]

In other words, a universal tale of freedom, a move in the 18th and 19th centuries from status to contract, the emergence of the – metaphorically – self-made man, becomes one written on one side of the page alone; women and women's bodies are not so much in the margins or on the verso, they are *other bodies* capable, unlike the men, of remaining owned *by others*. While the male body may have been rendered external to the male, the female remained firmly under Locke and key. This was shown not just in the relation of women to owning property, in the so called 'public' sphere, but also in the conjugal site of the family: '... for women to exclude others from their physical beings would mean the end of life ... female property-in-self would put an end to the ability of male self-proprietors to control the means by which they perpetuated themselves and their property.'[40]

Finding *where* I own my body, as I have proposed in my titular question, is then no easy thing. It is little beneficial use looking in Locke; Kantian ethics and his account of autonomy also afford poor return, and a gendered reading of the emergence of modern contract law discloses that any favours that body ownership might be thought to bestow were to be bought at the stall of Cartesian dualism, but only by those with the calling card of masculinity. How has the common law responded to these claims?

---

37 *Op cit*, Naffine, fn 33, pp 201–02.
38 Below, Chapter 5.
39 *Op cit*, Naffine, fn 33, p 202.
40 *Op cit*, Naffine, fn 33, p 204.

ENGLISH COMMON LAW

The rights that individuals may have to control the use of their bodily products is one which occurs from time to time in English law, in areas such as donation of organs and tissue. But to what extent, if any, can it be said that an individual might have a right of ownership over his or her body or bodily parts, and where is it suggested that such rights come from? The classical position of the English common law (described as 'a bit thin on the ground' by Andrew Grubb)[41] has been that the body and its parts are not property at all.[42]

The Nuffield Council on Bioethics, in their report *Human Tissue: Ethical and Legal Issues*, 1995, summarised their view of the present position in English law:

9.3 No claim by statute is available to the person from whom tissue is removed. Indeed, the implication of the Human Tissue Act 1961, the Human Organ Transplants Act 1989 and the Anatomy Act 1984, though not expressly stated, is that the tissue removed pursuant to these Acts is given free of all claims; eg is an unconditional gift. The Human Fertilisation and Embryology Act 1990 is less straightforward. Donors of gametes or embryos may impose conditions on use and may vary or withdraw any consent given. By adopting a scheme of consents, however, the Acts avoid vesting any property claim in the donor.

9.4 At common law the issue has not been tested in English law. It is instructive to enquire why the question of a claim over tissue once removed has not received legal attention. The answer seems simple. In the general run of things a person from whom tissue is removed has not the slightest interest in making any claim to it once it is removed. This is obviously the case as regards tissue removed as a consequence of treatment. It is equally true in the case of donation of tissue whether, for example, blood, bone marrow or an organ. The word donation clearly implies that what is involved is a gift.

9.5 It is true of course that an appendix or gallstone may be returned to a patient who may refer to it as *her* appendix or gallstone. But, this says nothing about any legal claim that she may have to the appendix. In fact, in the case of the returned appendix, one view of the legal position may be as follows: the patient consents to the operation which involves the removal of her appendix, on removal the appendix acquires the status of a *res* (thing) and comes into the possession of the hospital authority prior to disposal; in response to a request by the patient that it be returned, the hospital gives the appendix to the patient as a gift; the appendix then becomes the property of the patient.

---

41 Grubb, A, 'I, me, mine: bodies, parts and property'(1998) 3 Med Law International 299, p 313.

42 See, eg, Coke, 3 Co Instit 203; Blackstone, 2 Bl Comm 429, 4 Bl Comm 429; 2 East PC 652; Stephen, JF, *Digest of Criminal Law*, 5th edn, 1877, London: Macmillan, Art 318, p 252, etc, oft repeated by modern commentators.

However, this accepted orthodoxy has been questioned by Paul Matthews:[43]

> If one looks at human tissue simply as physical matter, its characteristics are those of other animal tissue, about which there is no argument, but which is clearly property in the physical sense. If on the other hand we are concerned in defining 'property' to analyse the nature of the rights persons have in relation to particular specimens of human tissue, then all we can mean by 'property' is a bundle of concepts, rights, duties, powers, liabilities and so on.[44]

Of *Haynes' Case*,[45] Matthews avers:

> The classical writers of the common law, then, for the most part agree that there is no property in corpses, but either they cite each other or the case of a buried corpse where the question did not even arise, much less was decided.

The traditional approach from the 18th century was that human organs and tissue are not susceptible to claims of ownership. In 1749, it was decided that there was no property in an unburied corpse. This was based on an understanding of one of the first institutional writers of English law (but note, not Scots), Sir Edward Coke, who wrote in his *Institutes* that a cadaver was *nullis in bonis*. It has been argued by Matthews that, not only might Coke have got it wrong, but at best his statement was properly limited to buried corpses, because Coke was, at that time, considering *cara data vermibus* (flesh given to worms). However, it seems to have been widely accepted since then that, at English law, buried or not, rightly or wrongly, the dead human body is subject to the 'no property' rule. In Scotland, however, it seems that an alternative rule applies, and that a corpse can, at least before burial, be stolen.[46]

In one of the few decided and reported cases (until recently) in which the orthodox view has been challenged, one member of the High Court of Australia can be found to apply an essentially Lockean notion of the acquisition of property rights. The dissenting judge in the case of *Doodeward v Spence*,[47] Higgins J, affirmed that no one could have property in another human being – alive or dead. One of the two majority judges, Barton J, did not challenge this fundamental proposition, but held that, on the facts of the case, a stillborn fetus did not constitute an unburied corpse within 'the general rule'. Only Griffith CJ enunciated a different formulation:

> If ... there can, under some circumstances, be a continued rightful possession of a human body unburied, I think that the law will protect that rightful possession by appropriate remedies. I do not know of any definition of property which is not wide enough to include such a right of permanent

---

43 Matthews, P, 'Whose body? People as property' [1983] Current Legal Problems 193 and 'The man of property' (1995) 3 Med L Rev 251; Harris, JW, 'Who owns my body?' (1996) 16 OJLS 55.

44 *Ibid*, 'Whose body?', p 194.

45 (1614) 12 Co Rep 113; (1614) 77 ER 1389.

46 *HM Advocate v Dewar* 1945 SC 5.

47 (1908) 6 CLR 406.

possession. By whatever name the right is called, I think it exists, and that, so far as it constitutes property, a human body, or a portion of a human body, is capable by law of becoming the subject of property ... I entertain no doubt that, when a person has by the lawful exercise of work or skill so dealt with a human body or part of a human body in his lawful possession that it has acquired some attributes differentiating it from a mere corpse awaiting burial, he acquires a right to retain possession of it, at least as against any person not entitled to have it delivered to him for the purpose of burial.[48]

It has been assumed that certain body products such as blood and urine once separated from the body become property that can be stolen. Thus, in *R v Welsh*[49] and *R v Rothery*,[50] the courts without trouble applied a property analysis, in convicting motorists who had disposed of bodily samples taken for the purposes of providing evidence of statutory traffic offences. In the former case, Brabin J for the court wrote that 'the theft of the urine ... is in its way a technical offence, namely emptying his own sample down the drain'.[51] In the second case, the counts charged, *inter alia*, that the defendant stole a capsule and container being the property of the police authority. Both the trial judge and the Court of Appeal spoke in judgment of the theft of the specimen itself. Matthews writes of these cases that 'it would be an extremely poor legal system which could not ascribe to such matters having physical substance the capability of being 'property'.[52] In the broad sense of there being some rights to possession of these products, they are obviously 'property'. And, commenting, Matthews asks: 'Why should not blood, at any rate once removed from the donor's body, be treated as property, protected by the law against theft?'[53]

These rules came to be discussed in two recent English cases: *Dobson v North Tyneside HA*[54] and *R v Kelly*.[55] Peter Gibson LJ, giving the judgment of the Court of Appeal in *Dobson*, said that the 'facts of this case are unusual'. Deborah Dobson had died at the age of 22 suffering from brain tumours. She had collapsed at work, been taken to hospital and examined. A report suggesting liability to primary generalised epilepsy was made and she was discharged, without a CT scan having been taken. Two months later she became very ill, was admitted and a CT scan showed two brain tumours. She died four hours before a scheduled operation. During the course of an autopsy, her brain was removed and preserved in paraffin while the rest of her

---

48 (1908) 6 CLR 414.
49 [1974] RTR 478 (urine).
50 [1976] RTR 550 (blood).
51 [1974] RTR 478, p 480.
52 *Op cit*, Matthews, 1983, fn 43, p 223.
53 *Op cit*, Matthews, 1983, fn 43, p 225.
54 [1996] 4 All ER 464.
55 [1998] 3 All ER 741.

body was returned to her family for burial. It was ascertained that she died of natural causes, but no histological tests were carried out on the brain and it was subsequently disposed of.

Her mother brought proceedings against the hospital in which Deborah died, claiming that had the tumours been benign Deborah's life could probably have been saved by an earlier CT scan. Secondary proceedings were brought against the health authority for failure to preserve the brain and consequent loss of the opportunity to adduce histological evidence relating to the tumour.

The court held that there was no property in a dead body unless it had undergone a process or application of human skill such as stuffing or embalming. The preservation of the brain in paraffin was not a process that resulted in the plaintiffs acquiring property in it. Although an executor or administrator of an estate may have the right to custody and possession of a dead body until burial, no such persons had been appointed here prior to the burial.

There was no duty on the hospital to preserve body parts indefinitely after the conclusion of an inquest and post mortem.[56] Peter Gibson LJ cited *Clerk v Lindsell* to the effect that:

> Once a body has undergone a process or other application of human skill, such as stuffing or embalming, it seems that it can be the subject of property in the ordinary way; hence it is submitted that conversion will lie for a skeleton or cadaver used for research or exhibition, and the same goes for parts of and substances produced by a living person.[57]

On this, he commented that, while he was prepared 'to accept that proposition is properly arguable', that was not on the basis of *Doodeward v Spence*. The court's analysis in *Dobson* proceeds on the basis that the brain, specimen or other tissue is *lawfully* recovered from the body; but that in order to satisfy the arguability of the proposition in *Clerk v Lindsell*, more would have to be shown. Thus, the mere recovery of a brain from a body for the purposes of post mortem examination is not, without more, sufficient to give rise to a claim that the next of kin should be entitled to possession of the tissue, *still less* that they ever acquired property in it:[58]

> There is nothing in the pleading or evidence before us to suggest that the actual preservation of the brain after the post mortem was on a par with stuffing or embalming a corpse or preserving an anatomical or pathological specimen for a scientific collection or with preserving a human freak such as a double-headed foetus that had some value for exhibition purposes. There was no

---

56 If the brain had still been in existence, they could have been obtained during the process of discovery in the action: RSC Ord 24; or Supreme Court Act 1981, s 34 (and RSC Ord 24 r 7A) if the second defendant was not a real party to the action.

57 [1996] 4 All ER 464, p 478.

58 *Ibid*, p 479h.

practical possibility of, nor any sensible purpose in, the brain being reunited with the body for burial purposes.[59]

The crucial consideration here is that it must be possible to *show some practical value or possible sensible purpose in retaining the specimen for future use* such that it makes sense to recognise a proprietary or possessary interest.

The second case concerned Anthony-Noel Kelly, an artist. One of the features of his work was the agreed drawing of anatomical specimens held by the Royal College of Surgeons. Kelly asked a junior technician employed at the College to remove some 40 of the specimens from which Kelly then made casts. Most of the body parts were buried in a field, although part of a leg was found in Kelly's attic and some parts in the basement of a flat belonging to friends.

Kelly and the technician were charged with theft: s 1(1) of the Theft Act 1968 provides that 'a person is guilty of theft if he dishonestly appropriates property belonging to another with the intention of permanently depriving the other of it'.

At their trial, they submitted in defence that body parts were not capable in law of being property and hence could not be stolen. The judge rejected those arguments, and the jury convicted the defendants (Kelly was originally sentenced to nine months, reduced to three on appeal), who then appealed to the Court of Appeal, where the judgment was given by Rose LJ.

The specimens had been preserved or fixed by staff of the College or by some other medical agency. All were subject to a regular scheme of inspection and preservation and most of them had been subjected to further prosecution – expert dissection so as to reveal the inner workings of the human body. This work would have involved many hours, sometimes even weeks, of skilled work. Kelly argued that, owing to the age of many of the specimens, which antedated the provisions of the Anatomy Act 1984, he had believed that they were merely intercepting body parts which were 'on their way to the grave'. Nonetheless, the judge ruled at trial that the specimens were property *because of an exception* to the general common law rule, as to no ownership of the body or body parts, based on *Doodeward v Spence*.

Rose LJ observed[60] that 'however questionable its historical origins' it has been part of the common law for 150 years that neither a corpse nor any part of a corpse are in themselves and without more capable of being property protected by rights. However, 'parts of a corpse are capable of being property within s 4 of the Theft Act' *if they have acquired different attributes* by virtue of *the application of skill*, such as dissection or preservation techniques, for exhibition or teaching purposes. The importance then is that the application of

---

59 [1996] 4 All ER 464, p 479g–h.
60 [1998] 3 All ER 741, p 749.

skill (rather than accident of nature; for example, suppose corpses of conjoined twins which become separated when dropped on the floor from a table) should lead to the acquisition of the 'different attribute'.

And, in an important *obiter*, Rose LJ[61] observed that it was important to recall that the common law does not stand still:

> It may be that if, on some future occasion, the question arises, the courts will hold that human body parts are capable of being property for the purposes of s 4, even without the acquisition of different attributes, if they have a use or significance beyond their mere existence.

Three clear examples of this might be:

(a) if the body part is intended for use in an organ transplant operation;

(b) if it is intended for use in extracting DNA;

(c) if it is intended for use as an exhibit in a trial.

These are intended only as examples of what in Rose LJ's judgment might be relevant; it is not an exhaustive list, and it may be possible to add to it, either now or in the future, in ways which are not yet realised or realisable.

BODY SHOPPING

Why do these questions appear now?

Andrew Grubb, in a discussion of these more recent cases, has concluded that the fear of consequential commercial dealings in bodies or body parts has inhibited the recognition of other, more limited property rights in parts of the body.[62] And he has sought to reassure us that while some may feel that these fears may be well grounded, they need not *necessarily* entail the development of more limited, protective proprietary interests. He quotes Paul Matthews' conclusion:[63]

> ... all the societal pressures which a century ago pointed away from lawfully possessing and using human tissue now point towards it. The non-property solutions of yesterday are inadequate to the task of today.

Why is this; and why have these questions and this pressure surfaced now?

One simple answer is, of course, that body parts are coming to be recognised as being, in themselves, or in certain states, rather valuable. In other words, they are something to which, increasingly perhaps, we can attach

---

61 [1998] 3 All ER 741, p 750.

62 *Op cit*, Grubb, fn 41, p 313; an inhibition that may be well founded: see (2001) *The Daily Telegraph*, 26 January, p 3 on the scale of thymus glands.

63 Expressed in his article 'A man of property', *op cit*, fn 43, p 256.

economic value. 'The questions are particularly important today as developments in the medical and other sciences increasingly permit and create therapeutic uses for human bodily material.'[64] The central question, not perhaps so much the central legal question, but certainly an important social and ethical one, is how cynical (in the Wildean sense) that is; how much, in coming to know the price of everything, we discover that we know the value of nothing.

Let me briefly offer five examples of the 'value' presently attaching to body parts as a way of exploring the reason for the emergence of these issues:

- the payment of donors of sperm (and eggs);
- payments for other organs;
- the status of the embryo, and related questions;
- the commercial exploitation of tissue or cell lines recovered from patients; and
- the question of 'ownership' of genetic information.

My purpose is not to conduct a comprehensive examination of the *substantive* questions, legal or ethical, involved or disclosed here. Rather, I want merely to illustrate why I believe this issue has arisen now and, in part, to suggest what hangs on its resolution.

The first example, then, concerns the payments (in money or money's worth) presently made for gametes: for sperm, eggs and embryos. The question of payments for gametes has been controversial throughout the 1990s, certainly since the inception of the Human Fertilisation and Embryology Authority under the Human Fertilisation and Embryology Act 1990.[65] Abandoning the payment of 'donors' was one of the Authority's earliest announced policy goals.

Legally, a number of issues arise, of which one is whether the donation of gametes and eggs is a supply of goods or provision of services? Or both? The importance of this question arises if it is argued that an action against a donor or a clinic could lie not just with respect to negligence in respect of defective gametes, but also under the strict liability regime of the Consumer Protection Act 1987 for defective products. Body products, such as blood or sperm, once separated from the body and in the control of someone, are capable of being owned: *Welsh* and *Rothery*. But whether sperm, eggs or fertilised ova are 'products' for the purposes of the 1987 Act is not settled. The American courts in the early 1970s began to hold that blood was a product for the purposes of tortious liability, often to be reversed by the legislature declaring it to be a service incident to treatment. However, some courts have responded by

---

64 *Op cit*, Grubb, fn 41, p 302.
65 For further more detailed discussion, see Morgan, D and Lee, RG, *Human Fertilisation and Embryology: Regulating Revolutions*, 2001, London: Blackstone, Chapter 2.

distinguishing between the supply of blood from a commercial blood bank and from a hospital. Where the supply is the primary objective of the commercial concern and only an incidental concern of the service provided by the hospital, a blood bank has been found liable in contract for the supply of defective blood.[66]

The second example comes from, perhaps, the more usual source of this debate: the shortage of organs for use in transplantation operations and the related purported benefits of establishing a 'market in organs'.[67] Consider whether the sale of organs should be allowed. As Ken Mason has suggested, effectively the issue resolves into whether, on the one hand, the State has a duty to protect its more vulnerable citizens from exploitation or whether, on the other hand, an individual's right to autonomy extends to the disposal or, I would add, use of body parts as and when the owner wishes. The Human Organ Transplant Act 1989, drafted and enacted in response to the revelation that a Turkish peasant had sold a kidney for £5,000, which was used by a British surgical team to transplant into a private patient in the UK, has been castigated by Mason as:

> ... little more than a rather hurried and intuitive recoil from what appears to be a fundamentally degrading process which is likely to have adverse effects on society's values as a whole.[68]

And, as Hansmann objects, the ruling out of a market in organs 'has been adopted casually, without serious examination of the potential advantages or disadvantages of compensation systems'.[69] '[T]he issue of organ transplants is far too important to be left to unreflective moralising.'[70] I do not presently want to enter that debate, to engage on the 'reflective moralising' that Hansmann calls for. Suffice it to say that the debate has costs as well as sacrifices that its resolution one way or the other affords. On one side, as some see it, are the lives of the thousands who die each year because a transplantable organ is not 'salvaged' and used; on the other, as some would see it, society's soul.

The third example which has pushed the legal status of body parts, organs and tissues up the public agenda has been the potentially far more controversial issue of the status of the embryo. I consider this question at greater length in a later chapter, and there is no reason to give a full repeat performance of the arguments rehearsed there.

---

66 See *Cunningham v MacNeal Memorial Hospital* 266 NE 2d 897 (Ill 1970) and *Belle Bonfils Memorial Blood Bank v Hansen* 579 P 2d 1158 (Colo 1978).

67 For one such proposal, see Hansmann, H, 'Markets for human organs' and the reply by Bernat, E, 'Marketing of human organs', in Mazzoni, CM, *A Legal Framework for Bioethics*, 1998, The Hague: Kluwer, pp 145 and 161 respectively.

68 Mason, K, in Dyer, C (ed), *Doctors, Patients and the Law*, 1992, Oxford: Blackwell, p 125.

69 *Ibid*, Hansmann, p 146.

70 *Ibid*, Hansmann, p 159.

The point has not yet arisen in the UK, but a related, potentially far more controversial issue arises in asking whether the embryo is a person or a chattel. Lord Hailsham pleaded in debate that:

> It is wrong to try to define a human embryo in terms of established legal definitions which are plainly inapplicable to human embryos. Why must an embryo be one or the other? Why cannot it be just an embryo?[71]

In the US, in *Del Zio v Presbyterian Hospital*,[72] the US District Court for the Southern District of California appeared to treat the embryo as though it were a chattel, whereas, in the first instance Tennessee case of *Davis v Davis*,[73] the embryo was clearly understood to be a person. The legal importance of these questions can be seen in *York v Jones*, where a couple who wished to transfer from Virginia to California frozen embryos attempted to discover whether this amounted to interstate commerce and what consequences might follow. In Europe, such questions arise as whether we are dealing with the free movement of goods under Arts 30–36 of the Treaty of Rome, or the free movement of persons. Does a frozen embryo need a passport, immigration papers, or an import/export licence? In the Act, the embryo is nowhere given a status either as a chattel or as a person. Warnock observed that:

> Until now the law has never had to consider the existence of embryos outside the mother's uterus. The existence of such embryos raises potentially difficult problems as to ownership. The concept of ownership of human embryos seems to us to be undesirable. We recommend that legislation be enacted to ensure that there is no right of ownership in a human embryo.[74]

And yet, as Kennedy and Grubb remark, Warnock gives to the couple who have stored an embryo rights to use and dispose of it (paras 10.11 and 12); rights of sale of gametes and embryos where licensed (13.13); and limited circumstances where drug testing may be carried out on embryos created specifically for that purpose (para.12.5). In light of this they pointedly ask:

> What *special* status does an embryo have if it may be the object of research during the first 14 days of gestation and thereafter destroyed? What is ownership if it is not the right to control, including to dispose of by sale, or otherwise?[75]

It seems consistent with the approach taken in the Act, especially if the arguments as to totipotentiality of the cells up to the appearance of the primitive streak are accepted, that only after that time does the legal category of person even begin to emerge. This is not to say that it is then possessed of

---

71   House of Lords, *Official Report* col 751, 6 February 1990.

72   74 Civ 3588 (SD NY 1976).

73   (1989) (reversed on other grounds on appeal, see 842 Sw 2d 588 (1992), *York v Jones* 717 F Supp 2d 421 (Va 1989)).

74   Para 10.11.

75   Kennedy, I and Grubb, A, *Medical Law: Text and Materials*, 1989, London: Butterworths, p 682.

legal personality. Indeed, it seems from *R v Tait*[76] and later cases[77] that a fetus is not a person for the purposes of the Offences Against the Person Act 1861. *A fortiori*, then, an embryo before that time will not be. It is indeed consistent with this scheme to regard the pre-embryo, sperm and eggs as more like property than anything else, although we may refuse to recognise a full sense of property in relation to them, in the sense that we may regard them as something to which obligations and responsibilities are owed, but which cannot be owned in the full sense of the ownership of other chattels.

Thus, it is not possible straightforwardly to say whether an embryo can be stolen, bequeathed, kidnapped or, perhaps most controversially, patented. Certainly, in respect of genetically engineered plants and animals, both the US and the UK, and other European countries, have allowed patenting, and genetically engineered mice, known as 'Oncomice', are available for sale in the US. And if a cryopreservation facility were destroyed in a fire, would a claim on the centre's insurance policy, which limited claims to loss or damage to property, include the embryos held in storage? Or not?

The question of legal rights in dead or extracted human tissue has traditionally been answered, as we have seen, by averring that there are no property rights in a dead body in England and Wales, and it was thought, by analogy, no such rights in dead human tissue. However, as Grubb has suggested, that is in the process of change: '*Kelly* is the first case in which an English court has held that parts of a dead body are capable of being stolen.'[78]

Until this, there had been no directly applicable UK case. Legal excitement or consternation had been provoked in the US where the Supreme Court of California considered the question of ownership of body parts in *Moore v Regents of the University of California*.[79] Moore suffered from hairy cell leukaemia, underwent a consensual splenectomy, and on several occasions had samples of blood, skin and bone marrow removed. His cells were used for research purposes, from which his clinician had developed a commercially valuable cell-line. Moore argued, *inter alia*, that he owned his cells and hence retained the right to direct their use in potential research and should be entitled to share in any profits thereby generated. The Supreme Court denied Moore's argument that he retained any ownership claim in respect of the cells taken from his body. Even if Moore could be said to own his own cells, this was distinct from the resulting cell-line that was sufficiently distinct and

---

76 [1989] 3 All ER 613.

77 *AG's Reference (No 3 of 1994)* [1997] 3 All ER 936.

78 *Op cit*, Grubb, fn 41, p 307.

79 793 P 2d 479 (1990); for discussion of the issues involved in the case, see Lavoie, J, 'Ownership of human tissue' (1989) 75 Va L Rev 1363; for a comprehensive discussion of the position in France, see Fagot-Largeault, A, 'The ownership of the body', International Program in Bioethics Education and Research, First Meeting, Research Paper, Nijmegen, 17–22 May 1992.

produced by the University doctors. The court majority observed that any property rights in the cell-line to the benefit of Moore would inhibit research and that the grant of such rights was a matter solely within the competence of the legislature. The court did hold, however, that the disposal of the tissue was governed by the doctrine of informed consent and that this, in turn, depended on a fiduciary duty to disclose all relevant information to the patient. Although there is no such fiduciary duty between doctor and patient in English law, it is thought that a court in this jurisdiction would hold that the prospect of monetary gain was something so obviously necessary to an informed decision by the patient that no reasonably prudent professional clinician would fail to mention this in seeking consent, such that a failure to do so would amount to negligence.[80] It is possible that a patient would additionally be entitled to a claim in equity for a share of the profits generated from an enterprise to which his or her contribution was a prerequisite, on the basis of the action for unjust enrichment.

Finally, consider the question of the ownership of genetic information. There is no specific provision in the law of England and Wales which covers the question of ownership of genetic information, although it is clearly a matter of great importance. Who has access to the DNA marker results? Can a relative be forced to donate a blood sample[81] for a linkage test to be performed for a relative? Who owns the DNA and the genetic information obtained from it once it is in the laboratory?

The question of principle involved is whether *information* can, in English law, be regarded as property. The subsidiary question is whether parts of one's body, such as tissues, or, as in this case, cells, can be the subject of claims of ownership. The derivative question is whether, in the case of body part(s) themselves (as, say, with blood), the information derived from an analysis of that matter can similarly be the subject of ownership claims.

One temptation against which we must specifically guard is that of torturing the provisions of existing common law and statute to breaking point to see if they will yield up any protection of genetic privacy. While it may be true that 'no surveillance technology is more threatening to privacy than that designed to unlock the information contained in human genes', we must address the urgent questions which this poses in a robust and mature fashion. The 'surveillance society' should not allow those 'modern explorers [who] have set sail on voyages into the genetic microcosm, seeking a medically powerful but potentially dangerous treasure'[82] to cross uncharted seas without the benefit of maps which at least define the outlines of areas where there be dragons and contain some preliminary consideration of whether the

---

80 See Lord Bridge in *Sidaway v Board of Governors of the Bethlem Royal Hospital and the Maudsley Hospital* [1985] AC 871, p 900 (HL).

81 Cf, for children with paternity testing, *S v S* [1972] AC 24.

82 Privacy Commissioner of Canada, *Genetic Testing and Privacy*, 1992, Ottawa: Ministry of Supply and Services, pp 3, 2.

seas flow to the edge of a world which is flat or round. We need to debate whether we are rushing headlong to disaster or are set upon a course where the Scylla and Charybdis are at least clearly identifiable in outline, even if their precise shapes, contours and terrain cannot yet be sketched.

If, as a matter of principle, English law holds that these matters cannot be the subject of ownership claims what – if any – protection does the law afford to individuals in respect of genetic matter or data generated from their body? Taken together, these may be thought to generate the major questions concerned with the privacy interests which an individual may have in respect of genetic information, which may regarded as a species of ownership right. The notion of 'genetic privacy' has two dimensions: protection from the intrusions of others and protection from one's own, hitherto unknown, secrets.[83] The basic questions comprise: 'Who is collecting and using (and for what purposes) genetic information about identifiable persons, and to whom is the information being disclosed?'[84]

CONCLUDING REMARKS: SHOPPING THE BODY

The traditional starting places for the discussion of the philosophical bases of self-ownership, it is now clear, do not disclose either the authority or the neutrality, the universalisability, that they have often times been mistaken for doing. To admit the notion of body ownership may provide some limited rights and limited protections of individuals in some circumstances. It is also another invitation to engage the further juridification of social spheres which Gunther Teubner has identified,[85] further to see 'law abounding', as Marc Galanter has cautioned,[86] a further twist of the role of law in Beck's 'risk society',[87] a further stage in de Sousa Santos' paradigmatic transition, the representation of technological rationality through claims of self-ownership.[88]

Questions about body ownership create new uncertainties. Cultural explicitness revolutionises former combinations of ideas and concepts; the more we give legal certainty to social concepts, the more we cut from under our feet assumptions about the intrinsic nature of those social concepts themselves. Whether or not all this is a good thing is uncertain. What *is* certain

83 *Op cit*, Privacy Commissioner of Canada, fn 82, p 4.

84 *Op cit*, Privacy Commissioner of Canada, fn 82, p 25.

85 Teubner, G, 'Juridification: concepts, aspects, limits, solutions', in Teubner, G (ed), *Juridification of Social Spheres*, 1987, Berlin and New York: Walter de Gruyter.

86 Galanter, M, 'Law abounding' (1992) 55 MLR 1.

87 Beck, U, *Risk Society: Towards a New Modernity*, Ritter, M (trans), 1992, London: Sage.

88 de Sousa Santos, B, *Toward a New Common Sense: Law, Science and Politics in the Paradigmatic Transition*, 1995, London: Routledge, p 34.

is that it will not be without consequence for the way people think about one another.[89] Questions about body ownership *are* questions about society's attempts to understand and control threats to its stability and identity; what kind of society it is.

---

89   After Strathern, M, *Reproducing the Future: Anthropology, Kinship and the New Reproductive Technologies*, 1993, Manchester: Manchester UP.

PART III

INTROS: ENTRANCES AND ARRIVALS

CHAPTER 7

THE LEGAL STATUS OF THE EMBRYO AND THE FETUS

The question of control over genetic products and the limits to be imposed creates problems in terms of both application of existing legislation and principles of law, and respect for the fundamental principles and values of our society: in particular, individual freedoms and human dignity.[1] In this chapter, I return to an early attempt to work through some of the questions posed by the legal status of the embryo and the fetus. Since then, various courts in various jurisdictions have indeed addressed this issue,[2] and there has been a wealth of commentary too, which I have considered elsewhere. Because they add little to the analysis presented here, I have considered that this chapter can stand more or less as it was originally written, although I have made passing reference to an important discussion of the main point in a House of Lords' decision in 1995.

EARLY ATTITUDES TO THE FETUS

Legal attitudes to fetuses and newborns have varied over time, some cultures proscribing abortion and infanticide, some early codes giving the fetus indirect protection by prohibiting the striking of a woman so as to cause the death of her unborn child.[3] In other cultures, abortion and infanticide were seen as acceptable resolutions of dilemmas posed by scarce resources, birth defects or sexual balance. Neither ancient Greek nor early Roman law forbade abortion, the latter not regarding the unborn child as a living human being. The common law has long drawn a fundamental distinction between the fetus and the child following birth. Recent developments in common law jurisprudence have, however, seen the recognition of interests – notice the importance of that term, interests, not rights – against harm to the 'child' before its birth.

It is perhaps important to distinguish at this early stage between law, philosophy and public policy. The distinguished American jurisprudent Oliver Wendell Holmes wrote that 'the life of the law is not logic but

---

1   Council of Europe, *Human Artificial Procreation*, 1989, Strasbourg: COE, Art 11.

2   Some of these cases and the consequential literature are reviewed in Morgan, D and Lee, RG, *Human Fertilisation and Embryology: Regulating the Revolution*, 2001, London: Blackstone.

3   Codes: Sumerian 2000 BC, Assyrian 1500 BC, Hittite 1300 BC and Persian 600 BC.

experience'.[4] Put another way, law is not so much the handmaiden of philosophy as the servant of public policy. There is, indeed, a tension between the analytic demands of philosophy, the pressures of public policy and the service which law provides. The pragmatism, so often remarked, of English common law, lends more to the requirements of public policy than to dissection by philosophy. Thus, Andrew Grubb, in one of the few domestic attempts to grapple with this question, has suggested that:

> When a court is seized of a case ... [it] would have no choice but to treat an extra-corporeal embryo as either a person or a chattel. The likely outcome is that it would be held to be a chattel. Such law as exists points in this direction and the pragmatism of the common law would see that to treat an extra-corporeal embryo as a chattel is more consistent with common sense than for it to be given the rights of a person.[5]

Unfortunately, the notion of common sense to which Grubb appeals is not here made explicit. The general point, however, is that the pragmatist of the common law will often want to know, in advance of her answer, who is asking the question and for what purposes. Thus, if asked 'what is the legal status of the embryo and the fetus?', the usual reply of the English common lawyer will be in the form of a question, rather than a direct reply. What is remarkable about this pragmatism is that it is often prepared to endure philosophical, and indeed sociological obloquy, hostility and approbation, in order to avoid answering directly a question posed, or to avoid answering it in a way which would seem to provoke hostility from the prevailing currents of political values.

The main questions with which a lawyer, confronted with determining the status of the embryo, will be concerned are: Who has control over the frozen embryo? In what way, if at all, is that control restricted? And what limits apply to the way in which gametes and embryos can be used? The Human Fertilisation and Embryology Act 1990, although not commonly seen in this way, was a major piece of restrictive legislation. It imposed limits on the use and control of embryos where none had effectively operated before. The limitations on the research use of the embryo, the restrictions on their use in the provision of treatment services and the protection given to children subsequently born alive who can show that they have suffered injury as a result of the negligent handling of gametes or embryonic material, are all major steps forward in the legal recognition given to the embryo.

That this is not always apparent may be gauged from some of the responses to the recommendations of the Warnock Committee.[6] Recall that the

---

4   Holmes, OW, *The Common Law*, 1881, Cambridge, Mass: Harvard UP, p 1.

5   Grubb, A, 'The legal status of the frozen human embryo', in Grubb, A (ed), *Challenges in Medical Care*, 1991, Chichester: Wiley, p 69.

6   Warnock Committee, *Report of the Committee of Inquiry into Human Fertilisation and Embryology*, Cm 9314, 1984, London: HMSO.

Committee had concluded that the embryo of the human species was entitled to special consideration and yet recommended that the couple who have stored an embryo should have rights to use and dispose of it;[7] that there be rights of sale of gametes and embryos where licensed,[8] and limited circumstances where drug testing may be carried out on embryos created specifically for that purpose.[9] This led Ian Kennedy and Andrew Grubb pointedly to ask:

> What special status does an embryo have if it may be the object of research during the first 14 days of gestation and thereafter destroyed? What is ownership if it is not the right to control, including to dispose of by sale, or otherwise?[10]

First, I shall briefly identify some legal conundrums to which the embryo has given rise and introduce a short philosophical excursus. Secondly, I shall set out what may be thought of as the 'classical' view of the fetus and the embryo. This is followed by a survey of recent jurisprudence. Turning first to the provisions of the Human Fertilisation and Embryology Act 1990, I examine the limitations on research which the Act introduced, the 'consent' requirements established under Sched 3 for the use of embryos and gametes and, finally, the additional legal protections for any child injured in the course of the provision of infertility treatment services.

Legal conundrums and philosophical excursus

Before the 1990 Act, there were a number of cases which might have arisen where the status of the embryo would be critical in determining its fate; some of these conundrums may have survived the legislation. First, suppose that a clinician deliberately destroys an embryo, created from A and B's gametes, in a fire at an IVF clinic:

- Does s/he kill the embryos?
- Does s/he convert them?
- Is the claim on any insurance policy for damage to goods or loss of life?
- Can A and B claim for post-traumatic stress disorder caused by the loss of the embryos?

The point of this example is that the clinician's act operates against the genitors', but especially the woman's interests; thus, recognising the embryo as a 'person' would hardly interfere with any interest which she has; on the

---

7   *Op cit*, Warnock Committee, fn 6, paras 10.11 and 12.

8   *Op cit*, Warnock Committee, fn 6, para 13.13.

9   *Op cit*, Warnock Committee, fn 6, para 12.5.

10 Kennedy, I and Grubb, A, *Medical Law: Text with Materials*, 1989, London: Butterworths, p 682.

contrary, it would serve to protect or preserve it. Additionally, the clinic would be likely to carry insurance against the loss.

These two remarkable features – that allowing the claim would not interfere with any interest of the woman and liability insurance would cover any general damages recoverable – are the salient features of the single exception to general maternal immunity to suit from a fetus and 'furnishes a rare instance of a legal duty owed directly to the unborn infant'.[11] In this hitherto unique case, a child born with congenital disabilities as a result of injuries incurred as a result of its mother's negligent driving has a direct cause of action against her; in reality, of course, against the company with which she has placed the risk against which she must by law insure. While we may conclude that, even in our hypothetical case, the law would not recognise the embryo as a 'person', this is merely symptomatic of the blindness of English law to the need to make supportable distinctions based on the sort of interest which requires protection.[12]

Secondly, suppose that a clinic storing a couple's gametes or embryos is faced with an eventuality which had not previously been contemplated. For example, suppose that the clinic receives a demand from one of them that stored embryos be allowed to perish, either because the relationship has ended in divorce or death of one of the parties, or because the genitors now disagree about proceeding with the treatment service.[13] A variant would be that, on the death of one of the parties, the clinic is faced with a demand from the survivor to release to them their partner's stored gametes or embryos for use.[14] Or on the death of both parties?[15] Finally, imagine a dispute between the clinic C and the couple about release of stored embryos for the couple's continued use against the clinical judgment of those in charge of the clinic.[16] What, in each case, should be the response of the clinic?

Happily, the Human Fertilisation and Embryology Act 1990 provides that these questions must at least be addressed. There is then some temporary legal finality to some questions of the status of the human embryo. But, there will hardly be ethical agreement. I do not want to rehearse the debates about embryo research or the different philosophical traditions upon which they rest; I have attempted that task elsewhere.[17] For the present, it is sufficient to

---

11 Brazier, M, 'Embryos' "rights": abortion and research', in Freeman, MDA (ed), *Medicine, Ethics and the Law,* London: Stevens, 1988, p 21, n 14.

12 Wells, C and Morgan, D, 'Whose fetus is it?' (1991) 18 JLS 431.

13 *Davis v Davis* 842 Sw 2d 588 (1992).

14 *Parpalaix v CECOS* (1984) Trib Gr Inst De Créteil, 1 August, Gaz Pal 1984.II.560.

15 See Smith, GF, 'The *Rios' Embryo* case: Australia's frozen "orphan" embryos: a medical, legal and ethical dilemma' (1985–86) 24 J Fam Law 27.

16 *York v Jones* 717 F Supp 2d 421 (Va 1989)).

17 *Op cit,* Morgan and Lee, fn 2.

recall one example from each wing of the philosophical plane to illustrate the general tenor of the debate and the flights of fancy sometimes involved. On the linguistic turn complained of in the invention of the term pre-embryo, Jonathan Glover has, in my view quite rightly, observed that 'any right a pre-embryo may have is not diminished by calling it a pre-embryo rather than an embryo'. More contentiously, he then goes on to argue that:

> ... no one denies that [the pre-embryo] is alive, and that it is surely a member of our species rather than any other. But the problem with this argument is that it applies equally to the unfertilized egg or to the human sperm cell. This argument easily enough proves that the embryo or fetus is a human being, but it is not clear that the status 'human being' in this minimal sense brings with it any moral rights. It is widely assumed that qualifying as a human being is sufficient to guarantee the possession of a right to life. But this assumption is questionable, and perhaps derives much of its plausibility from our thinking of 'human beings' in terms of our friends and neighbours. An embryo is not the kind of human being you can share a joke with or have as a friend.[18]

The essential fallacy with this sort of argument is that there may be many of one's friends or colleagues about whom one might say the same thing; in short, this objection shows us nothing of any moral substance. And notice what the argument entails: it is clear that we have a human being, but it is not clear that the status 'human being' brings with it any moral rights. That may be thought by many to be offensive and morally outrageous in itself. It is indeed widely assumed that qualifying as a human being is sufficient to guarantee the possession of a right to life. The history of the centuries shows us that it is when we begin to think of the status 'human being' as being insufficient to guarantee a certain moral respect that many of our troubles and ills have begun. As events in the Balkans, the former Soviet Union and countries in Africa disclose, it is precisely when we begin to regard one another only as human beings of a particular sort that our woes begin to multiply.

The argument that an embryo is a person is based upon the proposition that life begins at conception when a genetically unique entity with the potential for development comes into existence. Of course, there are those for whom the prospect of research upon, as they see it, living human beings in their embryonic form, is of the highest moral repugnance and that in sanctioning non-therapeutic research Parliament, in the 1990s, took a step across a Rubicon for which there is no return ticket. For example, Lord Rawlinson posed this question in a House of Lords' debate on the Human Fertilisation and Embryology Bill which proposed to allow research until the appearance of the 'primitive streak' 14 days after the onset of the process of conception:

---

18 Glover, J, *Fertility and the Family: The Glover Report on Reproductive Technologies to the European Commission*, 1989, London: Fourth Estate, p 96.

The question is asked: 'When does life commence?' Surely, if it has commenced, the killing is not acceptable. To those who reply 'after 14 days' I say '14 days after what?'.[19]

This position has been upheld by the Tennessee Circuit Court in *Davis v Davis*, at least two US States' legislatures, and has been ruled to be a constitutional declaration of State policy in the Supreme Court's decision in *Webster v Reproductive Health Services*.[20] It formed the basis of the Danish legislation of 1987, establishing its Council of Ethics, which was charged by the legislation to proceed on the basis that human life begins at the time of conception.[21]

In *Davis v Davis*, Judge Dale W Young at first instance awarded 'custody' of seven cryopreserved fertilised ova to a now divorced woman in a divorce suit and declared that she should be 'permitted the opportunity to bring these children to term through implantation'. He held that the embryos were, in law, persons, because life began at conception such that 'the manifest best interest of the children, *in vitro*, [is] that they be made available for implantation to assure their opportunity for live birth'. Among the reasons for his ruling were that 'Human life begins at conception ... and Mr and Mrs Davis have produced human beings, *in vitro*, to be known as their child or children'.

On appeal, the court remanded the case to the Circuit Court to enter judgment vesting joint control in the former husband and wife (both now remarried) and giving them equal voice over their disposition. The Appeals Court held that awarding sole custody to Mary Sue Davis, such that she could attempt implantation without her former husband's consent, was impermissible State action. Judge Franks, writing the leading opinion, held that such an award infringed Junior Davis' constitutionally protected rights concerning procreation; in particular, that it might force him to become a parent against his will. The Appeals Court could find no compelling State interest to justify ordering implantation against the will of either party. To this extent, the lower court's action usurped the exercise by Junior of 'the decision whether to bear or beget a child [which is] a constitutionally protected choice'. However nascent, this seems to recognise an emergent sphere of men's' rights to control their fertility and conception, which will lead to a direct clash with women's rights (as in this case) and any emergent notion of fetal rights.

Grubb, commenting on Judge Young's initial ruling, writes:

... the biological reality added to the philosophical imperative gave rise to a legal determination that the embryos were persons ... there is no silliness in the question 'what should be the fate of the frozen embryos?' Nor necessarily is

19 *Hansard* col 953, 8 February 1990.
20 492 US 490 (1989).
21 See Morgan, D and Nielsen, L, 'Dangerous liaisons; law, technology and European ethics: an Anglo-Danish comparison', in McVeigh, S and Wheeler, S (eds), *Medicine, Law and Regulation*, 1992, Aldershot: Dartmouth.

there any foolishness in the answer that their custody should be awarded to [the woman who wanted the implantation to proceed]. Instead, the defect in the judgment lies in the reasoning process which equates biological life with legal personhood and, as a consequence, treats embryos and children alike.[22]

It may be that Grubb dislikes the conclusions which flow from Young's ruling, but it is hardly correct to object that the reasoning discloses a *non sequitur*. Indeed, the transition from equating biological life with legal personhood, to treating embryos and children alike is – on one view – a smooth, defensible progression and not a *non sequitur* at all. On this view of legal personhood, it does indeed follow that embryos and children should be treated alike. Grubb's objection, then, should be directed towards the premises or assumptions that Young makes, and not the relationship between the variables. Of course, it would be possible to hold a third view, one close to that which I hold myself, which is that, even though there is a close relationship between biological life and personhood, it does not follow from that that research on human embryos should be legally proscribed or indeed is morally impermissible (which, again, may be two very different things).

But, it is indeed the potential consequences of Judge Young's ruling to which Grubb really takes objection. Although the judge's conclusion was set aside by the Tennessee Court of Appeals (awarding joint custody), the 'person analysis' leads to the conclusion that the party seeking custody for the purposes of implantation should be awarded it. Grubb again: '... there is no room for flexibility and there is no room for manoeuvre.'[23] In a definitional sense, that is probably correct, but in terms of what one may lawfully do with the embryos, that is another matter:

> ... the knock-on consequences of the trial judge's reasoning make his position very unattractive for the normal pragmatism of the common law judge. Some of these consequences would be as follows: embryo research leading to death could be murder; embryos could not be harmed in any way; hence research of all kinds (except the purely observational) would be unlawful; inheritance rights would seem to exist even before implantation.[24]

This kind of objection is shared by the jurists who composed the sadly now defunct Law Reform Commission of Canada. In their commentary on the trial judge's ruling, they wrote: '... the ruling ... in the *Davis* case illustrates the dangers of absolutism.'[25] Unfortunately, the LRCC here falls into the familiar trap of equating 'dangers' with 'consequences which I don't personally like'. The absolutism is 'dangerous' only if you want to try to produce some other result; if those are the consequences that flow from the 'absolutist' position,

---

22 *Op cit*, Grubb, fn 5, p 74.

23 *Op cit*, Grubb, fn 5, p 74.

24 *Op cit*, Grubb, fn 5.

25 Law Reform Commission of Canada, Working Paper No 64, *Medically Assisted Procreation*, 1992, Ottawa, pp 139–40.

then, arguably, those are the consequences. For myself, I do accept that those are the consequences that flow inexorably from that position, but I do not want to be detained longer on this excursus than I have already.

The classical common law position

Whatever the philosophical proposition that life begins at conception, it is not a position adopted by the English common law. The classical position is quite clear: a fetus, still less an embryo, is not a person. This is not the same, of course, as saying that it enjoys no legal protection whatsoever. The embryo, or at least the child *en ventre sa mère*, as the common law would have it, has some protected interests, such as the right to inherit,[26] and to be classified as a dependant for the purposes of the Fatal Accidents Acts.[27] But, in both cases, the interests crystallise only on the fetuses' live birth and are at best contingent rights. And, as I shall later show, further protected interests have been recognised by statute and, latterly, the common law, which have implications not only for this abstract analysis in which I am now engaged, but also for the practice of fetal medicine and infertility treatment services.

The 'classical' view was restated by the Warnock Committee in their Report:[28]

> We examined the current position of the *in vivo* embryo in law. The human embryo *per se* has no legal status. It is not, under law in the United Kingdom, accorded the same status as a child or an adult, and the law does not treat the human embryo as having a right to life. However, there are certain statutory provisions that give some level of protection in various respects.

They then cited the Offences Against the Person Act 1861, the Abortion Act 1967 (abortion is a criminal offence save in some cases provided for in the legislation), the Infant Life (Preservation) Act 1929 (the protection of the life of a child 'capable of being born alive') and the Congenital Disabilities (Civil Liability) Act 1976, which allows, in limited circumstances, an action for damages where an embryo or fetus has been injured *in utero*. Each of these provisions might be thought of as extending some forms of indirect benefit or protection under the law. None of this, of course, related to the *in vitro* embryo; the Offences Against the Person Act, which contains the still extant abortion provisions in England and Wales, does not apply to the extra-corporeal embryo because it speaks of the 'procurement of a miscarriage'. An embryo *in vitro* is never carried by a woman, and hence it falls outside the

---

26 Administration of Estates Act 1925, s 55(2).
27 *The George and the Richard* [1871] LR 3 A & E 466.
28 *Op cit*, Warnock Committee, fn 6, para 11.16–17.

law's ambit in this regard. As Margot Brazier wrote of the embryo before the passage of the 1990 Act, 'it exists and dies in a legal limbo'.[29]

No such limbo attended the fetus outwith these limited, but exceptionally important statutory enactments. That a fetus is not a person has been reiterated on a number of occasions when the issue has arisen in a variety of ways in common law courts. Some early examples will illustrate this point:

- In *Paton v BPAS*,[30] discussing a husband's attempt to prevent his wife seeking an abortion, Sir George Baker said: 'A fetus cannot, in English law, in my view, have any right of its own at least until it is born and has a separate existence from the mother.'

- In *Re F (In Utero)*,[31] on an attempt to make a fetus a ward of court to guard its health against feared harm from its mother's behaviour, the Court of Appeal held that an unborn child lacks legal personality to be made a ward of court because it would be incompatible with the rights of the mother. It has been suggested by John Keown that that case establishes nothing about forms of protection which could have been made available to the *in vitro* embryo before the 1990 Act. In particular, he suggested that, because it was *in vitro*, no question of conflict with the mother's rights arose, and hence it could be possible to make such an embryo a ward of court.[32] This view is strongly challenged by Andrew Grubb, according to whom:

    ... it would be quite wrong to see the cases as only failing to recognise the legal status of the unborn child because to do so would lead to a certain conflict with the pregnant mother's interests ... if an unborn child is not a legal person, it cannot seriously be argued that a frozen two-, four- or eight-cell embryo is a legal person with all the legal consequences stemming from such recognition by the law.[33]

Although I suspect that Grubb is right, it is again on the level of pragmatism more than principle. Of course, to recognise the wardship jurisdiction over an embryo would interfere with the genitor/parents' interests, and that may be sufficient reason to deny it legal status.

- In *C v S*,[34] where a putative father attempts as next friend of the fetus to prevent his former girlfriend from having an abortion, Heilbron J, in holding that a child injured while in the womb may be the subject of a legal action by the child once it is born, said: '... the claim crystallises on

---

29 *Op cit*, Brazier, fn 11, p 23.

30 [1979] 1 QB 276.

31 [1988] 2 All ER 193.

32 Keown, J, 'Creative criminals', paper presented at *Assisted Conception and the Law: A Medical/Legal Forum*, 1989, London: Royal Society of Medicine.

33 *Op cit*, Grubb, fn 5, p 75.

34 [1988] 1 QB 135.

the birth, at which date, but not before, the child attains the status of a legal persona; and thereupon can then exercise that legal right.'

- A variant view has been suggested by Lord Prosser in *Hamilton v Fife*[35] at first instance, challenging not the view that the fetus is not a person, but the view that any rights which are nascent, crystallise on the child's subsequent live birth. Lord Prosser said that for the purposes of s 1(1) of the Damages (Scotland) Act 1976, personal injuries had to be seen as sustained at the time when they first came into existence. If that time was before birth and only injuries sustained by a person were within the scope of the section, then the pursuer's claim would fail. Here, the child had died as a consequence of injuries sustained when he was a fetus; thus, he was not a 'person dying in consequence of personal injuries sustained by him'. Although Scots law has long adopted the fiction of the civil law that, in all matters affecting its interests, the unborn child *in utero* should be deemed to be already born,[36] the defenders submitted that, while the child might have invoked the fiction so as to have himself deemed to be already born at times prior to his birth, that fiction could not be invoked in the interests of third parties such as the pursuer (his parents). Lord Prosser thus held that the words used in s 1 of the Damages (Scotland) Act 1976 did not cover the situation where injury was sustained by a fetus rather than a person. Lord Prosser's judgment was appealed, and was independently rejected by Lord Morton in *McWilliams*,[37] who held on similar facts that injury sustained in the womb could give rise to a relevant claim.

- This position has now been supported by recent Court of Appeal authority in England in *Burton v Islington HA* and *de Martell v Merton and Sutton HA*.[38] Both cases involved damage done to a fetus in the womb prior to 1976 when Parliament passed the Congenital Disabilities (Civil Liability) Act; both cases involved a claim against hospital authorities for negligence in the performance of an operation (in the first case a D and C, and in the latter, while the plaintiff's mother was in labour). At first instance in *de Martell*, Phillips J observed that:

> The human being does not exist as a legal person until after birth. The fetus enjoys no independent legal personality ... An unborn child lacks the status to be the subject of a legal duty. If injury is done to an unborn child, no duty is broken. If injury is negligently caused to a newly born babe, liability in negligence arises ... In law and logic no damage can have been caused to the plaintiff before the plaintiff existed. The damage was suffered by the plaintiff at the moment that, in law, the plaintiff achieved personality and inherited the damaged body for which the defendants (on the assumed

---

35 1993 SC 369, Court of Session, Outer House.
36 *Elliot v Joicey* 1935 SC (HL) 57.
37 *McWilliams v Ministry of Defence* 1992 SC 220.
38 [1992] 3 All ER 833.

facts) were responsible. The events prior to the birth were mere links in the chain of causation between the defendant's assumed lack of skill and care and the consequential damage to the plaintiff ... The lack of legal status of the unborn child poses a peculiar problem in the law of negligence.[39]

On appeal, in a case joined with *Burton v Islington HA*, Dillon LJ said that the civil law maxim that an unborn child shall be deemed to be born whenever its interests require it could have been applied directly to these two cases, such that the two plaintiffs were treated as lives in being at the times of the events which injured them as they were later born alive.[40] However, Dillon LJ held that it was not necessary to do this. Citing and approving the main Commonwealth authority of *Watt v Rama*[41] and the reasoning of Winneke CJ and Pape J, Dillon LJ held that, on birth:

> ... the relationship crystallised and out of it arose a duty on the defendant in relation to the child ... as the child could not in the very nature of things acquire rights correlative to a duty until it became by birth a living person, and as it was not until then that it could sustain injuries as a living person, it was, we think, at that stage that the duty arising out of the relationship was attached to the defendant ...

The injury whilst *en ventre sa mere* was but an evidentiary incident in the causation of damage suffered at birth by the fault of the defendant.[42]

What the court was not prepared to do in this case was to go as far as some American States and hold that this theory of contingent rights can apply to the case of a child who is stillborn:

> The effect of the post-1945 decisions is that the courts of every American State have now held, as a development of the common law and despite previous decisions to the contrary, that a child can recover damages for a pre-natal injury, and even that damages can be recovered by the estate of a stillborn child. It is wholly unnecessary to go that far in the present case ...[43]

One final point is worthy of note in the context of the development of theories of fetal rights or legal interests. One objection which had been put in argument by Counsel for the defendant health authorities, if the fetus on live birth acquired standing to sue for injuries negligently inflicted while in the womb, was the danger to which this could give rise of potential conflict between mother and child. Without here commenting at length on the desirability or otherwise of this – I think, in fact, it is highly undesirable – Dillon LJ observed in response that if this opened the way to a flood of claims, Parliament could intervene, although he doubted

---

39 [1992] 3 All ER 820, pp 830–32.
40 [1992] 3 All ER 833, p 839.
41 [1972] VR 353, pp 360–61.
42 *Burton* [1992] 3 All ER 820, p 841, *per* Dillon LJ, citing Gillard J in *Watt, ibid*, pp 374–75.
43 [1992] 3 All ER 820, pp 839–40.

whether there would be many cases now outstanding which are not statute barred, in respect of children stillborn before 22 July 1976 (when the Congenital Disabilities (Civil Liability) Act 1976 came into force) or any children born before that date, 'who are locked in litigation with their mothers over whether the mother tasted alcohol or followed a diet other than that recommended by the current phase of medical opinion during pregnancy'.[44]

- In *AG's Reference (No 3 of 1994)*, Lord Mustill said that:

> The emotional bond between the mother and her unborn child was also of a very special kind. But, the relationship was one of bond, not identity. The mother and the fetus were two distinct organisms living symbiotically, not a single organism with two aspects. The mother's leg was part of the mother, the fetus was not ... It is sufficient to say that it is established beyond doubt for the criminal law, as for the civil law that the child *en ventre sa mere* does not have a distinct human personality, whose extinguishment gives rise to any penalties or liabilities at common law.[45]

The House of Lords ruled both that the Court of Appeal had stretched the concept of transferred malice too far, and that it was wrong, to treat the fetus as part of the mother rather than a unique organism. Nonetheless, their Lordships suggested that it would be open to the jury to find the accused guilty of manslaughter. This was on the basis that the required *mens rea* for manslaughter was an intention to do an unlawful and dangerous act. Thus, it was possible to establish the necessary *mens rea* in stabbing the mother, and that the child on birth could fall within the scope of that *mens rea*. This was on the following basis:

> For the fetus life lies in the future, not in the past. It is not sensible to say that it cannot be harmed, or that nothing can be done to it that can never be dangerous. Once it is born it is exposed like all living persons to the risk of injury. It may also carry with it the effects of things done to it before birth which, after birth, may prove to be harmful ...[46]

THE HUMAN FERTILISATION AND EMBRYOLOGY ACT 1990

Finally, I can turn to look at the statutory provisions of the Human Fertilisation and Embryology Act 1990. Although the embryo is nowhere given a status as either a chattel or as a person, the Act introduces, through the licensing scheme to be overseen by the Human Fertilisation and Embryology Authority (HFEA), the most comprehensive statements as to how embryos are to be treated. Recall that Warnock had observed that:

---

44 [1992] 3 All ER 820, pp 843–44.
45 *AG's Reference (No 3 of 1994)* [1996] QB 581.
46 [1997] 3 All ER 936, p 957, *per* Lord Hope.

> Until now the law has never had to consider the existence of embryos outside the mother's uterus. The existence of such embryos raises potentially difficult problems as to ownership. The concept of ownership of human embryos seems to us to be undesirable. We recommend that legislation be enacted to ensure that there is no right of ownership in a human embryo.[47]

The ensuing legislation does not take such an opportunity, although in debates on the Human Fertilisation and Embryology Bill, Lord Kennet moved Amendment 9A in the House of Lords Committee consideration of the Bill. That amendment provided: 'For the avoidance of doubt it is hereby declared that the embryo shall have the legal status of a person.' The opening words of the amendment are salutary; they do not suggest that we have forgotten that the embryo is a person, they remind us that the legal status of an embryo (and the amendment did not distinguish between extra-corporeal embryos and those *in vivo*) is a doubtful and difficult concept with which lawyers and others have to struggle, although the amendment fell.

The ensuing debate brought this intervention from the former Lord Chancellor, Lord Hailsham:

> An embryo is not a chattel, and to destroy it if it were would be a trespass to someone else's property. A human entity which is living is not a chattel and neither is it a person in the ordinary sense. Most extraordinary results would follow if it were ... It would be able to bring an action for personal injury if it were damaged. I suppose the loss of expectation of life might be among the general effects for which general damages could be awarded ... It is wrong to try to define a human embryo in terms of existing legal definitions which are plainly inapplicable to human embryos. Why must an embryo be one or the other? Why cannot it be just an embryo?[48]

It may be that developments in the future will render the question of excess embryos irrelevant, in that technologies or practices will advance to such an extent that superovulation will be unnecessary or that cryopreservation of ova will achieve all that the production of surplus embryos now achieves in terms of treatment without the on-cost questions about embryo research, although more recent developments in stem cell research now make that unlikely.

General prohibitions

Section 3 defines activities which are beyond the power of the HFEA to licence. The Authority may not authorise the use or retention of a live human embryo after the appearance of 'the primitive streak'.[49] Unless the embryo is stored by way of freezing, this is taken to be 'not later than the end of the

---

47 *Op cit*, Warnock Committee, fn 6, para 10.11.

48 *Hansard* vol 515, col 750–51.

49 Human Fertilisation and Embryology Act 1990, s 3(3)(a).

period of 14 days beginning with the day when the gametes are mixed'.[50] This much criticised pragmatic solution had been adopted by the Warnock Committee as the point when human life begins to matter morally.[51]

Similarly, the Authority may not authorise the placing of a human embryo in any animal, keeping or use of an embryo where regulations prohibit this or nucleus substitution, sometimes referred to as cloning.[52] This is where the nucleus of the cell of an embryo (which contains the hereditary genetic material) is removed and replaced with the nucleus taken from a cell of another person, embryo or later developed embryo.[53] This latter technique has been claimed to hold important prospects for work with genetically inherited disease and the production of immunologically identical organs for transplantation purposes. But, it is said to raise the spectre of the production of genetically identical humans, clones, or humans with specific characteristics. The Authority will not presently be able to licence such work. Section 3(3)(b) prohibits 'placing an embryo in any animal'.

Schedule 2 'treatment licences' may authorise a variety of practices designed 'to secure that embryos are in a suitable condition to be placed in a woman or to determine whether embryos are suitable for that purpose',[54] which may look uncommonly like research.

Section 4 provides more contentious reading. Sections 4(1)(a) and (c) provide for offences in respect of storing gametes (ova and sperm) and cross-species fertilisation using live human gametes without an HFEA licence.

Human embryo research

Originally, there was nothing in the Human Fertilisation and Embryology Bill that would have prevented unlicensed 'research' up to the point of syngamy. Section 1 was amended to deal with this; it adopts a scientific understanding as its definition of an embryo; in s 1(1) it provides that references to an embryo are to a live human embryo 'where fertilisation is complete', but that references to an embryo 'include an egg in the process of fertilisation'.[55] Fertilisation is not complete 'until the appearance of a two-cell zygote'.[56] I shall return to the problems that this drafting has disclosed in respect of cell nucleus transfer below, Chapter 10.

---

50 Human Fertilisation and Embryology Act 1990, s 3(4).
51 *Op cit*, Warnock Committee, fn 6, paras 11.2–11.9.
52 I return to these questions in Chapter 10, below.
53 Human Fertilisation and Embryology Act 1990, s 3(3)(b), (c) and (d).
54 *Ibid*, s 1(1)(d).
55 *Ibid*, s 1(1)(a) and (b).
56 *Ibid*, s 1(1)(a) and (b).

A licence authorising specific research under the 1990 Act may be granted by the HFEA for a maximum period of three years.[57] Any research licence may be made subject to conditions imposed by the HFEA and specified in the licence.[58] Each research protocol must be shown to relate, broadly, to one of the existing categories of research aim[59] and then again only if the Authority is satisfied that the use of embryos is 'necessary for the purposes of the research'.[60] These aims are:

(a) promoting advances in the treatment of infertility;

(b) increasing knowledge about the causes of congenital disease: an amendment seeking to limit this to life threatening or severely disabling conditions was withdrawn;

(c) increasing knowledge about the causes of miscarriage;

(d) developing more effective techniques of contraception: an amendment condemning this as 'frivolous' was defeated;

(e) developing methods for detecting the presence of gene or chromosome abnormalities in embryos before implantation.

New purposes may be specified in regulations, but only for the purpose of increasing knowledge about the creation and development of embryos or enabling such knowledge to be applied.

THE CONSENT REQUIREMENTS OF THE ACT

The consent requirements, which are elaborated in Sched 3, play an important part in the determination of some substantive points of principle and practice which arise. Failure to observe the provisions of Sched 3 by proceeding (for example) without an effective consent is one ground for revocation of the licence under s 17(1)(c). The consents provisions of Sched 3 are not just limited to the formal process of protecting the providers of treatment services. All consents must be in writing, and before consents to use or storage of gametes or embryos are given, a person must be given a 'suitable' opportunity to receive 'proper' counselling about the implications of such a step and 'such relevant information as is proper'. Paragraph 4(1) provides that the terms of any consent in the third Schedule may be varied or withdrawn at any time, unless the embryo has already been used in providing treatment services or for research purposes. Consents for the use of any embryo must specify to what use(s) it may be put and specify any associated conditions to that

---

57 Human Fertilisation and Embryology Act 1990, Sched 2, para 3(9).

58 *Ibid*, Sched 2, para 3(7).

59 *Ibid*, Sched 2, para 3(2).

60 *Ibid*, Sched 2, para 3(6).

consent.[61] An example might be whether gametes or embryo may be used only for the consent giver, or for any other people requiring treatment services or for the purposes of research.

In respect of gamete or embryo storage, the maximum period of storage must be specified in the consent. In addition, and importantly, the consent must address the question of what is to happen to stored gametes or embryos if the consent-giver dies or becomes incapacitated and is, therefore, unable to revoke or vary their consent. The Act does not provide for what should happen, it requires only that the consent-giver(s) address the issue. This provision is inserted to obviate difficulties exemplified by requests for use of the embryos or gametes after the death of one consent-giver[62] and also in the *Rios' Embryos* case. In the *Rios* case, the Rios were Californian citizens and parents of frozen embryos held in store in Melbourne when they were killed in a plane crash. They died intestate and the Californian intestate succession laws appeared to apply, giving a share of the estate to Mr Rios' son by a previous marriage and to Mrs Rios' mother. In December 1987, the Californian Superior Court declared Mrs Rios' mother to be the sole heir. The Medical Center in Melbourne then declared that the embryos would be thawed and allowed to perish. This led to an outcry, culminating in the intervention of the State Minister of Health, who had to make special provision for them. In the event, the embryos were to be held in storage until a suitable recipient could be found, although the chances of survival were put at less than 5%.

It seems desirable that the powers granted to the Authority under para 3(3) of Sched 3, to provide for other matters which must be dealt with in the consents, include that specific questions should be answered. For example, in the event of death, does the surviving partner have the right of access to the gametes or embryos? While s 27(4)(b) provides that a man whose sperm, or an embryo derived in part from his sperm, is used after his death is not to be treated as the father of any resulting child, this is not directly relevant to the point here. Similarly, should the gametes or embryos be allowed to perish, or may they be used by the Authority?

An important point of difference arises in respect of consent when dealing with embryos created *in vitro* and those obtained from a woman following lavage (recovering the embryo by flushing the uterus) or laparoscopy (a microsurgical technique which permits the recovery of the embryo instrumentally). The continued storage of embryos will depend on how the embryos were 'brought into being'. With an embryo created *in vitro* following gamete donation, the embryo may not be kept in storage without the effective consent (written consent which has not been withdrawn) of both gamete

---

61 Human Fertilisation and Embryology Act 1990, Sched 3, para 2(1).
62 The *Parpalaix* case, discussed above, p 110. Although the effect of this has now to be considered in the light of the case of *R v HFEA ex p Blood* [1997] 2 All ER 687.

donors.[63] Withdrawal of the consent of either donor to the embryo's creation means that it must be allowed to perish.

Where the embryo has come into being in the uterus and is subsequently extracted, not only may it not be used for any purpose unless the woman alone gives consent for that use,[64] it may not be stored unless there is an effective consent by her, and her alone.[65] This appears to be the Government's chosen way of avoiding the litigation spawned over cryopreserved embryos in the divorce proceedings of *Davis v Davis*.

The lessons from mistakes made in that case have clearly been learnt. For example, there was no discussion between the Davises and the Center about the consequences of separation or divorce occurring while the ova remained frozen, nor were the Davises required to sign any agreement about the terms of storage or disposition at the time the fertilised ova were cryopreserved. The 1990 Act attempts to address these questions. In the first case, where the embryo is brought about outside the body, the woman's partner can, by withdrawing his consent, effectively require that the embryo perish. In the second case of an embryo recovered by lavage, he cannot. In both cases, the women can achieve this result.

Posthumous treatments

The effect of reading together ss 14(1)(b) and 4(1)(b) is that where a clinic decides, or the treatment services contract or agreement provides, that the death of one of the partners is to terminate the provision of treatment services, the other partner will have no right to insist on the clinic making available to them any stored gametes or embryos. If the clinic decides that it will, for example, honour the wishes which the now deceased partner was required to express as to use of stored gametes or embryos following their death (Sched 3, para 2(2)(b): written consent 'must ... state what is to be done with the gametes or embryo if the person who gave the consent dies') that appears to be a matter for the exercise of clinical judgment and discretion.[66] Otherwise, an embryo created *in vitro* may only lawfully be kept 'in storage' with effective consent of both partners, whereas an embryo which was formed within the woman's body and subsequently recovered surgically (by lavage or laparoscopy), may only be stored with the consent of the woman from whom it was obtained.[67]

---

63 Human Fertilisation and Embryology Act 1990, Sched 3, para 8(2).
64 *Ibid*, para 7(1).
65 *Ibid*, para 8(3).
66 Again, subject to the apparently 'one off' litigation in *Blood*.
67 Human Fertilisation and Embryology Act 1990, Sched 3, para 8(2) and (3) respectively.

CIVIL LIABILITY: CONGENITAL DISABILITY

The Congenital Disability (Civil Liability) Act 1976, which replaced any previous common law, provides for civil liability in the case of children born disabled in consequence of the intentional act, negligence, or breach of statutory duty of some person prior to the birth of the child. The Act covers liability for children born alive; 'born' here meaning reaching the point at which the child has life separate from its mother and surviving for 48 hours.[68] The defendant is answerable to the child if that defendant was liable, in tort, to one or both of the parents in respect of the matters which gave rise to the disability at birth. Such matters could arise either before conception, or during the pregnancy of the mother or the process of childbirth. In relation to matters arising before conception, this would clearly cover an injury to the parent which, at the time of conception, was transmitted to the child. Note that, under the 1976 Act, liability on the part of the mother to her own child is excluded, but the liability of the father is not. Such preconception or pre-implantation liability is now additionally provided for in s 44 of the Human Fertilisation and Embryology Act 1990.

The 1990 Act, by s 44(1), introduces a new s 1A to the 1976 Act specifically to provide for actions that might arise in the course of providing assisted conception. It follows the scheme of the 1976 Act, and introduces for children born as a result of assisted conception the same sort of regime in respect of statutory conditions for liability as that Act did for natural conception. It applies to any case where:

(a) a child has been born disabled following the placing in a woman of an embryo, or sperm and eggs, or following her artificial insemination;

(b) the disability results from an act or omission in the course of the selection of the embryo or the gametes used to bring about the embryo; or

(c) the disability results from some act or omission in the keeping or use of the embryo or gametes outside the body;

(d) the defendant is (or would, if sued in time, have been) liable for negligence or breach of statutory duty to one or both of the parents, irrespective of whether they suffered actionable injury as long as there was a breach of duty which, if injury had occurred, would have given rise to liability.

This section clearly covers damage caused by the keeping or storage of the embryos or gametes, whether they have been frozen or not. It also applies to the procedure of selection of the embryos for implantation, although so little is known about this process that it is more of a morphological check than a scientific screening procedure. There are, on the face of it, some difficulties.

---

68   Congenital Disability (Civil Liability) Act 1976, s 4(2), and see *Rance v Mid Downs HA* [1991] 1 All ER 801.

For example, it is not clear that it applies to an act or omission which causes damage to an embryo being recovered from a woman by lavage for subsequent implantation in another woman who gestates the child subsequently born injured. It is arguable that the recovery of the embryo could be regarded as a 'selection', but it is probable that that wording would be more strictly confined to the selection of one rather than another embryo for transfer to the woman's uterus.

The 1976 Act provides a number of defences to an action. A significant one is that if the parents, or either of them, knew the risk of the child being born disabled and accepted that risk, then the creator of the occurrence carrying that risk is excused liability. Clearly, this applies only to matters that precede conception.[69] This defence is not available to the father acting as defendant, where he, but not the mother, had no knowledge of the risk. For present purposes, however, s 1(5) also provides a significant defence. Section 1(5) states that:

> The defendant is not answerable to the child, for anything he did or omitted to do when responsible in a professional capacity for treating or advising the parent, if he took reasonable care having due regard to then received professional opinion applicable to the particular class of case; but this does not mean that he is answerable only because he departed from received opinion.

Section 44(1)(a)(3) provides a defence to an action by a child where, at the time of the treatment, either or both of the parents knew the risk created by the particular act or omission of their child being born disabled. The other defences available under the 1976 Act are also available in this extended action (s 44(1)(a)(4)).

Section 44(1)(a)(3) provides the same defence in respect of parental knowledge as in the 1976 Act. Thus where, at the time the embryo, or sperm and eggs were placed in the woman, or at the time she was inseminated, either or both of the parents knew the particular risk created by the act or omission of their child being born disabled, then the defendant (a 'person answerable to the child') under s 44(1)(a)(2) is not answerable to the child. It will be interesting to monitor the way in which infertility clinics attempt to discharge their liability under this section. It has been suggested by some clinicians that a blanket warning as to risks of handicap as a result of infertility treatment would be sufficient to exculpate from liability. It will probably develop as practice to include some provision in the consents form which the woman or the couple will sign at the outset of the treatment.

Where a surrogacy arrangement within the provisions of s 30 (parental orders section) has taken place and the genetic parent(s) apply for an order, the provisions of the congenital disabilities section will still apply for the benefit of the child. It is clear that, in a number of instances, for the purpose of

---

69 Congenital Disability (Civil Liability) Act 1976, s 1(4).

instituting proceedings under s 1 of the 1976 Act, it would be necessary to identify the genetic father or mother of the child. Suppose, for example, a complete failure of genetic screening at a treatment centre resulted in the birth of a child disabled within the meaning of the 1976 Act. If a mother were then to make a claim that the failure of genetic screening at the centre 'affected ... her ability to have a normal, healthy child' since she was introduced to a donor whose sperm was always likely to give rise to a disabled child, it might be necessary for evidential purposes to trace that donor. Similarly, the donor himself might be liable where, knowing that he was HIV positive, he nonetheless allowed his sperm to be used for infertility treatment. As the Act places liability upon 'a person (other than the child's own mother)', it is clear that there is nothing in the 1976 Act itself which would exempt the donor, even if considered as father, from liability. Again, however, the problem would be identifying the donor. Finally, the state of the father's knowledge may be relevant to the s 1(4) defence considered above. But who is the 'father' for these purposes?

A new s 4(4) of the Congenital Disabilities Act is included to allow that where, as the result of assisted conception, a child carried by a woman is born disabled, then references within the 1976 Act to a 'parent' will include a reference to a person who would be a parent but for ss 27–29 of the 1990 Act. Also, in an attempt to resolve some of the difficulties of identifying parents, s 35(1) states that where, for the purposes of initiating proceedings under the 1976 Act, it is necessary to identify a person who would or might be the parent of a child (cf the wording in s 30(4)) but for ss 27–29 of this Act, then the court may, on the application of the child, make an order requiring the HFEA to disclose registered information under s 30 of the Act such that the person could be identified. Most importantly, this will include sections such as ss 27(1) and 28(6), which provide that donors (other than the couple receiving treatment) are not to be treated ordinarily as either the mother or the father of the child in question. Note that this is only available on a court order which requires the Authority to disclose such information.

CONCLUSION

The Human Fertilisation and Embryology Act is a complex piece of legislation and, as the 10 years since its inception have shown, continues to provoke controversy. The common law and statute are both now clear that neither the fetus, nor the embryo *in vitro*, enjoys legal status, although both enjoy significant legal protections. These stop (a long way) short of providing that the fetus may not be lawfully killed in a termination of pregnancy, or that the embryo may not be the subject of destructive human embryo research. The law even provides that the embryo may be specifically created only for the purpose of being the subject of research. It is there, and not in other matters of their status, that controversy over the fetus and the embryo will continue to rage. As the advent of 'therapeutic cloning' and cell nucleus substitution has shown, that controversy is not only likely to continue, it is going to throw up new legal and ethical conundrums too.[70]

70 See below, Chapter 10.

CHAPTER 8

LEGAL AND ETHICAL DILEMMAS OF FETAL SEX IDENTIFICATION AND GENDER SELECTION

The case of Louise and Alan Masterton of Dundee, who want to use IVF technology to ensure the birth of a daughter following the death of their three year old, Nicola, is a tragic reminder of the continued appeal of gender selection.[1] The techniques which enable this to be done have developed greatly over the past 20 years, and pre-implantation genetic diagnosis is seen by many as an important strategy in the struggle with inherited genetic disease. In this chapter, I focus on two slightly different legal issues:

(a) prenatal screening, prenatal diagnosis and genetic information and the termination of a pregnancy disclosing a 'handicapped' fetus;

(b) whether the use of termination once sex has been diagnosed in a pregnancy is unlawful, as is widely claimed. I conclude that it is not, while recalling that whether gender or sex selection is a wise or acceptable technique is, of course, a different question.

The first question might be, and has sometimes been, condemned as part of the search for the perfect baby, while the second might involve what, for some, is thought to be the search for the perfect society.

DIAGNOSTIC ISSUES

Gender denotes legal, social and economic distinctions that follow from biological difference. Sex denotes the biological classification of human beings into two broad categories.[2] And, the possibility of the use of technology to ensure sex selection has long been foreseen:

> ... it would be possible, using *in vitro* fertilisation, to allow a number of eggs to develop to a stage at which the sex of each organism could be determined. Those of the unwanted sex could be jettisoned, and one of the desired sex implanted. Rather as with a litter of kittens, one could keep the boys and throw the girls away, but long before birth ... Obviously, the use of such a procedure in human beings raises in acute form questions of the sanctity of life. In the broad human sense, nothing has been lost: a person who wished to procreate

---

1   October 2000. It has been reported that the Mastertons are considering a challenge to the advice of the HFEA, which has set itself against the use of IVF in a case such as this.

2   O'Donovan, K, *Sexual Divisions in Law*, 1985, London: Weidenfeld & Nicolson, p xi.

has done so. In a narrow sense, thousands, even millions of potential organisms have been sacrificed.[3]

The economic dilemma of modern medicine arises partly from the fact that many medical advances improve the survival of people with chronic disabilities, and so lead to increasing service needs. Largely because of this, in the absence of prevention, the cost of treating patients with inherited diseases (such as cystic fibrosis, sickle cell disease, phenylketonuria, haemophilia, thalassaemia and Huntington's chorea) will double in the next 20–30 years. Unlike many other branches of medicine, medical genetics has a built in means through genetic counselling and prenatal diagnosis for limiting its own expansion.[4]

What I am primarily concerned with in this chapter are issues of *gender*, in which the sex of the embryo or fetus is 'identification evidence' on the basis of which other decisions are taken. To be sure, the balance between the emphasis given to sex and that to gender is not a constant, fixed one. When I am discussing the use of diagnostic and screening procedures for the identification of X-linked inherited disease, I am primarily concerned with the question of the sex of the fetus. But, even in this case, I contend that the conclusions that are drawn are based upon a series of assumptions or beliefs which are intimately connected with economic and social, as well as moral and legal values and judgments. When I move to discuss fetal sex identification and abortion, I am primarily and explicitly concerned with questions of gender.

A preliminary point needs to be addressed here. Prenatal diagnosis and genetic screening, fetal gender identification and questions of random reduction of multiple pregnancies raise a range of legal and ethical questions. In this chapter, I am going to concentrate on only some of the legal issues, notably, fetal sex identification and abortion, and only a selective range of the ethical dilemmas. It may be appropriate, however, to identify part of the broader range of questions which a full consideration of this topic would demand. For example, with diagnosis and screening, it needs to be recognised that these have wider ethical and legal implications than those flowing simply from diagnosis and screening based on sex. Other important consequences flow for chromosomal and multi-factorial diseases. In addition, each of these areas raise questions, sometimes different questions, of counselling and negligence, counselling and confidentiality, and actions based upon a claim for wrongful life.

There are a group of ethical questions associated with diagnosis and screening, which might be roughly reduced to questions about societal attitudes to handicap and disability more generally. I believe that it can

---

3   Rattray Taylor, G, *The Biological Timebomb,* 1968, New York: World, p 42.
4   Royal College of Physicians of London, *Prenatal Diagnosis and Prenatal Screening: Community and Service Implications,* 1989, London: RCP, para 6.13.

properly be argued that questions of diagnosis and screening can, and indeed should, be properly separated from attitudes towards handicap and disability, or towards people with different learning and other social abilities. It is sometimes suggested that attitudes towards testing, screening and even appropriate treatment regimes for severely handicapped neonates is somehow *necessarily* connected with the way in which we view, provide for or abuse disabled or differently capable people in modern Western society. It would be foolish to suggest that such a paradise already existed, and probably an able-bodied and able-minded fool at that. But, this need not, indeed should not, shield us from the fact that there can be attitudes towards handicap which are not based on discrimination, but on compassion, that technology and screening can bring understanding as well as ignorance, hope as well as despair. To achieve the necessary balance between the benefits which technology and knowledge can bring and the reinforcement of attitudes of repugnance and discrimination is not an easy task. But it confuses, rather than clarifies, the issue to claim that screening, diagnosis and, say, abortion, *necessarily* reinforce negative attitudes.[5] Of course, they may do, and any tendencies towards that should be resisted. Without these understandings, we assume awesome power without responsibility. And, unless we are to accept a totalitarianism of the able bodied, we should rightly want to guard against and reject this.

HOW CAN SEX BE DETERMINED?

Attempts to realise techniques of sperm selection have been long practised; a team at Keio University in Japan was reported in the late 1980s as having used a centrifugal system to isolate the differential densities of X and Y chromosomes carried in sperm in order to produce an X chromosome rich fraction. This sperm was then used to artificially inseminate six women who specifically wanted to bear a daughter.[6]

A second method involves the sexing of embryos prior to, or soon after, implantation. This can be done by taking a small piece of tissue from the developing embryo or by dividing the eight-cell stage embryo into two and, using DNA probes to recognise part of the Y chromosome, examining one half while the other is freeze-stored pending the outcome of the DNA examination. A variation on these cumbersome DNA procedures is PCR – Polymerase Chain Reaction. This involves amplifying specific segments of the DNA code exponentially, without the necessity of cloning the DNA into a vector, such as a virus or bacterium, which was previously done. Two small pieces of DNA –

---

5   See Maclean, A, *The Elimination of Morality*, 1993, London: Routledge, p 31; see, also, below, Chapter 9.

6   See (1989) 321 Nature 720.

primers – are stuck to and flank the DNA region to be amplified. These primers are used to synthesise the copy. Between 20 and 40 cycles of amplification are performed, with the DNA doubling at each cycle. One early reported application[7] of this technique produced fetal sexing for X-linked conditions. This was achieved from a single cell from a human embryo at the 6–10 cell cleavage (about three days after *in vitro* fertilisation). The cell was broken open in a test tube and the DNA released. A section was then taken on the Y chromosome and amplified up using PCR. This produced sufficient DNA to observe it with conventional analytical techniques. One result of this sort of application is that it becomes possible to sex a *single cell*, because the Y-specific fragment will give no signal from a female cell, whereas there will be one from a male cell. The advantages of PCR are that it does not interfere with the development of the embryo; intervention can be performed at a very early stage of development, with the prospect of speedy results of the DNA analysis (for carriers of cystic fibrosis genes, results have been tendered in 10 hours). PCR has also been applied to individual sperm, but the presence of dust particles (usually human skin) have been shown to produce a lot of false negative and positive results. 'Using this method, population screening will be possible using single hairs, or cells from mouth washings, thus saving the time and expense of taking blood samples.'[8] These techniques could also be used for pre-implantation diagnosis of the early ovum or blastocyst *in vitro* before return to a woman's uterus. The limitations presently are that little is known about the resilience of the pre-embryo under such manipulation.

Thirdly, there is a group of diagnostic procedures which may involve determining fetal sex during pregnancy, or which may be used solely for diagnostic purposes. Five such techniques can be identified here:

(a) Amniocentesis: this involves drawing off amniotic fluid from the amniotic sac in which the developing fetus is harboured and culturing the fetal cells so obtained to distinguish between the XX (female) and XY (male) cells so obtained. Despite claims made by some clinics, notably in Northern India, it is not possible to produce a result from amniocentesis quickly. Culturing the cells takes several weeks and, as amniocentesis can only be performed after the 16th week of pregnancy, any resulting decision in relation to abortion is well into the 20th week of the pregnancy.

---

7   See Handyside *et al* (1989) *The Lancet*, 18 February.
8   See Lench, N *et al*, 'Simple non invasive method to obtain DNA for gene analysis', cited in *op cit*, RCP, fn 4, para 3.6.

(b) Chorionic villus sampling (CVS) demands the biopsy of a few cells from the fingers of tissue (the villi) which grow from the chorion (the membrane, derived from the early embryo surrounding the fetus) into the wall of the uterus. Such sampling can be done after six to eight weeks of pregnancy, and the results of the DNA analysis can be made available within 48 hours, although the time taken for diagnosis can range from three days to three weeks.

(c) Fluorescence-activated cell sorting (FACS) involves the identification of fetal blood cells that have crossed the placenta into the mother's blood or the use of blood samples taken directly from the fetus. It can be performed safely only after the 17th week of pregnancy. The technique now practised of ultrasound guided transabdominal needle puncture of the fetal cord insertion also allows fetal skin and liver biopsies, selective feticide of one discordant twin and intrauterine transfusions.

(d) Ultrasound scanning can be used in order to determine the sex of the fetus, but only after the development of external genitalia, during the third trimester of pregnancy, and even then, identification of the relevant organ is difficult, even to a trained operator. Whereas the other methods identified can be used with relatively high success rates, the use of ultrasonography for sex identification purposes is not particularly reliable.

(e) DNA methods of examination and diagnosis have been introduced above. These are increasing greatly the range and accuracy of prenatal and carrier diagnosis for inherited disease. The chromosomal locations of defective genes that cause many single gene disorders have now been identified.[9]

What might selection be used for?

There are three potential reasons for the use of sex selection:

(a) the negative eugenic elimination of sex-linked disease;

(b) the establishment of a unisex society or community;

(c) a preference for sons (or daughters).

In this chapter, I want primarily to concentrate on the first and the third of these as raising linked issues. The second clearly is related, but raises somewhat different concerns.

---

9   Further description of these techniques is found in *op cit*, RCP, fn 4.

PRENATAL SCREENING, PRENATAL DIAGNOSIS AND GENETIC INFORMATION

Prenatal screening can be used to identify from among a population of apparently healthy individuals those whose risk of a specific genetic disorder that may affect the fetus is sufficiently high to justify a subsequent diagnostic test or procedure. Prenatal diagnosis is used to confirm or reject whether a specific genetic abnormality which might affect the fetus is present in an individual pregnant woman at high risk.

One to two per cent of all newborns have a major congenital or genetically determined disorder. Few can be treated satisfactorily, management if possible is burdensome, expensive and often thought to be unsatisfactory. Two to three per cent of couples are at high and recurrent risk of having children with an inherited disorder. These include: dominant disorders (where disease occurs even if only one copy of the two copies of each gene inherited by an individual is defective), such as Huntington's chorea, neurofibromatosis, multiple polyposis coli or adult polycystic kidney disease; X-linked disorders, which are determined by genes located on the X chromosome, hence sex-linked traits, such as fragile mental retardation, Duchenne muscular dystrophy and Haemophilia A; and finally recessive disorders (where disease occurs only if both copies of an inherited gene are affected), such as cystic fibrosis and phenylketonuria, and, in certain ethnic groups, thalassaemia sickle cell disease and Tay-Sachs disease. Carriers of many of these diseases may increasingly be detected by biochemical or DNA methods. According to the Royal College of Physicians, the goal of genetic and prenatal diagnostic provision must be 'to help these couples make an informed choice, one which they feel is best for themselves and their families'.[10]

The diagnosis of a dominant disorder in one individual implies a risk for all first degree relatives of carrying the same pathological gene and of developing the same disease and transmitting it to their offspring. The vast majority of abnormal genes carried in human populations are recessive and most people carry at least one such potentially lethal gene.[11]

Screening for congenital malformations

Congenital malformations may be screened for in one of three ways: infectious causes; maternal alphafetoprotein estimation; or ultrasound scanning. The main source of infectious congenital malformation is the rubella virus. Although only about 20% of exposed fetuses will be affected, evidence of maternal exposure often leads to termination of the pregnancy.

---

10 *Op cit*, RCP, fn 4, Preface.
11 *Op cit*, RCP, fn 4, paras 1.9, 1.11.

Screening for chromosomal abnormalities

The diagnostic method most used here is amniocentesis or CVS followed by chromosomal analysis (karotyping). Because there are obstetric risks and karotyping is a skilled and labour-intensive procedure, prenatal testing for fetal abnormalities is usually only offered to women at more than 0.5–1.0% risk of bearing an affected child; indeed, most children with, for example, Down's syndrome are born to young mothers, not typically thought to be at such risk.[12]

Screening for inherited diseases

The feasibility of carrier detection is an important limiting factor here. It is presently possible to detect before pregnancy only for relatives of patients with a limited number of dominant or X-linked disorders, and for recessively inherited haemoglobin disorders and Tay-Sachs disease. The possibilities using developing DNA methods are, however, immense. More recent developments will bring specially constructed genetic probes to detect carriers and provide prenatal diagnosis for the commonest inherited diseases. In addition, PCR will make this work much cheaper and, potentially, far less invasive.

Cystic fibrosis is the most common recessively inherited disease in the UK. Prenatal diagnosis is possible with an assay of amniotic fluid at 19 weeks' gestation or DNA analysis in the first trimester, and PCR. Although there is an increasing demand for the service, it has only a small effect on the birth rate of affected children because no carrier testing yet exists and prenatal diagnosis can only be offered to couples retrospectively, that is, after the birth of a first affected child. Prospective carrier diagnosis would require the prior testing of the whole population before they have children. As the RCP Report expresses it: 'Important advances are now pending for cystic fibrosis, the gene for which is carried by about 5% of the UK population. When a DNA-based method for carrier screening becomes available, the high incidence of carriers *implies that screening should be offered to all people prior to reproduction.*'[13] This raises issues of compulsion, compellability and confidentiality, all major sources of ethical disquiet. I shall return to consider these points later.

The use of diagnosis for the elimination of such sex-linked diseases as haemophilia (carried on the X chromosome) or Duchenne muscular dystrophy, and of sex determination techniques in the identification of

---

12 *Op cit*, RCP, fn 4, para 1.17.
13 *Op cit*, RCP, fn 4, para 3.7, emphasis added.

individuals at risk of passing on dominant disorders, or chromosome disorders, such as Down's syndrome and Edward's syndrome, could hardly be described as uncontested. For many people, however, they probably represent one of the acceptable faces of genetics.

The search for the perfect baby?

While it may be true that the development of these techniques has already brought the relief of much pain and suffering to the lives of identifiable human subjects, they nonetheless raise issues of acute ethical difficulty. They raise, in Jonathan Glover's memorable phrase, the question: 'What sort of people should there be?' What characteristics should those who are yet to be born possess? We may find a large degree of agreement about the answers given to some parts of that question; areas of divergence to others. We have to find ways of mediating these different responses, of approaching our own responses defensibly, and of drawing boundary lines which, while having all the appearances of arbitrariness, can be defended, if not logically, then at least consistently.

The only effective way of putting to practical use the findings of many of these diagnostic techniques is to abort an identifiable fetus. For some opponents of abortion, this fact is sufficient in itself to render the process morally indefensible. Indeed, there is evidence which suggests that some women are put under pressure by their attendant physicians to consider abortion as a prerequisite of any testing:

> In a mistaken attempt to justify the obstetric risk and expense involved in prenatal testing, women are often asked for an undertaking to terminate the pregnancy should the fetus prove to be affected. Insensitive handling during termination of pregnancy is common. If pregnancy is to be terminated, the need for support and for subsequent contact is the same as that required for high risk conditions.[14]

As the RCP Report comments, it is perhaps not surprising that there is some public anxiety about the medical application of genetic knowledge.[15] While the legality of such diagnostic procedures and, indeed, the subsequent abortion of an affected fetus is not in doubt under English law, the ethical

---

14 *Op cit*, RCP, fn 4, para 5.23.
15 *Op cit*, RCP, fn 4, para 5.23.

questions are sorely contested. The legal position is governed by what I once called 'the unexamined ground' of abortion law.[16]

Section 1 of the Abortion Act 1967 (as amended by s 37 of the Human Fertilisation and Embryology Act 1990) provides, in its material sub-section:

1(1) Subject to the provisions of this section, a person shall not be guilty of an offence under the law relating to abortion when a pregnancy is terminated by a registered medical practitioner if two registered medical practitioners are of the opinion formed in good faith ...

(d) that there is a substantial risk that if the child were born it would suffer from such physical or mental abnormalities as to be seriously handicapped.

It is important to notice that the Act does not say that a fetus may be aborted if it is carrying undesirable genes. Section 1(1)(d) requires that the physician decide that there is a 'substantial' risk that the physical or mental abnormalities are such that the child, if born, would be 'seriously' handicapped. Of course, termination on the grounds of fetal abnormality might additionally be justified under s 1(1)(a), that the woman is so worried about continuing the pregnancy that it seriously affects her mental or physical health, but that is not the point with which I am immediately concerned. I am interested to know what sufficiency is required for a termination under s 1(1)(d) alone.[17]

The question arises, what standard is to be applied when deciding on the degree of 'serious handicap'? One immediate analogy which could be drawn upon is provided by the neonate. In a number of cases, the Court of Appeal has had to consider in what, if any, circumstances a severely handicapped infant might be allowed to die. Presently, the two most useful are *Re C*[18] and *Re B*.[19] In *Re C*, a baby born with an unusually severe form of hydrocephalus and with a poorly formed brain structure was allowed to die. She was physically handicapped, including generalised spastic cerebral palsy of all limbs, probable blindness and deafness and an inability to absorb food. In the first judgment of its kind, the High Court acknowledged *and condoned* the paediatric practice of managing some neonates towards their death rather than striving with heroic interventions to save or treat at all costs. The review by the Court of Appeal decided that the criteria against which a non-treatment

---

16 [1990] Crim LR 687.

17 The *[Lane] Committee Report on the Working of the Abortion Act 1967*, Cmnd 5579, 1974, London: HMSO observed that 'the decision to be made as to an abortion under [s 1(1)(d)] by the mother and father and the medical advisers may be among the most difficult under the Act, for example where it is known that there is a risk but that it is not of a high order. We do not think that it would be appropriate to try to define this statutory ground more precisely and we make no recommendation with regard to the wording of the section' (para 211).

18 [1989] 2 All ER 782.

19 [1981] 1 WLR 1421.

decision may be taken is a legal question for determination by the courts, the actual taking of that decision is one for the parents and the medical team dealing with a particular case.

Re C fleshed out the skeletal approach which the Court of Appeal had said should be brought to these cases in its earlier judgment in *Re B*. There, the court had established that these cases could only proceed under a 'best interests' (in that case, of the ward) test and, secondly, only in a case where the prognosis established that the child's future life was going to be 'demonstrably ... so awful' and where there was no lingering doubt that a non-treatment order would be appropriate. This would include cases of severe proved damage, where the future was so uncertain that the court would be driven to conclude that non-treatment was appropriate. Such cases would not, however, arise, where the prognosis or information about the damage was 'still so imponderable' that it would be wrong for the baby to be allowed to die. In *Re C*, Ward J at first instance, in a part of his judgment which does not appear to have been questioned by the Court of Appeal, identified two criteria, relational and physiological, which will ensure that non-treatment orders will be narrowly drawn. He said that the ward had suffered 'severe and irreparable damage' and that she was 'permanently unable to interact mentally, socially and physically'. Tying these standards to the extensively rehearsed facts of the case gives an indication of the sort of case in which the courts are going to hold non-treatment to be appropriate and acceptable *in the child's own best interests*.

There are two points here which need clarification. First, in drawing this analogy between the 'treat to die' cases and the fetal ground of s 1(1)(d), I am not suggesting that all fetuses necessarily demand the same protection as all children and adults, a point I have elaborated on other occasions.[20] Although *Re B* and *Re C* were both concerned with babies in their early months, nothing in those decisions straightforwardly suggests that they are applicable only to newborns. However, sound arguments could be adduced to support a position which placed fetuses and neonates in a band of protection which differed from that accorded to older children and adults. Secondly, in addition to the unarticulated limits of these cases is the court's failure to acknowledge that neonates are regularly 'not-treated' in neonatal units on broader criteria than those approved and applied in the cases.[21] If it is accepted that neonates may attract different protection from that afforded to older children and adults, it may be argued (it does not follow, of course) that there should be

---

20 See Morgan, D, 'Judges on delivery' (1988) JSWFL 197 and, in an extended form, 'Judges on delivery: change, continuity and challenge in obstetric regulation', in Chard, T and Richards, M (eds), *Obstetrics in the 1990s: Current Controversies*, 1992, Oxford: MacKeith, pp 24–42.

21 I have reviewed the supporting data for this assertion and the arguments to which they give rise with Wells, C, in 'Medicine, morals, money and the newborn' (1989) J Social Welfare Law 57–62.

some consistency between the interpretation given to s 1(1)(d), paediatric practices and the judicial criteria for non-treatment.

The point of this excursus is simple, but important. In considering what serious handicaps qualify under s 1(1)(d), it is at least arguable that it covers *only* those where it can be shown that the child's life will be so demonstrably awful that it will be in the *child's interests for it to be aborted while a fetus*. This would follow if one accorded to the fetus a status similar to, or comparable with, the neonate, or the severely handicapped neonate. If those states are not to be equated, grounds for differentiation need to be adduced. Of course, if we eschew the notion of a metaphysical frontier, there is the possibility that, say, abortion and non-treatment should be treated differently, perhaps because the reasons supporting them are of different weight, in just the same way that, say, abortion and embryo research may be treated differently.[22] Glanville Williams has suggested that the fetal ground for abortion relates to the welfare of the parents, whose lives may be 'blighted by having to rear a grossly defective child', and 'perhaps secondly by consideration for the public purse'.[23] His supporting reasoning is questionable. Morally, as Williams points out, this seems to involve the commitment that the fetus is not the same as a child, for the killing of children because of their handicap is not permitted. But, as I have shown, such killing is indeed condoned, *where it can be shown to be in their own best interests*. This qualification is not observed by Williams.

It is clear from *Re B* and *Re C* that 'treating for dying' is justified as being in the child's best interests. That is not what Williams has suggested is contemplated under the Abortion Act. He has argued that the welfare to be considered is that of the parents. If this is correct, and that is not conceded, my argument is this. If the ground on which a child can be relieved of the burden of life in its own interests is narrowly drawn, as it is under *Re C* and *Re B*, it is arguable that the necessary conditions to be satisfied for relieving *others* under the 'fetal abnormality' grounds of the Abortion Act should be comparable. It is arguable that they ought, at the very least, to be no more widely drawn; arguable that they should be drawn in the same place, and even arguable that they should be drawn more narrowly than criteria which are to be applied in deciding on treatment for the *child's own interests*.

However, many of those who argue that handicapped neonates can properly be allowed to die (and, as I argue above, the same argument could apply *a fortiori* to fetuses) do so on grounds which *combine* the interests of the neonate and her family. If this were not so, and the only interests which fell to

---

22 See Glover, J et al, *Fertility and the Family: The Glover Report on Reproductive Technologies to the European Commission*, 1989, London: Fourth Estate, p 101.

23 Williams, G, *Textbook of Criminal Law*, 2nd edn, 1983, London: Stevens, p 297.

be considered were those of the fetus or neonate, it might be difficult to resist an argument for the compellability of an abortion *against a pregnant woman's wishes*, which most people would find objectionable. This is discussed below. Furthermore, Williams' contention that a relatively low risk of a relatively severe handicap would justify termination under s 1(1)(d)[24] cannot be sustained. In all cases, the ground is clear: it has to be shown not merely that there is a chance or even a risk of the fetus developing into a child which would suffer from such physical or mental abnormalities as to be seriously handicapped, but that there is a *substantial* risk (that is, much greater than 50% risk) that this will be the case.

It follows from this that the *lawfulness* of a termination on the grounds of, say, carrying an X-linked disease is not straightforward, and cannot be justified on s 1(1)(d) grounds *alone* merely on the basis of its existence. This legal question is, of course, itself independent from the ethical dilemmas to which genetic screening and prenatal diagnosis give rise. Two types of ethical dilemma might be identified: I will call them the internal ethical dilemma and the external ethical dilemma.

The internal ethical dilemma

One 'internal' dilemma I take to be generated by such practices as that which the RCP Report rebuked. It is axiomatic that it cannot be acceptable, for example, that women should be harried towards decisions on the grounds of cost, convenience or conscience of the doctor. The RCP Report recognises this when, in its review of ethical aspects of the practices considered, it states that women must have the right to refuse testing,[25] that couples should never be pressed to terminate an affected pregnancy and that a doctor opposed to abortion may not deprive a pregnant woman of access to prenatal diagnosis.

Secondly, it is a difficult question of whether, once the information about genetic make-up is available, there is a moral or legal duty to use that information, and to whom it should be circulated. Similarly, once genetic screening techniques are available, there may arise liability in negligence on behalf of either a counsellor or doctor for either a failure to alert a patient to this, or for carrying out a screening procedure in such a negligent fashion that it fails to disclose the presence of an affected fetus. Interestingly, the White Paper *Human Fertilisation and Embryology: A Framework for Legislation* did not address the questions of prenatal screening and diagnosis directly. It described the genetic manipulation of the embryo to allow the creation of human beings with certain predetermined characteristics as one which 'society would clearly regard as ethically unacceptable'[26] and s 3 of the Human Fertilisation and Embryology Act 1990 attempted to prohibit this. Beyond that, however, the

24 *Op cit*, Williams, fn 23, p 298.
25 *Op cit*, RCP, fn 4, para 8.5.
26 See Cm 259, 1987, para 37.

concerns of the White Paper and the 1990 Act are concerned more with questions related to assisted conception and research than with the central matters of this chapter. It may be that the framework established within that specific context of assisted reproduction will form the blueprint for legislative consideration of genetic disease screening more generally, and in 2000 the HFEA did issue a consultation paper on pre-implantation genetic diagnosis.

A third type of internal question addresses the *scope* of research on genetic disorders. Here, controversy focuses on disorders which may also have an environmental impact, such as coronary heart disease, diabetes, some malignancies, manic depressive disorders and schizophrenia. The arguments concern whether these are environmentally or socially caused or created, that genetic mapping has nothing to offer here whatsoever and that, if there are environmental causes or contributory causes, these should be examined or avoided before prenatal diagnosis is introduced. There is also what the RCP Report calls the 'borderline situation', such as the carrier state for familial hypercholesterolaemia or the emphysema-producing form of alpha-1 antitrypsin deficiency or a strong disposition to diabetes, where the 'possibilities for accurate prediction of risk for multifactorial diseases will increase'. They conclude that 'ultimately the attitudes, experience, and wishes of parents and society at large will determine their application for prenatal diagnosis'.[27]

The external ethical dilemma

This is a useful introduction to the wider 'external' issues which are at stake here. They resolve, essentially, into the familiar 'If it can be done, should it be done?' question. Again, there is no ethical consensus. The 'external' question addresses the charge made by opponents of some or all such testing, that it represents a quest for the 'perfect baby', often translated into the popular imagery of the doctors 'playing God'. This now merits attention. The core of the ethical dilemma revolves around, first, whether fetuses and embryos are entitled to the same protection and treatment as other people, such that the appropriate standards to be applied to their care are those equivalent to those established in *Re B* and *Re C*. Secondly, the question follows, if fetuses, embryos and other human beings are not fully comparable, whether it still amounts to discrimination against handicapped people genetically to engineer the embryo or abort the handicapped fetus.

For some people, the argument that fetuses should be aborted on any grounds is morally unthinkable. Others hold that abortion on any grounds is permissible at the request of the pregnant woman. Others hold that the

---

27 *Op cit*, RCP, fn 4, para 3.12.

interests of the State, whether in the genetic pool, or in the demands made on the Treasury by handicapped people, entail the compulsory screening for genetic disease and handicap and the enforced sterilisation of affected individuals in order to ensure that they do not procreate. My task in this section will be to try and discover on what principle the goal of prenatal genetic screening and diagnosis can justify the abortion of genetically damaged fetuses and the non-treatment of severely handicapped neonates and yet be defended against the charge that this discriminates against the handicapped.

One possibility is to consider the fetal interests argument. Here, we are drawn to a distinction made by Ramsey between abortion and fetal euthanasia.[28] The right to live an intolerable and painful existence or to choose to die is one which should be accorded to a fetus as much as to a neonate or to an adult. It follows from this, as Mason has pointed out, that the claim for wrongful life, denied in *McKay*,[29] should be available to the child wrongly forced to live, as much as to its parents, wrongly forced to care for the child.[30] This much is straightforward. The enormous difficulty to which this fetal interests argument gives rise is the increasing recognition of the fetus as a legal person independent of its mother. The dangers of doing this are rehearsed elsewhere,[31] and I believe that this conclusion should be avoided.

The fundamental issue at stake in this external argument is whether therapeutic abortion on the grounds of fetal handicap or abnormality discriminates in an objectionable way against handicapped people generally, and whether it enforces a view about 'acceptable' babies and people. The 'therapy' applied in these cases eliminates the disorder by eliminating the patient. But to deny, as we rightly should, that a handicapped person *necessarily* will have a less fulfilled life, does not mean that we are committed to the view which adduces no grounds for preferring the birth of a normal child to a handicapped one. As Glover has pointed out,[32] if we conceive of a case in which we deliberately cause a child to be born handicapped, most would consider this a 'monstrous' thing to do, although we must be careful, even in these circumstances, that we identify 'handicap' appropriately. For example, do two deaf parents who do not consider their deafness a handicap and who ask for the *deliberate* manipulation of an embryo to ensure that they have a deaf child behave 'monstrously'?

---

28 See his 'Reference points in deciding about abortion', in Noonan, JT (ed), *The Morality of Abortion*, 1970, Cambridge, Mass: Harvard UP.

29 *McKay v Essex AHA* [1982] QB 1166.

30 See Mason, K, 'Abortion and the law', in McLean, S, *Legal Issues in Human Reproduction*, 1988, Aldershot: Ashgate, p 73.

31 See the literature cited in *op cit*, Morgan, fn 20.

32 *Op cit*, Glover, fn 22, p 128.

None of this commits us to saying that handicapped children or adults are less worthy of respect or love or care or to saying that we may rightly choose to produce a child who is not handicapped rather than one who is. And, as Ruth Chadwick has noted, the important boundary is not that between the handicapped and the healthy, but between fetuses and adults. It is not the case that only handicapped fetuses are aborted, for healthy fetuses are similarly if they constitute a threat to the health or welfare of the mother. 'The thinking behind eugenic abortion is not necessarily that genetically handicapped people are less valuable in some overall sense than others. The idea may be that fetuses are not yet people and we are still in some sense deciding what sort of child to have.'[33]

It seems to be the case that, all things being equal, we do indeed have a preference for being born without a handicap than with a handicap. If it makes sense for people to see death as being in their interests, there is a parallel possibility of parents or doctors thinking that not being born at all may be in the interests of a potential child. One difficulty with this analysis, of course, is that the grounds for so thinking may vary, from those which are very narrowly drawn, for example, serious genetic disease or handicap, to those which are very widely drawn, such as parental unfitness (howsoever defined) to raise and care for the child.

Glover provides what is, in my view, a promising way forward. The difficulty, he adduces, in identifying what harm a handicapped person has suffered by being born with a handicap rather than not at all misses a vital component:

> ... reproductive ethics seems to be a field in which there are 'impersonal' harms and benefits. Harm can be done without there being identifiable people who are worse off than *they* otherwise would have been. In explaining why it is better to avert the conception of someone with a severe medical condition, we can use the idea of impersonal harms, without having to resort to metaphysical claims about benefits to a particular non-existent person.[34]

To be sure, this does not answer all the questions, for it requires us then to decide what sorts of handicap and disability are sufficiently grave to justify entertaining the notion that it is preferable for no person to be born at all than a person with this given handicap. In these circumstances, it seems to me, it is part of what being a parent *is* that this decision should be left to the individuals concerned, with the advice and support of their doctors and nurses, to make such a personal, individual reproductive decision.

The more distant issues concern forms of genetic engineering that can produce particular genetic features for individuals. The European Parliament has argued that there is a right 'to genetic inheritance which has not been

---

33 See her *Ethics, Reproduction and Genetic Control*, 1987, London: Routledge, p 111.
34 *Op cit*, Glover, fn 22, p 132.

artificially interfered with, except for therapeutic purposes'.[35] Again, as Glover has convincingly argued, those whose genes had been altered to make them more intelligent or attractive might not feel that a right which they had had been interfered with, or indeed if it had, that they had been deleteriously interfered with: 'there is a suspicion that the 'right' has been plucked out of the air to settle a difficult issue at great speed.'[36] The vast ethical questions raised by positive genetic engineering are outwith the general scope of this paper.[37] The problems of technological risk, governmental control and the potential for abuse, the frequent selection of certain characteristics and the potential for discrimination against those not so selected, the difficulties of deciding who should make decisions of positive genetic engineering, are for many of sufficient weight to ensure the ethical dubiety of such engineering, whatever its potential benefits. As Bernard Williams has pointed out, there are deep questions of personal identity involved with genetic engineering, especially where its use is contemplated in the State-directed eugenic sense: '... we might well wonder *who were* the people.'[38] We may well have learned enough in the last 150 years to believe that positive genetic engineering is too fraught with difficulties and danger presently to be contemplated.

FETAL SEX IDENTIFICATION, ABORTION AND THE LAW

Reproductive technologies have forced many difficult and pressing questions on to the social and legal agendas. One of the most contested is the use of different techniques for the purposes of sex selection or sex predetermination of intended children. Media reports over the past years have highlighted the existence of a number of controversial practices; in this part of the paper, I want to concentrate on the use of sex determination for the purpose of selective abortion of female fetuses.

How prevalent is sex selection?

One estimate has suggested that up to 100 abortions each year are performed in the UK on the ground of fetal sex alone, but the figure is very difficult to verify. What can be confidently stated is that the practice is much more widespread, particularly among Indian and Asian communities, than has been

---

35 Council of Europe Recommendation 934, 1982, Strasbourg: COE.

36 *Op cit*, Glover, fn 22, p 139.

37 But, they are covered with characteristic panache by John Harris in his book *Wonderwoman and Superman: The Ethics of Human Biotechnology*, 1992, Oxford: OUP.

38 In his *Problems of the Self*, 1973, Cambridge: CUP, p 246. For further discussion of these issues, see *op cit*, Glover, fn 22, pp 137–40; *op cit*, Chadwick, fn 33, pp 119–27; and Yoxen, E, *Unnatural Selection? Coming to Terms with the New Genetics*, 1986, London: Heinemann.

thought or acknowledged, and that if the abortion cannot be achieved in this country, women fly to India, on a prearranged package, for the abortion. In an article called 'The mania for sons', Ramanamma and Bambawale published their investigation of two hospitals in India where, in the late 1970s, amniocentesis had been used for the selective abortion of female fetuses. Of 400 women consulting one hospital in 1976–77, 92 were prepared to indicate that their reason for wanting to know the sex of the fetus was for the purposes of termination if it were female. At the other hospital, of 700 women attending the hospital in one year, 450 were told they were carrying a female fetus, of which 430 aborted.[39] Traditionally, the Chinese have believed that only a son can worship ancestors and continue a family line. Evidence offered by *The Washington Post* in 1985 suggested that 300,000 cases of infanticide occurred in 1982 and 345,000 in 1983. In 1983, the *People's Daily* reported that 'At present the phenomenon of butchering, drowning and leaving female babies to die is very serious'. In one report, Mirsky suggested that the registration of birth figures disclosed that up to 20% of female infants were being killed.[40] Similarly, Colin Thubron's reportage of his Chinese journey records accounts of female infanticide:

> [Being sold off as a young bride] was better than being killed in infancy. I heard of them being killed in other villages. It was quite common. The peasants would just drop them into the water and drown them ... You see, they don't think. They just drop it in. They just say 'It's a girl! It's worthless!' Girls are not *descendants*, you understand. They're not viewed that way. It's boys who continue our line.[41]

> It's wrong to limit babies. I've heard about these one-child families in the towns, and the children growing up to be little emperors. Spoilt. And what do you do if you only have a girl? Confucius said your first duty was to give your parents heirs – to carry on the name. It's terrible to have no son. People die out that way ... I said: 'So what happens to the girl babies?' But I knew, of course, what sometimes happens. The custom of killing them is inveterate. In the last century missionaries often came upon baby girls, sometimes still alive, pitched over town ramparts to the rubbish and pariah dogs below. The man said: 'Occasionally girl babies are abandoned on the town streets, and people adopt them. There's no penalty attached to adopting. But out here everyone wants sons. Girls can't do the same heavy work ... So, sometimes, secretly, the girl babies are drowned.'[42]

Abortions on such grounds as fetal sex are said to be in direct conflict with advice tendered in a Department of Health and Social Security letter of 17 December 1985, that such abortions in the UK would not be protected by the terms of s 1 of the Abortion Act 1967. That letter, sent to all proprietors of

---

39 'The mania for sons' (1980) 14 Social Science and Medicine 107.
40 Quoted in Trombley, S, *The Right to Reproduce: A History of Coercive Sterilisation*, 1988, London: Weidenfeld & Nicolson, p 233.
41 Thubron, C, *Behind the Wall*, 1988, Harmondsworth: Penguin, p 25.
42 *Ibid*, p 276.

nursing homes registered under the Act, was prompted by allegations made in a London Weekend Television programme earlier that year, taken up by *The Daily Mail*.[43] In May 1989, *The Sunday Times* carried an article purporting to disclose further abuses of the Act,[44] and the US-based weekly, *Time*, highlighted the prevalence of sex preselection as a gathering alternative to female infanticide in India, China and South East Asia, where, in all but the most remote provinces, infanticide has been curbed.[45]

The mania for sons

Son-preference has roots implanted as firmly in Western as in other cultures. The surviving extent of son-preference in Western societies helps to explain the importance of the issues being addressed here. Many surveys have concluded that women express more disappointment about having daughters than sons, when this information is acquired *at birth*. In 1954, Dinitz, Dynes and Clark reported that 62% of the males surveyed and 58% of the females expressed a preference for a firstborn son, with the respective percentages increasing to 92% and 66% if the question related to the sex of an only-born child. Only 4% expressed a desire for a firstborn daughter. By 1971, a similar survey revealed male/female preferences of 80% and 79% for a firstborn son and 12% for a daughter, and in 1984, a survey response of 62% expressed a preference for a son compared with 6% for a daughter.[46]

Research reported in 1983, since the more public advent of reproductive technologies, has tended to reinforce these earlier findings. Respondents were asked whether, if the technology were available, they would avail themselves of sex predetermination techniques. Of those replying 'yes', 81% of the women and 94% of the men preferred firstborn sons. It is instructive to compare these preferences with those disclosed by women who are themselves pregnant. In 1971 an American survey (a 46% son preference, a 32% daughter preference and a 22% no preference) discovered no statistical difference amongst 81 women pregnant for the first time. Similarly, a British study in 1978 conducted by Ann Oakley revealed figures of 54%, 22% and 25% among pregnant women and a further study in 1984 has recorded figures of 25%, 7% and 48%, respectively. In 1983, one study for the first time demonstrated a preference for firstborn girls. Surveying 140 women pregnant for the first time, and in the

---

43 (1985) 25 June.

44 Mahmood, M and Penrose, B, 'Doctor tells family to lie to gain an abortion' (1989) *The Sunday Times*, 11 May, p 3.

45 (1988) *Time*, 4 January, p 46.

46 See Steinbacher, R and Holmes, HB, 'Prenatal and preconception sex choice technologies', in Corea, G *et al* (eds), *Man Made Woman*, 1985, London: Hutchinson, pp 52–57. See, also, Katz Rothman, B, *The Tentative Pregnancy: Prenatal Diagnosis and the Future of Motherhood*, 1988, London: Pandora, pp 133–43.

last three months of their pregnancies, it suggested that, of those expressing a preference for the sex of their baby, 57% would choose to have a firstborn girl. Three hypotheses to explain this finding are suggested:

(a) that American society is becoming less biased, and that male and female infants are equally highly valued;

(b) that women actually have an underlying preference for girls, and that the research has managed to detect this;

(c) that expectant mothers in the 1980s, aware of the cultural thrust towards equality, are reluctant to make inappropriate looking choices and express sexual stereotypes in their questionnaire responses.[47]

The tenor of these findings is reflected in an independent study by Barbara Katz Rothman. Of 50 women learning the sex of their babies following amniocentesis, 10 expressed disappointment. All were carrying males. Rothman's conclusion, having adjusted for factors which might have influenced these women's desires, was that:

> It's one thing to have given birth to a son. It's another to be told that the fetus growing inside your body is male ... To have a male growing in a female body is to contain your own antithesis. It makes of the fetus not a continuation and extension of self, but an 'other'.[48]

These differing research findings suggest, then, that we must approach with caution presenting reasons for abortion following the identification of fetal sex. Whose reasons for wanting the abortion are we really considering, and what factors should and may lawfully be taken into account?

What is the ambit of the Abortion Act 1967?

Recall that the operative section of the present Abortion Act in England and Wales, s 1, provides that no abortion offence is committed when a pregnancy is terminated by a registered medical practitioner if two such doctors in good faith form the opinion that:

> (a) ... the pregnancy has not exceeded its 24th week and that continuance of the pregnancy would involve risk, greater than if the pregnancy were continued, to the life of the pregnant woman, or of injury to the physical or mental health of the pregnant woman or any existing children of her family.

In assessing the risk to which s 1(1)(a) refers, s 1(2) provides that 'account may be taken of the pregnant woman's actual or reasonably foreseeable environment'. I want to suggest here that those provisions quite clearly can be used to demonstrate the *legality* of abortion following the identification of fetal sex. In so doing, it needs to be clarified that I am not presently concerned with

---

47 *Op cit*, Steinbacher and Holmes, fn 46.
48 *Op cit*, **Katz** Rothman, fn 46, p 150.

abortions performed following the disclosure of a mental or physical fetal abnormality such that there is a substantial risk that the fetus will be born seriously handicapped, as additionally provided for in s 1(1)(d), which I discussed above.

Three separate factors persuade me of this view. First, the Act, as drafted, allows for termination if it can be shown that the risk to the pregnant woman's health is greater if the pregnancy is allowed to continue compared with the risks attendant on termination. As abortion technology has become more and more sophisticated, the risks associated with its use have fallen, to the point where the risks of serious injury to, or death of, the pregnant woman are lower in almost all abortions, but particularly early abortions, than the risk of death in childbirth.[49] The comparative risk balance of s 1(1)(a) now offers more protection to the pregnant woman.

The second reason relates to the risk of 'injury to the physical or mental health of the pregnant woman taking account of [her] actual or reasonably foreseeable environment'. The Act does not suggest that the source of the risks to the pregnant woman's mental or physical health must be the pregnancy itself. It is sufficient that the continuance of the pregnancy is more likely to expose her to those risks than its termination. Indeed, it is widely accepted that s 1(2) permits a wider range of factors affecting the health of the woman to be taken into account than the pregnancy.[50] The fact that the termination will relieve those risks does not affect the legality of performing the operation for those reasons. The Act does not attempt to limit the source of the risks to which the woman might be exposed: '... it is really quite clear that the Act is intended to provide for the overburdened mother.'[51] The threat to her physical or mental well being by virtue of the fact of the hostility which the birth will occasion is demonstrably within the scope of the section.

Finally, the Act additionally provides that an abortion may be performed 'where the continuance of the pregnancy would involve risk ... of injury to the physical or mental health of ... any existing children of her family, greater than if the pregnancy were terminated'. In families where existing female children are already regarded as a financial, social and cultural burden, the addition of yet another female child might not only deleteriously affect the woman and the child she is then carrying, but also those existing children. Each successive child may become a greater burden on the family's purse, prestige and power. Termination in such circumstances may, at least, be arguable to safeguard the physical and mental health of the woman's present children; this might be thought the arguable ground.

---

49 *Op cit*, Williams, fn 23, p 299; Mason, JK and McCall Smith, A, *Law and Medical Ethics*, 5th edn, 1999, London: Butterworths, Chapter 5.

50 *Ibid*, p 301.

51 *Ibid*.

I have been concerned in this section not with the ethics of abortion on the grounds of fetal sex, but with its legality. Contrary to the advice tendered to the Department of Health and Social Security in 1985 and circulated to registered abortion clinics, I have suggested that the abortion of a healthy fetus on the grounds of its sex alone is permissible under the Abortion Act 1967.

REPRODUCTIVE ETHICS: THE SEARCH FOR THE PERFECT SOCIETY?

When the Warnock Committee presented its report in 1984, they evidenced a number of potential uses to which the existing and developing techniques of sex-selection might be put, and some of the consequences of such uses. Paralleled with the development of reliable and simple sex prediction tests which can be self-administered before fertilisation, they recommended that the 'whole question of the acceptability of sex selection should be kept under review'.[52] Warnock resiled from making any recommendations on the control of sex-selection techniques beyond this general overview, however, because 'of the difficulty of predicting the outcome of any such trend'.[53] They did feel dubious about their use on a wide scale, however, because of the negative image of women which use of the techniques would continue to promote; existing evidence which establishes the benefits which firstborn siblings enjoy over later children; and the unknown effects on the ratio of males to females.

What is wrong with gender selection? John Harris has argued that it could be used, along with methods of artificially inducing parthenogenesis, to produce an all-female society in which the inhabitants were all like their mothers, to the extent that genetic differences had not been engineered in.[54] But Harris is in the minority in thinking that this is how gender selection would, in fact, work. Edward Yoxen, reviewing some of the demographic data available, has concluded that if sex predetermination were practised on any scale in Western societies, the population ratio would not shift significantly, that there would be fewer families of all boys or all girls, but that fewer girls would be firstborn children.[55] Ruth Chadwick has surveyed different accounts of the effects of gender choice and the sex ratio, and the fears to which this has given rise. These range from the hypothetical Manland society of Joanna Russ through the apocalyptic vision of Roberta Steinbacher and

---

52 Cmnd 9341, para 9.11.

53 *Ibid.*

54 *The Value of Life: An Introduction to Medical Ethics*, 1985, London: Routledge and Kegan Paul, pp 166–73.

55 *Op cit*, Yoxen, fn 38, p 113.

Helen B Holmes. In the first, Chadwick identifies the self-defeating argument.[56] This proposes that if all women were eliminated from a future society, some men would be assigned female roles. The same point is made in Harris' preview of an all female society. On the other hand, Steinbacher and Holmes' fears are more immediate:

> However devalued, controlled, feared or exploited woman have been, their indispensability to the contribution of the human race has remained a stubborn fact ... now, for the first time in history, the power is at hand to negate that indispensability ... There is, to be blunt, the possibility of femicide.[57]

If my argument that abortion following the identification of fetal handicap does not *necessarily* entail or lead to discrimination against the 'handicapped' is correct, am I not led to the same conclusion in respect of gender grounds for abortion? There, I argued that sometimes, sex-selection has a medical justification and, although there is no consensus, can be defended. Do not the same arguments apply here? I think not. The point of that argument was that such abortion was justified where it could be shown to be in the interests of the fetus or its mother that it should be relieved of a life that would be a burden *above and beyond that which life imposes on all of us*. Gender selection *simpliciter* carries no such rationale. Although it might be said that abortion on the grounds of gender relieved the fetus of possible infanticide following its live birth, or that abortion relieved its mother of physical or psychological abuse for the production of a daughter, these reasons are qualitatively different from those adduced earlier. Indeed, the major objection to such femicide is that it legitimates desires and preferences that we might want to regard, at best, as objectionable, at worst as abhorrent. While such selection would extend the ambit of choice which parents have, we need to look carefully at the preferences involved. Gender is not a disease. There is, as the examples quoted illustrate, the danger that gender selection is used to reinforce attitudes of sex prejudice that we might want to work to undermine rather than satisfy. This does, indeed, entail a commitment to denying some parental choices. But we may be prepared to ask precisely what sorts of choice we are committed to if gender selection is one of them. What sort of people are we and what sort of people do we want to become?

At the very least, it may be said that gender selection violates a principle of equality between males and females and the psychological importance to parenting of an unconditional acceptance of a new child by its intended parents. Furthermore, gender selection may become a precedent for genetic manipulation which encourages parents to select other desired characteristics for their children. Of course, that then leaves us with the problem of how to control or limit, or, if we prefer, encourage gender selection. Yoxen has argued

---

56 *Op cit*, Chadwick, fn 33, p 128.
57 'Sex choice, survival and sisterhood', in *op cit*, Corea *et al*, fn 46, p 52.

that reproductive freedom entails a commitment to as great a range of unrestrained choices as possible. But, with gender selection, there is the fear of what 'the values of a possible society' might entail.[58] Nonetheless, he concludes that prohibition only encourages evasion and that, as a responsible society, we need to face the arguments and respond with argument, not with legislative restriction. Glover reaches the same conclusion: that the desires behind the choice of sex will often be ones society would do better to discourage and that 'our best hope is the erosion of attitudes which make sex choice seem so important'.[59]

How adequate are these responses? There is a final note which is appropriate to sound here. It, too, is committed to the search for the perfect society, but it differs from the sort of society in which fetal sex identification and selection is a necessary feature. Individuals living in a society often have little choice. This, indeed, lies at the root of fetal abortion on the grounds of sex alone. Rothman has put it thus: '... the question then becomes, not whether individual choices are constructed, but how they are constructed.'[60] While 'rights' of access to information, such as fetal sex and fetal health, may be necessary for a society in which reproductive choices can be made, they are not a sufficient guarantee that reproductive autonomy, let alone freedom, has been secured, nor that it will be exercised autonomously, let alone responsibly.

---

58 *Op cit*, Yoxen, fn 38, p 116.
59 *Op cit*, Glover, fn 22, p 144.
60 Rothman, BK, 'The meaning of choice in reproductive technology', in Arditti, R *et al* (eds), *Test Tube Women: What Future for Motherhood?*, 1984, London: Pandora, pp 32–33.

PART IV

ATTEMPTS AND FAILURES IN MEDICAL LAW: THE CASE OF GENETICS AND RISK SOCIETY

THE TROUBLED HELIX:
LEGAL ASPECTS OF THE NEW GENETICS

> Sorcerers are too common; cunning men, wizards, and white witches as they
> call them, in every village, which, if they be sought unto, will help almost all
> infirmities of body and mind.[1]

EPISTEMOLOGY, ETHICS AND GENETICS

Developments in genetics 'pose challenging questions for the application of
traditional legal principles'.[2] This much was recognised, for example, at the
Asilomar conference in 1975, where a group of molecular biologists
recommended a moratorium on genetic manipulation while arrangements
were made to regulate recombinant DNA techniques.[3] Without precedent, the
scientific research community was inviting regulation from the legislature for
its own activities. Indeed, writing in 1971, James Watson (the elucidator, with
Francis Crick, of the structure of DNA) had suggested, of the possible
developments in human reproductive research, that techniques for the
manipulation of human eggs *in vitro* were likely to be in general medical
practice, capable of routine performance in many major nations, within some
10 to 20 years, and that international agreement was a preferred method of
control. On some matters, there might even be 'a sufficient international
consensus ... to make possible some forms of international agreement before
the cat is totally out of the bag'.[4]

The particular difficulties that lawyers and ethicists will want to address
are the functional analogue of the difficulties that the genome project discloses
in general:

> Physically, printing the names of the three billion base pairs would require the
> number of pages in at least 13 sets of the Encyclopaedia Britannica, and this
> does not take into account the heterogeneity of human beings. The

---

1   Burton, R, 1621, cited in Thomas, K, *Religion and the Decline of Magic: Studies in Popular
    Beliefs in Sixteenth and Seventeenth-Century England*, 1973, Harmondsworth: Penguin.

2   Kennedy, I and Grubb, A, *Medical Law: Text with Materials*, 2nd edn, 1993, London:
    Butterworths.

3   Maddox, I, 'New genetics means no new ethics' (1993) 364 Nature 97.

4   Watson, JD, 'Potential consequences of experimenting with human eggs', paper
    presented at the 12th meeting of the Panel on Science and Technology, Committee on
    Science and Astronautics, US House of Representatives, Washington, 1991, cited in
    Gunning, J and English, V, *Human In Vitro Fertilization: A Case Study in Medical
    Innovation*, 1993, Aldershot: Dartmouth.

epistemological consequence of this huge amount of information is unforeseeable.[5]

As it is for society, so it is for individuals; the consequences of knowing so much about oneself, about others and about all humans are unforeseeable. One apparent danger is that, because genetic conditions are often regarded as immutable hereditary traits, 'overly deterministic interpretations of genetic information can readily distort genetic risk and become enshrined in institutional policies of social isolation and discrimination'.[6]

One of the difficulties in assessing the human genome project and the associated, but independent industry of genetic screening is that we are limited in our assessment because, as Bryan Wynne has written of a cognate area, we 'cannot in any significant sense assess the technology itself for its full "factual" impact' and thus 'we have to assess the *institutions* which appear to control the technology'.[7]

Nevertheless, it has been argued that the development of the human genome project itself raises no new ethical difficulties and perhaps few legal problems,[8] and that such problems as there are arise from the use and development of genetic testing and screening as a therapeutic opportunity rather than the mapping and sequencing of the genome.[9] Even here, John Maddox (the editor of *Nature*) has counselled caution in creating 'new' ethical dilemmas: '... the availability of gene sequences, and ultimately of the sequence of the whole genome, will not create ethical problems that are intrinsically novel, but will simply make it easier, cheaper and more certain to pursue certain well established objectives in the breeding of plants, animals and even people.' It might be objected that it is in this elision between plants, animals and people, in the apparent ease of the assumption that (however well established the fantasy of breeding people scientifically) we are dealing with nothing more than linear progressions of scientific vectors, that the real challenges lie. But Maddox's argument belies the transparency that he has himself claimed for it. He argues that, while the molecular causes of conditions such as sickle cell disease, various thalassaemia, Huntington's disease, fragile-X syndrome and cystic fibrosis have all been determined in the past few years, 'this new knowledge has not created novel ethical problems, only ethical simplifications'.

5   Rix, BA, 'Should ethical concerns regulate science? The European experience with the Human Genome Project' (1991) 5 Bioethics 250.

6   Jecker, N, 'Genetic testing and social responsibility of private health insurance companies' (1993) 21 J Law, Medicine and Ethics 109.

7   Wynne, B, 'Technology, risk and participation: on the social treatment of uncertainty', in Conrad, J (ed), *Society, Technology and Risk Assessment*, 1982, London: Academic.

8   *Report of the [Clothier] Committee on the Ethics of Gene Therapy*, Cm 1788, 1992, London: HMSO.

9   *Op cit*, Maddox, fn 3.

Eschewing such formulations, George Annas has suggested that the uniqueness of the human genome project is not its quest for knowledge. The history of science is filled with little else. What is unique, he claims, is an understanding at the outset that serious policy and ethical issues are raised by the research, and that pre-emptive steps ought to be taken to try to assure that 'the benefits of the project are maximized and the potential dark side is minimized'.[10] Annas has suggested that there are three levels of issues that the human genome project raises: (a) individual/family; (b) society; and (c) species. Most attention on genetics to date has been at the individual/family level, where questions of genetic screening and counselling predominate. Thus, negligence in failing to offer or to perform properly these tests has already resulted in lawsuits for wrongful birth and wrongful life,[11] and standards for genetic screening and counselling have indeed been discussed.[12]

Issues at the second level implicate society more directly. For Annas, the human genome project gives rise to three major societal issues: population screening; resource allocation and commercialisation; and eugenics. More specifically, he asks: '... to what uses should the fruits of the project be put in screening groups of people, such as applicants for the military, government workers, immigrants and others?'[13]

How, if at all, should intellectual property laws such as patents be invoked? What funding and resource allocation decisions are there to be made?[14]

The results of the EC human genome analysis may lead to enhanced possibilities in the prevention and treatment of disease, through new methods of genetic testing and screening. Access to genetic information may also improve the quality and efficiency of public authorities outwith health care; in particular, those in the fields of criminal justice, social security and public health and in immigration cases. Each of these areas raises discrete difficulties in terms of protection of individual privacy and integrity, and it may be here that the quantitative difficulties for law will arise.[15]

Third-level issues are more speculative, and involve how 'a genetic view of ourselves could change the way in which we think about ourselves'.[16] And, importantly, others: it may affect the way in which we come to view

10 Annas, G, *Standard of Care*, 1993, New York: OUP, pp 149–50.
11 See *Allen v Bloomsbury HA* [1993] 1 All ER 651.
12 Chadwick, R and Ngwena, C, 'The development of a normative standard in counselling for genetic disease: ethics and law' (1992) JSWFL 276.
13 *Ibid*, Annas.
14 McLean, S and Giesen, D, 'Legal and ethical considerations of the Human Genome Project' (1994) 1 Med Law International 159.
15 Nielsen, L and Nespor, S, *Genetic Test Screening and Use of Genetic Data by Public Authorities in Criminal Justice, Social Security and Alien and Foreigner Acts*, 1993, Copenhagen: Danish Centre of Human Rights.
16 *Ibid*, Annas.

relatedness, otherness and difference. Marilyn Strathern and her colleagues have, in a cognate area, argued that the deployment of reproductive technologies is affecting assumptions we bring to understandings not only of family life, but to the very understanding of family itself and cultural practice:[17] 'The way in which the choices that assisted conception affords are formulated, will affect thinking about kinship. And the way people think about kinship will affect other ideas about relatedness between human beings.'[18] And, I would add, the way in which we think about relatedness between human beings will affect the way in which we think about the relationship between individuals, groups and the State.[19]

Let me test quickly the hypothesis that underlies my thesis by returning briefly to Maddox's argument. Discussing the possibility that a gene for schizophrenia may confer advantages not yet recognised on those in whom the overt disease does not manifest, he suggests that not only will it be a long time before the genetics of psychiatric conditions is understood, but, more importantly, 'geneticists themselves are likely to be the first to recognize the dangers of interfering with the natural flow of genes within a population before the social implications are understood'.[20] Thus, he appears to be suggesting an essentially biological or genetic subset of dangers that are divorced, or separate, from the social implications of what may transpire. To this, I want to take exception. Secondly, he avers that 'only geneticists can recognize the dangers'. Herein, it seems to me, lie the seeds of the first new, or radically transformed, ethical dilemma: not simply asserting a professionally proprietorial attitude to knowledge (which would not be new), but additionally to *understanding and application*. This, taken with changes within ethical debate itself, has radical potential.

I want to focus now on three specific manifestations of the 'new' genetics: (a) the regulation of the use of information derived from genetic testing, taking merely as an example the use by the insurance market; (b) questions raised by information derived from an individual's genetic make-up, including in this context consent, especially where children are concerned; (c) the particular application of that knowledge in the context of abortion based on fetal anomalies.

---

17 Foucault, M, *The Order of Things*, 1970, London: Tavistock; Thomas, K, *Man and the Natural World*, 1983, Harmondsworth: Penguin; Strathern, M *et al*, *Reproducing the Future: Anthropology, Kinship and the New Reproductive Technologies*, 1993, Manchester: Manchester UP.

18 *Ibid*, Strathern *et al*.

19 Beck, U, *Risk Society: Towards a New Modernity*, Ritter, M (trans), 1992, London: Sage.

20 *Op cit*, Maddox, fn 3.

GENETIC INFORMATION AND PRIVACY

> The use of information about genetic variability in relation to life insurance, health or social security raises fundamental questions of discrimination against those with genetic risks and of confidentiality of personal health information. These issues need urgent attention.[21]

Genetic privacy, what Erving Goffman once identified as 'the right to reticence',[22] is essential, if we are to avoid creating a zone in which privacy is earned 'only by having nothing to hide'. We live increasingly in the surveillance society and the global village – panoptic planetary people – in which we are watched over in the bank, the store, the petrol station, the telephone booth; day and night surveillance is facilitated by the possibilities of chip technology. The video camera that can control and entertain our children can imprison and impoverish them; information about our movements, our tastes, pleasures and purchases can be transmitted almost instantaneously from one side of the globe to the other.

Genetic knowledge is a form of information technology, and as such it poses three types of disquiet: (a) in facilitating intrusions on personal privacy; (b) in providing the means for institutions to exercise particular forms of control; and (c) in encouraging practices that threaten certain values. Allied with the biotechnological imperative, which has come to replace nuclear power as the symbol of 'technology out of control', information technologies can directly affect particular economic interests; they may be a source of risk, and for some, they are a moral threat. Indeed, Dorothy Nelkin has suggested that biotechnology raises many of the same problems as nuclear power; the hazards are invisible and there remains uncertainty about the health effects of low level, long term exposure. Like nuclear power, biotechnology evokes images of warfare and fantasies of monsters and mutations, demons and chimeras.[23] The challenge that recent developments in genetic science presents is to obtain all the benefits of the knowledge while minimising or eliminating the risk.

The question of genetic information about one person, which may identify or suggest a genetic disorder or trait in another, poses a particular dilemma in the physician-patient relationship. MAM de Watcher has suggested that:

> Genetic medicine ... is greatly expanding ... views [of privacy and bodily integrity] into a wider concept of corporate ownership of familial and ethnic autonomy. It now seems that the totality of a person's physical existence exceeds the limits of a single person's body. Some already say that genetic

---

21 European Commission, Working Group on the Ethical Social and Legal Aspects of Human Genome Analysis (WG-ELSA), *Final Report*, 1992, Brussels.

22 Goffman, E, *Stigma: Notes on the Management of Spoiled Identity*, 1964, Harmondsworth: Penguin.

23 Nelkin, D, 'Against the tide of technology' (1993) The Higher, 13 August.

information is the common property of the family as 'corporate personality'. Are we then entering a new era of medicine ... an era where information is governed not only by rules of individual confidentiality but also by duties of common solidarity?[24]

Four particular pitfalls are evident: mere biological links may be insufficient to promote the intrusion into the psychosocial components of privacy; it is difficult to draw the line between information relevant to genetic counselling and that which is not; as more diseases appear to contain hereditary components, possible compromises of confidentiality appear unlimited; removing all control of data from people who are screened may be counterproductive and dissuade them from entering family screening programmes. As genetic tests become simpler to administer and their use expands, a growing number of individuals may be 'labelled' on the basis of predictive genetic information. The use of predictive genetic diagnoses creates a new category of individuals who are not ill, but have reason to suspect they may develop a specific disease sometime in the future: 'the healthy ill'.[25] The loss of autonomy and privacy, which fears of genetic testing have foreshadowed, can be 'the genesis of a life-long psychological prison – the prison of one's perceived genetic "programming"'.[26]

Crude genetic screening has been used for many years by taking into account family history, such that the current health state of an individual is thought to be a useful (if not completely reliable) indicator of that individual's life expectancy and the extent to which he or she is likely to consume health and other resources in the future. Whereas, in the past, one might have said that an individual's state of health was a combination or amalgam of heredity, environment, behaviour and luck, one of the radical changes that genetic testing introduces is the question of responsibility for health. Over 4,000 Mendelian inherited disorders have been identified: some determined wholly by single gene mutations and inheritances; some causing disease before birth, or shortly after, others observed only in adulthood. Understanding of polygenic conditions (those determined by sets of genes) and predispositions to diseases (where disease onset is determined by a combination of genetic and environmental factors) is growing. Mapping the genome may increase the scientific and medical ability to predict, understand and eventually to prevent or to cure human diseases. This also gives rise to questions as to how this information should be used, and the necessary background laws and norms that will either be applied or will become more clearly perceived to direct and control, to regulate the use of this information, either by individuals or by

---

24 Bankowski, Z and Bryant, J, *Health Policy: Ethics and Human Values: European and North American Perspectives*, 1989, Geneva: CIOMS.

25 *Ibid*.

26 Privacy Commissioner of Canada, *Genetic Testing and Privacy*, 1992, Ottawa: Ministry of Supply and Services, p 30.

societies generally. With the advances in the scope and reliability of genetic testing, information relating to an individual's genetic predisposition will be of considerable use to a potential insurer in that such information is indicative of the risk to the insurer that that individual represents. More than that, the influence that this knowledge, directly and indirectly, could exert over lifestyle and life choices is manifest and major. The knowledge that a woman is at risk of giving birth to a genetically damaged child may ensure that she is unable to obtain insurance cover for the child and hence lead to tacit pressure to have an abortion.

In the European Community Programme for 'Predictive Medicine',[27] it was acknowledged that, for a large number of common Western diseases, such as cancer, coronary heart disease, diabetes, autoimmune diseases and major psychoses, there is a strong environmental component. Given that we are unlikely to be able to remove those environmental factors entirely, the development of information about genetically determined predisposing factors is critical if we are to be able to identify high risk individuals. The controversial nature of some of the genome research is evident in the reworking of the European 'Predictive Medicine' project: the initial aim of going directly from the discovery of genetic abnormalities to the use of prenatal diagnosis and abortion to prevent their inheritance has been dropped from the programme, although it remains as a clear, if controversial, backdrop to its development and implementation.

One response in the European Parliament has been to urge that the requirement to submit to genetic screening as a condition for obtaining insurance should be prohibited. In an amendment to the Pompidou Report from the Energy, Research and Technology Committee[28] (which had recommended that disclosure of genetic information should be strictly regulated), it has been proposed that 'insurers should not have the right to require genetic testing or to inquire about the results of previously performed tests as a precondition for the conclusion or modification of an insurance contract'. The prohibition on inquiring about previous tests could have a dramatic effect on the insurance industry, described by Brett and Fischer[29] as 'dangerous'.

The National Heritage Committee has proposed the introduction of a Privacy Bill, and the Third Report of the House of Commons Science and Technology Committee, *Human Genetics: The Science and its Consequences*[30]

---

27 European Commission, *Adopting a Specific Research and Technological Development Programme in the Field of Health: Predictive Medicine*, 1989, Brussels.

28 Pompidou, A, 1993, A3-0000/93; Doc EN/PR/218992 I, March 1993.

29 Brett, P and Fischer, EP, 'Effects on life assurance of genetic testing' (1993) *The Actuary*, July, pp 11–12.

30 July 1995, HC 41-I, p 22.

called for the misuse of genetic information to be both a criminal and civil offence. Attempts to legislate in the US have taken the form of Bill HR 5612, which first entered the US Congress in September 1990 as the Human Genome Privacy Act, to be succeeded later by a modified Bill in April 1991. More recently, Bill HR 2045, virtually identical to Bill HR 5612, has been presented to the House of Representatives. Salient sections of the Bill specify that:

2(b) The purpose of this Act is to provide an individual with certain safeguards against the invasion of personal genetic privacy by requiring agencies, except as otherwise provided by law, to:

1   permit an individual to determine what records pertaining to him or her are collected, maintained, used, or disseminated by such agencies;

2   permit an individual to prevent records pertaining to him or her obtained by such agencies for a particular purpose from being used or made available for another purpose without his or her consent;

3   permit an individual to gain access to records, to have a copy made of any or all portion thereof, and to correct or amend such records;

4   collect, maintain, use, or disseminate any record of identifiable personal genetic information in a manner that assures that the information is current and accurate for its intended use, and that adequate safeguards are provided to prevent any misuse of such information;

5   permit exceptions from the requirements with respect to genetic records maintained anonymously for research purposes only; and

6   be subject to civil suit and criminal penalties for any damages which occur as a result of negligent, wilful, or intentional action which violates any individual's rights under this Act.

The Bill defines genetic information (s 101(2)) as 'any information that describes, analyses or identifies all or any part of a genome identifiable to a specific individual'.

Unlike the US law, English law knows no general concept of privacy. In the sense that it gives limited access and ability to be able to control the divulgence of facts or information about oneself, English law may be said at best to afford some tangential recognition of privacy interests, but it admits as yet of nothing so strong as a right of privacy. It is evident, however, that the use of genetic information by insurance companies for the purpose of deciding whether, or at what level, to grant insurance should be debated and resolved before widespread piecemeal applications of genetic testing take place[31] to forestall the creation of what Nancy Jecker has identified as an 'underclass of medically uninsurable people'.[32]

---

31   Beauchamp, T and Bowie, N, 'Corporate social responsibility', in Beauchamp, T and Bowie, N (eds), *Ethical Theory and Business*, 2nd edn, 1983, Englewood Cliffs, NJ: Prentice Hall; *op cit*, Jecker, fn 6.

32   *Op cit*, Jecker, fn 6.

Widespread genetic discrimination in the private insurance market would furnish a compelling argument for instituting a public insurance programme or instituting across-the-board regulation of the private insurance market. Those who are dismayed by the reaction of insurance companies to the availability of genetic information might be relatively indifferent to which alternative avenue of public or private provision was preferred, but one ever present fear is of the creation of at least a two-track insurance system. As Jecker has suggested, any society's attraction to retaining a private health insurance market depends upon private health insurers affirming and meeting responsibilities to the wider society. She argues that how a society and the insurance industry respond in the face of new genetic testing capabilities will be a moral guidepost indicating how we, as a society, should devise and implement health care reform.[33]

If an individual in the UK currently has had a genetic test, the results will be included in that person's medical records. Insurers can already demand access to those reports as a condition of offering cover. The fear that insurers voice is that, as genetic tests become more readily available, cheaper and thought to be of greater predictive accuracy, more people will have them. Individuals may then use this knowledge adversely to select against insurers, who in turn may respond by demanding, first, access to the results of those tests, as was the early experience with testing methods of seropositivity of HIV. Secondly, and in the more troublesome projections, insurers may then oblige proposers to undergo genetic testing as a condition precedent to insurance cover being underwritten, with premiums then set according to the specific risk that each individual presents. At this point, the principle of risk-pooling will begin to evaporate and most people would be unable to obtain many forms of insurance or mortgage cover at standard rates, which are currently applied to some 95% of the insured population.[34]

Clarification of the position of British insurers came in a letter from Mark Boleat, Director General of the Association of British Insurers, in response to an article in *The Independent* where Perutz had argued that confidentiality in respect of genetic matters was of paramount importance.[35] Boleat wrote: '... if an individual wishes to obtain life insurance, the insurance company must know as much about the risk it is taking on as the individual ... This is fair both to the individual and to other policy holders in the insurance fund.' Although the principle of general fairness to other policy holders may be implicitly acknowledged by reference to general Aristotelian principles, the

33 *Op cit*, Jecker, fn 6.
34 *Op cit*, Brett and Fischer, fn 29.
35 Perutz, A, 'The right to know your own genes' (1993) *The Independent*, 21 August, p 28.

fairness in this arrangement to the individual concerned (who, in the extreme case, may discover that he or she is uninsurable in the prevailing market) is left unstated.

Boleat concluded his letter by arguing that genetic information is no different from other medical information that may be held in an individual's medical record, and observed that existing records probably contain references to family history and illnesses. Such information may already be used in making differential assessments of risk, and to allow withholding of genetic information 'distorts such equitable treatment and ... is akin to offering motor insurance while letting drivers withhold information on their accident record'. This assertion contains a number of assumptions that would need to be explored elsewhere. Importantly, the analysis appears to ignore the possibility that a number of key issues confront the family, the geneticist and society in connection with the genetic counselling process which may ensue following the initiation of what we may call the 'genetic viewing' process. The point has been well put by Ian Pullen: 'What at first sight may seem to be a simple enough transaction, is beset with ethical and legal problems.'[36] These issues include: (a) what is genetic information? Does it apply to family history information and to blood tests? (b) How *are* insurers to be protected against adverse selection? (c) Should an underwriter be permitted to request genetic screening when it has not previously been performed? Pullen concludes that there are more *ethical* problems surrounding genetic tests than present day medicals, from which he argues that 'it is likely' that regulations will be introduced to restrict an insurer's liability to request a genetic test.[37] Aside from this jurisprudential observation, however, Pullen's point is central: present medical tests can reveal a disorder that a person already has, whereas genetic tests can disclose disorders that a person may get in the future. What liabilities is the underwriter to assume in respect of counselling and follow-up services?

Although there is no extant British legislation, there have been calls for legislation to be introduced to regulate this market in medical futures. Urging continued vigilance in respect of those who would make use of genetic knowledge for personal, political or economic interests and leverage, David Suzuki and Peter Knudtson recall the 'endlessly shifting balances of power that are the inevitable consequence of scientific knowledge and its

---

36 Pullen, I, 'Family genetics', in Sutherland, E and McCall Smith, A (eds), *Family Rights: Family Law and Medical Advance*, 1990, Edinburgh: Edinburgh UP.

37 Kennedy, I, 'Law and ethics', paper delivered in *Proceedings of the Second Symposium of the Council of Europe on Bioethics: Ethics and Human Genetics*, Strasbourg, 30 November–2 December 1993; Morgan, D, 'Problems and possibilities: the case of regulating United Kingdom health care', paper prepared for the AAAS NATO Advanced Workshop, *Developing an Infrastructure for Science and Technology in Eastern Europe: The Role of Scientific and Technical Societies*, Visegrad, Hungary, 27–31 October 1994.

application'.[38] Suggestions have included general welfare provision through the establishment of a common insurance fund to cover genetic high risk individuals, a quota system forcing all insurers to underwrite a fixed number of high risk cases, or a State funded insurance pool to prevent the emergence of uninsured individuals. In Canada, the recent report of the Privacy Commissioner has argued for there to be *no* right to inspect an individual's genetic information without consent. It would allow, however, that while there should continue to be a general air of restraint in collecting personal medical information, where a case for collection can be made, 'genetic testing (but *only* with the consent of the subject) may be an appropriate means of acquiring the information'. This type of testing should be subject to strict conditions.[39] Thus, the Commissioner suggests that:

(a) a person should have the option to be tested by any means that will provide reliable information, including genetic information;

(b) the type of information obtained should be strictly controlled, such that they caution strongly public and private sector institutions 'against acquiring more personal information through genetic tests than they would have acquired using other methods';

(c) only the information needed to tell whether the person meets the required standard should be collected.

As the Privacy Commissioner concludes: '... the very availability of intrusive technology seems to whet mankind's appetite for its use.'[40] In the process, privacy becomes a casualty. Genetic technology has appeared alongside other biotechnological developments and threatens to surpass them all in its ability to intrude:

> Benevolence can be vulnerable to fear, prejudice, irrationality and the blind drive for efficiency. Taken individually, decisions by employers and insurers to employ biotechnology to their advantage may appear logical. On a societal level, however, they are not. Nor are they necessarily humane.[41]

It is the demystification of health futures through genetic testing that is imposing tremendous costs in the insurability market. Because ignorance meant that luck (or superstition) was ever present, even in families where there was already genetic risk, insurance could function satisfactorily. It is as though insurers have themselves become frightened of the power that genetic tarot readings offer and have begun to react against adverse selection in the way which they have. This may be described as a radical form of discounting: the chromosomal 'commodification' of fetal futures.

---

38 Suzuki, D and Knudtson, R, *Genetics: The Ethics of Engineering Life*, 1988, London: Unwin Hyman.

39 *Op cit*, Bankowski and Bryant, fn 24.

40 *Op cit*, Privacy Commissioner of Canada, fn 26.

41 *Op cit*, Jecker, fn 6.

Medical confidentiality and the public interest

Of course, once having obtained information about an individual in respect of his or her genetic make-up, doctors and other health care workers have an established duty not to disclose this information learnt in the course of their practice.[42] This extends to any information about a patient that the doctor has learnt directly or indirectly in the course of the professional relationship or capacity.[43] The obligation arises out of the relationship, although it may be reinforced by the nature of the information.[44] The public interest in obtaining information in order to secure public health indicates that certain kinds of information, such as may be obtained by certain kinds of testing, give rise to an obligation of confidence on all concerned.[45] This might extend the duty of confidence not only to the health care professionals primarily concerned, but also to laboratories and other paramedicals involved in the analytical process. Patients may have a concomitant duty to their doctors in certain circumstances.[46]

The further question arises of whether a health care professional may be entitled to or become obliged to reveal genetic knowledge to relatives of a primary patient, where that discloses information whose absence would be harmful to those other individuals. And, they may have an obligation to do this *despite the objections of the primary patient* about or from whom they have gathered the initial data. Clearly, once a duty to pass on medical information – or, as here, genetic information – becomes established, the health carer becomes implicated through having that knowledge. A number of circumstances may arise in which information may have to be disclosed to a third party.

The first is where, in the course of legal proceedings, a breach of confidence is required by a competent court[47] or where disclosure is otherwise authorised by statute – as under the Abortion Act 1967 and its regulations, or the Public Health (Infectious Diseases) Act 1984. Secondly, information may, in its nature, come to lose the necessary elements of confidentiality, such that further disclosure would no longer represent a harm to the person to whom it related.[48] Thirdly, there may be circumstances in which the disclosure is expressly or impliedly authorised by the person to

---

42 *W v Egdell* [1990] 1 All ER 835 (CA).

43 General Medical Council, *Professional Conduct and Discipline: Fitness to Practice*, 1989, London: GMC, para 80.

44 *Langside v Kerr* [1991] 1 All ER 418 (CA).

45 See *X v Y* [1982] 2 All ER 648, p 653; Grubb, A and Pearl, D, *Blood Testing Aids and DNA Profiling: Law and Policy*, 1990, Bristol: Jordan.

46 *Latham v Stevens* [1913] Macq Cop Cas 83 (1911–16).

47 *Ibid*, Grubb and Pearl.

48 *AG v Guardian Newspapers Ltd (No 2)* [1988] 3 All ER 545 (HL).

whom it relates – in a way, this is an example of the information having lost its necessary element of confidence. Finally, there may be circumstances in which, through the behaviour or some other act or omission of the relevant party, it is in the public interest that otherwise confidential information be disclosed.[49]

The case of *W v Egdell* discloses 'in an unusually stark form' the question of the nature and quality of the duty of confidence owed to a patient. Having forwarded a copy of his psychiatric report on W to the Home Secretary without W's permission, Egdell was the subject of an action by W for breach of confidence. The High Court and the Court of Appeal refused W's claim against Egdell. In the Court of Appeal it was said, again, that there were competing public interests, W's in seeking advice and assistance from an independent doctor and a countervailing interest in public safety. In view of the nature and number of killings for which W had been detained, it was vital for those responsible for W's treatment to be provided with full, relevant information concerning his condition.

The Court of Appeal accepted that to justify disclosure there must be:

- ... a real risk *of danger* to the public;
- a risk of serious or substantial harm; and
- that disclosure be made to and confined to the proper authorities.

The circumstances in which these conditions will be fulfilled in respect of genetic information are likely to be very rare and to constitute, at most, narrow exceptions to a general duty of confidentiality.[50]

A final question here is whether there may be circumstances in which a doctor may be held liable to a person for failure to disclose to them risks materialising from information that they have gained in their professional capacity as clinicians involved in the care of another. This has arisen in the American case of *Tarasoff v Regents of California*,[51] which confronts the question of whether a doctor who, in treating a psychiatric patient, becomes aware of a serious risk to others, is under a duty to warn those others of that risk. The Supreme Court of California held that a psychologist owed a duty of care to a woman murdered by a psychologist's patient. The patient had expressed an intention to kill the woman. The court accepted that there was a balance to be drawn between the public interest in effective treatment of mental illness and the consequent requirement of protecting confidentiality, and the public interest in safety from violent assault. Duties to warn of contagious diseases have also been recognised by American courts and State legislatures; this has been particularly the case involving fatal conditions such as HIV. The argument has been, and has been accepted in some States of the US, that (at least) the sexual partners of A should be informed of A's seropositivity by the

---

49 *AG v Guardian Newspapers Ltd (No 2)* [1988] 3 All ER 545 (HL).

50 *R v Crozier* [1991] Crim LR 138.

51 *Tarasoff v Regents of California* 551 P 2d 334 (1976).

doctor who has care of A. It has been argued by many commentators in the UK that disclosure would be justified to known sexual partners and needle sharers if the patient himself or herself would refuse to make the disclosure.[52]

If the limiting conditions of this advice are extracted, it is clear that it is only in the most limited circumstances – a serious and identifiable risk to a specific and existing individual and not a potential victim in the future – that a duty to disclose might conceivably be imposed on a doctor or other genetic counsellor. This limited scope is in line with developments in the *Tarasoff* doctrine itself, where the duty is anyway narrowly drawn. First, the therapist should not be encouraged to reveal such threats routinely. Secondly, the Californian Supreme Court has itself distinguished *Tarasoff* in a case where a patient made *general* threats against children. In *Thompson v County of Alabama*,[53] the court said that *Tarasoff* was limited in that that case involved a specific threat to an identifiable, specifically foreseeable, victim.

There is doubt whether the general principle in *Tarasoff* would be applied in the UK: in *Holgate v Lancashire Mental Hospitals Board*,[54] a hospital was held liable for negligently releasing on licence a dangerous patient who had been compulsorily detained. The patient entered the plaintiff's home and assaulted her. The trial judge seemed to assume that there would be a duty of care, which may be justified by the degree of control exercised by the hospital over the patient, analogous to that exercised by a prison over a prisoner. Genetic counsellors and other medical professionals do not exercise this degree of control over their patients and the bases of liability now applied by the common law courts – of proximity, foreseeability and justness in imposing liability on the defendant[55] – do not militate in favour of such liability.

Genetics and existence: the abortion section

Ruth Chadwick has reminded us that the practice of rejecting 'defective' babies (as she calls them) has a long human pedigree. The Spartans exposed to the elements those neonates deemed unsuitable, and Plato recommended that those babies that did not 'fit' established guidelines should be hidden in a dark and secret place.[56] Contemporary practice with handicapped neonates has sometimes led to the prosecution of the medical staff involved, although a line of jurisprudence has emerged according to which it may be permissible to

---

52 *Op cit*, Grubb and Pearl, fn 45.

53 *Thompson v County of Alabama* 614 P 2d 728 (1980).

54 *Holgate v Lancashire Mental Hospitals Board* [1937] 4 All ER 19.

55 *Caparo Industries v Dickman* [1990] 1 All ER 568.

56 Chadwick, R (ed), *Ethics Reproduction and Genetic Control*, 1987, London: Croom Helm, pp 93–135.

treat some babies for dying, rather than to intervene to keep them alive.[57] And, the Abortion Act 1967, since its inception, has allowed for termination of pregnancy on the ground of fetal abnormality. As Chadwick writes:

> Although, of course, abortion is itself by no means uncontroversial, the fact of handicap is generally regarded as one of the best reasons for having one.[58]

That this *need not* imply a eugenic policy or preference is clearly articulated by Anne Maclean, who reminds us that there is an important distinction between abortion suggesting that handicapped men and women's lives are not worth living and suggesting that an individual person cannot cope with a handicapped child. 'It is not the case ... that the decision to abort a handicapped fetus implies or presupposes any view about what makes life valuable in the metaphysical sense'.[59] It is important to examine the approach of English law on this point, because the fetal abnormality ground, which is the subject of this part of the chapter, is frequently viewed in precisely this way.

Section 37 of the Human Fertilisation and Embryology Act 1990 amended the Abortion Act 1967 in a number of significant ways. It introduced into the legislation an explicit time limit (24 weeks) after which an abortion would not be lawful, unless special grounds were shown. Those grounds were reformulated and, in a move that surprised many observers, were enacted without time limit. There are now three specific grounds on which an abortion may lawfully be performed up until term: one of these is the fetal abnormality ground. The Abortion Act 1967 (as amended) in s 1 now provides that:

(1) ... a person shall not be guilty of an offence under the law relating to abortion when a pregnancy is terminated by a registered medical practitioner if two registered medical practitioners are of the opinion formed in good faith –

...

(d) that there is a substantial risk that if the child were born it would suffer from such physical or mental abnormalities as to be seriously handicapped.

This provision is not without its difficulties, as I shall discuss, but let me dismiss one potential apprehension first. Suppose that a doctor terminates a

---

57 For one of the most publicised (and discussed) prosecutions, see *R v Arthur* (1981) 12 BMLR 1 (Crown Court), and for the leading case on 'treatment for dying' see *Re J (A Minor) (Wardship: Medical Treatment)* [1990] 3 All ER 930 (it would be lawful to withhold life saving treatment from a very young child in circumstances where the child's life, if saved, would be one irredeemably racked by pain and agony). For a discussion of some of the earlier legal cases and clinical assessments, see Wells, C, 'Otherwise kill me: marginal children and ethics at the edges of existence', in Lee, RG and Morgan, D (eds), *Birthrights: Law and Ethics at the Beginnings of Life*, 1989, London: Routledge, p 195; for an examination and criticism of the most widely announced philosophical arguments brought to play in this area, consider Maclean, A, *The Elimination of Morality: Reflections on Utilitarianism and Bioethics*, 1993, London: Routledge, esp Chapters 2 and 3.

58 *Op cit*, Chadwick, fn 56.

59 *Ibid*, Maclean, p 31.

pregnancy believing, in all good faith, that if the fetus were born it would suffer from 'such physical or mental abnormalities as to be seriously handicapped'. It later transpires that she has made a mistake, and that the fetus was, in fact, in perfect health (there is, of course, a nice ambiguity in describing a fetus in this way). The doctor does not lose the protection of s 1 for an honest mistake, although she may still be open to an action in negligence at the suit of the woman or would-have-been parents.

The fetal handicap provision, now in the reformulated section, had been examined by the Select Committee of the House of Lords on the Infant Life (Preservation) Act 1929, chaired by Lord Brightman.[60] That Act, which had introduced the so called 28 week time limit for abortions,[61] had been subject to much debate, and the Committee had taken the opportunity of its review to make comments on wider issues in relation to termination. Of the fetal handicap ground, they observed that if a fetus was diagnosed as:

> ... grossly abnormal and unable to lead any meaningful life, there is in the opinion of the Committee no logic in requiring the mother to carry her unborn child to full term because the diagnosis was too late to enable an operation for abortion to be carried out before the 28th completed week.[62]

Leaving aside the philosophical or ethical inquiries to which this might give rise, for present purposes we can abstract from this observation the concept of a fetus being so 'grossly abnormal and unable to lead any meaningful life' as being the closest that we come to an interpretation of the fetal handicap sub-section. For it remains the case that, despite being the 'abortion ground that is likely to command the most widespread sympathy', it remains the most difficult to interpret and, as I have elsewhere called it, is 'the unexamined ground'.[63]

This explanation by the House of Lords Select Committee comes close to those guidelines that have been suggested in the common law courts when judicial sanction has been sought for medical decisions affecting the dissolution of neonatal life. In *Re J*,[64] the Court of Appeal was concerned with a pre-term baby born at 27 weeks' gestation, weighing 1.1 kg at birth. Placed immediately on a ventilator, given antibiotics and put on a drip, he was removed a month later from the ventilator. He suffered recurrent convulsions and episodes of apnoea. Four attempts to wean him from the ventilator successively failed and over the following 12–13 weeks, although his condition stabilised, any improvement was from a baseline which was, in the words of Lord Donaldson, 'abysmally low'. He had suffered severe brain

---

60 House of Lords Papers (1987–88) HL 50.
61 Morgan, D and Lee, RG, *Blackstone's Guide to the Human Fertilisation and Embryology Act 1990: Abortion and Embryo Research – The New Law*, 1990, London: Blackstone, pp 43–47.
62 *Ibid*, House of Lords Papers.
63 See above, Chapter 8.
64 [1990] 3 All ER 930.

damage, and the most optimistic assessment of his prognosis was that he would develop serious spastic quadriplegia, be unable to sit up or hold his head upright, and that he was likely to be blind, to all intents mute, and unlikely to develop even limited intellectual abilities:

> Most unfortunately of all, there is a likelihood that he will be able to feel pain to the same extent as a normal baby ... It is possible that he may achieve the ability to smile and cry. Finally, as one might expect, his life expectancy has been considerably reduced at most into his late teens, but even Dr W would expect him to die even before then.

This case differed from those that the court had considered earlier, in which guidance had been given about the appropriate approach to the medical treatment of children who are imminently dying and whose deaths can only be postponed for a short while.[65] In a case such as *Re J*, the question was whether there could be anything to be balanced against the principle of the sanctity of life, and if so, what that right consisted in. Lord Donaldson said:

> What doctors and the court have to decide is whether, in the best interests of the child patient, a particular decision as to medical treatment would be taken which *as a side effect* will render death more or less likely ... *Re B*[66] seems to me to come very near to being a binding authority for the proposition that there is a balancing exercise to be performed in assessing the course that is to be adopted in the best interests of the child. Even if it is not, I have no doubt that this should be and is the law.

The critical question that then arose, of course, was whether anything could displace or question the 'very strong presumptions in favour of a course of action which will prolong life'. Lord Donaldson concluded that it was manifest and appropriate:

> ... that account has to be taken of the pain and suffering and quality of life which the child will experience if life is prolonged. Account also has to be taken of the pain and suffering involved in the proposed treatment itself.[67]

If, in interpreting s 1(1)(d) of the Abortion Act we suggest that account has to be taken of the pain and suffering and quality of life which the child will experience if life after birth is prolonged, then we may be able to suggest a narrow but consistent reading of the abortion ground (which has still not been adequately explored).[68] Importantly, it is one that avoids stipulative conditions about the sorts of people that we are prepared to admit that there may be (a primary concern of those who are worried about the potential for eugenic uses that prenatal diagnosis and other fetal screening programmes offer). It is pre-eminently one that, if given the restricted meaning for which I

---

65 *Re C (A Minor) (Wardship: Medical Treatment)* [1989] 2 All ER 782.

66 *Re B* [1981] 1 WLR 1421.

67 *Re J* [1990] 3 All ER 930.

68 Mason, K, *Medico-Legal Aspects of Pregnancy and Parenthood*, 1990, Aldershot: Dartmouth, pp 105–07.

have sketched one interpretative mechanism, reflects compassion for the child that would be born and not (which is a typically eugenic framework) its failure to pass some test which would have secured it the prize of 'entitlement to life'.[69] In other words, an appeal to the interests of the child, in the way I have argued, is not an argument about the fetus' 'entitlement to life', but one that considers the kind of life that the fetus would have as a child if it were to be born. This argument sees s 1(1)(d) as primarily a fetal interests provision. Others have suggested, on the contrary, that the fetal ground really relates to the welfare of the parents, or to the public purse.[70]

Suppose that this were the preferred reading of the section. It still does not follow that the primary importance of the fetal ground is eugenic. It is true that the care of handicapped people is costly, and it is in part a desire to cut costs that lies behind programmes that screen for the certain handicaps. But whether for the individual woman or for the National Health Service itself, offering the screening and the termination services *does not necessarily imply* that the individual woman or the Health Service planners believe people with handicaps to be less 'entitled to life' than people without. While we may be morally censorious (of course, we may not be: that is a different argument), we may nonetheless accept that the individual decision, like the institutional decision, is based, and based alone, on a *preference* not to raise or care for a handicapped child. In other words, this would be a decision with which the individual may prefer not to have to *cope* without thereby presupposing any view about what makes life valuable in the metaphysical sense, let alone that some people are 'less entitled than others to life'.[71]

An alternative reading of this story, of course, suggests that what we are witnessing (or, rather, are failing to see or are wilfully blind to) is a shifting rationality, a moving gradient of responsibility, which may have an explicitly eugenicist slide to it. It is an interesting question for the common lawyer whether this is a new development or merely a continuation of policy that the common law has long adopted.[72] As technology expands and develops, the very nature of the definitional aspects of questions change. Lene Koch, in a related area (of infertility), has shown how the nature of what constitutes a rational decision may also be metamorphosed.[73] Thus, the danger might be, with the audacious cocktail of reproductive technologies in societies in which the cult of beauty is tyrannical,[74] that the more sophisticated the instruments

---

69   *Op cit*, Maclean, fn 57.

70   Williams, G, *Textbook of Criminal Law*, 2nd edn, 1987, London: Stevens.

71   *Op cit*, Maclean, fn 57.

72   McVeigh, S, comment at the Socio-Legal Studies Association Annual Conference, Nottingham, April 1994.

73   Koch, L, 'IVF – an irrational choice?' (1990) 3(3) Issues in Reproductive and Genetic Engineering 235.

74   This alluring phrase is from Richards, S, *Epics of Everyday Life. Encounters in a Changing Russia*, 1991, Harmondsworth: Penguin, p 132.

of prenatal diagnosis, the more sophisticated the possibilities of diagnosis, the greater the possibility that a defect may be discovered, and the greater the range of possible anomalies that might be disclosed. This, it has been averred, may even have a *preventive* aspect, in which the moral obloquy of abortion is undercut by resort to genetic screening and perhaps replaced by assisted conception. Responsible parents of the future may ask themselves whether 'their own "hereditary material" meets contemporary requirements, or whether it would be preferable for them to resort to ovum or sperm donors, who would of course be carefully selected'.[75]

Elizabeth Beck-Gernsheim has argued that there are two powerful forces underpinning the trend towards '"quality control" of progeny'. The first is that, in a socially mobile society, parents are exposed to heavy pressure and do all in their power to give the best opportunities to their children from the outset. In other words, a corresponding need for 'genetic engineering' already exists.[76] Secondly, the history of technology teaches that a new technique often itself contributes to the creation of a further need. The promise is followed by growing desire, or, as Hans Jonas has put it, 'appetite is aroused by the prospect'.[77] These possibilities have led Beck-Gernsheim to suggest a new and increasing pressure for prospective, responsible parents. Taken together, techniques of assisted conception such as test tube fertilisation with embryo transfer and techniques of prenatal diagnosis and increasingly sensitive genetic testing may lead to responsible parents of the future being unprepared to accept that their children may have a handicap: '... must they not rather do all in their power to make sure that no impairment exists?'[78]

Children and consent

In this final section, I shall turn to explore whether existing children can lawfully be used in a predictive way to gain information about the genetic health of their present and putative siblings and other genetic relations. English law generally admits no principle of altruism, and, in respect of young children, who may well be the subject of predictive testing for themselves or others, the courts have evolved and guarded jealously the legislatively adopted principle of the welfare of the individual child. In protecting and advancing the best interests of the child, the courts have worked with a conservative standard which, on occasions, health care and other professionals have found to be frustrating and occasionally obstructive.

---

75 Gernsheim-Beck, E, 'Changing duties of parents: from education to bio-engineering' (1990) 42 Int J Social Science 451.

76 *Ibid*. See above, Chapter 2, fn 72.

77 Jonas, H, *Philosophical Essays: From Ancient Creed to Technological Man*, 1985, Englewood Cliffs, NJ: Prentice Hall.

78 *Ibid*, Gernsheim-Beck.

Generally, the law is jealous of health care decisions for those unable, through age, to see through the consequences of what they might themselves otherwise decide, or, *in extremis,* be unable to decide. It has time and again been castigated as paternalistic and out of step with modern notions of young people's needs (let alone demands) for autonomy.[79] I do not wish, generally, to enter those arguments, but I shall briefly summarise the principles upon which the courts have proceeded, and then apply them in the context of genetics. But, one caveat: this has become a motile area of legal development. Commentators have on more than one occasion in the recent past expressed surprise, if not dismay, at the direction of the currents, let alone the strength in the jurisprudential tide. Attempts to crest along this should, then, be treated with some temporal caution.

The general position in the law of England and Wales stems from s 8 of the Family Law Reform Act 1969, and the landmark decision of the House of Lords in the celebrated case of *Gillick v West Norfolk and Wisbech AHA.*[80] In relation to a person who has reached the age of 16, health professionals may presume that consent to treatment will be as valid as if the person was 18. This presumption is vulnerable if the person is not, as a matter of fact, competent to consent. Below the age of 16 (the '*Gillick* competent' test), health care professionals must assess the capacity of each person to consent in relation to the proposed treatment or intervention. If the person under 16 is capable of understanding the consequences of their decision, then their consent will be sufficient to render the treatment lawful. If the person cannot understand the question, or if they refuse treatment, then in the first case, parental consent will usually be required, and in the second case, either a parent or the court may give the appropriate approval, which again will have the effect of rendering the treatment or intervention lawful. In addition, ss 43(7) and 44(7) of the Children Act 1989 sought to provide that a person under 16 may refuse to submit to a medical or psychiatric assessment if 'of sufficient understanding' to make an informed decision.[81] Nothing in the Family Law Reform Act 1969 (which introduced a number of important measures in respect of capacity and age, including lowering the so called age of majority from 21 to 18) affected common law powers of parental consent (s 8(3) of the Family Law Reform Act 1969). The effect of this is that a parent may provide consent to medical treatment for their child until the latter is 18. It was at first thought that this meant that they could consent where the person was incapable of doing so, a line of reasoning that appeared to be confirmed in *Gillick.* But, in a series of controversial decisions, the Court of Appeal, in

---

79 Alderson, P, *Choosing for Children: Parents' Consent to Surgery,* 1990, Oxford: OUP.

80 *Gillick v West Norfolk and Wisbech AHA* [1985] 3 All ER 402.

81 This summary may be deduced from a patchwork of (more or less controversial) cases following from *Gillick;* the more important are *Re R* [1991] 4 All ER 177, *Re E* [1991] 1 FLR 386 and *Re W* [1992] 4 All ER 627.

panels headed by the then Master of the Rolls, Lord Donaldson, the courts decided that the effect of s 8(3) of the 1969 Act was that parents could consent to treatment of their children under the age of 18 even when the children themselves were capable of doing so, and in some cases even where the 'child' was clearly refusing treatment. So, where consent is needed, but cannot (or occasionally will not) be given by the child, the consent of one of the parents must be sought. But, as Jonathon Montgomery has expressed it, 'this apparently simple requirement gives rise to three areas of difficulty'.[82] These concern who is a parent; what happens when parents disagree; and what limits there are to parental consent.

I shall not review each of these (what turn out to be) complex questions here. For the present purpose, it is sufficient to draw the following conclusions. In the question of consent to genetic testing, the first question that the health care professional must ask is whether the child's parents are married. If they are, the consent of either parent will suffice. If they are not, then *prima facie* the greater authority will lie with the child's mother, unless the father has one of a number of requisite court orders. In the event of a disagreement between the parents, if the woman consents to any genetic testing, then this will effectively protect the health care worker for any properly performed intervention. Where she refuses her consent, but apparent consent is given by the child's father, then caution will be appropriate where the mother and father are unmarried. This is because, under the Children Act 1989, where parents are married they will both have parental responsibility for their child or children, but where they are not, the mother will have automatic parental responsibility but the father will not, unless acquired by court order.

In the case of operations and the giving of consent in respect of very young children, Lord Donaldson again has set out the philosophy of the common law most clearly:

> It is sensible to try to define the relationship between the court, the doctors, the child and its parents. The doctors owe the child a duty to care for it in accordance with good medical practice recognised as appropriate by a competent body of professional opinion ... This duty is, however, subject to the qualification that, if time permits, they must obtain the consent of the parents before undertaking serious invasive treatment. The parents owe the child a duty to give or withhold consent in the best interests of the child and without regard to their own interests.

Where the 'intervention' (and here we may explicitly include the question of genetic testing) is expected to benefit the child, the parents may consent to most treatments. For the present, it is only sterilisation of a 'minor' that is thought to give rise to such difficult considerations that such an operation should be referred to the court. And, following from Lord Donaldson's

---

82 Montgomery, J, 'Consent to health care for children' (1993) 5 J Child Law 117.

opinion just quoted, Montgomery has proposed that: 'Parental consent may be valid because even where care is not expected to benefit the child, the parents have the power to consent if it is reasonable and in the child's best interests to do so.'[83]

The most obvious area in which this is likely to arise is testing for genetic orders that may not affect the child, or at least not until much later in adult life, or may be likely only to affect the putative 'family' of siblings. And, in the light of our previous caution about altruism, Montgomery's advice on the question of genetic testing and best interests is salutary. Three considerations are of particular importance:

(a) in all cases there must be a balancing of the risks of the intervention and the expected benefits *to the subject of the intervention* in assessing the reasonableness of the parental consent;

(b) the urgency of the intervention, or the benefits that it is sought to realise, should be considered; thus, an operation to remove a healthy organ for transplantation into a dying sibling might be more favourably regarded – even in the absence of a duty of altruism – than a genetic test where the 'beneficiary' would be the not-to-be-born sibling and the subject of the intervention, to whom additional parental attention might be expected to flow;

(c) even where the child is (legally) incapable of taking the decision, her or his wishes should be accounted, and, if the intervention can be postponed until the child can make it, then it would reasonable for that to be done.

From this brief review, it can be concluded only that difficult questions can arise for individual children, their mothers and fathers and the health care professionals working with the family group. The best that the law currently offers is a form of flexibility in the advice that it offers. In any case of doubt, the geneticist, whether clinician or counsellor, is best advised to act cautiously and to make use of formal court procedures in the cases of greatest doubt or difficulty. This analysis does, however, underline the importance to be attached to sensitive handling of genetic information; not everyone wants to be co-opted into the fast lane of the genetic superhighway, and the wishes of those whose demand for ignorance represents the bedrock of their caution should be respected.

---

83   *Re J* [1990] 3 All ER 930, *per* Lord Donaldson; *op cit*, Montgomery, fn 82.

CONCLUSION

As I have previously argued, Ulrich Beck has suggested the dangers of uncontrolled or unregulated uses and developments of science and technology. He has suggested that, while the latest research results constantly open up possible new applications, because this happens at such a rapid, exponential rate, the process of implementation is practically uncontrolled. A variant on this which I would add is that, where it is controlled, countervailing arguments are more easily marshalled on the basis of benign experience or supposed individuation of consequences. Accordingly, although medicine supposedly serves health, it has in fact 'created entirely new situations, has changed the relationship of humankind to itself, to disease, illness and death, indeed, it has changed the world'.[84]

Thus, an analysis of medical progress as itself institutionalised discloses that there has been a 'revolution of the lay public's social living conditions without its consent'.[85] Indeed, in an arresting phrase, Beck describes this process as a 'secret farewell to an epoch of human history' in which the principles of technological feasibility and arrangement encroach on the subjects in such a way that the very foundations of a model of 'progress' that implicates a subject who is supposed ultimately to benefit from the process, are cancelled. Recalling the basic principles of democratically based societies in which central issues of public policy affecting the future of society are the subject of public debate to shape the political resolve, he fears that the developments of modern technology have set in motion processes that undermine the 'idea of democracy from inside'. Technology, medicine, and reproductive technologies are becoming the instruments of uncontrolled 'sub-politics', where, in the sub-politics of medicine, there is no parliament and no executive in which the consequences of a decision might be examined before it is taken:

> There is not even a social locus of decision making ... the highly bureaucratised developed Western democracies check every act for its conformity with legal requirements, terms of reference and democratic legitimation; at the same time it is possible to escape all the bureaucratic and democratic controls and to take closed decisions despite the hail of general criticism and scepticism in a world which escapes parliamentary control and in which the very bases of existing life and previous patterns of social control can be completely neutralised.[86]

Although there are the beginnings of regulatory regimes now in place in many countries of the European Union, one of the fears is well expressed by Elisabeth Beck-Gernsheim: parliamentary and other official committees find

---

84 *Op cit*, Beck, fn 19, p 204.
85 *Op cit*, Beck, fn 19, p 206.
86 *Op cit*, Beck, fn 19, p 208.

themselves faced with immense and completely innovative issues, which never respect the patterns of scientific disciplines. The struggle to find answers is correspondingly complex. And then a great deal of time is necessary to negotiate, amend and reformulate draft Bills, which are passed backwards and forwards in the power struggle between departments. Thus, years are wasted. But, the genetic engineers do not wait until the material and statutory provisions have been clarified. In their laboratories, they have been fertilising and generating life *in vivo* and *in vitro* by homologous and heterologous means.[87]

A vital task for medical law and medical lawyers is to be engaged with assessing the most appropriate deployment of the law in these massively changed circumstances.

---

87 *Op cit*, Gernsheim-Beck, fn 75.

CHAPTER 10

AFTER GENETICS

The genetic revolution has come and gone. This essay is the first draft of an attempt to understand the modern legal history of a revolution which occurred, like the first English revolution, recalled in Christopher Hill's memorable phrase, 'in a fit of absence of mind'.[1] And it has occurred in memorable times; times in which, as Eric Hobsbawm has suggested, a global concern with ethics appears to have become almost the defining stigmata of the late 20th century.[2]

Genetics is, in many ways, the paradigm of Beck's notion of 'unplanned excess', not in the sense of planned excess which has been exceeded by design or deception, but one which is, in large part, due to the very different methodologies of science and statutory law. I want to ask, given that the scientific front of the genetic revolution occurred at the time of hyper-regulation, juridification, the questioning of the basis of ethics, in the 'land of metamorphoses', precisely how it is that genetics, as it were, 'got away'; how it is that genetics has, by and large, not been the subject of the sort of statutory regulation that we have seen in other aspects of medical life. I shall, for the most part, refrain from observing whether I think this absence of a particular sort of regulation to be a good or bad thing, positive or negative. But, I think that my emphasis might be more towards suggesting or registering surprise at that absence. I want to suggest that two or three of the reasons why the regulatory hound has not barked, are part of the very metamorphoses that I have identified, that is, metamorphoses in the nature of the patient, of ethical debate and of the role and nature of law. From this, I believe, genetics has appeared largely to benefit.

Yet, I think that there is something in the nature of a paradox here; that on closer examination, one of the reasons why we *appear* not to have regulated the genetics revolution in the ways which we would have expected to do is because of these very metamorphoses; because of the exponential nature of change, because of what Ulrich Beck has identified as the *unplanned* nature of the excesses which modern biotechnological research thrusts upon us. The changes in the world which modern medicine has brought about have come to be seen as 'normal', 'naturalised', part of the natural part of the world without much public notice or attention. Genetics is now so much more part

---

1   *The Intellectual Origins of the English Revolution*, 1965, Oxford: Clarendon, p 1.
2   Hobsbawm, E, *Age of Extremes: The Short History of the Twentieth Century 1914–1991*, 1994, London: Michael Joseph, p 287. Ethics are not only 'global', they are apparently of 'universal' concern, in that they are found in and across many disciplines.

of the fabric than the fabulous that what had previously been unthinkable (not in terms of what we might achieve or what we might countenance, but in terms of what we should aspire to and discuss is now commonplace).

GENETICS: THE REGULATORY QUADRILLE

Monitoring and regulation of genetics in the UK has been undertaken largely by the Gene Therapy Advisory Committee (GTAC), the Advisory Committee on Genetic Testing (ACGT) and the Human Genetics Advisory Commission (HGAC). The Government published, in May 1999, a report of its review of *The Advisory and Regulatory Framework for Biotechnology*, in which it concluded that the current regulatory and advisory arrangements are (necessarily) complex and difficult for the public to understand and that they do not, therefore, always reflect the broader ethical and environmental questions, nor the views of all potential stakeholders. Accordingly, the Government announced the establishment of a Human Genetics Commission and an Agriculture and Environment Biotechnology Commission. It envisaged that these bodies will take a strategic advisory role, such that they may sit alongside rather than replace the existing committees, or be the primary committees to which other committees concerned with keeping developments in genetics under review should report.

The new strategic commissions have wide ranging remits to include strategic analysis of biotechnological developments, address broader issues including ethical considerations regarding the acceptability of genetic modification, identify gaps in the regulatory and advisory framework and to build up a wider picture from that obtained by individual regulatory bodies. The establishment of the strategic bodies is a recognition that the regulatory and advisory framework in genetics (and, perhaps, other aspects of the biotechnological sciences) must serve two functions: first, that of reviewing and considering whether to grant approvals to individual products and processes, and, secondly, that of setting a strategic framework within which the development of technology in the UK may, should or must proceed. It is possible that, if taken and co-ordinated together, these bodies could effectively discharge the function of the Human Genetics Commission, called for in 1995 by the House of Commons Science and Technology Committee, *Human Genetics: The Science and its Consequences*.[3] Until now, as the Government has acknowledged, the regulation of genetics has followed a subject or outcome specific approach; the GTAC was established in 1993 (*inter alia*) 'to consider and advise on the acceptability of proposals for gene therapy research on human subjects'. This was followed by the ACGT, established in 1995 to

---

3   HC 41, 1995.

consider and advise on the ethical, social and scientific aspects of genetic testing, both within clinical practice and those sold directly to the public, and the HGAC, which was established in 1996 to take a broader view of developments in human genetics and to consider policy issues in relation to the application of genetics. In February 1997, when the Commission first met, it identified its initial priorities as cloning, insurance, privacy and genetics services provided by the NHS.

Aspects of genetics or genetics services are also the subject of a plethora of reports from, or reviews by, other professional, statutory and advisory bodies. Thus, the development and assessment of medicinal products and devices are regulated by the Medicines Control Agency and the Medical Devices Agency; pre-implantation diagnosis is within the remit of the Human Fertilisation and Embryology Authority (HFEA); genetic research involving humans must be approved by a Research Ethics Committee, under principles discussed above; the use of genetic testing in employment is monitored by the Health and Safety Commission's Occupational Health Advisory Committee, which has a group specifically dedicated to genetic screening (and, in appropriate cases, the use of pre-employment genetic screening may give rise to complaints under various anti-discrimination legislation); the Association of British Insurers (ABI) has issued a code of practice (believed, to the Government's evident annoyance, to be widely flouted (see various newspaper reports, 1 August 1999)) on the use of genetic information by members of the ABI.

A number of additional reports have been issued by the Department of Health, the Royal College of Physicians, the Royal College of Obstetricians and Gynaecologists, the Royal College of General Practitioners, the Nuffield Council on Bioethics, the British Society for Human Genetics and the Genetic Interest Group.

The Government announced, in April 1999, the establishment of a Genetics and Insurance Committee (GAIC) to oversee the use of genetic information by the life insurance industry, and the establishment of a review committee to consider further the recommendations made in 1998 in a joint report of the HGAC and HFEA, *Cloning Issues in Science, Reproduction and Medicine*, on the possible application of non-reproductive 'cloning' of stem cells.

In the same way that there are suggestions that the development of the human genome project itself raises no new ethical difficulties and perhaps few legal problems, there are many distinguished voices who observe that the regulatory mechanisms that we have in place – the responses, in other words, that the common law has made and is capable of making – are, at the very least, adequate and better for responding appropriately to the genetic revolution. Thus, in an Australian context, Loane Skene has argued that:

> The possibilities of genetic diagnosis and engineering do not alter our notions of parental and medical responsibility towards the child, and towards other members of the family. Genetic diagnosis and treatment offer new and

improved ways to care for children and to improve their welfare. I do not see them as reducing human dignity. In view of the copious and complex legislation that we now have in Victoria on ART and research in this area, I believe that there is much to be said for limiting the role of the State to determining legal status issues, such as parentage and information, and leaving the day to day operation of ART programs to be governed by the common law, in the same ways as other medical procedures. Some Australian jurisdictions (notably New South Wales) have adopted this approach.[4]

One of the difficulties which I believe this 'watch my lips: no new ethics' presents is the static nature of the State and the modern responsibilities properly directed by it which it proposes. A second difficulty, perhaps allied with, or consequential upon, the first in part, is that the situational changes which encompass genetic medicine – the various metamorphoses which I have attempted to identify – themselves suggest a vastly changed contextual landscape against which our genetic pictures are now framed.

Others, of course, view the nature of the changes brought about by genetics less sanguinely and doubt the ability of the common law to handle or manipulate such metamorphoses in line with public concern and resultant public policy. Thus, Louis Waller has observed that there is 'little in Australia by way of legal principles, standards and rules which affect directly and specifically, and unequivocally control' genetic research.[5] But, as he continues, we are no longer startled – it is an arresting assessment, but one that, with a little historical reflection, is entirely justified – that is, we have become accustomed to 'accounts of tissue transplants, including major single organs, nor surprised by the prospect of more and more spare parts being manufactured to replace worn-out or damaged elements in the human engine'.[6]

Waller then asks: 'Is the combination of common law rules, derived especially from the recent decisions of the High Court of Australia, and the NHMRC Guidelines a sufficient framework of regulation for this area of scientific research and its medical applications?' He concludes, after a detailed and thoughtful analysis, that it would not:

> [T]his area of human activity calls for careful regulation and control through the medium of legislation. In a country which has multiple legal systems, but where there are no significant differences in values, and in medical research

---

4   Skene, L, 'Genetics: an Australian report', in Deech, R, Mulders-Klein, T and van Dickerbroeke, P (eds), *Artificial Reproductive Technology and Genetics*, 2001, The Hague: Kluwer.

5   Waller, L, 'Controlling genetic research', in Smith, RG, *Health Care, Crime and Regulatory Control*, 1998, Sydney: Hawkins, Australian Institute of Criminology, p 204.

6   *Ibid*, p 205; *mutatis mutandi* in the UK.

and clinical practices, from Broome to Brisbane and from Darwin to the Derwent, it would be proper that such legislation should be national.[7]

I think further that, while the common law may have, indeed probably must have, an *interim* role to play in the legal responses to genetics, it lacks, for a variety of reasons, the necessary resources properly to represent a full response. Of course, there is a legal *contribution* which the common law can make. At one level, the clearest legal issues appear to be regulation of the uses of the fruits of genetic knowledge. Such fruits might come in at least two palettes:

(a) changing or modifying existing practices or behaviour, whether in relation to foodstuffs, animal welfare, genetic 'fingerprinting' of human beings and criminal detection;

(b) regulation of the information which genetically based methods can discern, whether in relation to health, medical or related insurance, medical records and family history (and, in each case, access to such information), individual predisposition to genetically inherited diseases, the patenting of the products of bioengineering, including human cells or human cell lines.

These are the fairly standard concerns of lawyers who have addressed questions of genetics. With them come several contributions (usually and necessarily derived from moral philosophy) to understandings of human dignity, 'personhood', and consequential matters relating to the medical or genetic interventions at the beginning or, less frequently, the ending of life.[8]

Thus, the US National Institute of Health has identified some of the following as important questions or considerations which need to be addressed:

• questions of fairness in the use of genetic information, especially with respect to insurance, employment, the criminal justice system, the education system, adoptions and family formation and the military;

• the impact of genetic information on the individual, including questions of stigmatisation, ostracism, labelling and individual psychological responses;

---

7 *Op cit*, Waller, fn 5, p 211.

8 The major legal concerns will focus on DNA fingerprinting as a legal tool, the legal regulation of research, ownership of genes, cells and embryos and the patenting of genetic information. Other legal difficulties concern ownership of the genetic information: genetic counselling and the legal responsibilities which this discloses, the legality or otherwise and grounds of access to abortion, and the question of commercial exploitation of the results of the human genome mapping project – which is also linked with issues of ownership through questions of intellectual and industrial property law. See, eg, Brahams, D, 'Human genetic information: the legal implications', in *Human Genetic Information: Science, Law and Ethics*, 1990, Chichester: John Wiley, p 149.

- the privacy and confidentiality of genetic information, including questions of ownership and control of that information, and consent to disclosure and use of that information;

- issues raised by genetic counselling, specifically in areas such as pre-natal testing, pre-symptomatic testing, carrier status testing, testing when no therapeutic remedy is available, counselling and testing for polygenic disorders, and population screening compared with testing;

- issues raised by reproductive decisions influenced by genetic information (which might be considered an adjunct of the privacy question), such as the effect of genetic information on options available and the use of genetic information in the decision making process;

- issues raised by the introduction of increased genetic information into mainstream medical practice, including questions of professional standards of care and quality control in acquiring and using genetic information, the qualifications and training of health professionals involved in genetic testing and counselling, the impact on the physician-patient relationship, standards for appropriate patient education, and education of the general public with respect to availability and accessibility of genetic services;

- the uses and misuses of genetics in the past and their current relevance, that is, the eugenics movement, problems arising from screening for sickle-cell trait and other examples in which screening or testing sometimes achieved unintended or unwanted outcomes, and the misuse of behavioural genetics to advance eugenics or prejudicial stereotypes;

- questions raised by the commercialisation of the products of the human genome project, particularly intellectual property rights, property rights, the impact on scientific collaboration and candour, and the accessibility of data and materials;

- a range of conceptual and philosophical issues raised, such as the implications for concepts of personal identity and responsibility, the concepts of determinism and reductionism, and the concepts of health and disease.

I think, however, that there is particular value in evolving statutory responses to genetics, in all its different guises, whatever masks it adopts or is adorned with. Thus, when Biotechnology Australia, in its September Discussion Paper, *Developing Australia's Biotechnology Future,*[9] discloses that new legislation to regularise the Interim Office of the Gene Technology Regulator is being developed co-operatively with State and Territory Governments, and co-ordinated through the IOGTR, and that:

---

9   Canberra, Commonwealth of Australia, September 1999, p 7.

> All jurisdictions share the aim of ensuring that the legislation is passed by all
> State, Territory and the Commonwealth Governments to provide a national
> regulatory framework,

that is merely writing on one national page a story which could be written on all.

I believe, however, that while these are necessary responses, they are also responses that are *necessarily* insufficient. This is a part of my thesis which, I would warrant, would need further elaboration and defence, and that is the burden of this present argument. More immediately, I want to suggest that the reason, the main reason, why we need to move from common law to statute, why there needs to be some commonality about our legal approaches to the genetic revolution, is primarily one of imagination. The biotechnological metamorphosis is a global one; the reassurance of insulation and isolation is something which genetics, fundamentally, will not permit – it almost prohibits it. The legal responses which we will need to make, which lawyers will be called upon to fashion, are the fairly standard concerns of lawyers who have addressed questions of genetics. These standard concerns, informed by moral philosophies, will, necessarily, reflect the traditions of moral philosophy in which the legal system exists. Domestic regulation, aided and abetted when the circumstances arise, as, for example, in the early applications of telemedicine, by the doctrines of private international law, will effectively amount to no regulation. Our early experiences with that other global revolution, the internet, are a precursor to that.

The common law will be insufficient to this task because there is no response that the common law can effectively make to global changes; again, our experiences with climate change and environmental law suggest this. There is nothing in the common law *imagination* that equips it to be fashioned for our use in this brave new world. But, presently, let me suggest only that a statutory response, one directed and delivered by government, is necessary to regulate (and I do not *necessarily* imply by that restriction, limitation or prohibition) the genetic revolution in an imaginative international order; an order which is called for, almost which is called forth, by the nature of modern science. Statutory responses are the only way, it seems to me, to generate that commonality of response which genetics calls for, or forth, globally. The common law, for all its protean strengths, knows nothing of a 'common' law, in the sense of one which is necessarily common *to* all States, let alone one common to all common law States. Our various approaches to the development of the law of torts, the different entries in our criminal calendar, are but two examples of this. It is perhaps only in certain aspects of the law of commercial contracts that a truly international *system* can be identified, and only in the legal response to changes of distance and imagination called forth by that earlier revolution of the 20th century – air travel – that a global, international *response* can be identified.

A *statutory* domestic suite of responses is called for before we can even begin to approach melding those responses together into a global international response. The alternative is fairly clearly seen by some commentators: '... in the end, international borders can do little to impede the reproductive practices of couples and individuals.'[10] And, as Lee Silver observes:

> ... the market place – not government or society – will control cloning. And if cloning is banned in one place, it will be made available somewhere else – perhaps on an underdeveloped island country happy to receive the tax revenue. Indeed within two weeks of Dolly's announcement, a group of investors formed a Bahamas-based company called Clonaid (under the direction of a French scientist called Dr Brigitte Boiselier) with the intention of building a clinic where cloning services would be offered to individuals for a fee of $200,000.[11]

Silver goes on to argue that the Roslin patent application was purposely worded to be inclusive of human cloning so that 'the inventors could use it as a legal vehicle to try to prevent this particular application from being used by anyone else'. However, Silver is doubtful that the fear of patent infringement will have any effect on cloning enterprises that operate in countries that refuse to accept World Intellectual Property Organisation rulings; and, in any case, 'the patent expires in 2017'.[12]

This scepticism stands in contrast to the emergence of other demands for supranational regulation of biomedicine and the identification of appropriate fora which have come to occupy the international community in the last decade. Possible responses to those demands, an understanding of intellectual forces which have produced them and the mediation of differences of form and substance, comprise what I have called *biomedical diplomacy*.[13] This concept can be located within a wider theoretical construct, identifying shifts in the nature of philosophical practices, and the development and deployment of new forms of regulation which both supplement and represent a challenge to the increasing juridification (the danger of the uncritical and unreflective appeal to and of law) of social and technical practices.[14]

The genetic revolution is over, as far as law is concerned, because it *cannot* be regulated. Common law regulation can address the usual palettes, but it lacks the imagination to 'control', let alone to 'direct', the vectors of the

---

10 Silver, L, *Remaking Eden: Cloning, Genetic Engineering and the Future of Humankind?*, 1998, London: Weidenfeld & Nicolson, pp 114–15.

11 *Ibid*, p 144; and see www.clonaid.com.

12 *Ibid*, p 347.

13 See above, Chapters 1–3.

14 See Teubner, G, 'Juridification: concepts, aspects, limits, solutions', in Teubner, G (ed), *Juridification of Social Spheres*, 1987, Berlin: Walter de Gruyter, pp 3–48; Galanter, M, 'Law abounding' (1992) 55 MLR 1; Beck, U, *Risk Society: Towards a New Modernity*, Ritter, M (trans), 1992, London: Sage, p 204.

fabulous world of global science. Statute is the only *form* that could be appropriated to address the genetic revolution, but there are already sufficient examples to suggest that, at the *instrumental* level, the ability of statute effectively to patrol the chromosomal commons is limited.

Let me offer two examples.

(a) Identity issues: the strange case of nucleus substitution

Licences under the Human Fertilisation and Embryology Act 1990 may not authorise the nucleus substitution (replacement) of an embryo (s 3(3)(d)). A licence is required for the creation of an embryo outside of the body (ss 3(1)(a) and 1(2)), where an embryo is defined as a live egg that has been fertilised or is in the process of fertilisation (s 1(1)(a) and (b)). Quite clearly, this prohibits cloning, where the techniques involve replacing the nucleus of a cell of an embryo *with a nucleus taken from elsewhere*, such as a person, or another embryo:

> A licence cannot authorise ... replacing a nucleus of a cell of an embryo with a nucleus taken from a cell of any person, embryo or subsequent development of an embryo [s 3(3)(d)].

Until recently, it was assumed that any cloning by nuclear substitution would entail such a replacement of the *nucleus* of an embryo, or replacing the nucleus of an egg with a *nucleus* from an embryonic cell. Indeed, Dolly had been preceded at birth by Morag and Megan, but they had been born following the use of an embryonic or fetal cell. The Dolly technique, however, involved nucleus substitution into an *egg* and not an embryo. A donor cell *was taken from an adult animal* (here, an udder cell) and cultured in a laboratory. A donor *cell* was taken from the culture and 'stored' in a medium which kept it just alive; the reason for this was to slow down or shut down the activities of the cell and send it into a period of dormancy (or 'quiescence'; scientifically called the G0 or Gap Zero cell stage). The G0 cell was then placed alongside a sheep *egg cell* (an oocyte, *not an embryo*) from which the nucleus had been removed. An electric pulse was used to fuse the two cells and activate embryo development, which after five to six days' further development in a laboratory was implanted in the surrogate mother ewe, Dolly's 'mother'.[15] Some 150 days later, to public astonishment and incredulity, Dolly's birth was announced in the scientific literature.[16]

The 'Dolly technique' not only stormed the popular imagination and gave the *Boys from Brazil* their greatest exercise in the last 15 years, it again appeared

---

15 Wilmut, I, Campbell, K and Tudge, C, *The Second Creation: The Age of Biological Control by the Scientists who Cloned Dolly*, 2000, London: Headline.

16 'Viable offspring derived from foetal and adult mammalian cells' (1997) 385 Nature 881.

to shake the foundations on which the Human Fertilisation and Embryology Act had been built; the scientific rocks on which the legislative house had laid its foundations were being battered by the waves of scientific endeavour and coming increasingly to resemble the shifting sands on which public policy's slippery slopes have their first outing; law was surfing again the turbulent seas of chaos theory. Later, a team of scientists in South Korea reported in 1998 that they had achieved nuclear replacement in a human ovum and then cultivated the fertilised egg to an early embryonic stage, although other scientists doubted the veracity of the report.[17]

The Warnock Committee made the assumption that the vast majority of embryos used in research would be spare embryos, created in the course of *in vitro* fertilisation treatment, but no longer required for that purpose. The tiny minority of embryos created specifically for research would have been produced by similar techniques (that is, mixing sperm and egg in the laboratory to achieve fertilisation outside the body). The creation of embryos by means other than by fertilising an egg with sperm was not possible when the issues were debated by the Warnock Committee and in Parliament. This gives rise to at least two immediate questions; what are Dolly, Millie, Christa, Alexis, Carrel and Dotcom? At one level, they are, respectively, one sheep and five pigs. But, created as they were outwith the established fertilisation boundaries – either 'naturally' or 'scientifically' – sparked into life after an electrical pulse, have they been born from a *new kind of embryo, morally* speaking? Secondly, what is the *legal* status of such a creation?

The moral argument

The suggestion explored here, that in creating an embryo by the process of cell nucleus replacement a new type of embryonic life has been created as a matter of moral judgment, comes from examining the stress previously laid by moral philosophers and theologians on the significance of fertilisation. Thus, Leon Kass has argued that:

> While the egg and the sperm are alive as cells, something new and alive *in a different sense* comes into being with fertilisation ... there exists a new individual with its unique genetic identity.[18]

This has drawn forth the following from Professor of Molecular Biology, Lee Silver. 'All non-religious objections to the cloning of human beings,' he has suggested:

---

17 (1998) *The Guardian*, 17 December.

18 Kass, L, 'The meaning of life – in the laboratory', in Alpern, KD (ed), *The Ethics of Reproductive Technology*, 1992, New York: OUP, pp 98–116, emphasis in original.

19 *Op cit*, Silver, fn 10, p 305.

... evaporate when a child is born through the fusion of cloned embryos. Such a child will not be genetically identical to either of her progenitor-parents and thus there cannot be any violation to her so called 'right to genetic uniqueness' ...[19]

Silver's argument, while a good example of many of the *non sequiturs* which abound in this debate, illustrate clearly the role that will need to be assumed here by law in what we might call its declamatory function – marking out the boundaries (or merely a temporary fence) to the people whom we say we are and those that we want to become. In fact, as I try to show later, the importance of the resolution to this moral debate has more than the usual significance for the legal regulation of embryo research: to paraphrase Margot Brazier, it is more than just an ethicist's tiff. Suppose that, morally, we conclude that an embryo created following cell nucleus replacement is not fundamentally a different *type* of embryo because, like all other embryos, it is (a) undoubtedly human embryonic life and (b) could develop into a human being. If, indeed, we regard this as a morally compelling reason for treating the cell nucleus replacement created embryo more or less like any other embryo, or certainly *sufficiently* like an embryo created either *in vivo* or following *in vitro* fertilisation, this is to take what might be called a 'purposive' (or resulting) moral view of the embryo. That is, that the moral status of the embryo is given from what results and not (although some once thought and wrote differently) from the mechanisms or processes – or even some particular point in that mechanism or process – by which it comes into existence. If this moral point or argument is defensible, then contrary to Beykveld and Pattinson, Brazier and Silver, in arguments I review shortly, the legal position based upon a purposive interpretation of the 1990 Act is similarly defensible.

Margot Brazier has aired her worries on this particular question: '... nuclear substitution challenges our understanding of what a human embryo is and what its moral claims may be.'[20] While this is one of the first essays in the UK in which this 'moral status' has been publicly raised, I suspect that it will not be the last. What Brazier means in her question is that many opponents of embryo research centre their opposition to destruction of embryos on the view that, from the creation of a zygote – after the process of fertilisation between the egg and sperm – a new genetic person comes into being. It is the fusion of egg and sperm which begins a new human creature. When the embryo is created by the cell nucleus replacement technique and not from the fusing of sperm and egg, *when fertilisation never takes place*, in what (moral) sense is an embryo as a genetically unique entity created?

The use of cell nuclear replacement to produce human embryos might be thought to create a new form of early embryonic life – one that is genetically virtually identical to the donor of the cell nucleus. This prospect goes further than that contemplated by either the Warnock Committee or Parliament when it debated these issues. The creation of embryos in this way is not ruled out

20 Brazier, M, 'Regulating the reproduction business?' (1999) 7 Med L Rev 189.

under the 1990 Act, provided that any research use to which it is proposed to put the embryo is for one of the five existing purposes. Although these embryos differ in the method of their creation, they are undoubtedly human embryonic life, which, given the right conditioning, could develop into a human being. But are they the same kind of embryo – morally speaking – as that which deserves respect as a member of the human species as Warnock originally thought and as the 1990 Act decreed? As Brazier asks: 'What is the fundamental nature of cloned cell tissue or organs?'[21]

The legal argument

It is important here immediately to observe three things:

(a) *cell nucleus replacement* is not specifically prohibited by the 1990 Act;

(b) the same is true of 'embryo splitting', which occurs naturally at a very early stage of embryonic development in the formation of identical twins. This can also be done *in vitro* in some species at the 8-cell stage and identical 'cloned' embryos may develop;

(c) the so called Dolly technique, where the nucleus of an egg cell is replaced with a nucleus of a somatic cell taken *from an adult* was beyond the bounds of scientific credibility, at least when the 1990 Act was passed.

The HFEA gave careful consideration to embryo splitting as an additional possible form of infertility treatment in 1994, when its potential use at the 2- or 4-cell embryonic stage was discussed. After considering the social and ethical issues involved, the HFEA decided to ban embryo splitting as a possible fertility treatment and additionally indicated that it would not license research towards the development of cloning as a form of treatment. However, the Authority did not then make a similar prohibition in respect of cell nuclear replacement research. Somatic cell nuclear transfer, then, raises at the very least a new legal question on the ambit of the Human Fertilisation and Embryology Act; as the technique involves nucleus substitution into an egg and not an embryo, and this is not specifically covering by the wording of s 3(3)(d) of the Act, is it prohibited? And, as fertilisation is not then involved, such that s 3(1) ('No person shall bring about the creation of an embryo ... except in pursuance of a licence') does not apply either, is it regulated at all by the Human Fertilisation and Embryology Act?

The HGAC and the HFEA, in their consultation paper on cloning and the subsequent report, *Cloning Issues in Human Reproduction* (1998), rejected the arguments implicit in both of these questions which would have left cell nucleus substitution outside the regulatory ambit of the Act. Rather, following

---

21 *Op cit,* Brazier, fn 20.

counsel's advice, they declared that, depending on the method used, cloning is either prohibited or subject to licensing. The Report observed that, while 'embryo splitting and the nuclear replacement of eggs are not expressly prohibited ... both involve the use or creation of embryos outside the body'. Hence, they concluded: '... they fall within the Human Fertilisation and Embryology Act and therefore come under the jurisdiction of the HFEA.'[22] Clearly, this relies on taking a 'purposive' rather than a 'literal' interpretation of the 1990 Act and the meaning assigned in the legislation to the term 'embryo', and the HFEA have made it clear that it will not issue a licence for any research 'which has reproductive cloning as its aim'.[23]

It has not been (indeed, it is far from) settled that the application of the Dolly technique to humans would fall on the narrowly drafted provisions of the HFEA. At least three objections have so far been publicly registered; from Deryck Beykveld and Shaun Pattinson, from Margot Brazier, and from the All-Parliamentary Pro-Life Group. First, Beykveld and Pattinson have insisted that using the Dolly technique does not involve the creation of an embryo at all, because an embryo is defined under the Act as 'a live human embryo where fertilisation is complete', including 'an egg in the process of fertilisation'. Indeed, as they aver, Wilmut has himself suggested that '[t]he oocyte is an egg but it has not been fertilised and it *never is fertilised* because the nucleus is transferred to it'[24] (emphasis added), although they do add their belief that 'in practice, it is very likely that the term "fertilisation" will be judicially construed to include the nuclear substitution of an egg, especially since the HFEA seems to be acting according to the construction of this term'.[25]

Secondly, Margot Brazier has offered a similar interpretation: 'I would contend that nuclear substitution into an egg cell is unregulated in the United Kingdom today.'[26] Using the analogy of plant breeding, she argues that cell nucleus substitution constitutes propagation, not fertilisation. Section 3(1) (requiring a licence from the HFEA to bring about the creation of an embryo) is subject to the definition of an embryo in s 1: that provides that 'embryo means a live human embryo' and, if that is all that it said, then cell nucleus

22 HGAC and HFEA, *Cloning Issues in Reproduction, Science and Medicine*, 1998, London: HGAC/HFEA, para 3.4.

23 *Ibid*, para 5.4, p 11.

24 Beykveld, D and Pattinson, S, in Beykveld, D and Haker, H, *The Ethics of Genetics in Human Procreation*, 2000, Aldershot: Ashgate, p 232, offer a second example of difficulties with legislative interpretation. The German Embryo Protection Act (*Embryonenschutzgesetz*) 1990 is clearly intended to prohibit cloning; s 6 renders it an offence to create an embryo that is genetically identical to another embryo, fetus or any living or dead person; but the Act does not define the term 'genetically identical', so it is questionable whether it is wide enough to encompass a clone produced by somatic cell nuclear transfer.

25 *Ibid*, p 233.

26 *Op cit*, Brazier, fn 20, p 189.

replacement would clearly be within the statutory scheme of the 1990 Act. But the Act says more, as the All-Parliamentary Pro-Life Group have shown. They have challenged the interpretation offered by the joint consultation paper issued by the HFEA and the HGAC of April 1998. Repeating the Authority and the Commission's view that embryo splitting and nuclear replacement of the eggs fall within a purposive interpretation of the legislation, the Parliamentary Group object that the Human Fertilisation and Embryology Act defines an embryo as 'a live human embryo where fertilisation is complete', and observe that:

> ... the clear intention of Parliament was to prohibit the creation of cloned human embryos, both for research and reproductive purposes ... since a cloned embryo has not undergone fertilisation, it might be argued that a cloned embryo is not an embryo for the purposes of the Act. If the courts were to adopt this interpretation, it would follow that the HFEA has no power to regulate the creation or keeping of embryos [paras 1.3.2–1.3.3].

They conclude that it is questionable that 'work which would create cloned human beings cannot lawfully be carried out', as the Government had concluded, and called for the Act to be clarified to ensure that such a prohibition was unassailably in place.

Let me add to this my own view, shortly. Recall that I have already argued that, at least from a moral point of view, and taking what we might call a purposive or result oriented approach, it may be possible to reconcile the cell nucleus substitution embryo with embryos created *in vitro* in what, astonishingly, we might now call 'the ordinary way'. From this, it would follow, contrary to Brazier and Beykveld, that there is no particular difficulty in accepting the view to which the HFEA works, that the creation of embryos by cell nucleus substitution is *already* brought within the scheme of the Human Fertilisation and Embryology Act by an extended interpretation of s 1.

So far, what I have quoted from s 1 throws doubt on the advice received by the HFEA and HGAC, which is the advice from the Department of Health. But, that is not all that s 1 says. It is limited not just in the one way that Beykveld and Brazier have pointed out, but in an additional way too. Correctly, they have reminded us that an embryo in s 1 means 'a live human embryo where fertilisation is complete', whereas with an embryo created by cell nucleus substitution (CNR), fertilisation never has taken place, so it is difficult to accept that an embryo within the meaning of the Act has been created. And herein lies the second difficulty.

Section 1(1)(a) in full reads:

> In this Act, *except where otherwise stated*: (a) embryo means a live human embryo where fertilisation is complete.

The emphasised words make it plain that the legislator could have provided separately for embryos created other than by *in vitro* fertilisation to be included within the statute, but evidently they did not. To read the statute as providing for embryos created by cell nucleus replacement is to read it as providing that an embryo means a live human embryo where fertilisation is complete, *unless the context otherwise requires*. And that, decidedly, the Act does not do.

The fundamental problem with adopting the purposive approach to the interpretation of s 1 which has been commended to the HFEA is that, as a matter of statutory interpretation practice, the purposive approach can only be relied upon when there is an ambiguity produced by a literal interpretation of the provision in question. On the face of the Act, there does not appear to be any such ambiguity. However, the way in which a court might be persuaded to approach this difficult question might well depend on *context*. Imagine two cases in which this question of the legal status of the CNR embryo and the ambit of the 1990 Act might come to be argued.

First, suppose that an embryologist advised of the 'literal interpretation' argument decides, without more, that he or she will proceed to create CNR embryos without reference to the HFEA, does so, and conducts experiments on those embryos without applying to the HFEA for a licence, and is then prosecuted under ss 3(1) and 41(2) for carrying on without a licence an activity for which it is said a licence was necessary. Conviction on indictment on such a charge carries a possible term of imprisonment of up to two years. The usual rule in a criminal prosecution would enable the embryologist to claim the benefit, and here the protection, of the literal interpretation of the 1990 Act argued for above. A court might be somewhat more reluctant to adopt this sympathetic approach with an embryologist who had kept, and perhaps even conducted experiments that entail keeping, the CNR embryo long beyond the appearance of the 'primitive streak' (the '14 day rule', as provided for in s 3(3)(a) and (4)), but, if this 'literal' argument is correct, such experiments would not be unlawful *under the 1990 Act*. Whether the embryologist might commit an offence under another enactment is a moot point.

Suppose, however, in a second example, that a case comes before the High Court by way of an application for judicial review, the HFEA having refused to grant a (particular) licence on application to conduct experiments set out in a research protocol on CNR embryos or, perhaps more realistically, attaching conditions to a licence providing that CNR embryos are not be used in the project or that the CNR embryo is not to be kept beyond the statutory period. Here, the embryologist's argument is that he or she is being unlawfully deprived of a research opportunity by the HFEA, which it is alleged is acting beyond its powers. The strength of the case for a literal, rather than a purposive, interpretation of the Act is far less compelling. It may seem less than extraordinary that a provision such as s 1 of the Human Fertilisation and Embryology Act might be open to competing interpretations; it is the essence of statutory *interpretation* that words do not interpret themselves. It might

---

27 See, eg, *Coventry Waste Disposal v Solihull BC* [1999] 1 WLR 2093.

seem more unlikely that the interpretation to be settled on might depend on the circumstances of the case first bringing the question to the court, but this *contextual* argument has some weight of legal experience behind it.[27]

(b) The legality of taking and storing ovarian tissue and gametes

For the second example of my argument, the relevant provisions to consider are ss 4(1), 12, 14, Sched 3 (consents) and Sched 3, s 2(2), para 8(1) (storage) of the Human Fertilisation and Embryology Act 1990, and the HFEA Code of Practice, paras 3.39–3.42.

The general rules in relation to the removal and storage of ovarian tissue and testicular tissue are set out in guidance from the HFEA, given its understanding of the common law and the provisions of the Human Fertilisation and Embryology Act. They can be summarised as follows.

Oocyte preservation and ovarian tissue storage

- A person who keeps or uses gametes in contravention of the Act is guilty of an offence.

- If ovarian tissue contains gametes as understood by the HFEA, then the licensing provisions of the Act apply and a storage licence is generally required.

- Gametes are understood by the HFEA to be:

  ... a reproductive cell, such as an ovum or a spermatozoon, which has a haploid set of chromosomes and which is able to take part in fertilisation with another of the opposite sex to form a zygote.[28]

- If the ovarian tissue which is taken does *not* contain gametes as understood by the HFEA (and a practical difficulty is that the best results appear to be obtained using oocytes taken from the largest follicles, which are, therefore, already the most mature *in vivo*)[29] then it may be stored (as

---

28 *Storage and Use of Ovarian Tissue*, 1990, London: HFEA. The Human Fertilisation and Embryology Act 1990, s 1(4), is the closest that the legislation itself comes to a definition: '... references to gametes or eggs do not include eggs in the process of fertilisation.'

29 Health Council of The Netherlands, Committee on *In Vitro* Fertilisation, *IVF-Related Research*, 1998, Rijswijk, p 41, para 3.2.2.

30 Because s 2(2) does not apply by virtue of s 1(4); for the notion of 'fertility insurance' see *ibid*, HFEA, p 47, para 3.4.3.

31 Family Law Reform Act 1969, s 8: '(1) The consent of a minor who has attained the age of 16 years to any surgical, medical or dental treatment which, in the absence of consent, would constitute a trespass to his person, shall be as effective as it would be if he were of full age; and where a minor has by virtue of this section given an effective consent to any treatment it shall not be necessary to obtain any consent for it from his parent or guardian.'

a non-licensable activity) in, say, prospective oncology treatment as a form of 'fertility insurance'[30] (if the HFEA is correct):

o with the consent of the woman if over 18, as with any other adult;

o if 16–18, with consent by the girl herself;[31]

o with the consent of the girl herself if she is under 16 and 'Gillick competent';[32] or

o if not Gillick competent, then with the consent of her parent(s) or another person with parental responsibility.[33]

• It is possible that autografting pieces of ovarian tissue which have been excised and cryopreserved would enable a woman to attempt to conceive without IVF, but, if the immature gametes are later taken from the tissue and matured in vitro,[34] then the Act will apply even if the oocytes are to be used for the woman's own benefit. Ovarian tissue grafting carries a risk, of course, which is not present with use of frozen mature oocytes, of reintroducing the cancer cells with the transplant.

Merely because the tissue is stored in the course of an unlicensed activity does not mean, however, that it is free from legal control, especially not at the behest of the tissue provider. Thus, where the unlicensed activity takes place – as most will do, I suspect – in a clinic outside the NHS, there will be an express or implied contract between the gamete provider and the clinic. The contract might expressly provide what is to happen to the tissue, although the enforceability of a detrimental term against a minor would be highly unlikely. More likely might be a claim against a clinic for wrongful disposal of the tissue, including a claim that the tissue disposed of belonged – in a proprietary sense – to the provider. Any such (contractual) claim could include a claim for damages for any personal distress caused to the provider by the dealing with the tissue (for example, apparent use or disposal of the tissue without the provider's consent or in breach of the implied terms of the contract).[35]

What would need to be shown is that there is 'some practical value or possible sensible purpose in retaining the specimen for future use such that it makes sense to recognise a proprietary or possessary interest'.[36] A

---

32 Gillick v West Norfolk and Wisbech AHA [1985] 3 All ER 402.

33 For the concept of 'parental responsibility', see the Children Act 1989, s 3.

34 IVM: in vitro maturation of oocytes.

35 Bliss v South East Thames RHA [1987] ICR 700; Hayes v Dodd [1990] 2 All ER 815.

36 Dobson v North Tyneside AHA [1996] 4 All ER 464.

cryopreserved or otherwise stored immature gamete probably comes as close to illustrating such a consideration as any other tissue is likely to do.

The Human Tissue Act 1961

There is a further issue concerning the applicability of the Human Tissue Act to immature oocytes and their use subsequent to the death of the provider. Mature oocytes, or gametes, are of course within the statutory scheme of the Human Fertilisation and Embryology Act 1990. Gamete donation is within Sched 3, para 2(2) of the Act. But ovarian tissue, on the HFEA's definition of 'gametes', is not, though it does probably fall within the 1961 Act.[37] The relevant section of that Act is s 1:

(1) If any person, either in writing at any time or orally in the presence of two or more witnesses during his last illness, has expressed a request that his body *or any specified part of his body* be used after his death for therapeutic purposes ... the person lawfully in possession of his body after his death may, unless he has reason to believe that the request was subsequently withdrawn, authorise the removal from the body of any part, or as the case may be, the specified part, for use in accordance with the request.

(2) ... the person lawfully in possession of the body of a deceased person may authorise the removal of any part of the body for the said purpose if, having made such reasonable enquiry as may be practicable, he has no reason to believe that:

    (a) the deceased had expressed an objection to his body being dealt with after his death and had not withdrawn it; or

    (b) that the surviving spouse or any other relative of the deceased objects to the body being so dealt with.

Section 1(1) thus contemplates the direction by a person in their last illness to the use of a part of their body after death for therapeutic purposes. Where this concerns the recovery of immature oocytes through follicle puncture or through ovarian tissue biopsy, this may be a way for a person about to undergo therapy which, in the event, they do not survive, effectively being able to 'donate' immature oocytes for the use by another woman.[38]

- Where a licence for storage is needed, the effective consents provisions of the Act must be complied with. Such consent can only be provided by the person whose gametes are to be stored; there is no provision in the Act here for substituted consent. Neither the parents of a girl unable to provide an effective consent, nor any one else with parental responsibility, can provide an effective consent in such circumstances.

---

37 Department of Health, *Review of the Common Law Provisions Relating to the Removal of Gametes and of the Consent Provisions in the Human Fertilisation and Embryology Act 1990,* (the MacLean Report), 1998, London: DOH, p 21, para 3.13.

38 For present purposes I *assume* that there is no other doubt as to the technical viability of such grafting.

- Thus, if it is intended to take ovarian tissue containing gametes *for storage* as understood by the HFEA, the following steps must be complied with. It may be stored *only* if there is an effective consent:
  - by the woman (if over 18); or
  - by the woman between 16–18; or
  - by a young woman under 16 who is *Gillick* competent *herself* to give consent to the storage.

The consent of no one else to the storage will suffice. With adolescent girls, this will mean that, in each case, the doctor must be satisfied that the girl is capable of understanding the *implications* of the proposed course of action. This will mean that the mere written recording of agreement is not sufficient, effective consent properly understood will mean that the decision has been arrived at on the basis of information and discussion, and if the clinician concludes that a young woman cannot understand the information or is unable to participate in a discussion concerning the proposed treatment and the implication of the storage (including the possibility that the gametes may later have to be allowed to perish) then, although he or she might conclude that the girl would be *Gillick* competent for a range of *other* therapeutic interventions, the doctor may yet have to conclude that the young woman is not *Gillick* competent for this proposed intervention. Finally, it will mean that that the provisions of Sched 3 to the Human Fertilisation and Embryology Act have been complied with. Again, this entails that:

> A consent under this Schedule must be given in writing and, in this Schedule, 'effective consent' means a consent under this Schedule which has not been withdrawn ...

And, crucially:

> 2(2) A consent to the storage of any gametes ... must:
>
> (a) specify the maximum period of storage (if less than the statutory storage period); and
>
> (b) state what is to be done with the gametes ... if the person who gave the consent dies or is unable because of incapacity to vary the terms of the consent or to revoke it; and
>
> (c) may specify conditions subject to which the gametes ... may remain in storage.

The possibility of *reintroducing* the cancer from the tissue with immature oocytes would need to be raised, if not at the time of taking then at some later time; with frozen oocytes there is, of course, no such risk of transmission.

- Whether ovarian tissue contains gametes in any given case will need to be decided by the clinician according to the woman's menstrual cycle or testing of the tissue itself.

This reading of the scope of the Act leads to the conclusion, undesirable as it may be, that there are circumstances in which it would be perfectly lawful to *recover* ovarian tissue containing gametes, or even gametes themselves, at common law (as being in the 'best interests' of someone who was incapable of consenting to their taking), but where it would be unlawful to store them in any way.[39] While this may be less of a problem in respect of ovarian tissue or oocytes, it is undoubtedly a very great problem in respect of post-Tanner Stage 2 boys who are, nonetheless, judged not *Gillick* competent for the purposes of giving effective consent to storage within Sched 3.

Indeed, it might be thought that this anomaly, as Professor McLean describes it, where gametes might be *lawfully*[40] recovered as being in a person's best interests but may not be stored until such time as they can exercise their own determination as to what they believe their best interests to be might be, provides a clear indication of a provision in a UK statute which is incompatible with Arts 8 and 12 of the European Convention on Human Rights. In relation to any relevant challenge, British courts will be required under the Human Rights Act 1998 to pay attention to these provisions.

Indeed, an attempt to preserve gametes prior to the export to another Member State for the purpose of longer term storage with a subsequent view to the use of treatment services there, might also be thought to be in contravention of the relevant provisions of the EC Treaty (as amended). Here, we run into the wider reaching effects of the decision of the Court of Appeal in *Blood*.[41] In deciding that infertility treatment services unequivocally fall within the scope of Arts 59 and 60 (free movement of services – now Arts 49 and 50, respectively),[42] and in doing so in the way in which they did, the Court of Appeal has opened a number of interesting lines of inquiry.

Lord Woolf, in the Court of Appeal, concluded that, in a case where a woman wished to receive artificial insemination using sperm of her late husband, 'it is artificial to treat the refusal of permission to export the sperm as not withholding the provision of fertilisation treatment in another Member State' and said that, from a functional point of view, the ability to provide those services 'is not only substantially impeded but made impossible'. The HFEA's original refusal to permit the export of Mr Blood's sperm 'prevents Mrs Blood having the only treatment which she wants'.[43]

---

39 And recall that s 2(2) of the Act regards cryopreservation as merely one method of storing within the Act. Of course, this is not applicable to immature oocytes, as defined by the HFEA.

40 This limitation is crucial; see the McLean Report, *op cit*, fn 37, para 2.9.

41 *R v HFEA ex p Blood* [1997] 2 All ER 687 (CA). There is a note of the case by Morgan and Lee in (1997) 60 MLR 840.

42 The jurisprudence of the ECJ on these questions appears quite unequivocal: 'Where rules impede market access by suppliers based in other Member States, they must be objectively justified. That the court has not been deterred from developing this principle despite Art 60(3) [permitting the supply of services to be regulated by the host State on "the same conditions as are imposed by the State on its own nationals"] testifies to its determination to construct a core set of principles of Community trade law, drawing together the separate Treaty provisions, most of all Arts 30 and 59.' Weatherill, S, *Law and Integration in the European Union*, 1995, Oxford: Clarendon, p 253.

43 [1997] 2 All ER 687, pp 700 and 698.

Mutatis mutandi, in respect of the storage of gametes or ovarian tissue containing gametes otherwise lawfully recovered which it is said cannot be lawfully preserved. The effect of the consent schedule – otherwise of laudable ambit – produces, in the case of someone unable to give effective consent to the storage of that tissue even where it would be *therapeutically* justified – and this is the important limiting condition of this argument – a restriction on them having access to the only treatment which they might (later) want. This would infringe, as it did in Mrs Blood's case, not only the freedom from restriction to *receive* services (itself a right derivative from the freedom to provide services), but also their implied freedom from restriction on the export of *resources necessary to secure those services* (that is, in such cases as the cryopreserved or otherwise stored gametes).

LAW, SCIENCE AND PUBLIC POLICY

These brief but complex examples illustrate that the time may be approaching when it is right for a wholesale review of the Human Fertilisation and Embryology Act 1990. This may be necessary in an innovative field such as this anyway, but also better to be able to understand the nature and type of regulation which is properly called for in this sensitive area. I am strengthened in this belief by the recent conclusions of the review by the HGAC and the HFEA in their consultation report, *Cloning Issues in Reproduction, Science and Medicine*.[44] At para 9.7, they observe:

> ... because of the pace of scientific advances in the area of human genetics, the HGAC and the HFEA believe that the issues need to be kept under regular review to monitor scientific progress. We therefore recommend that the issues are re-examined again in, say, five years' time, in the light of developments and public attitudes towards them in the interim.[45]

I am also convinced in this view by Bill Bryson. I am a great believer that the field of medical law, as much as medical ethics, should conform so far as possible with Bill Bryson's first rule of shopping: you should never buy anything which is too heavy to make the children carry home.[46] In other words, medical law, so far as possible, should be simple and straightforward and capable of ready understanding in everyday use in the High Street as much as in the High Court. With assisted conception and embryology, the law

---

44 1998, London: HFEA/HGAC.

45 This is a device adopted by other European jurisdictions, eg, Denmark and France, in their legislation concerning assisted conception procedures and their regulation. For a recent review of the French legislation of 1994 (Loi 94–654) as required by that Act, see *L'Application de la Loi No 94–654 du 29 juillet 1994* (No 1407 Ass National; No 232 Senat; Office Parlementaire d'Evaluation des Choix Scientifiques et Technologies, 1999).

46 Bryson, B, *Notes From a Small Island*, 1995, London: Doubleday.

is coming closer, I venture, to Flanders and Swann's view of the second law of thermodynamics than Bryson's more accommodating rule. It is becoming more and more complex and being made to dance upon the heads of embryological spindles:

> Legislative assemblies have not, however, been particularly quick or successful in their attempts to introduce legislation. This is not because assisted reproduction is thought to be uncontroversial or to lack priority. It is because it has proven to be too controversial. Ironically, those countries which have failed to legislate (such as Italy and Belgium) are by default the most 'permissive'.[47]

Of course, it does not follow from this that we should abandon altogether attempts to put into statutory form our present aspirations for the regulation of genetic sciences, nor that we should abandon those attempts any more at an international or even global scale than at a domestic one. We might want to continue to do this, or at least strive to continue to do this, for other, let us call them symbolic or declarative reasons. But the law of copyright is a good enough example of the difficulties associated with policing even very traditional scientific resources globally (with different levels of protection for traditionally recognised 'works' according to the level of observance of the individual States). These difficulties and differences are amplified when the system for protecting intellectual property is confronted with a new addition to the bundle of rights to be assessed (for example, the copyright protection of computer programs). It is not apparent whether the shape and nature of the arrival suggests that it is a lawful visitor, a licensee or a trespasser.

Genetics duplicates these questions exponentially, occupies new territory in the risk society, and is establishing adverse possession. The nature of the scientific shift which genetics imported demanded a similar paradigm shift of law, and we (have) lacked the 'lengthened foresight' to respond. To Giddens' assessment of risk society as one characterised as 'after nature' and 'after tradition', we should now also add 'after genetics'.

---

47 *Op cit*, Beykveld and Pattinson, fn 24.

PART V

OUTROS: EXITS AND DEPARTURES

TRAGIC CHOICES AND MODERN DEATH: SOME *BLAND* REFLECTIONS

Doctors ... are almost the only people we allow to talk directly of death ... a doctor is given leave to sit and talk to you in detail about your dying, if not your being dead. Everyone else, you soon discover, whether sad, concerned, excited (and that does happen) or merely anxious that you go without leaving a mess behind you, tends to talk to you about everything else except death ... No one minds talking about death as a statistic in Bosnia, or hospices for the terminally ill, or quoting a poet or two ... or even Woody Allen, but no one feels comfortable talking about *dying and being dead*.[1]

ON RITES

Euthanasia is an endless debate; likewise physician assisted suicide. Proponents are frequently portrayed as playing fast and loose with the sanctity of human life. Opponents are painted as fanatical do-gooders intent on imposing their enduring spiritual views on increasingly secular Western societies. Both caricatures have elements of farce and fairness in them, in an old debate where, too frequently, fiction takes the place of fact, where fable does the work of narrative and where demons and panics abound.

Thoughts of death are always a distraction from life and, as the years pass – for each of us – there is less and less time for them.[2] Yet, death has not required us to keep a day free.[3] The life cycle of ethical argumentation encompassing euthanasia and other terminal questions, approximating to what Guido Calabresi once identified as the endless movement of 'tragic choices',[4] oscillate around quality, sanctity and value. The framing of legal questions about death and the emergence of the language of rights *is* new. And there have also been important social and cultural changes which have brought the debate about euthanasia and other moments of dying to the banks of a Rubicon for which, supporters and opponents of euthanasia and its closely related cousins appear to agree, there is no return ticket. The morality

---

1   Dessaix, R, *Night Letters*, 1996, Sydney: Macmillan, p 110, emphasis in original.

2   Mortimer, J, *Murderers and Other Friends*, 1995, Harmondsworth: Penguin, p 74.

3   Cronin, A, *Samuel Beckett: The Last Modernist*, 1997, London: Flamingo, p 143, on Beckett's book on *Proust* (1931). Or, as Emily Dickinson has memorably put it: 'Because I could not stop for Death / He kindly stopped for me', quoted *ibid*, Dessaix, p 110.

4   Calabresi, G with Bobbitt, P, *Tragic Choices: The Conflicts Society Confronts in the Allocation of Tragically Scarce Resources*, 1978, New York: WW Norton.

plays of death are now received in theatres with increasingly ageing populations. The scarcity of resources which it is thought appropriate that health care should bear has become a pressing debate, the 'tragic choices' debate. Coupled with deepening scepticism about claims to professional independence from external scrutiny and supervision, increasing bureaucratisation and institutionalisation of medical decision making, and a growing awakening of global concerns about ethics and human rights, euthanasia and physician assisted suicide has hit new ground.

This chapter has an exploratory, if not experimental purpose. I am genuinely agnostic about the moral and ethical questions involved in some of the debates. For some people, of course, identifying an agnosticism to, say, euthanasia or physician assisted suicide is sufficient to condemn the implicit thesis that that must contain: that one could believe that, *in circumstances*, euthanasia could be accepted. Indeed, I do hold to the view that I could be persuaded that, *in circumstances*, euthanasia could be justified, just as I hold to the view that, *in circumstances*, what we habitually call murder, manslaughter or killing could be justified. The same should, in all fairness, be said to those of the opposite persuasion; those for whom, say, arguments and appeals to rights are sufficient to do *all* the work involved. Here, I am also agnostic; I am, like many, I suspect, lulled by the rhetoric of rights; but I have read John Hart Ely's pithy *dictum* too frequently (and cited it too often in footnotes) to be more than sceptical about the particular purchase that rights might afford, at least in the jurisprudence of health care and medical law. Ely has cautioned us to:

> ... watch most fundamental rights theorists start edging towards the door ... when someone mentions jobs, food, or housing: those are important, sure, but they aren't fundamental.[5]

In this chapter, I do not want to undertake yet another examination of the morality of euthanasia or physician assisted suicide, mercy killing and selective non-treatment. That ground is amply and adequately covered in other places.[6]

Rather, I want to offer some reflections about what I think these questions may have to show us about the place and purpose, the concerns and cautions, of modern medical law. I do want to investigate something of the rhetoric of *the right to die* which, like all advertising slogans and expressions, both debases as well as encapsulates something larger,[7] and to reflect upon the place of law in the making of tragic choices in death.

---

5   Ely, JH, *Democracy and Distrust*, 1980, Cambridge, Mass: Harvard UP, p 59.

6   The best general introductions of which I am aware remain Keown, J, *Euthanasia Examined*, 1995, Cambridge, CUP; Symposium, 'Physician assisted suicide' (1999) 109(3) Ethics 497; and Dworkin, R, *Life's Dominion*, 1993, London: HarperCollins. Margaret Otlowski's magisterial volume *Voluntary Euthanasia and the Common Law*, 1997, Oxford: Clarendon and John Griffiths' *Euthanasia and the Law in The Netherlands*, 1998, Amsterdam: Amsterdam UP are respectively the best account of the comparative legal position and the most sustained and informed analysis of and reflection upon the most controversial legal developments and reforms in The Netherlands.

7   Charlesworth, M, *Bioethics in a Liberal Society*, 1993, Cambridge: CUP, p 34.

Leon Kass has captured the lexical hopelessness of a narrowly conceived, literally constructed notion of a right to die.[8]

And John Finnis has dismissed as mere sloganising the use of the term 'euthanasia' devised, he claims, 'for service in a rhetoric of persuasion' because it has 'no generally accepted and philosophically warranted core of meaning'.[9] Max Charlesworth, on the other hand, has identified much of the prose for which the 'right to die' stands as a shorthand expression. Seen as the expanded notion of controlling the manner and the means, the geography and the grail of one's death, 'this developing recognition of the right of a person freely to determine and control, so far as is possible, the mode of his death'[10] is part of the attempt to recapture the right to preside at one's death, the loss of which is bemoaned by writers as diverse as Ivan Illich and John Gray.[11]

If concern with death, dying and euthanasia is really nothing new, what has brought about this change in the engagement?[12]

There are, I think, really two central points to the movement of the compass which are definitive: the second as a response to movements in the first. There have been, first, as remarked upon by so many before, changes in *the medicalisation of death* (if not life more generally). The medical management of death and dying is, perhaps, the single most salient change in the general practice of Western medicine in the past century. More and more people now die after an explicit decision has been made, either to withdraw or not start treatment. In clever technological societies, fewer and fewer people die at home; the final movements of life are played out in the theatres of death – the hospital. Those whose death could formerly have been foretold, chronicled with the most precision, the condemned, have been replaced by the sick in critical condition. At least, that is the argument of Ivan Illich:

> ... society, acting through the medical system, decides when and after what indignities and mutilations he shall die ... Western man has lost the right to preside at his act of dying ... mechanical death has conquered and destroyed all other deaths.[13]

---

8   Kass, L, 'Is there a right to die?' (1993) 23(1) Hastings Center Report 34.

9   'A philosophical case against euthanasia', in *op cit*, Keown, fn 6. Or, as otherwise put, 'When *I* use a word', Humpty Dumpty said, in a rather scornful tone, 'it means just what I choose it to mean – neither more nor less'. 'The question is,' said Alice, 'whether you *can* make words mean so many different things.' 'The question is,' said Humpty Dumpty, 'which is to be master – that's all.' Carroll, L, 'Humpty Dumpty', in *Through the Looking-Glass*, in Gardner, M (ed), *The Annotated Alice*, 1965, Harmondsworth: Penguin, pp 268–69.

10 *Op cit*, Charlesworth, fn 7, p 37.

11 I discuss these views in Chapter 12, although it might be objected that they at least as easily and happily belong here.

12 Callahan, D, in *op cit*, Keown, fn 6, p xiv offers his own interesting reflections on this particular question, while concluding that 'there is no clear and obvious explanation'.

13 Illich, I, *Limits to Medicine: Medical Nemesis: The Expropriation of Health*, 1976, Harmondsworth: Penguin, p 210. And see Nietzsche, F, 'The twilight of the idols', in *The Complete Works of Frederick Nietzsche*, p 88, quoted in *op cit*, Dworkin, fn 6, p 212.

Whether or not this is, in fact, the case, and I suspect that there is a good deal of rhetoric and hyperbole there, there has certainly been a fear, an apprehension, that this might have become the case. Much modern medical death *is* hospitalised and turns on decisions as to the *time* of dying: '... many of the problems ... about death and dying arise from the fact that the majority of people now die in hospitals which are centres of sophisticated medical technology.'[14]

Hence, modern medicine is frequently portrayed as bringing indignity, uncertainty and confusion in the closing passages of what is always the heroic struggle for life. Such a perception, accurate in outline as it may be, may damage the very real work which doctors and nurses do with individual patients. And yet, there are celebrated examples where the fear has all too palpably turned to horrific reality. One is captured in the remarkable and poignant book, *The Diving Bell and the Butterfly*, written while suffering in a 'locked in' state by Jean-Dominique Bauby.[15] In an early, moving passage, he describes his condition and his response, which needs to be quoted in full:

> Up until [Friday] I had never even heard of the brain stem. I've since learned that it is an essential component of our internal computer, the inseparable link between the brain and the spinal cord. I was brutally introduced to this vital piece of anatomy when a cerebro-vascular accident put my brain stem out of action. In the past it was known as a 'massive stroke' and you simply died. But prolonged resuscitation techniques have now prolonged and refined the agony. You survive, but you survive with what is aptly known as 'locked in syndrome'. Paralysed from head to toe, the patient, his mind intact, is imprisoned inside his own body, but unable to speak or move. In my case, blinking my left eyelid is my only means of communication.[16]

It is those words 'in the past', 'simply' and 'prolonged and refined the agony' that have, I think, contributed in large part to the changing nature of the debate.

The hospital, as Michel Foucault has shown, is a fairly recent cultural invention, being perhaps no more than 200 years old. The emergence of the hospital, for Foucault, is linked with 'rènférnment' or 'enclosure', and the appearance of the asylum, the factory, the modern prison, the school and the family; all forms of 'institutional enclosure', as Charlesworth calls it.[17] For Foucault, of course, this is connected with the increase of State surveillance and control from the 18th century onwards. Allied with this was a significant shift, perhaps we might call it the first *significant modern shift*, in 'knowledge of the body':[18]

> Medical curricula and practice were shaped around what was easily standardised and defined in technological models. To work appropriately and

14 *Op cit*, Charlesworth, fn 7, p 55.
15 Bauby, JD, *The Diving Bell and the Butterfly*, 1997, London: Fourth Estate.
16 *Ibid*, p 12.
17 *Op cit*, Charlesworth, fn 7, p 57.
18 Which forms one of the themes of this collection.

to claim expertise in the late 19th and early 20th centuries was to work with standardised objects defined in isolation from their social context. The body became a standardised object, and the medical curriculum organised around standardisable skills.[19]

Hence, according to Charlesworth, death was transformed from a human and religious phenomenon into 'a problem of bodily function'. Attention was directed to the body and – as with many aspects of nature in what we were to come to call the 'biomedical model'[20] – it became 'a machine susceptible to repair and intervention'.[21]

Allied with the emergence of the hospital has been an increasing scepticism about the claims of the 'biomedical model'. Since at least the time of Illich, we have been sensitised to the limits and lamentations of modern medicine and the extent to which it has – rightly or wrongly – intentionally or inadvertently – necessarily or uncontrollably – trespassed beyond what might have been thought to be its proper bailiwick. Indeed, Thomas McKeown alerted us to the limited extent to which classical clinical medicine practised according to what is now regarded as the biomedical model, could properly claim to have secured 'improvement' in the general level of the public's health. The individualised measures which alleviate particular symptoms, circumvent or replace particular malfunctions or palliate particular pain,[22] when compared with what is called 'public health', improvements in sanitation and preventive medical care, working and living conditions and matters generally outwith the expertise, experience or economy of medicine, have been, he shows, of far less significance.

Illich's first role was to alert us to the changes in modern life which medical care was promising – not all of them, to be sure, ones which commanded or now command universal assent or approval. Since then, Beck, in an arresting phrase, has calibrated the extent to which modern medical practice (we may hesitate always to call it care, since that is precisely what is at issue), has brought about a 'noiseless social and cultural revolution'[23] of which practices attendant upon the manufacture of death provide but the most outstanding incidents. One particular example stands out.

---

19 Mischler, EG *et al* (eds), *Social Contexts of Health, Illness and Patient Care*, 1981, Cambridge: CUP, quoted in *op cit*, Charlesworth, fn 7, p 57.

20 On which, see Chapter 5.

21 *Op cit*, Charlesworth, fn 7, p 57. Parenthetically, notice that this was the time of the mechanisation metaphor: Le Corbusier was to christen houses as 'machines for living in' and Picasso's fabulous 'Girl with a mandolin' (1910) was to take Cézanne's theory of variability and stability to its astounding logical conclusion and present the human figure simplified – reduced to geometry – interacting on a par with the space around it, treated like architecture. The human figure in the Mandolin has become dehumanised, a metaphorical representation of the body in biomedicine.

22 McKeown, T, *The Role of Medicine*, 1979, Oxford: Basil Blackwell.

23 Beck, U, *Risk Society: Towards a New Modernity*, Ritter, M (trans), 1992, London: Sage, p 202.

In 1983 or 1984, the precise date eludes me, I reviewed a pamphlet, it really was no more, for a weekly legal publication. In the review, I commented on a remarkable development. I observed that an extraordinary metamorphosis had taken change within medical law, without the loss of a jot of judicial blood, without the spillage or staining of a drop of legislative ink. At the time, I confess, I probably failed to see the long term importance of the pamphlet; indeed, I introduced the review by cautioning readers not to laugh, this being a serious subject. The review was of a short document, it is of no more than 50 pages, by Dr Christopher Pallis, called *The ABC of Brain Stem Death*. The incongruity of the title disguises the most fundamental shift which had taken place in the practice of modern medicine in the previous 30 years, 40 years, or perhaps many more. Death had been redefined. Quietly, simply and alone, by doctors meeting in 1968 at the conference of medical colleges at Harvard.[24]

No trespassers here from law, whether limping along a little in the rear[25] or fleet of foot; no squatters – as they were soon to be described in the *British Medical Journal* – from the tenements of philosophy,[26] then believed to be arrogantly billeted in the very belfry of the ivory tower ringing clarions which were only muffled from their long use in the discordant chimes of linguistic philosophy; no ill-informed, untutored members of the public expressing nothing more than their gut feelings – a sentiment with a perfectly respectable anthropological lineage, as Mary Douglas has convincingly demonstrated.[27]

In response to these metamorphoses of death and dying, its contours and its co-ordinates, there has been an increasing trend, a slide, towards what I might call *an individuation of ethics* and the consequent *allure of rights*. I address, in various places in this collection, aspects, attractions, limitations and uncertainties of rights-based arguments.[28] What is certain is that they have not bypassed death and dying. And, there is one particular example of the consequent change in attitude which this metamorphosis has produced. Consider the contemporary welcome afforded a claim advanced in the English Court of Appeal less than a decade ago, in a case that was to be reported as *Re T*.[29] The sub-editor of Clare Dyer's report in *The Guardian* heralded: 'Court to rule on zealot's right to die.'[30] As subsequent events have

---

24 See 'Report of the Ad Hoc Committee of Harvard Medical School' (1968) 205 J Am Medical Association 337; 'Report of the Conference of Medical Royal Colleges and their faculties 1976' (1976) 2 BMJ 1187.

25 The phrase is that of Windeyer J in *Mount Isa Mines v Pusey* (1970) 125 CLR 383, p 395.

26 Davis, JA, 'Whose life is it anyway?' [1986] BMJ 1128.

27 In her monograph *Purity and Danger: An Analysis of the Concepts of Pollution and Taboo*, 1996, London: Routledge.

28 Specifically in Chapter 4, where, drawing on some of the important work of Jonathon Montgomery, I explore what I have there identified as the 'opportunity costs of rhetoric', and, in Chapter 1, I explore some of the further dimensions of rights arguments.

29 [1992] 3 WLR 782.

30 (1992) *The Guardian*, 15 July, p 2.

shown, the headline was accurate in only one respect; that, indeed, the court had been asked to rule on the refusal of medical treatment by a Jehovah's Witness. Otherwise, the transformation from 'zealatory' to rights has been smooth (like the spread of calumny in Beaumarchais' *Barber of Seville*: *pianissimo, piano piano, rinforzando, crescendo*)[31] and remarkably swift.

ON RIGHTS[32]

I need to say a little more about rights-based arguments here. Ian Kennedy, amongst others, has reminded us of the moral basis of medical practice and the extent to which this *necessarily* involves its practitioners in the world of practical, normative ethics for which their education and training has traditionally little prepared them. This has not gone without drawing stinging ripostes and more thoughtful reasoned responses.[33] But we have – properly – insisted on the practice of modern medicine involving, implicating, indeed *being* the practice of contemporary morality so it can really come as no surprise (indeed, it may be thought to be a cause of celebration) when debates about contested practices within the art of medicine come to be conducted in essentially moral terms, and that changes in medical practice come to be rehearsed in moral language. Thus, the recent debate concerning the 'right to die' has engaged fundamental (if, in some judicial pronouncements, mistaken) understandings of philosophical, ethical and theological canons. But, to speak of a right to physician assisted suicide looks only to the question of need and demand and not also or instead to that of supply, and whether those with especial or particular skills do not also have a right to decide (morally) how those skills might or might not be deployed, or whether they may choose to

---

31 Beaumarchais, P-A, *The Barber of Seville*, Act 2 (Wood, J (trans), 1964, Harmondsworth: Penguin, pp 61–62). As Bazile (a music master) explains to Bartholo (a physician), one of the best ways of destroying a man is to destroy his reputation by 'nasty rumour'. Scandal, calumny, as he explains, is remarkably effective: 'Believe me, there's no spiteful stupidity, no horror, no absurd story that one can't get the idle minded folk of a great city to swallow if one goes the right way about it – and we have some experts here! First, the merest whisper skimming the earth like a swallow before the storm – *pianissimo* – a murmur and it's away sowing the poisoned seed as it goes. Someone picks it up and – *piano piano* – insinuates it into your ear. The damage is done. It spawns, creeps, and crawls and spreads and multiplies and then – *rinforzando* – from mouth to mouth it goes like the very Devil. Suddenly, no one knows how, you see calumny raising its head and hissing, puffing, and swelling before your very eyes. It takes wing, extending its flight in ever widening circles, swooping and swirling, drawing in a bit here and a bit there, sweeping everything before it, and breaks forth at last like a thunder clap to become, thanks be to Heaven, the general cry, a public *crescendo*, a chorus universal of hate, rage and condemnation. Who the deuce can resist it?'

32 Again, much of this analysis follows Montgomery.

33 Of which the most thoughtful is Maclean, A, *The Elimination of Morality*, 1993, London: Routledge, esp p 187ff.

deploy them in certain ways at all. The language of rights can properly be met with that of denial based on rights or morality too.

But, the fainthearted paternalist in me objects to the reduction of all aspects of care to strong rights claims which involve nothing more than the need not to be treated as an infant, but as the autonomous person that we believed we were before the accident or illness. It is here that the damage of rights rhetoric can become the most severe; for who when healthy can become a foot?[34] Who can know at the time of the disease or the illness or the treatment what their wants and desires may be? Of course, I do not say that there is no place for arguments drawn from the jurisprudence of rights in the shaping, consideration or determination of medical law generally or specifically dying. But they need some careful articulation and accommodation if they are to avoid the criticisms of exclusivity and individuation generally levelled at rights-based arguments. Rights are not, and should not be, the only foundation for the practice of modern medicine.

LAST RIGHTS

What I want to do in the third part of this chapter is to map onto these shifting contours – of medicalisation and the attendant rights discourse – a brief review of the reception of variously formulated 'right to die' arguments in the US, Canada, New Zealand and then England and Wales. This review is in a way tangential to the main burden of what I want now to say, but it allows for an illustration of the various ways in which courts have addressed and responded to rights claims in death and dying.

(a) In *Cruzan v Director, Missouri Department of Health*,[35] the US Supreme Court held that there is a liberty interest in rejecting unwanted medical treatment, including the provision of food and water. The court held that it is constitutional for a State to impose a requirement that, where a person is incompetent, life sustaining treatment could only be withdrawn where there was clear and convincing evidence that that was, or would be, the wish of the person. This was followed by the Patient Self-Determination Act 1990, which in particular gave legal force and moment to the introduction of advance directives, where people could set out in advance their wishes, views and objections to treatments of particular types of medical intervention.[36] The Oregon Death with Dignity Act 1994,[37] which

---

34 The line is that of WH Auden, from his poem 'Surgical ward', in *The Penguin Poets: WH Auden*, 1958, Harmondsworth: Penguin, p 56.

35 497 US 261 (1990).

was enacted after a popular referendum and eventually came into force in 1998, has been the only statute successfully introduced by a State legislature despite further attempts to do so in California, Iowa, Maine, New Hampshire, Washington and Michigan. Yet the repeated (and, until 1999, unsuccessful) prosecutions of Dr Jack Kervorkian showed that opposition to physician assisted suicide was not universal. The issue came to the US Supreme Court in joined appeals in the cases of *Washington v Glucksberg*[38] (on appeal from *Compassion in Dying v State of Washington*)[39] and *Quill v Vacco.*[40]

In *Compassion in Dying v State of Washington*, a majority of the Court of Appeals for the Ninth Circuit held that a Washington statute rendering assisted suicide unlawful was unconstitutional under the Due Process clause of the 14th Amendment to the US Constitution. Reinhardt J, for the 8:3 majority, wrote that the 'liberty interest' decisions of the US Supreme Court (marriage, procreation, family relationships, childrearing and education, consensual non-procreational intercourse, termination of pregnancy) 'involve decisions that are highly personal and intimate as well as of great importance to the individual':

> These matters involve the most intimate and personal choices a person may make in a lifetime; choices central to personal dignity and autonomy are central to the liberty protected by the 14th Amendment. At the heart of liberty is the right to define one's own concept of existence, of meaning, of the universe and of the mystery of human life. Beliefs about these matters could not define the attributes of personhood were they formed under the compulsion of the State.[41]

Cruzan, said Reinhardt, is consistent with a finding that a competent person has a liberty interest in determining the time and manner of their death. The State, he said, had a legitimate interest (a compelling interest which might override a liberty interest) in preserving life generally, preventing suicide, and avoiding the use of third parties and arbitrary, undue or unfair interest, but not in protecting family members and loved ones, nor protecting the integrity of the medical profession, nor in slippery slope arguments based on potential adverse consequences if the statute was declared unconstitutional.

However, the State's interest was dramatically diminished in the case of a terminally ill person:

---

36 I consider the advance directive more closely in Chapter 12.
37 The operation of the Act having been until then injuncted; see *Lee v State of Oregon* 891 F Supp 1429 (1995).
38 138 L Ed 772 (1998).
39 79 F 3d 790 (1996).
40 138 L Ed 834 (1998), on appeal from 80 F 3d 716 (1996). For an excellent review of the appeal courts' judgments see Sunstien, C, 'The right to die' (1997) 106 Yale LJ 1123.
41 79 F 3d 790 (1996), p 824.

> In the case of a terminally ill adult who ends his life in the terminal stages
> of an incurable and painful degenerative disease, in order to avoid
> debilitating pain and a humiliating death, the decision to commit suicide
> is not senseless, and death does not come too early.[42]

Assessing the weight of the interests, the court balanced the State interests
and the degree to which the State infringes the liberty interest of the *'right
to determine the time and manner of one's death'*.[43] As the prohibition on
assistance of suicide is absolute, the majority held that the State's interests
were insufficient to outweigh the interest of the individual.

In *Quill v Vacco*, the majority of the Appeal Court of the Second Circuit
invalidated a New York statute prohibiting physician assisted suicide as
unconstitutional in offending the Equal Protection clause of the 14th
Amendment, deciding that it improperly distinguished between those
who are terminally ill and on a life support machine and those who are
terminally ill and not in need of life support. Calabresi J, in a concurring
opinion, would have also been prepared to hold that the law offended the
Due Process clause, but argued that the statute should be sent back to the
New York legislature for reconsideration before the court struck it down.

The New York Court of Appeals in *Rivers v Katz*[44] had held that the right
to bring on one's death by refusing medical treatment is a 'fundamental
common law right'. In *Quill v Vacco*, the court reasoned that, because a
competent person could direct the removal of a life support machine, or a
respirator, which would bring about their further demise and eventual
death, and an incompetent person could not do so, this improperly
distinguished between the competent and the incompetent terminally ill.
The court failed to find any distinction between allowing a person to direct
an end to life supporting treatment and receiving medication which they
might self-administer to bring about their death:

> The writing of a prescription to hasten death after consultation with a
> patient involves a far less active role for the physician than is required in
> bringing about death through asphyxiation, starvation and/or
> dehydration. Withdrawal of life support requires physicians or those
> acting at their direction physically to remove equipment and often to
> administer palliative drugs which may themselves contribute to death.
> The ending of life by these means is nothing more nor less than assisted
> suicide.[45]

In turning to the question of whether the State had a compelling interest
sufficient to override or limit any interests of the dying person, the court
summarily disposed of this in observing:

---

42 79 F 3d 790 (1996), p 828.
43 Emphasis added.
44 67 NY 2d 485 (1986).
45 *Quill v Vacco* 80 F 3d 716 (1996), p 742.

At oral argument and in its brief, the State's contention has been that its principal interest is in preserving the life of all its citizens at all times and under all conditions. But what interest can the State possibly have in requiring the prolongation of a life that is all but ended? Surely the State's interest lessens as the potential for life diminishes (*Quinlan*). And what business is it of the State to require the continuation of agony when the result is imminent and inevitable? What concern prompts the state to interfere with a mentally competent patient's 'right to define [his or her] own existence, of meaning, of the universe, and of the mystery of life' (*Planned Parenthood v Casey* (1992)) when the patient seeks to have drugs prescribed to end life during the final stages of a terminal illness? The greatly reduced interest of the State in preserving life compels the answer to these questions: 'None.'[46]

On appeal to the Supreme Court, *both* holdings were *unanimously* reversed. In *Washington v Glucksberg*, the court failed (or refused) to find a fundamental constitutional right to assistance with suicide in either US history or in what it called the concept of 'constitutionally ordered liberty'.[47] What was claimed to be the 'right' to physician assisted suicide, said the court on examination of the Ninth Circuit's decision, was, in fact, a much broader entitlement to permit surrogate decision making and, where the patient could not act personally, perhaps even the administration of a lethal injection by a physician or a family member. The State of Washington was, therefore, required only to show, and succeeded in doing so, that the ban on assistance in suicide was 'rationally related' to 'legitimate government interests'.[48] Such interests encompassed the preservation of human life; the prevention of suicide; the protection of the integrity and ethics of the medical profession; the protection of vulnerable groups; and guarding against the start of a slide to voluntary and even involuntary euthanasia.[49]

In *Quill v Vacco*, Rheinquist CJ announced that the unanimous court did not find that the prohibition on assisting suicides in New York offended the Equal Protection clause, as the Second Circuit had done:

> *Everyone*, regardless of physical condition, is entitled, if competent, to refuse unwanted lifesaving medical treatment; *no one* is permitted to assist suicide.[50]

Hence, there was simply no equal protection question.

(b) In Canada, two cases have defined this area. In *Nancy B v Hotel Dieu de Quebec*,[51] B sought an injunction to require the hospital to disconnect her artificial respirator. She suffered from Guillian Barré syndrome, was

---

46   *Quill v Vacco* 80 F 3d 716 (1996), p 746.
47   138 L Ed (1998), p 792. For a valuable review of the decisions, see Freeman, MDA, 'Death, dying and the Human Rights Act' (1999) 52 Current Legal Problems 218.
48   138 L Ed (1998), p 792.
49   *Ibid*, p 795.
50   *Ibid*, p 841.

unable to move and could breathe only with the assistance of the respirator. She remained conscious and her intellectual capacity was unaffected. The Quebec Superior Court granted the injunction, finding that keeping her ventilated without her consent constituted an intrusion and violation of her person. However, in *Rodriguez v British Columbia*,[52] the Supreme Court of Canada by, 5:4, *refused* to hold that laws prohibiting assisted suicide were unconstitutional. The court dismissed a claim by a 42 year old woman suffering from Lou Gehrig's disease, which caused progressive loss of physical ability including, eventually, swallowing and breathing. Ultimately, she would come to be dependent on a respirator and artificial feeding, although she would remain conscious and aware of her condition. The Supreme Court found that the law prohibiting assisted suicide did infringe her right to liberty and security of the person, guaranteed under the Canadian Charter of Rights and Fundamental freedoms, but *not* in a way which was contrary to the principles of fundamental justice.

Sopinka J, writing in the majority, observed that:

> ... Canada and other Western democracies recognize and apply the principle of the sanctity of life as a general principle which is subject to limited and narrow exceptions in situations in which notions of personal autonomy and dignity must prevail. However, these same societies continue to draw distinctions between passive and active forms of intervention in the dying process ...[53]

(c) Strangely, the High Court in Australia has yet to consider any comparable case,[54] although the 'death and dying' issue has arisen in New Zealand. There, Thomas J, in *Auckland Hospital v AG*,[55] considered another Guillian Barré (locked in, locked out) syndrome case.[56] The patient was described by the medical witnesses as the worst case they had ever encountered; his brain was no longer connected to his body although it may have retained some visual pathways. Thomas J held that it would be justifiable for the doctors to remove the ventilator, which would result in the patient suffering a cardiac arrest. The doctors were under no obligation to continue medical treatment where it would have no therapeutic or medical benefit. Recognising the deep-rooted nature of the sanctity of life, the judge observed the wording of s 11 of the New Zealand Bill of Rights Act

---

51 (1992) 86 DLR (4th) 385.

52 (1993) 107 DLR (4th) 342.

53 *Ibid*, p 409.

54 Although there is an excellent discussion of applicable principles and possible authorities in Magnusson, RS, 'The sanctity of life and the right to die: social and jurisprudential aspects of the euthanasia debate in Australia and the United States' [1997] Pacific Rim J Law and Policy 1.

55 [1993] 1 NZLR 235.

56 For a tragic description see *op cit*, Bauby, fn 15.

('Everyone has the right to refuse to undergo any medical treatment') and said that:

> Human dignity and personal privacy belong to every person, whether living or dying. Yet, the sheer invasiveness of the treatment and the manipulation of the human body which it entails, the pitiful and humiliating helplessness of the patient's state, and the degradation and dissolution of all bodily functions invoke these values.[57]

(d) Finally, let me turn to consider the relevant line of authorities in England and Wales where these propositions have been contested.[58] The recent starting point must be the judgment in *Re T*[59] of Lord Donaldson MR, where he observed that:

> An adult patient who ... suffers from no mental incapacity has an absolute right to choose whether to consent to medical treatment, to refuse it or to choose one rather than another of the treatments being offered ... This right of choice is not limited to decisions which others might regard as sensible. It exists notwithstanding that the reasons for making the choice are rational, irrational, unknown or even non-existent ... The fact that, 'emergency cases' apart, no medical treatment of an adult patient of full capacity can be undertaken without his consent, creates a situation in which the absence of consent has much the same effect as refusal.

Where the treatment of patients lacking capacity to consent are concerned, the House of Lords in *Re F (Mental Patient: Sterilisation)*[60] held that such a person may nonetheless be examined or treated if a responsible body of medical opinion believes it to be in their best interests. Thus, to summarise: a voluntary refusal of life prolonging treatment by a competent adult must be *absolutely* respected.[61] Where a patient has a lost the *capacity* to make a decision, but has a valid advance directive refusing life prolonging treatment, this too must be respected.[62] A valid advance refusal has the same legal authority as a contemporaneous refusal. In England and Wales and Northern Ireland, no other person has the power to give or to withhold consent for the treatment of an adult who lacks decision making capacity, but the treatment may be provided without consent if it is considered to be necessary and in the best interests of the patient. The same principles apply when decisions are taken in relation to a woman who is pregnant with a viable fetus.[63]

---

57 (1993) 1 NZLR 235, p 251.

58 The law in Scotland differs in many important respects; discussed in *Law Hospital v Lord Advocate* 1996 SLT 848.

59 [1992] 3 WLR 782.

60 [1990] 2 AC 1.

61 *Re MB* [1997] 2 FLR 3; *St George's NHS Trust v S (No 2)* [1998] 3 WLR 936.

62 *Re C* [1994] 1 WLR 290.

Some argue that the same moral duties are owed to babies, children and young people as they are to adults, although depending on their capacity it may be open to and appropriate for parents to take decisions on behalf of their children. Those with parental responsibility for a baby or young child are legally and morally entitled to give or withhold consent to treatment. Their decisions will usually be determinative[64] unless they conflict seriously with the interpretation of those providing care about the child's best interests, when it may be challenged and possibly overridden.[65] Treatment may, however, be given where there is consent from someone authorised to give it, whether the competent young person themselves, a parent, a court, or a person with parental responsibility. A young person's *refusal* may not, in law, necessarily take precedence over the consent of their parents or the court.[66]

Further guidance about the scope and process of decision making was provided in the case of *Re R (Adult) (Medical Treatment)*.[67] R was 23 years old and had been born with a serious malformation of the brain and cerebral palsy. He developed severe epilepsy, had profound learning difficulty and had not developed any formal means of communication or any consistent social interactions. He was unable to walk, was believed to be blind and deaf and had a range of other health problems. In the expert clinical evidence provided, it was stated that R was believed to be operating cognitively and neurologically at the level of a newborn infant. The health care team were in agreement that, should R have a further life threatening crisis, cardio-pulmonary resuscitation or antibiotics should not be provided, as this would be of no benefit to him. This assessment of R's best interests was challenged by a third party on the basis that the decision to withhold care was 'irrational and unlawful in that the decisions to withhold CPR and antibiotics permit medical treatment to be withheld on the basis of an assessment of the patient's quality of life'. The court dismissed the appeal, and made clear that decisions should be made on the basis of whether a particular treatment would confer benefit on the patient – taking into account both medical factors and whether the treatment was able to provide a reasonable quality of life for the patient – rather than a blanket decision to provide no treatment. The court clarified that 'the decision as to withholding the administration of antibiotics in a potentially life threatening situation is a matter fully within the

---

63 *Re MB* [1997] 2 FLR 3; *St George's NHS Trust v S (No 2)* [1998] 3 WLR 936, overruling *Re S* [1993] Fam 123.

64 *Re T* [1997] 1 All ER 906.

65 *Re C* [1998] 1 FLR 384; *Re A (Children) (Conjoined Twins)* [2000] 4 All ER 961.

66 *Re R (Wardship: Consent to Treatment)* [1991] 4 All ER 177; *Re W* [1992] 4 All ER 627.

67 *Re R (Adult) (Medical Treatment)* [1996] 2 FLR 821.

responsibility of the consultant having responsibility for treating the patient'.[68]

These principles, taken together with the two leading cases of *Re T* and *Re F*, lay the foundation for the case that I want to make the focus of the remaining observations in this chapter, *Airedale National Health Service Trust v Bland*.[69]

THE CASE OF TONY BLAND

Bland was a victim of a severe crushing injury who had lived thereafter in a persistent vegetative state (PVS) for four years.[70] He was fed artificially and, although he had no upper brain function, his brain stem continued to function (and hence he was not 'dead' on the 'Harvard' criteria). There was no doubt that he could be kept alive in this state for many years. The House of Lords held that the artificial hydration and nutrition amounted to medical treatment and could be discontinued provided that responsible and competent medical opinion was of the view that it would be in his 'best interests' not to prolong his life by continuing that form of treatment because it was futile and would not confer any benefit on him.

Lord Goff said that 'the sanctity of life must yield to the principle of self-determination',[71] and Lord Keith that 'a person is completely at liberty to

---

68   *Ibid*, p 828.

69   [1993] AC 789.

70 A person living in PVS has been described as having 'a body which is functioning entirely in terms of its internal controls. It maintains temperature. It maintains heart-beat and pulmonary ventilation. It maintains digestive activity. It maintains reflex action of muscles and nerves for low level conditioned responses. But there is no behavioural evidence of either self-awareness or awareness of the surroundings in learned manner'; *In the Matter of Jobes* 529 A 2d 434 (NJ, 1987), p 438, quoting an expert witness, and cited by Giesen, D, 'Dilemmas at life's end: a comparative legal perspective', in *op cit*, Keown, fn 6, p 214, n 8. In the same volume, Brian Jennett, one of the authors of the term, describes what he calls 'the medical facts' in this way: 'The vegetative state is a term coined ... to describe the behavioural features of patients who have suffered severe brain damage that has resulted in the cerebral cortex being out of action. Without the thinking, feeling, motivating part of the brain these patients are unconscious, in the sense that they make no responses that indicate any meaningful interaction with their surroundings, and remain unaware of themselves or their environment. They never obey a command, nor speak a single word. More primitive parts of the brain that are responsible for periodic wakefulness and for a wide range of reflex activities are still functioning, giving the paradox of a patient who is at times awake but always unaware. When open, the eyes roam about but do not fix or follow for long, whilst the spastic paralysed limbs never move voluntarily or purposefully. They can, however, withdraw reflexly from a painful stimulus which may provoke a grimace or a groan – but there is no evidence that pain or suffering is experienced. Occasional yawning, smiling, weeping and sometimes even laughing can occur, but these are unrelated to appropriate stimuli. Reflex swallowing, chewing and gagging occur and breathing is normal with no need for a ventilator.' (Jennett, B, 'Letting vegetative patients die', in *op cit*, Keown, fn 6, p 171.)

decline to undergo treatment even if the result of his doing so is that he will die'.[72] Despite the inability of Tony Bland to consent to this, the hospital and physicians responsible for treating and attending upon him might lawfully discontinue all life sustaining treatment and medical support measures designed to keep him alive in PVS including the termination of ventilation, hydration and nutrition by artificial means. Not all of the judges were attracted by the conclusion, even that in which they agreed, that it was lawful to withdraw hydration and nutrition – an omission (to continue treating) – but that it would be unlawful to end Bland's life by a positive act. Thus Lord Browne-Wilkinson complained that:

> The conclusion I have reached will appear to some to be almost irrational. How can it be lawful to allow a patient to die slowly though painlessly, over a period of weeks, from lack of food but unlawful to produce his immediate death by a lethal injection, thereby saving his family from yet another ordeal ...? I find it difficult to find a moral answer to that question. But it is undoubtedly the law.[73]

Lord Mustill believed that 'the foundations of the courts' unanimous decision is morally and intellectually misshapen'.[74]

Bland appears to decide that, in England and Wales and Northern Ireland, proposals to withdraw artificial hydration and nutrition from a patient who is in PVS or in a very low state of awareness should – at least until a body of professional opinion has developed – be referred to the court.[75] In Scotland, this referral is not required.[76] Predictably, *Bland* has been followed by other cases.[77] The most important of these have been cases such as *Frenchay Healthcare NHS Trust v S,*[78] *Re G,*[79] and *Swindon and Marlborough NHS Trust v S.*[80] These cases formed the backdrop to the BMA's recent advice on decisions

---

71   [1993] AC 789, p 864.

72   *Ibid*, p 857.

73   *Ibid*, p 880.

74   *Ibid*, p 887.

75   *Airedale NHS Trust v Bland* [1993] AC 789. Between 1992 and 1998, 18 such cases were so referred. The courts have not specified that court authorisation should be sought for patients who are not in PVS, and a body of opinion has developed that such action would be appropriate in some cases – such as patients who have suffered a severe stroke or have severe dementia.

76   *Law Hospital v Lord Advocate* 1996 SLT 848.

77   The BMA's *Guidance for Decision Making: Withholding and Withdrawing Life-Prolonging Medical Treatment*, 1999, London: BMA/BMJ, p 44, recalls that 18 cases have been taken to the High Court since the House of Lords' decision in *Bland*.

about withholding or withdrawing artificial nutrition and hydration.[81] The BMA proceeded to its conclusions in this way:

> The primary goal of medical treatment is to benefit the patient by restoring or maintaining the patient's health as far as possible, maximising benefit and minimising harm. If treatment fails, or ceases, to give a net benefit to the patient (or if the patient has competently refused the treatment), the primary goal cannot be realised and the justification for providing the treatment is removed. Unless some other justification can be demonstrated, treatment that does not provide net benefit may, ethically and legally, at least in the UK, be withheld and withdrawn and the goal of medicine shifts to the palliation of symptoms. Prolonging a patient's life usually, but not always, provides a health benefit to the patient, and although it may be emotionally easier to withhold treatment than to withdraw it once it has been started, there are no legal and necessary morally relevant distinctions between the two actions.[82] Treatment should never be withheld, however, where there is a possibility that it will benefit the patient simply because withholding it is considered easier than withdrawing it.

NEGOTIATING DEATH AND TRAGIC CHOICES

These are indeed times of change and renegotiation in one area of life that had once seemed to be fixed and certain; that of death. It may be because of the symbols and forms with which we surround death that it is very difficult for the law to allow that, for some, life and death may be indistinguishable, or that death may appear preferable to life. This is not to say that the law treats all deaths the same, any more than the law treats all lives the same way. What, then, might these cases, cases such as *Bland*, *Quinlan*, *Rodriguez* and *Quill v Vacco*, tell us about the legal system and attitudes to modern death and dying? It is to that question that, finally, I turn.

Perhaps every generation of every legal system needs a fulcrum around which stigmata choices, which define and distinguish how and where a

---

78   [1994] 2 All ER 403, holding that reference to the court in all cases of PVS is not necessary, and in cases of emergency (eg, where a gastrostromy tube had become disconnected and the question arose whether it should it be re-inserted) even a second medical opinion to confirm that the patient is definitely in PVS is not always required.

79   [1995] 2 FCR 46, where a disagreement arose between relatives as to the appropriate course for man in PVS for over two years, the High Court held that the doctor in whose care G lay had a duty to act in his best interests, and in reaching that decision had a duty to take into account the views of G's relatives, but that the opposition of his mother to discontinuance of treatment could not operate as a veto so as to prevent a course being followed which the doctor believed to be in G's best interests.

80   [1995] 3 Med LR 84: where a patient in PVS had been cared for at home for many years and the family reached a point where they felt further treatment was inappropriate, the wishes of the family were to be taken into account but were not determinative of whether care should be withdrawn.

81   Critically reviewed by Keown, J in 'Beyond *Bland*' (2000) 20 LS 66.

82   *Airedale NHS Trust v Bland* [1993] 1 AC 1, *per* Lord Goff.

society's central values are arranged and calibrated, are organised. Such cases require the articulation of the particular beliefs on which the legal system rests. There is an awful sense in which such cases *properly* force upon judges and jurists, professionals and public, the tragic choices (as Guido Calabresi has called them)[83] necessitated by the clash of absolutes.[84]

I want to argue that *Bland* (and these other cases) is situated firmly between the 'progressions', *between* the allocative choices and the legitimation process, that I identified in Chapter 1. That is the further dimension to the tragic choice which interests me here, one perhaps not always legitimately applied to individual cases or decisions but which – in a case such as *Bland* and also in the later case of *Blood* – so clearly marks it out as a stigmata case, a reference point for modern medical law. Recall that it is characteristic of tragic choices (unlike non-tragic ones) that the allocative decisions necessary in the first and second order determinations are made separately:

> This allows for the more complex mixtures of allocation approaches which are brought to bear on the tragic choice, and it permits a society to cleave to a different mixture of values at each order. Indeed, when the first order determination of a tragic choice appears to be no more than a dependent function of the second order, it will usually be the case that the connection is illusory, serving to obscure the fact of tragic scarcity and – while the illusion lasts – evading the tragic choice.[85]

In an example well known to his readers, Calabresi offers the suggestion that we can comfort ourselves in the belief that 'our society does not establish an acceptable number of auto deaths, but that this figure results from thousands of independent, atomistic actions'.[86] But, in this way, Tony Bland's death, like each auto death, was not only an accident waiting to happen, but a chronicle of another death foretold. There is a sense in which Tony Bland is a hostage to the fortune which the British public health service no longer has. Bland is part both of an apparently dependent second order decision and a first order one, in Calabresian terms. Each of the judges who addressed this point in the House of Lords and the Court of Appeal loudly proclaimed that resources were not in issue. But, unpalatable as it is, we must face the fact that Tony Bland is more expensive to maintain in PVS than he is to bury. Fiscally, at least, we save by deciding that Tony Bland has no interests worth further protection, that he is, to all intents and purposes, a wasting asset wasting assets. Of course, the courts do not speak in such terms; we might be outraged if they did. But, in *Bland*, the House of Lords obscures the fact (perhaps *must* obscure the fact) of tragic scarcity, by making the first order determination

---

83 *Op cit*, Calabresi and Bobbitt, fn 4.
84 Detmold, M, *The Unity of Law and Morality*, 1984, London: Routledge and Kegan Paul, pp 144–45, 249.
85 *Op cit*, Calabresi with Bobbitt, fn 4, p 20.
86 *Op cit*, Calabresi with Bobbitt, fn 4, p 20.

(how much health care should we produce?) appear to be no more than a dependent function of the second order (who should get this treatment?). That it is not in Tony Bland's best interests to receive futile (or indeed any other) treatment legitimates our decision not to produce enough health care to care for him anyway. The fact of the tragic scarcity is obscured – but only just, as the speeches of Lords Browne-Wilkinson and Mustill disclose – by an *illusion* of plenty on the horns of a legal and moral dilemma.

It may be trite to say, but every legal system needs its Tony Bland, in the same way that it needs its Diane Blood.[87] The long dying of a young man in PVS, trapped in the erosion of death,[88] provoked a re-examination of many questions of value which death provokes. When we read the speeches of the House of Lords,[89] there is a terrible sense in which we know that Tony Bland is already dead. Not in the dualistic (non)sense introduced by Sir Stephen Brown P in his judgment in the High Court,[90] but in the broader sense that we have already killed him. Tony Bland died because he no longer had interests which a family could care for, he had no continuing family interests. Bland may have been very far from the madding crowd, but he was certainly still much engaged in its ignoble strife. His case, *Airedale NHS Trust v Bland* (and the related cases that I have introduced), offers an opportunity to take stock, to re-examine the existing boundaries between the anomalous and the routine, between the normal and the pathological; to reflect upon the paradox that (to paraphrase the observation of Ulrich Beck and Elizabeth Gernsheim-Beck), while death may be a natural event: '... in the waning years of the 20th century nature no longer exists in the sense we mean it; nature is usually in the hands of the experts.'[91]

Bland, like *Blood*, raises the balance of personal interests and public interest. Both are also of interest to the public; in a very real sense there is an inquiry which asks, perhaps with some presumption, who *are* these people. They are subjects *of* the law's regulation, in that advances in modern science have delivered Tony Bland and Stephen Blood not only to the ward of the hospital, but also to the precincts of the court. One case raises questions where the capacity for meaningful life is said to be past, the other questions of what amounts to the meaningful capacity for life. In this, both cases challenge

---

87   *R v HFEA ex p Blood* [1997] 2 All ER 687.

88   Naturally, the phrase is taken from Marquez, GG, 'Death constant beyond love', in *Innocent Erendira and other Stories*, Rabassa, G (trans), 1981, London: Picador, p 62.

89   *Airedale NHS Trust v Bland* [1993] 1 All ER 821.

90   *Ibid*, p 832d, h: the withdrawal of artificial hydration and nutrition 'does not in my judgment alter the reality that the true cause of death will be the massive injuries which he sustained in what has been described as the Hillsborough disaster'.

91   Beck, U and Gernsheim-Beck, E, *The Normal Chaos of Love*, 1995, Oxford: Polity, p 116.

accepted notions and conceptions, in the one case of the limits and meaning of life and death, in the other on the limits and meaning of death and life.

Significantly, *Bland, Cruzan, Glucksberg, Quill* and so on, like *Blood*, force us to ask of the very basis of medical practice – not how, but why; goals rather than methods are the primary concern. These cases involve what would, until recently, have been thought to be unthinkable, the inconceivable. In the face of novelty and uncertainty, the reason and the security in which medical practice was once practised have begun to evaporate. *Bland* is a paradigmatic example of what Beck calls the secret farewell to an epoch, the noiseless social and cultural revolution in which the logic of progress has come to incorporate 'the possibilities for thoughtless and unplanned exceeding of limits'.[92] The second of Calabresi's 'moving progressions' is evident here, as the courts engage with deciding, rationalising and remaking tragic choices, part of the Calabresian meditation of a culture upon itself. New definitions of death (as much as new conceptions of family formation) challenge familiar assumptions about familial bonds, and the implication of the courts in these processes require that they develop a social, even a moral, vision of families and family relationships, of health care and medical treatment, so that they can determine the appropriate response to the social and moral dilemmas created by the cultural revolution of contemporary medicine.[93]

---

92 *Op cit*, Beck, fn 23, p 209.
93 For the identification of these themes see Dolgin, J, *Defining the Family: Law, Technology and Reproduction in an Uneasy Age*, 1997, New York: New York UP.

CHAPTER 12

ODYSSEUS AND THE BINDING DIRECTIVE: ONLY A CAUTIONARY TALE?*

ODYSSEUS AND AUTONOMY

Before Odysseus navigates the rocks on which live Scylla and Charybdis, he is lulled by the Sirens, promising advance disclosure of earthly adventures. Forewarned by Circe, he enjoins his crew first to contain him; later (on pain of death) to release him from the mast to which he is bound. Held to his originally expressed wishes, they refuse, and bind him more tightly.[1] In this way, Odysseus creates what may have been one of the first advance directives. Its enforcement illustrates one of the concerns which have latterly been expressed about making binding health care choices, possibly many years before they might take effect.

> People do not always mean what they say; they do not always say what they want; and they do not always want what they say they want. That much is, if not exactly clear, at least uncontroversial. What is controversial is, recognizing this, how to proceed.[2]

People change their minds.[3] The lesson which the Odyssian directive affords is that we may wish to bring to the consideration of advance directives a certain caution. As it happens, holding him to his previous wishes may be thought to have benefited Odysseus in this case. Some would argue that his autonomy was respected (even enhanced), not only in that his welfare was

---

*   This chapter was originally drafted as a paper for the First National Palliative Care Conference, Reading, September 1993. Versions of it have benefited from the critical attention of Tony Hope, Hugh Upton and Carol Brennan. Allan Hutchinson, characteristically, prevailed upon me to strengthen the concluding comments, and I have taken his counsel as well. The final draft of this article was written while I was a Visiting Researcher at Det Retsvidenskabelige Institut C, University of Copenhagen. I am grateful to Joseph Lookofsky, Head of the Institute, and Linda Nielsen for their kindnesses to me as their guest. It needs hardly be stated that the usual caveat applies. But I will; it does.

1   Homer, *The Odyssey*, XII, 'Scylla and Charybdis', Rieu, EV (trans), Jones, PV (revised), 1991, Harmondsworth: Penguin, Chapter 11.

2   Elliott, C, 'Meaning what you say', in Emanuel, L (ed), *Advance Directives: Expectations, Experience and Future Practice* (1993) 4(1) J Clinical Ethics 61. Whether what Elliott describes as 'uncontroversial' can, without more, be agreed upon is, of course, contested; see Fish, S, *Doing What Comes Naturally*, 1989, Oxford: Clarendon and *There's No Such Thing as Free Speech (... and it's a good thing too)*, 1994, New York and Oxford: OUP for celebrated introductions to one body of the literature.

3   Several studies have shown how patients change their minds about decisions; see Emanuel, L, 'Advance directives: what have we learned so far?', in *ibid*, Emanuel, p 9, n 18. Of course, one must be careful here to distinguish between competence and sincerity, to which I return below.

protected, but also because a crucial dimension of autonomy might be thought to be the ability to enter into *binding* agreements. In trying to protect people from coming later to regret their previously expressed decisions, we may be refusing to treat them 'as an autonomous and responsible person'.[4] And, for some people, consideration of autonomy has come to occupy a central place, not just in the examination of the value and validity of advance directives, but in debates about medical law and jurisprudence more generally.

In an article generally cautious about the use of living wills, Joanne Lynn has suggested that there may be particular advantages to living wills in specific cases. These include where any form of legally sanctioned surrogate might be controversial (the mother or the long term partner of an AIDS patient); where a patient expresses particularly specific priorities or unusual preferences (such as never to be treated again in a particular hospital, or not to have a particular treatment option) and for those for whom laying anxiety to rest is a particularly important part of their care.[5]

But, as Allen Buchanan has suggested, this limited catalogue of benefits would be a seriously incomplete weighting of the value of advance directives. This appreciation is one which some of the members of the courts which disposed of the *Bland* case in 1992 and 1993 perceived and sought to address.[6] Importantly, Buchanan argues that advance directives might be seen to contribute to a new form of altruism; to ensuring that a person's 'surviving interests' are satisfied, thus, that their interests in general are enhanced and, thus, that their *present* interests are augmented or secured.[7]

There are problems and difficulties with advance directives, some of which I want to allude to here, and there are seen to be particular advantages in their development. The most frequently cited are that they allow for greater self-determination and afford protection from unwarranted or futile interventions

---

4 Wertheimer, A, 'Two questions about surrogacy and exploitation' (1991) 21 Philosophy and Public Affairs 237. Thus, we may hold that expressed wishes should be enforced even when they will do the person harm (or lead to their death). Alternatively, we may say that there are good reasons to depart from their wishes when it will do them harm. I do not enter that particular argument here.

5 Lynn, J, 'Why I don't have a living will', in Capron, A (ed), 'Medical decision making and the "right to die" after *Cruzan*' (1991) 19 Law, Medicine and Health Care 104.

6 [1993] 1 All ER 821; [1993] 2 WLR 316.

7 Buchanan, A, 'Advance directives and the personal identity problem' (1988) 17 Philosophy and Public Affairs 277; a person who takes an interest in the well being of others can use an advance directive to contribute to their own well being in two ways: (a) while still competent, the author's anxiety about the distress to which loved ones will be subjected in making difficult decisions without guidance will be reduced; (b) 'there is a sense in which our interests can survive us. I have an interest in how my family will fare after my death, and that interest survives me in the sense that whether or not it is satisfied will depend on events that occur after I am gone. An advance directive can help me ensure that my "surviving interests" are satisfied' (p 278, n 1). And see Dworkin, R, *Life's Dominion: An Argument about Abortion and Euthanasia*, 1993, London: HarperCollins, p 193, and Jecker, N, 'Being a burden on others' in *op cit*, Emanuel, fn 2, p 19.

at the end of life. It is, in part, in the fear of such interventions that the debate about other forms of intervention at the endings of life have been discussed.[8] I do not want, in this chapter, to trespass into the wider ground of euthanasia,[9] nor even to consider what is often seen as a corollary to the advance directive, a health care proxy or substitute decision maker.[10] My focus is exclusively on the advance directive, and what may be seen as some of the benefits and drawbacks of such a form of medical decision making.

However, the development and deployment of advance directives and medical treatment in English law illustrate one important movement in medical law and provide an opportunity to reflect on the place of law in medical jurisprudence and practice. Recall that it is less than 40 years since Patrick Devlin wrote of the 'pleasant tribute to the medical profession' that:

> ... by and large it has been able to manage its relations with its patients on the basis of such an understanding [that conduct be regulated by a general understanding of how decent people ought to behave] without the aid of lawyers and law makers.[11]

The living will is a gauge on which the contemporary strength of that tribute can be calibrated.

THE EXPERIENCE OF DYING AND THE 'VULGARISATION OF SURGERY'[12]

Traditionally, the person best protected from death in modern societies was the one whom society had condemned to die; authority might be challenged if convicts were to take their life before the appointed hour. Ivan Illich has argued that those who are best protected today from setting the stage for their own dying are the sick in critical condition:

> Society, acting through the medical system, decides when and after what indignities and mutilations he shall die ... Western man has lost the right to

---

8   House of Lords Select Committee, *Report of the House of Lords Select Committee on Medical Ethics*, HL Papers 21-I, 1994, London: HMSO, paras 186–203.

9   For a recent consideration, see *op cit*, Dworkin, fn 7, and *ibid*, rejecting arguments in favour of legalisation of euthanasia in the UK.

10 A full account of the role of law and medical practice at the end of life would, of course, have to consider the practice and scope of euthanasia or physician assisted suicide, and the role of health care proxies, without which there may exist only a partial understanding of the place of the advance directive. Both these are canvassed in the House of Lords' Report.

11 Devlin, P, 'Medicine and law', in *Samples of Lawmaking*, 1962, Oxford: Clarendon, p 103.

12 This phrase comes from Garcia Marquez, G, *Love in the Time of Cholera*, Grossman, E (trans), 1988, Harmondsworth: Penguin, p 10.

preside at his act of dying ... mechanical death has conquered and destroyed all other deaths.[13]

We do not live life to experience death; in Wittgenstein's classic expression, 'death is not an event in life. Death is not lived through'.[14] Yet death is an important and permanent aspect of the human condition, 'affecting the meaning and value of life'.[15] In an essay discussing the use and complications of cardiopulmonary resuscitation, John Saunders has illustrated how fear of dying, of the possible manner of death and, indeed, of death itself, are important parts of the human condition.[16] Recalling Paul Ramsey's essay, he suggests that awareness of dying constitutes an experience of ultimate indignity in and to the self who is dying.[17] In our dread, we are capable of doing much harm; in the case of CPR, this includes harm to patients, their families, the medical team and society at large. Robert Pearlman and his colleagues, in the latest in a series of studies of specific circumstances that people may consider to be worse than death, have reported that these include chronic pain, coma, and severe physical or mental dysfunction.[18] But, going beyond what they have called 'the traditional biomedical focus', they have also recorded that as between patients and physicians, disagreements often focused around the manner or location of death, social well-being and burden:

> Many respondent comments ... include concerns about hopelessness, becoming disaffected by the circumstances, remaining alive merely by virtue of sophisticated machinery, placing an undue burden on family members or caregivers, suffering, dying in an unfamiliar environment (such as a hospital or nursing home), no longer having anyone to love or be loved by, and the religious or spiritual meaning of life and death.[19]

They conclude that knowledge of circumstances under which patients 'would prefer to die rather than to remain alive has direct relevance to communication

---

13 Illich, I, *Limits to Medicine: Medical Nemesis: The Expropriation of Health*, 1976, Harmondsworth: Penguin, p 210. And see Nietzsche, F, 'The twilight of the idols', in *The Complete Works of Frederick Nietzsche*, 1967, New York: Random House, p 88, quoted in *op cit*, Dworkin, fn 7, p 212.

14 Wittgenstein, L, *Tractatus Logico-Philosophicus*, Ogden, CK (trans), 1922 (reprinted 1992), London and New York: Routledge, 6.4311. Developments in modern technology may cause us to question whether Wittgenstein's description remains accurate.

15 Hanfling, O, *Life and Meaning: A Reader*, 1987, Oxford: Basil Blackwell, p 2.

16 'Medical futility: CPR', in Lee, RG and Morgan, D (eds), *Death Rites: Law and Ethics at the End of Life*, 1994, London: Routledge, pp 72–90. The Royal College of Nursing, in evidence to the House of Lords Select Committee on Medical Ethics, suggested that 'many people are not necessarily afraid of death, but are afraid of the manner of death' (*op cit*, fn 8, para 187).

17 'The indignity of "death with dignity"' (1974) Hastings Center Report 47.

18 Pearlman, R, Cain, K, Patrick, D, Appelbaum-Maizel, M, Starks, H, Jecker, N and Uhlmann, R, 'Insights pertaining to patient assessments of states worse than death', in *op cit*, Emanuel, fn 2, p 34. Compare *op cit*, House of Lords Select Committee, fn 8, para 194.

19 *Ibid*, p 39.

about advance planning'.[20] Death is of overwhelming significance not only because, for better or worse, it brings experience to an end, but also because its nature and timing affect the quality of life as measured by a person's critical interests. It can be important for a person to live longer, even despite great pain, in order to finish her life project, or in order to be present at an important family event, or just in order to have fought well and struggled to the end.[21]

Central to Homer's allegory is that of Odysseus' refusal, like Sisyphus, to surrender to death at the end of his 'proper' term. The vulgarisation of surgery which has contributed to or dictated this raging against the dying of the light has brought a stinging riposte from an unusual contemporary critic of modern medicine, one of the principal theorists of British New Right politics, John Gray. In his essay 'An agenda for green conservatism', he has disputed that we are all going to die and pleaded that it cannot be the true office of medical care to thwart the course of nature. Rather, its proper disposition should be to assist and smooth its way; many, if not most episodic ailments are self-limiting and either the healing resources of the body cope with them or else death supervenes:

> Medical care ... cannot ... conjure away our mortality. When it attempts to do so, iatrogenic illness becomes a worse affliction than those that befall us in the natural course of things. Much modern medicine is pathological in its denial of death and reflects the broader culture of which it is a part in refusing to recognise that we may thrive in dying, even as our souls may perish in senseless longevity.[22]

From this he has argued that any reform of health care, in which he promotes the most liberal form of voucher or health credit scheme to help reverse 'the medicalisation of life that the omnicompetent authority of the medical guild carries with it',[23] must aim to promote responsibility and enhance dignity and must encompass measures enabling patients to reject medical care and to prevent their unwilling survival. No scheme of reform of health care is adequate which does not contain measures for enabling and empowering patients as agents in these decisions, through the legal availability of euthanasia, physician assisted where necessary, as provided for in a version of the 'living will' mandating termination of life under specified conditions.[24]

---

20 *Op cit*, Pearlman *et al*, fn 18, p 35.
21 Scanlon, T, 'Partisan for life' (1993) *New York Review of Books*, 15 July, p 49.
22 *Beyond the New Right: Markets, Government and the Common Environment*, 1993, London: Routledge, 167.
23 *Ibid*, p 169.
24 *Ibid*, p 171.

TERMINAL CONSIDERATIONS

The term 'advance directive' (of which a 'living will' may be thought to be one expression) is usually taken to mean 'a document which is intended to demonstrate that a patient has made an anticipatory decision, and the scope of the decision made'.[25] The Law Commission of England and Wales has distinguished this from a 'living will', which 'typically refers to an advance directive which is concerned with the refusal of life-sustaining procedures in the event of a terminal illness',[26] although they recognise that a living will is sometimes taken to mean rather more than that. It is 'sometimes used for advance directives which are concerned with other situations or which can be used to express a willingness to receive particular treatments.'[27] The House of Lords Select Committee's *Report on Medical Ethics* refers to advance directives as a means by which:

> ... autonomy can be extended to a situation when the patient has become incompetent, by stating in advance the types of treatment which the patient would or would not find acceptable in certain circumstances.[28]

Thus, advance directives (necessarily concerned with future states of incompetence) may be thought to be of two kinds:

(a) Those directed towards refusal of certain *treatments* when the maker is later unable or incompetent to express a view about it. Here, it is the treatment *itself* which is held to be objectionable *whether or not* the condition is otherwise life threatening. This might include the possible marginal cases where somebody has lots of tubes attached to them, or the maintenance of someone in a persistent vegetative state (PVS). Some hold that such states are offensive in themselves, although in these marginal cases, as I shall moot, the use of an advance directive may well be misleading.

(b) Those directed towards the management of certain deteriorating conditions *which are necessarily a matter of life and death* – such as Alzheimer's disease, when the director[29] intends that, when later incompetent, certain types of intervention (say antibiotics) should not be given in the event of some supervening, independent event. Thus, the director may forestall intervention in the contraction of an infection, in the

---

25   Law Commission, Consultation Paper No 129, *Mentally Incapacitated Adults and Decision Making: Medical Treatment and Research*, 1993, London: HMSO, p 29, n 18.

26   *Ibid.*

27   *Ibid.*

28   *Op cit*, House of Lords Select Committee, fn 8, para 181.

29   A term I use throughout to mean the person (patient or otherwise) who indicates certain pre-emptive concerns about their care.

knowledge that they will then die, even though the treatment itself is not otherwise inherently offensive.

In both cases, the director is seeking to avoid life in a certain condition. In the first, what we may call the 'treatment' case, the person is seeking to avoid living his or her life in a condition which for *them* is worse than death; in the knowledge that life has been bought at too high a price or against some higher commandment. The classic example is the refusal by Jehovah's Witnesses of blood transfusions.[30] This involves a real conflict between what those from the outside want and what the patient thinks. Here, there are two questions: does the individual have the 'right to die', and what procedures are needed to be sufficiently sure that the patient really does want this? And it is here, with the first question, that cases such as that of *Tony Bland*[31] and *Nancy Cruzan*[32] are often, and perhaps inappropriately, introduced.[33] The central issue in these cases is whether PVS is a state which has any value at all to the person (on which we may disagree)[34] and where the advance directive is being used to give some rather spurious support to switching off the ventilator or discontinuing hydration and nutrition based on patient autonomy.[35] A test of the 'autonomy' argument here is what Nancy Jecker has called the 'darker side';[36] if the patient autonomy argument was really important, it would imply that we should respect the wishes of a person who had executed an advance directive that they should be kept in a PVS. Jecker has asked 'how should we as a society respond to patients who *insist* that everything possible be done and who simply refuse to take burdens to others into account?'.[37] And to this question, British courts, at least, have given a clear and unequivocal answer.[38] Whatever may be the case with patients declining to

---

30 The observation of the BMA Ethics Committee here is pertinent: 'Although it is sometimes assumed that such examples occur more frequently in textbooks than in reality, the enquiries which the Association receives from members indicate that appropriate treatment of Jehovah's Witnesses is not merely a matter of academic concern, but rather of deep soul searching.' (*Medical Ethics Today*, p 161.)

31 *Airedale NHS Trust v Bland* [1993] 1 All ER 821; [1993] 2 WLR 316.

32 *Cruzan v Director, Missouri Department of Health* 497 US 261 (1990), discussed extensively in *op cit*, Dworkin, fn 7; see, also, Alldridge, P, 'Who wants to live forever?', in *op cit*, Lee and Morgan, fn 16, pp 11–36.

33 As Tony Hope, commenting on a draft of this chapter, put it: 'Advance directives are being used in too blanket a way and to solve too many problems at once. They seem to be part of a current obsession that difficult issues in medical ethics can almost always be solved with reference to patient autonomy.'

34 For an eloquent, critical assessment of the House of Lords' speeches in *Bland*, see Finnis, J, '*Bland*: crossing the Rubicon' (1993) 109 LQR 329.

35 I am grateful to Tony Hope for the clarification of this argument. And see *op cit*, Lynn, fn 5, p 102.

36 'Being a burden on others' in *op cit*, Emanuel, fn 2, p 19.

37 *Ibid*.

38 *Re J (A Minor)* [1992] 4 All ER 614; *R v Secretary of State for Social Services ex p Hincks* (1992) 1 BMLR 93; *R v Secretary of State for Social Services ex p Walker* (1993) 3 BMLR 32; *R v Central Birmingham HA ex p Collier* (1988) unreported, 6 January. I also consider these cases above, Chapter 4.

accept certain treatments or interventions, there is no legal basis on which patients can require or mandate their doctors to treat them in preference to another, or to treat them in a way which impugns their professional judgment.

The latter case, which we may call the 'condition' directive, seeks to ensure that a certain kind of dying can be assured, and may be applicable in a wide variety of cases, such as advanced degenerative damage of the nervous system, cancer, AIDS, severe and permanent brain damage or other comparable cases. Here, an advance directive may be thought to have its most pertinent, yet difficult role. The condition directive raises issues concerned with personal identity in a way that others do not, because here, there is still a person who is sensate and can experience pains and pleasures, even though they are not cognitively competent. This situation, therefore, raises the important question of whether I can now say 'I do not want to be remembered as a demented person; therefore, if I become demented, don't treat any illness that might kill me'. But then, when I become demented, I may no longer care about what people think about me in the long term and I may well have a happy, though somewhat simple existence.

I want to suggest that, while the latter 'condition directive' *appears to* present the starker objection to medical care, the usual legal deference to clinical judgment[39] is being departed from more radically, and *therefore* with more circumspection, in the former. 'Treatment directive' cases involve a recognition of patients' interests, even though the doctor would have arrived at a different decision, in directing their own life and destiny.[40] The patient requires the doctor to depart from his or her own judgment and common law, as we shall see, has recently decreed that he or she must observe the patient's clearly articulated wishes.[41] This, I believe, is one explanation for the cautious approach of the court in a case such as *Re T*. Thus, the doctor must be satisfied that the patient's will has not been overborne, that they have directed themselves precisely to the position that has now arisen and that the refusal of treatment, if expressed on a standard form, must be clear and unambiguous,[42] *because* the legal order is recognising the disruption that it is causing and sanctioning to medical authority. Hence, it will do so only on clear and unambiguous evidence.

---

39 Eg, *Re J (A Minor)* [1992] 4 All ER 614; the court would not force a doctor to treat a child in a way contrary to his/her clinical judgment.

40 See Schneiderman, L, Kaplan, R, Pearlman, R and Teetzel, H, 'Do physicians' own preferences for life-sustaining treatment influence their perceptions of patients' preferences?', in *op cit*, Emanuel, fn 2, p 303: 'Our data ... suggest that physicians are hampered not only by flawed communication, but also by limits to their ability to be empathic – that is, to imagine their patients' feelings and ideas.'

41 The proposals of the House of Lords Select Committee represent a retrenchment from that common law position; see the discussion, below, at text accompanying fn 74.

42 *Re T (Adult: Refusal of Medical Treatment)* [1992] 4 All ER 649; [1992] 3 WLR 782; (1992) 9 BMLR 46.

In the case of the condition directive, that 'natural' order is not being challenged in such a direct way and, as the *Bland* case illustrates, although deep and difficult moral issues are raised, they do not give rise to the same difficulties for the law because they do not disturb the usual treatment and decision making hierarchy in the same way or, indeed, so radically.[43] *Bland* is itself an illustration of the way in which that ordering is reinforced; Tony Bland's doctors wanted to discontinue the treatment that *they* had concluded was futile. That there were others in the profession who arrived at the opposite conclusion[44] serves only to underline the freedom which the law traditionally affords doctors. As long as a 'responsible body of medical opinion'[45] defends or promotes what is being proposed, the law is hesitant to intervene. Hence *Bland*'s controversial significance.

A LONG EXPERIENCE OF DYING AND THE DEVELOPMENT OF LIVING WILLS

(a) The US

According to Ronald Dworkin,[46] every State in the US now recognises some form of advance directive: either living wills – 'documents stipulating that specified medical procedures should not be used to keep the signer alive in certain specified circumstances'; or health care proxies – 'documents appointing someone else to make life-and-death decisions for the signer when he no longer can'.[47] In 1990, Congress adopted a law requiring all hospitals supported by Federal funds to inform any patient entering hospital, for howsoever minor procedure, of the States' law on advance directives and of any formalities to be followed if they wish to be ensured of treatment and management appropriate to their wishes.[48] The stimulus for this recognition has been augmented by a number of well known cases – such as *Karen Quinlan* and *Nancy Cruzan* – which have tested the limits of the doctor-patient

---

43 *Airedale NHS Trust v Bland* [1993] 1 All ER 821; [1993] 2 WLR 316.

44 In addition to his oral evidence at first instance, see, also, Andrews, K, 'Managing the persistent vegetative state' (1992) 305 BMJ, 29 August, 486.

45 The traditional formulation of the now hopelessly misused negligence standard as articulated in *Bolam v Friern HMC* [1957] 2 All ER 118.

46 *Op cit*, Dworkin, fn 7, p 180.

47 For a comprehensive review to 1991, see Areen, J, 'Advance directives under State law and judicial decisions', in *op cit*, Capron, fn 5, pp 93–97.

48 Patient Self-Determination Act 1990, effective from 1 December 1991; see Omnibus Reconciliation Act 1990, PL 101–508, ss 4206, 4751.104 Stat 1388. For a recent update on States' positions in respect of advance directive provisions, see *ibid*, Areen, pp 91–100.

relationship through a variety of arguments, the most important of which is the US Supreme Court case of *Cruzan*.[49]

The effect of *Cruzan is* often misunderstood, but its role as a catalyst in reform is difficult to overstate. Recall that Nancy Cruzan had been in a PVS since an accident in 1983, and would remain that way until her death. Her nutrition and hydration were delivered, like Tony Bland's, tubally. In assuming, without expressly deciding, that autonomous patients have a constitutionally protected 'liberty interest' in refusing unwanted medical treatment, a majority of the justices of the Supreme Court of the United States have been applauded as having given a ringing affirmation of the right to self-determination for competent patients. They are thought to have rounded off the circle first sketched by Cardozo J in *Schloendorff v Society of New York Hospital*[50] that:

> [E]very human being of adult years and sound mind has the right to determine what shall be done with his own body; and a surgeon who performs an operation without his patient's consent commits an assault for which he is liable in damages.

The reality is rather different. In the *Nancy Cruzan* case, the Supreme Court majority said that the States were entitled to insist on clear and convincing evidence – such as a living will or other formal document – before permitting hospitals to withdraw life support.[51] To this extent, they agreed with the Missouri Supreme Court, which had held that the State requirement for 'clear and convincing evidence' could have been satisfied by a living will, but not 'the informal, casual statements her friends and family remembered'.[52]

Larry Gostin, writing in *Law, Medicine and Health Care*, has illuminated the limitations of this approach. The court, he has argued, provides uncertain protection for the rights of autonomous patients and virtually removes any constitutional protection once a person is declared incompetent.[53] The 'liberty interest' to refuse treatment afforded to autonomous patients is of uncertain value in Supreme Court discourse, compared with a heightened standard of constitutional review known as 'strict scrutiny'. Thus, the majority were careful not to suggest that competent patients have a fundamental right to refuse treatment, which would be protected unless the State interest is compelling.[54] A liberty interest, on the other hand, can be outweighed by State concerns which sometimes appear weak or even abstract.

---

49 *Cruzan v Director, Missouri Department of Health* 497 US 261 (1990).

50 211 NY 125 (1914), pp 129–30.

51 *Op cit*, Dworkin, fn 7, pp 187–88.

52 *Op cit*, Dworkin, fn 7.

53 Gostin, L, 'Life and death choices after *Cruzan*', in *op cit*, Capron, fn 5, p 9.

54 *Skinner v Oklahoma ex rel Williamson* 316 US 535 (1942).

Cruzan almost 'abandons any Federal constitutional protection for incompetent patients',[55] because the Supreme Court held that a State is entitled, but not required, to insist that relatives prove by 'clear and convincing' evidence that the patient, if competent, would have refused to be treated. Illuminating what he considers to be the wages of these 'technological shackles', Gostin warns that the upholding by the Supreme Court of a clear and convincing evidence standard:

> ... is so exacting as to burden unconscionably the right of an incompetent patient to avoid unwanted medical technology ... The overwhelming majority of people do not anticipate the circumstances of their death with the exactness required under a clear and convincing evidence standard and do not plan their lives by creating formal legal instruments.[56]

Several North American studies have shown that patients and members of the public are, at least in theory, well disposed towards giving advance instructions.[57] Yet, despite the publicity generated by the *Cruzan* case, very few people have executed living wills. One poll reported by Dworkin showed that 87% of those interviewed in 1991 believed that a doctor should either be required or permitted to withdraw life support if the patient had signed a living will so requesting, but another suggested that only 17% of those interviewed had actually signed one.[58] There is, however, less enthusiasm for writing down instructions than for talking about preferences or designating a proxy. This may reflect inhibitions that people may feel about creating and using legal documents, or about the technology of writing itself.

Or, it may reflect other inhibitions. This reported dissonance between sentiment and action is characteristic of avoidance behaviours. Lynn has suggested one reason for this: a living will entails a construction that identifies, at any one time, a group of persons who are 'dying'. The rest of us, in this conception, are not:

> Classifying some persons as 'dying' functions to protect people, most of their lives, against recognising that there is a death in store for each of us. The boundary between being merely mortal (like all humans) and being in the 'dying' category is a boundary people want desperately to find (and to find themselves in the 'non-dying' group).[59]

This serves to remind us that talking about death and dying has become extremely difficult and unfamiliar in our culture.[60] Thus, much of what people ordinarily take to be important in their choices is shunned in the conventional living will and the process of writing it. 'There is little passion or

---

55   *Op cit*, Gostin, fn 53, p 10.

56   *Op cit*, Gostin, fn 53.

57   These are reviewed in *op cit*, Emanuel, fn 2, p 12.

58   *Op cit*, Dworkin, fn 7, p 254, n 1. And see *op cit*, House of Lords Select Committee, fn 8, para 185.

59   *Op cit*, Lynn, fn 5, p 102.

60   *Op cit*, Emanuel, fn 2, p 12.

pathos, only the clean, sterile black and white of choices made and enforced.'[61] If these various observations are correct, this would have important consequences for the wider development of living wills altogether.

(b) Advance directives and English law

The background dialogue

The academic and professional interest in the importance of advance directives has followed a remarkably similar judicial trajectory in the UK. The House of Lords Select Committee has observed that the legal status of advance directives has 'not been specifically tested', and that 'the law is obviously in a state of rapid development'.[62] Most commentators, however, would agree with the opinion of the Centre for Medical Law and Ethics in their evidence to the Committee that their legal validity and binding force is 'now beyond question'.[63]

The background to these developments in English law is surveyed by Jonathan Montgomery.[64] As he there recounts, views on the legality of living wills differed sharply in the late 1980s. On the one hand, the British Medical Association (BMA), in its review of euthanasia, concluded that advance declarations of patient intent should be regarded as neither legally nor ethically binding; the difficulties for medical autonomy were clearly appreciated and spelled out.[65] The Centre for Medical Law and Ethics of King's College London and Age Concern came to the opposite conclusion on the then legal position and expressed this in their report, *The Living Will: Consent to Treatment at the End of Life.*[66]

The BMA's opposition to legislation was based on a familiar and often expressed ground, repeated in their more recent *Statement on Advance Directives* and evidence to the House of Lords Committee, that mutual respect and common accord is better achieved without legislation.[67] And, in advice from the BMA's Ethics, Science and Information Division, it is affirmed that,

---

61 *Op cit*, Lynn, fn 5, p 102. I do not deal here with the mechanics of making and executing an advance directive, but we live increasingly in the surveillance society and the global village, panoptic places and societies in which our every move is watched.

62 *Op cit*, House of Lords Select Committee, fn 8, paras 183, 184.

63 *Op cit*, House of Lords Select Committee, fn 8, para 183.

64 Montgomery, J, 'Power over death: the final sting', in *op cit*, Lee and Morgan, fn 16, pp 37–53.

65 British Medical Association, *Euthanasia*, 1988, London: BMA, para 236, cited in *ibid*, Montgomery, p 38.

66 *The Living Will*, 1988, London: Edward Arnold, p 35.

67 British Medical Association, *Statement About Advance Directives*, 1992, London: BMA, p 4.

while respecting the patient's previous decision, doctors must be cautious about acting on instructions which can no longer be confirmed: '... the BMA recommends that full discussion of the provisions of any advance directive between patient and doctor forms a continuing dialogue.'[68] However, it is later asserted that 'the Association confirms its commitment to the fundamental right of patients to accept or reject, through advance directives, treatment options offered to them'.[69]

This question of dialogue is one that is returned to frequently by commentators. In a considered essay, Lynn[70] remarks that 'the text of a living will rarely tells the physician anything that was not nearly as likely to be true without it', and the presentation of a standard format living will (while perhaps indicating something of the person's seriousness of purpose, and maybe something of themselves) 'is best used as an opportunity to explore what he or she really means to avoid, what is really feared and hoped for, and who would be trusted to make decisions'. This, while exceedingly valuable, she says, requires no legal standing for the document, nor that it be treated as the definitive statement of what should be done. In conclusion, she suggests that 'the standard living will is thoroughly disappointing as a legal document'. It does not reliably shape the care plan as intended and carries risks of affecting the care plan adversely.[71] This point is echoed by Montgomery, whose evidence to the House of Lords Select Committee is quoted on this point. The introduction of legislation, he observed, would need to be accompanied by a precise definition of when advance directives are to take effect:

> The more precisely that the events are described, the more likely it is that the actual scenario would be different and that the declaration would be held to be inapplicable. Thus, the practical effect of increasing the force given to directives might be to reduce the number which would be effective.[72]

Of course, there are background assumptions here about the nature and role of law and what is seen as the proper relationship between law and the social practice which medical care constitutes. Lynn's may also be a jurisdictionally specific comment on the proper relationship between health carers and their patients. But, it informs the evidence put by the BMA before the House of Lords Committee and weighed in the Committee's deliberations. Thus, the

---

68 British Medical Association, *Medical Ethics Today: Its Practice and Philosophy*, 1993, London: BMJ, p 12; *op cit*, House of Lords Select Committee, fn 8, paras 188–89. Perhaps if this objection is to shape the future scope and development of advance directives, it would be better if, in the majority of cases, these were known as 'advance planning directives', the ongoing conversational basis of the choices being emphasised.

69 *Ibid*, BMA, p 161.

70 *Op cit*, Lynn, fn 5, p 101.

71 *Op cit*, Lynn, fn 5, p 102.

72 *Op cit*, Montgomery, fn 64, pp 37–53, cited in *op cit*, House of Lords Select Committee, fn 8, para 211.

BMA urged that dialogue was not only a potential benefit of the advance directive, but also a necessary part of the process; the initiative in formulating a living will should become 'part of a continuing dialogue between doctor and patient so that both are fully apprised of the other's opinion'.[73] Clearly, the paradigm of the advance directive to which this is directed is what I have earlier called 'the condition directive'. It is only in that case that the question of a *relationship* can be of *mutual* value. In that of the treatment directive, the patient, almost by definition, is not concerned with the doctor, his views, her judgment or their consciences. Here, we see the full force of the symbolic as well as actual threat which the advance directive suggests to the medical guild.

The symbolic threat is to the world of doctor-patient relationships as once we might have known it; the evidence cited and the Committee's reactions are as pictures from a bygone age, and not one which has necessarily been sought by patients. Thus, the BMA 'welcomes advance directives as an aid to doctors, in acquainting them with their patient's view [which] could be of particular value when the patient is *otherwise unknown to the doctor*'.[74] And when is that? Almost all the time, I would venture to suggest, at least in one of the cases where the advance directive is to be of any particular force – the emergency treatment department. And when, in that setting, the doctor and patient are most likely to have had no prior contact, communication or relationship, the Committee resolves that 'there should be no expectation that treatment in an emergency should be delayed while enquiry is made about a possible advance directive'.[75] And, for good measure, the Committee imports from English land law the protections traditionally reserved for the *bona fide* purchaser without notice: 'A doctor who treats a patient in genuine ignorance of the provisions of an advance directive should not be considered culpable if the treatment proves to have been contrary to the wishes therein expressed.'[76] A basic consideration which might usefully have been imported from the otherwise much criticised Human Tissue Act 1961 is that a doctor might be obliged to make 'such enquiries as are reasonably practicable' to discover whether a patient had made any prior expression of their wishes.[77] A doctor who has a conscientious objection to complying with the directives of patients should 'make this clear at an early stage in [the preparation of the directive], so that patients may transfer to other doctors if they wish'.[78]

---

73 *Op cit*, House of Lords Select Committee, fn 8, para 188, citing BMA evidence. So much of this discussion proceeds as though a central feature to be taken into account here was not power and balance in the relationship, and as though information, let alone judgments, could be assigned to a value-neutral vacuum.

74 BMA evidence, quoted in *op cit*, House of Lords Select Committee, fn 8, para 189. Emphasis added.

75 *Op cit*, House of Lords Select Committee, fn 8, para 265.

76 *Op cit*, House of Lords Select Committee, fn 8, para 265.

77 And here, the value of a central registration system might be displayed, with advance directives available for recall on CD-ROM.

78 *Op cit*, House of Lords Select Committee, fn 8, para 265.

The model of the patient-practitioner relationship on which this builds is drawn on leaves taken straight from *Doctor Finlay's Casebook*. That for many people the ethically difficult and objectionable decisions may be taken at the outset of treatment or resuscitation means either doctors who have such objections will be denied the experience (and the chance of preferment) in casualty departments, or people's wishes about certain types or circumstances of medical treatment will be ignored wholesale. Similar disadvantages will attend professional para-medical staff who work in ambulance crews, where these decisions are even more difficult and, in practical outcome terms, perhaps more significant.[79] Provision could be made for these issues in the Code of Practice that the Select Committee recommended the colleges and faculties of all the health care professions jointly develop; resolving them by way of legislation would certainly have presented an equally difficult task. But, in the world of *Casualty* and *Health and Efficiency*, a person's relationship, even with what used to be called their family doctor, is unlikely to bear much relationship to that envisaged by members of the Select Committee.

Two views given in evidence (and not to be attributed to the BMA) make plain what is effectively being hinted at in what I have called this symbolic representation of the patient-doctor relationship. They lay bare the fact that advance directives might affect the real nature of the relationship. Thus, CARE opined that: '... it would be bizarre in the extreme to require a skilled, professional doctor to adhere to the stipulations of a living will which did not accord with his/her expert opinion of what would be in the best interests of the patient's health.'[80]

One commentator observed that in 'gravely' undermining the professional expertise and judgment of doctors, advance directives would 'make doctors nothing more than slaves of society'.[81] But, as Emanuel remarks on the significance of this type of colloquy, 'physicians are obligated to put their training and education to the service of patients, so that patient rights can be realized through suitable professional conversation and assisted decision making'.[82] Clearly, there are times when that is not discharged by setting out the wares available at the clinical Casbah and, in a feint of autonomy, settling back with the admonition: 'You choose.'[83] But, unfortunately, we have come to know enough about one version of the process of dying to be sceptically aware of

---

79 See a rare consideration of this important question in Irerson, KV, 'Forgoing hospital care: should ambulance staff always resuscitate?' (1991) 17 J Med Ethics 19.

80 Cited in *op cit*, House of Lords Select Committee, fn 8, para 196.

81 Cited in *op cit*, House of Lords Select Committee, fn 8, para 196.

82 *Op cit*, Emanuel, fn 2, p 12.

83 See Inkelfinger, FG, 'Arrogance' (1980) 304 New England J Medicine 150: 'I do not want to be in the position of the shopper at the Casbah who negotiates and haggles with the physician about what is best. I want to believe that my physician is acting under a higher moral principle than a used car dealer. I'll go further than that. A physician who merely spreads an array of vendibles in front of his patient and then says "Go ahead, you choose, it's your life" is guilty of shirking his duty, if not malpractice.' Cited in *op cit*, Saunders, fn 16, p 81.

the perceived need to avoid technological shackles. What is remarkable about the slavery view recorded by the House of Lords Committee is the recognition it requires that the medical and nursing professions have been as much a victim of the vulgarisation of surgery as the patient. The failure which the scalpel represented has been translated into the failure of the architecture and geography of dying. The hospital has become not a sanctuary of healing, but a palace of death.[84]

The legal voices

The Court of Appeal decision in *Re T*,[85] the House of Lords' speeches in *Airedale NHS Trust v Bland*[86] and the successful prosecution of Dr Nigel Cox for attempted murder[87] transformed, in the space of 18 months, the nature and impact of the debate in England and Wales. The first two decisions have also effected a dramatic change in, or clarification of, the legal position. Since then, the Law Commission has suggested the formal recognition of advance directives in England and Wales, and the common law developments broadly support the view taken by the Kings College/Age Concern *Living Will* report. From the course of judgments in the Court of Appeal and speeches in the House of Lords, it is now clear that English law, at least, recognises the validity and force of previously expressed intentions, in the form of advance directives, where medical treatment is concerned.[88]

Nonetheless, the House of Lords Committee (which contained several lawyers) was still cautious in its approach to the legal validity of advance directives, and those who, in evidence, urged the introduction of legislation frequently accompanied this opinion with the aspiration that this would remove 'any residual' or the 'remaining degree' of uncertainty. Such uncertainty is more apparent than real, although the Committee's *Report* correctly observes that this has not been the subject of any definitive consideration by a British court.

---

84 The work particularly of Philippe Aries is associated with a critical history of this development; see, *inter alia*, his *The Hour of Our Death*, 1982, New York: Vintage.

85 *Re T (Adult: Refusal of Medical Treatment)* [1992] 4 All ER 649; [1992] 3 WLR 782; (1992) 9 BMLR 46.

86 *Airedale NHS Trust v Bland* [1993] 1 All ER 821; [1993] 2 WLR 316.

87 *R v Cox*. An edited version of trial judge Ognall J's summing up to the jury is reported at (1993) 12 BMLR 38, and is the subject of commentary by Andrew Grubb at [1993] 1 Med L Rev 232.

88 This limitation in respect of medical treatment is, of course, important: if a procedure is medical treatment, its disposition, commencement and termination is a matter of clinical judgment and, in so far as an advance directive concerns medical treatment and care, it can only make directions which fall within that scope. It cannot impose a binding obligation on anyone to do something which would be unlawful or contrary to public health, such as excluding basic care.

Of most significance was the Court of Appeal decision in *Re T*, which involved the apparent refusal of consent to a blood transfusion by a former, lapsed or at best periodic Jehovah's Witness. She was, at the time, sedated with pethadine and said to have come under the heavy, but not undue, influence of her mother. Lord Donaldson observed that an adult patient who is mentally and physically capable of exercising a choice must, if medical treatment is to be lawful, consent to that treatment. Treating a person without consent (or despite a refusal) would constitute the civil wrong of trespass to the person and might constitute a crime:

> The patient's right of choice exists whether the reasons for making that choice are rational, irrational, unknown or even non-existent. That his choice is contrary to what is to be expected of the vast majority of adults is only relevant if there are other reasons for doubting his capacity to decide.[89]

On the question of advance directives, Lord Donaldson expressed the view that an anticipatory choice has the same effect as any other refusal of treatment if it is clear that the person making the decision (a) was competent, (b) clearly directed his or her mind to the issues or circumstances which have indeed arisen (in T's case, the court held that she had not done so), and (c) expressed an unequivocal and unrestrained (or untrammelled) view which was applicable in the circumstances.[90] Doctors faced with an anticipatory decision would have to consider the true scope and basis of the decision and whether, at the previous time it was made, it was intended by the patient to apply to the presently changed circumstances.

A refusal based on false premises or misunderstanding of the likely effect of the refusal, or of the seriousness of the consequences which would ensue, or of the realistic range of alternatives likely to be available when the anticipatory refusal's consequences ensued, might vitiate the apparent choice. *Re T* is itself an example of this. It appears that T was told that alternatives to a full blood transfusion were available, as indeed they are. But, her condition deteriorated to such an extent that, in emergency, *only* a blood transfusion would suffice; hence, said the court, the premise on which the directive was given had changed significantly. In addition, when T was told of the range of alternatives available, and of the likely consequences of her refusal, it was not then in the context of the emergency which had indeed developed. Thus, a refusal would be effective only strictly within the terms that it addressed.[91]

Courts in other common law jurisdictions, to which the English courts have looked in guiding them through the difficult legal and ethical questions which arise here, have taken a similar approach.[92] Their approach is echoed

---

89 *Re T* [1992] 4 All ER 649, p 653, *per* Lord Donaldson. I do not deal here with the question of whether choice has, by definition, to have a minimum content, such that as a matter of logic it is inappropriate for Donaldson to write of 'non-existent' reasons.

90 *Ibid*, p 797.

91 As Andrew Grubb points out, the anticipatory refusal thus has three elements: competence, scope and undue influence; see *op cit*, Grubb, fn 87, pp 85–87.

92 *Malette v Shulman* (1990) 67 DLR (4th) 321; *Fleming v Reid* (1991) 82 DLR (4th) 298.

by Lords Goff and Keith in the celebrated case of *Bland*, although the caution shown by the Missouri Supreme Court in *Cruzan* is more evident in the speech of Lord Mustill. Recall that Tony Bland was trapped in the mêlée at the Hillsborough football stadium in April 1989. Between then and his demise in 1993, following a long process of dying, attended with legal, medical, ethical and philosophical controversy, he existed in a PVS. Lord Mustill's is the key speech in determining the common law legality of living wills. Because of the disquiet which he expresses about the conclusion of the instant case,[93] this might affect the way in which his speech is studied on this narrower question.

Recalling that the American courts have sanctioned the discontinuance of life supporting medical care by developing the doctrine of informed consent, he observed that this has been achieved either by founding on the constitutional rights of the patient to due process or within the penumbra of the developing right to privacy. In what might then appear a limiting condition, he ventured that 'I cannot see that that doctrine [of informed consent] has anything to offer in the present case'. Commenting that this took two forms, he said that, in the first, where the court looked for the making of an antecedent choice by a patient, 'what has often been called a "living will" has been held sufficient for this purpose'. On this, he offered no critical comments or observations.[94] He reserved his more circumspect treatment for the much more difficult question of people who have left no explicit instructions, or instructions which can be deduced from clear and effective cross-examination of witnesses, as to their supposed wishes. In this second case, some American courts have developed limited theories of 'imputed choice'. Whilst this course is, in many ways, attractive, he considered that there were obvious dangers which may well be felt to justify the cautious attitude adopted by the courts of New York State in cases such as *Re Storar; Re Eichner*.[95]

Thus, there is nothing in Lord Mustill's speech which suggests an essential antipathy to the development of advance directives in England and Wales. Lords Goff and Keith are more explicit in their acceptance of the legal force of advance directives:

---

93   And which seems to have been critical in the setting of the terms of reference, if not the establishment of the House of Lords Select Committee (of which Lord Mustill was a member) to consider these issues.

94   [1993] 1 All ER 821, p 892b–d.

95   52 NY 2d 363 (1981).

... a person is completely at liberty to decline to undergo treatment, even if the result of his doing so is that he will die. This extends to the situation where the person, in anticipation ... gives clear instructions ...[96]

... a patient of sound mind may, if properly informed, require that life support should be discontinued ... the same principle applies where the patient's refusal to give his consent has been expressed at an earlier date.[97]

These *dicta* appear firmly to establish the existence and validity of advance directives in the curriculum of medical jurisprudence. The framework against which they will be manipulated is a question which will need careful observation. For the present, there are two particular questions of some difficulty to which brief attention needs to be directed: first, the troublesome question of competence; and, secondly, the related question of consultation with the next of kin when either competence is extinguished or the person's present wishes are unascertainable. A related issue is what I have called that of the 'committed directive'.

Competence

Among the groups of patients who cause 'greatest consternation'[98] regarding advance directives are those of questionable competence. Particular difficulty arises when people change their minds at the last minute, and the profound suspicion arises that 'the patient has lost connection with the narrative whole that constituted his life'.[99] Nonetheless, it is clear that demented patients can be competent for some decisions. Criteria and process for informed consent in such cases have been developed,[100] but additional considerations are necessary before they can be applied to advance directives. For example, competence may vary according to medication use or exacerbations in illness.[101] Thus, for some mentally ill patients, consent and competence as far as advance directives are concerned may not be a once-and-for-all possibility: '... it may be useful to sample the vicissitudes and potential validity of

---

96 [1993] 1 All ER 821, p 860a–b, *per* Lord Keith.

97 *Ibid*, p 866b–e, *per* Lord Goff. For the Court of Appeal's consideration of this point, see p 843a, *per* Butler-Sloss LJ; pp 835–36, *per* Sir Thomas Bingham; and pp 852–54, *per* Hoffman LJ.

98 *Op cit*, Emanuel, fn 2, p 11.

99 *Op cit*, Emanuel, fn 2, p 11.

100 For a good introductory discussion of the general principles involved, see Appelbaum, PS and Grisso, T, 'Assessing patients' capacities to consent to treatment' (1988) 319 New England J Medicine 1635. More comprehensive is Appelbaum, PS, Lidz, CW and Meisel, A, *Informed Consent: Legal Theory and Clinical Practice*, 1987, New York: OUP.

101 *Op cit*, Emanuel, fn 2, p 11.

advance directives by competing serial advance directives with assessment of competence at each statement.'[102]

A recent example of assessing competence in the case of a present refusal to consent to treatment and to project that forward to any anticipated intervention occurred soon after the conclusion of *Bland's* case, in *Re C*.[103]

The plaintiff, C, was 68 and had been diagnosed as a chronic paranoid schizophrenia patient. He was resident at Broadmoor, from whence he had been transferred to a local hospital following diagnosis of gangrene in the foot. He sought an injunction under the court's inherent jurisdiction to prevent the hospital from amputating his right leg following the consultant surgeon's assessment that he would die imminently if the operation was delayed. Thorpe J concluded that, while C was reduced by his mental illness, the decision as to whether he was so reduced 'remains marginal',[104] his rejection of amputation seeming to result from *'sincerely held conviction'*.[105] Following the direction of *Re R*[106] and *Re W*[107] in treatment decisions for minors, Thorpe J rejected the submission of C's counsel that the definition of capacity enabling an individual to refuse treatment was a minimal one, involving no more than 'the capacity to understand in broad terms the nature and effect of the proposed treatment'.[108] Rather, the question to be decided is whether the plaintiff's capacity was 'so reduced by his chronic mental illness that he does not sufficiently understand the nature, purpose and effects of the proffered amputation'. There were three ingredients in that decision: an ability (a) to take in and retain treatment information; (b) to believe it; and (c) to weigh that information, balancing risks and needs. Thorpe J glossed the second criterion, in adding that the plaintiff 'in his own way ... believes it and that in the same fashion he has arrived at a clear choice'.

What was of particular importance in making an *anticipatory* choice to refuse treatment was that 'in weighing the consequences of facing a future acute phase without amputation [C] has the experience of a recent acute attack to guide him'. And, importantly, Thorpe J said that the High Court has jurisdiction by way of injunction or declaration to rule that an individual is capable of refusing or consenting to medical treatment and to determine the effect of a purported advance directive, and that the judicial process was as much open to the individual patient as to the health care professional to seek such an order.

---

102 *Op cit*, Emanuel, fn 2.

103 [1994] 1 All ER 819.

104 *Ibid*, p 822c.

105 *Ibid*, p 823h, emphasis added.

106 *Re R (Wardship: Consent to Treatment)* [1992] Fam 11, p 26.

107 (1992) 9 BMLR 22.

108 A test drawn from *Chatterton v Gerson* [1981] 1 All ER 257 in respect of consent sufficient to avoid an allegation of battery.

The next of kin

The advantages of discussion with the next of kin, or an unequivocally clear and unambiguous directive, are palpable. But each has its limitations. Where people have not expressed their views in advance and are now incapable of doing so, seeking guidance from the next of kin might not be undesirable in practice, as long as this will not result in unnecessary delay in making treatment decisions about the patient. But this consultation may not be done as health care professionals sometimes mistakenly believe that 'because the next of kin has no legal right either to consent or refuse consent',[109] they have no role al all. Contact with the next of kin may, however, reveal the personal circumstances of the patient, the sorts of choices which they might have made if they had been in a position to do so and whether the patient has, in fact, made an anticipatory choice. Such information as gleaned from the next of kin could not, however, require a doctor to act against what he or she saw to be the best interests of the patient, nor could the information from the relatives permit him or her to do what the patient, albeit only orally, had required in advance that he or she should not do.[110]

> Neither the personal circumstances of the patient nor a speculative answer to the question 'What would the patient have chosen?' can bind the practitioner in his choice of whether or not to treat and how to treat *or justify him in acting contrary to a clearly established anticipatory refusal to accept treatment* but they are factors to be taken into account by him in forming a clinical judgment as to what is in the best interests of the patient.[111]

The committed directive[112]

The advantages of written, compared with oral, evidence, gleaned from the next of kin, are numerous. It goes to the heart of the evidentiary requirement that the advance refusal be 'clearly established' and it helps, but does not finally settle, the question of whether the refusal is truly that of the patient, as being an expression of their own, untrammelled wishes, and not overborne by or unduly reflecting those of another, significant other. The better course may be for advance directives to be written, although this technology has its own limitations and constructs its own exclusions, as I shall return to argue. Taking evidence from the next of kin is, as Grubb has suggested:

> ... by its very nature ... likely to be inconclusive. Doctors may feel that the relatives are not truly reflecting the patient's views or the patient's views may

---

109 *Re T* (1992) 9 BMLR 46, p 51, *per* Lord Donaldson.
110 *Ibid*.
111 *Ibid*, pp 50–51.
112 I use this term to encompass written directives and those committed to some other permanent form.

be insufficiently clear given the court's criteria for a valid anticipatory decision.[113]

The danger of this, as far as the patient's self-determination is concerned, is clear. It is spelled out by Donaldson: 'In case of doubt, that doubt falls to be resolved in favour of the preservation of life, for if the individual is to override the public interest he must do so in clear terms.'[114]

Given this approach, it seems likely that a living will is more likely to be validated if (a) drawn up in consultation with a doctor;[115] (b) at a time when the doctor and the patient have the latter's prognosis and treatment options in mind; and (c) it is more specific than general in its terms. The effect of this, Grubb suggests, is that:

A 'living will' is less comprehensive than would be a general statement of the patient's wishes. Provided that the specific situation contemplated arises, there is no legal problem; the advance directive is binding on the doctor ... If a different situation arises, however, the 'living will' may miss the mark and the patient's more general intention to, for example, forego life-sustaining treatment will be frustrated.[116]

The judicial reception of advance directives was supplemented by two Private Members' Bills which were introduced into Parliament early in 1993 to treat the question of living wills.[117] Although both were unsuccessful, they gave an indication of the way in which legislation might be framed in England and Wales. The Law Commission and the House of Lords Select Committee have offered their respective conclusions on these questions and on the desirability of legislation.[118]

There is a clear difference, however, between those bodies such as the BMA, which do not think that the introduction of legislation on advance directives is the preferred way forward, and the Law Commission. The latter has proposed the introduction of a statutory scheme to augment whatever common law validity such advance directives presently have. The Law Commission has, in preliminary conclusions, recommended that legislation should be introduced to provide for the scope and legal effect of anticipatory decisions, and that these should, if clearly established, be as effective as a

---

113 (1992) 9 BMLR 46.

114 *Ibid*, p 59.

115 Cf *op cit*, BMA, fn 68, p 162.

116 (1993) 1 Med L Rev, p 87

117 See the Termination of Medical Treatment Bill, HL 70, introduced by Lord Alport on 25 February 1992, and the more extensive and considered Medical Treatment (Advance Directives) Bill, HL 73, introduced by Lord Allen of Abbeydale and given its first reading on 16 March 1993.

118 In its Consultation Paper No 129, *Mentally Incapacitated Adults and Decision Making: Medical Treatment and Research*, 1993, London: HMSO, Pts V and VI. A full consideration of these proposals is beyond the scope of the present chapter.

contemporaneous decision taken by a mentally competent patient.[119] Two important limitations would be that such a decision would be ineffective to the extent that it sought to refuse pain relief or basic care, such as nursing care or spoon-feeding;[120] and that in cases of 'doubt or dispute' there should be 'a judicial forum ... to determine whether an anticipatory decision is clearly established and applicable to the circumstances'.[121] Such a forum might also be given power to override a clearly established and applicable anticipatory decision, although the Commissioners recognise the ambiguity of such a power and presently are not convinced of the need for a broad ranging power.[122]

The Law Commission suggested a formidable array of reasons why legislation is thought desirable, and there is indeed evidence that, absent a statutory regime, advance directives are not respected by health care providers, either because they are unaware of an advance directive or cannot reliably ascertain whether it is authentic.[123] Most importantly, the Law Commission believes that legislation could resolve uncertainty about the legal status of advance directives and clarify whether health care workers, and others, are bound by the expressed wishes of the patient, along the lines of models recently introduced in other common law jurisdictions.[124] A range of ancillary, but nonetheless significant issues are also addressed; these include statutory protection for a health professional who acts in accordance with an advance directive, even one later shown to have been invalid, as long as there was no question of *mala fides* in following the patient's apparent wishes. Limitations on the scope of directives could be canvassed, and penalties introduced for the wrongful concealment, alteration, falsification or forgery of such a directive.[125]

The Law Commission proposed that there should be a rebuttable presumption that an anticipatory decision is clearly established if it is in writing, signed by the director (or at his or her instance) and witnessed.[126] It could be revoked orally or in writing at any time when the director has the capacity to do so, and there would be no legislative provision, as some have

---

119 See *op cit*, Law Commission, fn 25, pp 28–33, a conclusion not since acted upon.

120 *Op cit*, Law Commission, fn 25, p 41; this is based on an argument by Andrew Grubb (*op cit*, fn 87, p 85) that a public policy prohibition on the refusal of nursing care should be enshrined in order to protect the interests of health professionals and other patients who would be affected by such a refusal.

121 *Op cit*, Law Commission, fn 25, pp 41–42.

122 *Op cit*, Law Commission, fn 25, p 42.

123 See Schucking, EL, 'Death at a New York hospital' (1985) 13 Law, Medicine and Health Care, cited also in *op cit*, Gostin, fn 53, p 11.

124 A prominent example here is the Canadian province of Ontario, which in 1992 enacted the Consent to Medical Treatment Act, which makes such provision, *inter alia*, in s 12.

125 *Op cit*, Law Commission, fn 25, pp 31–32.

126 *Op cit*, Law Commission, fn 25, p 36.

urged, for automatic time-based revocation.[127] The Commission does, however, recognise and address some of the common problems identified with advance directives, and these may be briefly summarised here. They include: (a) patients apparently demanding inappropriate treatment, or misdirecting doctors through an inadequate understanding of their circumstances or the evolution of new treatments; (b) what might be called the 'Odysseus problem', of patients who informally change their mind about refusing treatments; (c) the oral expression of what appears to be an impulsive or unconsidered view of future options, which affects the form in which advance directives might need to be expressed, and if they are valid, how they may be revoked; (d) whether there should be any limits placed on the recognition of anticipatory decisions, such that, for example, they should be confined only to those suffering from a terminal illness, or whether their scope should enable patients to exercise control over all the decisions made on their behalf while incapable, whether that incapacity is permanent or temporary.

There is a clear departure from these views in the conclusions of the House of Lords Select Committee on Medical Ethics.[128] While commending the development of advance directives, they recoil from recommending legislation and provide that the colleges and faculties of all the health care professions 'should jointly develop a code of practice to guide their members'.[129] Legislation, in the opinion of the Committee, is 'unnecessary' because doctors are increasingly recognising their 'ethical obligation' to comply with advance directives; case law is moving in the same direction and a doctor who acts in accordance with an advance directive where the clinical circumstances were such as the patient had considered 'would not be guilty of negligence or any criminal offence'.[130] In particular, they were persuaded by the judgment offered by Montgomery that:

> ... it could well be impossible to give advance directives in general greater legal force without depriving patients of the benefit of the doctor's professional expertise and of new treatments and procedures which may have become available since the advance directive was signed.[131]

More alarming is the conclusion which follows, that while the informing premise of any code should be that a directive must be respected as an authoritative statement of the patient's wishes, that is to be set alongside, or more accurately beneath, four different considerations. Thus:

> Those wishes should be overruled only where there are *reasonable grounds* to believe that the clinical circumstances which actually prevail are significantly

---

127 *Op cit*, Law Commission, fn 25, pp 44, 45.

128 *Op cit*, House of Lords Select Committee, fn 8, paras 181–215, 263–67.

129 *Op cit*, House of Lords Select Committee, fn 8, para 265. The Colleges requested the BMA to convene a working party in September 1994 to draft that Code. I accepted an invitation to chair that Committee.

130 *Op cit*, House of Lords Select Committee, fn 8, para 264.

131 *Op cit*, House of Lords Select Committee, fn 8.

different from those which *the patient has anticipated*, or that the patient had changed his or her views since the directive was prepared.[132]

Thus, in the first case, the wishes of the patient, howsoever clearly expressed, may be overtaken by clinical developments which, *even if the patient could have predicted them and would nonetheless have refused intervention*, have outpaced the form of words chosen to express the original intent. And, the judge of this case, we may predict from present judicial deference to medical wisdom, will be the *Bolam* doctor.[133] In other words, as long as a responsible body of medical opinion would conclude that the prevailing clinical circumstances are significantly different, a person's wishes may be overridden, even though another (perhaps larger) body of opinion would have respected them. Again, patients are sacrificed to the uncertainties of the heroic interventionists or the cavalier abstainers. The Committee's conclusions appear to be based on the fallacious assumption that doctors faced with an advance directive would thereby find no further avenue of communication with their patients or that, in the case of developments in medical practice, they would abandon them to the medical expertise of previous generations. The resulting conclusion of the Committee comes close to decontextualising the whole procedure; if the often expressed needs for the directive to be part of a process of consultation and advice mean anything, it cannot be that that conversation is interrupted at the moment that the patient believes the directive will become operative. In case it is replied to this objection that it has no force in the case of life-saving emergency treatment when a person is unable to participate in that discussion, the Committee pre-empts that, for it *separately* provides that 'there should be *no* expectation that treatment in an emergency should be delayed while enquiry is made about a possible advance directive'.[134] This primary ground for overriding the wishes of the patient is clearly directed, whether intentionally or inadvertently, to the wishes of a clearly conscious (albeit now perhaps incompetent) patient where the doctor would have arrived at a different decision if it had been their care which was in issue. But it is not.

The true scope of this first proviso is only really apparent when read in conjunction with the third independent ground for departing from a directive. Thus, the Committee additionally provides that 'A directive may *also* be overruled if it requests treatment which the doctor judges is not clinically indicated'.[135] So, even if the doctor, acting in accordance with a responsible body of medical opinion, concludes that reasonable grounds *do not* exist for departing from the patient's wishes, he or she may *nonetheless* manage the patient in the way *they think* is in the patient's best interests, if the formulation

---

132 *Op cit*, House of Lords Select Committee, fn 8, para 264, emphasis added.
133 *Bolam v Friern HMC* [1957] 2 All ER 118.
134 *Op cit*, House of Lords Select Committee, fn 8, para 264, emphasis added.
135 *Op cit*, House of Lords Select Committee, fn 8, emphasis added.

of the directive appears to call for one type of treatment, say 'nursing care only', and the doctor believes that more radical intervention is worth a try.

Finally, doctors may decline to institute the regime directed by the patient if it requests any illegal action. The second ground, that the patient has changed his or her mind, while largely uncontroversial, could have been used in an expanded and imaginative fashion to encompass much that the Committee wanted to achieve by way of protection for patients in the light of developments since the directive was last updated. If patient autonomy is the siren towards the Scylla of preventable or avoidable death, the hard place on which life may founder, the House of Lords have decidedly set course towards the Charybdis of medical zeal and paternalism. This yet threatens to smash the pearl of a meaningful life lived according to one's own preferences into a paste and imitation jewel which is given a counterfeit shine with the flannel of legislative quiescence.

A FRAIL REFLECTION?[136]

The assumption in the enthusiastic reception given by courts and commentators to advance directives is that if competent individuals have a virtually unlimited right to refuse immediate treatment, then the same choice ought to be respected when the competent individual makes it concerning a future consideration.[137] I want to examine that assumption and test against it several arguments. The first examines the basis of the argument from competent choices and explores possible asymmetries between present and future directions. The second involves a cluster of issues around identity, and arises most clearly in the case of neurological degeneration which affects personality, and whether, and to what extent, the personal identity of the advance director changes over time, in such a way that *it cannot be said that we are now speaking of the same person.* In which case, the direction given by P1 cannot bind P2, now described, even by those who knew them most intimately, as 'a different person'.[138] A third troubling issue might be thought

---

136 Lynn (*op cit*, fn 5, p 102) has warned that: '... the issues that have become conventional to deal with in extended-version living wills are but a frail reflection of the concerns that very sick patients actually express. In fact, some of their real concerns have almost completely lost a place in the discussion of any kind of formal advance directives. Many patients are concerned about the emotional, physical and financial burdens that their prolonged existence might entail for family. So often one hears, "I don't want to be a burden", and so often we fail to have the ability, within this culture, to acknowledge and explore that sentiment.'

137 This point is explicitly endorsed by a number of the judges in the cases of both *Bland* and *Re T*; see above. This assumption and the objections to which it may be subject are explored in *op cit*, Buchanan, fn 7, p 283, n 51.

138 Although I have not adequately dealt with this question in this version, attention will need to be given to the concerns raised by the arguments of Allen Buchanan in *op cit*, fn 7, pp 277–302.

to relate to the contested question of interpretation itself, and the difficulties inherent in 'a *genuine attempt* to identify the *true intentions* of the maker' of the advance directive.[139] Finally, there is a deep and contested question on the meaning of self-determination in respect of death, and the establishment of what has fashionably come to be called 'a right to die'. I cannot, presently, extensively treat each of these difficulties, but I can introduce the nature of the arguments involved.

Competent choices

The first argument is that competent and incompetent people simply do not have the same rights, or, for that matter, interests. In the case of Tony Bland, Butler-Sloss LJ averred that the principle of sanctity of life 'was not an absolute one'.[140] She rejected the approach which placed pain and suffering in a unique category and observed that the two exceptions which English law already admits (those of self-determination, and where the pain and suffering outweigh any concomitant benefit) should be supplemented by other factors, particularly how one will be thought of by others after death. This entailed that incompetent individuals should, and do, have the same rights as competent ones to refuse and terminate medical treatment.[141] Hoffmann LJ, Sir Thomas Bingham, Lord Goff, Lord Keith and the Ontario Court of Appeal all equate the conscious choice of a competent adult with one expressed to take effect at a future date contingent upon specified conditions.

One objection to this it that it looks to involve as much of a *non sequitur* as that committed by Brennan J in his dissenting opinion in the Supreme Court decision in *Cruzan*. Recall that Brennan J argued that, because competent people have the right to refuse medical treatment, and that because artificial feeding and hydration are medical treatments (all the justices – even the concurring ones – seem to agree on this point), and since being incompetent does not deprive people of their fundamental rights, it follows that Nancy Cruzan had a 'right' to have her earlier choice respected and thus to have the feeding tube withdrawn.[142] One commentator, Ron Stephens, has objected that this latter argument of Brennan J appears fallacious:

---

139 See *op cit*, Law Commission, fn 25, p 42, emphasis added.

140 [1993] 1 All ER 821, p 861g.

141 See *ibid*, p 847b, citing the majority opinion of Abrams J in the Massachusetts Supreme Court in *Guardianship of Jane Doe* 411 Mass 512 (1992). Later in her judgment (p 848a–b), she seems to suggest that an incompetent person might have the same interests as a competent one. 'We all, of course, recognise that a patient unable to choose cannot himself exercise his right of self-determination and he cannot make the irrational decision he might notionally have made if in possession of his faculties. But not to be able to be irrational does not seem to me to be a good reason to be deprived of a rational decision which could be taken on his behalf in his best interests ... A mentally incompetent patient has interests to be considered and protected ...'

142 *Cruzan v Director, Missouri Department of Health* 497 US 261 (1990), p 296.

... in that the basis of his first condition is competency, and it seems quite clear ... that the right to 'choose', or even 'refuse', uphold possibilities that are uniquely absent in the incompetent individual such as Nancy Cruzan. And while one can agree with his second condition, and reasoning, that is, incompetent patients are not to be deprived of their 'rights', it unhappily does not follow that competent and incompetent individuals have the same rights, particularly when the rights in question (by definition) inherently require competency (that is, the capacity to 'choose' or to 'refuse'). Consequently, Justice Brennan's concluding argument that Nancy has the right to 'refuse' artificial feeding is simply erroneous.[143]

This appears to be saying that, even if a competent choice gives us, in virtue of its being such, some reason to respect it at the time, this reason only persists as long as the chooser remains competent.

Stephens' argument is open to the strong objection that, in observing her wishes, the doctors are not upholding her fundamental right to '"refuse" artificial feeding' but, rather, a stronger claim not subject to the supposed fallacy. The 'fundamental rights' in question are not to have the feeding tube withdrawn, but rather to have one's (earlier) choices respected. The withdrawal of the feeding tubes is nothing more than an ancillary consequence of respecting that choice.[144] Of course, the demurrer which Stephens enters may be stronger than this. It may be that he is really observing that, if a competent choice gives us, in virtue of its being such, some reason to respect it at the time, *this* reason persists so long as the chooser *remains* competent. This, then, presents a more radical objection, which I consider below, that to respect an advance directive can only be justified if either (a) we are committed to respecting the wishes of the 'dead' (not in itself an insurmountable obstacle), or (b) we hold that the person, while competent, can bind the person when incompetent. This gives rise to what may be thought to be difficult questions of personal identity and interpretation to which I shall come.[145]

Second and subsequent objections to the 'equal rights assumption' are canvassed by Allen Buchanan, who has challenged it because:

> ... it overlooks several morally significant asymmetries between the contemporaneous choice of a competent individual and the issuance of an advance directive to cover future decisions.[146]

---

143 Stephens, RL, 'Duties to the incompetent: a specific examination of the morality of dealing with patients in a persistent vegetative state', unpublished MA thesis on file at University College Swansea, pp 12–13. I am grateful to Dr Stephens for permission to quote from this thesis.

144 Notice that Brennan speaks of the 'right to have the feeding tube withdrawn'; only Stephens of the 'right to refuse'.

145 I am grateful to Hugh Upton for his clarification of the views I have attempted to present in this paragraph. Whether he would recognise them is another matter.

146 *Op cit*, Buchanan, fn 7, p 278.

These asymmetries, he suggests, are, first, that therapeutic options and prognosis may change over time and that the director, as the House of Lords Committee following Donaldson in *Re T* were concerned, should make a decision on the proper basis of alternatives available. Secondly, the assumption that a competent person is the best judge of their own interests is weakened in the case of choice about future contingencies under conditions in which 'those interests have changed in radical and unforeseen ways'.[147] Again, as I have commented, this weighed with the Select Committee's *Report*. Finally, and perhaps of greatest force, is that:

> Important informal safeguards that tend to restrain imprudent or unreasonable contemporaneous choices are not likely to be present, or if present to be as effective, in the case of an advance directive.[148]

A competent patient might be urged to reconsider their decision, and the protective effects of family or close friends are less likely to be operative when the anticipated refusal is a distant or theoretical possibility. Nonetheless, the law might take the view that the dangers of medical paternalism robbing patients of the value of their future choices outweigh any perceived difficulties which these asymmetries suggest.

Let me reflect briefly on these objections. Buchanan's first two points may look the same – circumstances and interests may change – and it would be wrong for the executors not to assess decisions in the light of such changes. Thus, a person's choices about death carry a lot of weight but are, of course, open to review. This is true of all decisions to be acted on later when the decider is inaccessible for *any* reason. Accordingly, it is misleading to suggest that my status as a judge of my future interests is weakened, as though the status of others as judges of those interests are not affected in just the same way. The mere fact that the future is uncertain does not, in principle, weaken my status as a decider *in any way relevant to another deciding for me*, though obviously contingencies may make them or me the better informed. Buchanan's third point is puzzling. He suggests that we are less likely to take into account the views of others (as though we might be obliged to) when deciding for the distant future, and that we are therefore more likely to be imprudent and unreasonable. This may be the case, but it ignores the fact that the refusal (or choice) is not distant, it is taken now, when the advance directive is made.

The identity question

A far more troubling issue for Buchanan, however, is the question of personal identity, which represents a much more profound and potentially grave threat

---

147 *Op cit*, Buchanan, fn 7, p 279.
148 *Op cit*, Buchanan, fn 7, p 249.

to the moral authority of advance directives. This gives rise to the objection that:

> ... the very process that renders the individual incompetent and brings the advance directive into play can – and indeed often does – destroy the conditions necessary for her personal identity and thereby undercut entirely the moral authority of the directive.[149]

He seeks, then, to find a position which will enable the moral authority of advance directives to withstand such an assault, while not surrendering to what he calls dubious metaphysical theories of personal identity. In other words, he wants to rescue advance directives from the damage which a psychological continuity theory of personal identity might inflict if it were asked '*who* is dying?'.

The most difficult, and perhaps common, case is not that of PVS, but is presented by Alzheimer's disease, which results in such extensive, permanent neurological damage that the patient's memory is destroyed, cognitive processes are virtually obliterated, and all that remains is basic perceptual awareness. One argument, by Rebecca Dresser,[150] suggests that because one person's advance directive has no moral authority to bind another, and because psychological continuity may be so severely disrupted that the person who issued the advance directive no longer exists, therefore:

> ... in such cases the advance directive has no moral authority to determine what is to happen to the individual who remains after neurological damage has destroyed the person who issued the advance directive.[151]

Buchanan responds to this by suggesting that, just as where the threshold is set for decision making competence is a matter of choice, so too is the degree of psychological continuity regarded as necessary to speak about the destruction of a person.[152] Challenging Parfitt, who has suggested that the moral and social significance we attach to personal identity should reflect the fact that being the same person is not an either/or proposition, but a matter of more or less,[153] Buchanan contends that there is:

> ... nothing incoherent about designating a certain degree of psychological continuity as necessary for the presence of personal identity *and* recognizing

---

149 *Op cit*, Buchanan, fn 7, p 280.

150 'Life, death and incompetent patients: conceptual infirmities and hidden values in the law' (1986) 28 Arizona L Rev 379.

151 *Ibid*, cited in *op cit*, Buchanan, fn 7, pp 281–82.

152 *Op cit*, Buchanan, fn 7, p 282. A more radical formulation of the indeterminacy of personal identity is suggested in Allan Hutchinson in 'Identity crisis: the politics of interpretation' (1992) 26 New England L Rev 1173, pp 1212–13: '... by taking identity as something to be recovered and fixed, identity politics seems to freeze in place the positionality of people and reduce the options for personal and collective transformation ... For the postmodernist, the recognition of identity constitutes only a starting point, not an achievement, ambition or program.'

153 *Op cit*, Buchanan, fn 7, p 294, discussing Parfitt, D, *Reasons and Persons*, 1986, Oxford: OUP.

that psychological continuity is a matter of degree *and* admitting that psychological continuity is all there is to personal identity.[154]

It follows that there is nothing inconsistent in holding that the moral authority of an advance directive should diminish as the degree of psychological continuity decreases below the threshold, whether as a matter of judgment that is set at a high or at a meagre level. The importance of this conclusion is that it allows us to preserve the core of some of our most valuable practices and institutions: those which presuppose the use of all-or-nothing identity judgments, while acknowledging that:

> ... personal identity is simply a matter of psychological continuity and does not depend on some deeper, metaphysical fact. This compromise approach allows us to make a significant place for advance directives among our social institutions and practices without presupposing a dubious metaphysical theory of personal identity.[155]

These considerations do not appear to have disturbed the Select Committee's deliberations.

Identity and interpretation

I cannot here survey the literature to which the vexed question of interpretation has given rise in the past 30 years. I want only to recall that it has been argued that the relationship between author, text, reader and interpretation is a contested and controversial one. The point, in passing, is this: it cannot be assumed that the business of interpreting an advance directive, of discovering the director's true intent through genuine endeavour, is straightforward, uncontested or without particular significance or meaning.

One of the difficulties with living wills of a standard format is claimed to be that it attends to priorities that are not one's own, addresses procedures rather than outcomes, and 'requires substantial interpretation without guaranteeing a reliable interpreter'.[156] Written documents cannot easily capture the subtle cues that might give one cause to doubt whether a person does, in fact, mean what he says. Unfortunately, there is evidence that:

> ... substitute decision makers, even those who have had a long, intimate familiarity with a patient, may not be accurate predictors of patients' preferences. In the absence of better placed interpreters, we must make do with

---

154 *Op cit*, Buchanan, fn 7, pp 300–01.

155 *Op cit*, Buchanan, fn 7, p 301.

156 *Op cit*, Lynn, fn 5, p 101. This recalls the point made by Montgomery (*op cit*, fn 64) that the more precise the instructions given in an advance directive, and the more precise the grounds for triggering its implementation, the greater the likelihood that a general intention to avoid life sustaining procedures or treatments will be defeated. To this extent, living wills are in danger of being submerged into the Chancery Division mentality of charitable intention and the *cy-près* doctrine.

what the patient said, and perhaps more importantly, with how it says he behaved.[157]

The fact that a person took the time and the trouble to formulate and authenticate an advance directive and bring it to the physician's notice does imply something about that person's character and the seriousness with which he or she approaches these issues, 'but not much about the individual's preferences and priorities'.[158]

But, this search for the 'meaning' of a provision in a living will is not necessarily the starting point of the endeavour. In a more critical understanding:

> ... meaning is always to be argued for and never to be argued from. It is neither a sacred shard of archaeological excavation nor an ephemeral whim of narcissistic indulgence.[159]

When this is allied with the question of identity which Buchanan has discussed, the layers of complexity become more profound. Thus, a more radical response to Buchanan is that the notion of a psychological continuity theory of identity (from which he seeks to rescue living wills) is itself seriously contestable and a limited rendition of what identity might consist in. As Hutchinson has suggested, 'the relation between persons and their contexts is like that between writers and texts – *nothing necessarily follows*'.[160] Thus, identity 'is relative, not intrinsic; fluid, not fixed; perspectival, not neutral; and protean, not perfected'. To speak, then, of divining the 'true intent' of an advance directive when the question of identity may be fulcral may be a journey of Odyssean duration, direction and difficulty.

Directing what; advancing where?

Leon Kass has written that 'to speak of rights in the very troubling matter of medically managed death is ill suited both to sound personal decision making and to sensible public policy'.[161] In arguing from this premise, he concludes there is no firm philosophical or legal argument for a 'right to die'. 'My body and my life, while mine to use, are not mine to dispose of.'[162]

In contrast with this view is that of Ronald Dworkin, in his book *Life's Dominion: An Argument about Abortion and Euthanasia*.[163] Here, Dworkin has argued that there is no doubt that most people treat the manner of their deaths as of special, symbolic importance: they want their deaths, if possible, to

---

157 *Op cit*, Elliott, fn 2, p 61.

158 *Op cit*, Lynn, fn 5, p 102.

159 *Op cit*, Hutchinson, fn 152, p 1188.

160 *Op cit*, Hutchinson, fn 152, p 1192, note omitted.

161 Kass, L, 'Is there a right to die?' (1993) 23(1) Hastings Center Report 34.

162 *Ibid*.

163 *Op cit*, Dworkin, fn 7.

express and in that way vividly to confirm the values they believe most important to their lives. The idea of a good (or less bad) death is not exhausted by how one dies – whether in battle or in bed – but includes timing, and I would add geography, as well. It helps to explain the premium people often put on living to 'see' some particular event, after which the idea of their own death seems less tragic to them.[164]

It does not follow, however, that Dworkin would establish a right to die. While we almost all accept that human life in all its forms is sacred – that it has an intrinsic and objective value quite apart from any value it might have to the person whose life it is, we disagree about the source and character of that sacred value and, therefore, about which decisions respect and which dishonour it.[165] From this he suggests that, while many believe or concede that Lillian Boyes and Tony Bland were 'better off' dead, they nevertheless insist that killing her and letting him die were wrong, precisely because human life has this independent, sacred value.[166] But, this illustrates a fundamental distinction between morality and the State's responsibility for promoting, policing and enforcing law. Any legal regime which permits doctors and other health care workers to allow a patient to die – including those in which the person has made an advance declaration or stipulation of their wishes – must demand caution. It must be so structured as to protect the patient's 'real reflective wishes' and to avoid 'patients or relatives making an unwitting choice for death'.[167]

The crucial question may be not whether to respect the sanctity of life, but which decision(s) best respect it. Those who believe that being 'kept alive' permanently unconscious, sedated beyond sense, or in some other way grossly compromised, may believe that this degrades rather than respects life. As Gray forcefully pleads:

... the absurdity and moral horror in which we currently warehouse for survival those who would, often enough, vastly prefer to exercise the ultimate

---

164 *Op cit*, Dworkin, fn 7, p 211. As Tom Scanlon puts it in his review, 'Partisan for life' (1993) *New York Review of Books*, 15 July, pp 48–49: 'If experience is all that matters to our interests then we should be indifferent about what is done to us under [various] conditions. But most people are not indifferent. In order to make sense of what many people say about life and death, then, we must allow that the quality of a life can depend not only on the quality of the experience that makes it up but also the degree to which that life meets certain critical standards ... People differ in the particular standards that they want their lives to meet – in what Dworkin calls their "critical interests" – but almost everyone recognises some standards of this kind and many people care greatly about meeting them ... But this depends on what the person's critical interests are. Dworkin suggests that being kept alive in some circumstances can be contrary to a person's best interests not only when it is painful but also simply because it is so incompatible with the way that person wanted her life to go, and to end.'

165 *Op cit*, Dworkin, fn 7, p 25.

166 Of course, there are many who argue that the sacred value which these lives have is not confined to human animals and, for some, is not enjoyed by all human animals.

167 *Op cit*, Dworkin, fn 7, p 216.

form of exit option ... is not wisdom, conservative or otherwise, but rather a fetishisation of physical survival.[168]

Others counter that the abandonment of care is at the centre of decisions to end a patient's life or for the patient to seek assistance to do so, or to refuse what would otherwise be life-sustaining treatment or care.[169] The resolution of these issues by the State in the form or absence of law will, in part, disclose the relationships between law and morality of that society, but will also disclose whether the State believes it has the authority to impose views on its citizens in areas which, whatever their individual moral convictions, may be none of the law's concern.

WHO WANTS TO DIE FOREVER?

It may be that the advance directive will come to be seen as part of each human life. Addressing the question of how and when one wants life sustaining treatment withdrawn, or not commenced, will enable people to address that very fear of death and dying that, although part of the human condition, has become a subterranean concern.

The way in which the debate about living wills has come to proceed, in the form of treatment directives and condition directives, has focused attention on the patient's status (dying soon no matter what is done) and the procedures to be foregone (those that are artificial and 'only' serve to prolong dying) sometimes expressed as a list of medical procedures. These two attributes of the standard living will have been claimed subtly to distort good decision making. According to Joanne Lynn, this rests primarily in pursuing the best possible future from among those plans of care that can be effectuated. The notion of a 'best possible' plan must be defined from the patient's perspective to the extent possible. Nothing in this model, she avers, needs to turn on the proximity to death or the nature of the procedure involved, except as these considerations shape the desirability of various future courses to the patient:

> Sometimes ventilators are morally required, but sometimes even changing sheets is contra-indicated. For someone to be asked to decide in advance whether he or she would want dialysis, ventilator or feeding tubes, without knowing what using these procedures would yield, is incomprehensible.[170]

But, without advance directives, the physician and the family must face the tragic dilemma of determining how much suffering from intercurrent illness and its treatment the patient will undergo in order to continue a life already

---

168 *Op cit*, Gray, fn 22, p 171.
169 *Op cit*, Finnis, fn 34.
170 *Op cit*, Lynn, fn 5, p 102.

burdened with severe cognitive impairment.[171] Few doctors know at the relevant time of the existence of a living will and there is a very low rate at which they are honoured, especially without legislative or other legal sanction.[172] Doctors are notoriously hopeless communicators, at least when it comes to the patient, and however desirable or fashionable, the prospect of a real, effective dialogue, without at least a prompt from the patient, is a distant signal. The logistical and clinical barriers to having directives honoured impose further limits on the ability of instructional directives to protect a patient's wishes. The fear which many practitioners express is that the formal recognition of living wills or advance directives will not serve them or their patients well. Behind this lies another fear, which Martin Hollis has captured in characterising the doctor as 'caught with Kant and Bentham on the bookshelf, Hippocrates in his waiting room and the Ombudsman on the telephone'.[173] And, I might add, Blackstone at the bedside.

The advantages of a simple scheme are that the formalised standards envisaged by the BMA, the Law Commission and the Select Committee, whether underwritten by legislation or not, will impose a particular burden on people without sufficient education or economy. Legal formalities in drafting adequate advance directives will foreclose the exercise of 'rights' from those who are poor, illiterate or who have access to inadequate legal or other advice.[174] The option to determine one's own style of going off well must not be reserved for the well off. In our caution, we may be capable of doing as much harm as is often identified with medical zeal. If we need to exercise particular caution, it may be in ensuring that we do not turn the passage from life into a task of truly Odyssean labour.

The jurisprudence of the living will illustrates how the world has changed since Patrick Devlin's handsome tribute to the medical profession. We have moved far from the elysian pastures he identified and into the close where the madding crowd of contemporary professional priests of health and well being, doctors, philosophers, ethicists, lawyers and their critics have their stalls. Developments in science and technology, and their potential applications, have ushered into the judicial theatre dilemmas and conundrums which, while they may have been addressed by Plato and Hippocrates, have troubled all pretenders to high priesthood of this brave new world. In the short space of 30 years, the Supreme Court has been called upon to adjudicate the legality of surgical operations on an adult incapable of consenting;[175] forcing treatment upon an adult of sound mind for the benefit

---

171 Finucane, T, Beamer, B, Roca, R and Kawas, C, 'Establishing advance medical directives with demented patients: a pilot study', in *op cit*, Emanuel, fn 2, p 51.

172 See *op cit*, Emanuel, fn 2, p 13, n 55.

173 'A death of one's own', in Bell, J and Mendus, S (eds), *Philosophy and Medical Welfare*, 1988, London: Sage, p 14.

174 *Op cit*, Gostin, fn 53, p 11.

175 *Re F (Mental Patient: Sterilisation)* [1990] 2 AC 1.

of a full term fetus;[176] reviewing the circumstances and the parameters of a refusal to consent to treatment and the consequences which flow therefrom;[177] deciding whether the clinical judgment of a doctor can be reviewed at the behest of patients or their next of kin;[178] and, in the case of *Airedale National Health Service Trust v Bland*, in deciding whether the withdrawal of hydration and nutrition from a patient in PVS for whom further feeding was deemed to be medically futile would be lawful.

In so doing, the courts have been attendants at the birth of new medical powers and responsibilities, yet pall bearers at the graveside of patient interests and sovereignty. Death, once an immovable facet of life,[179] is, except in the context of catastrophic accident, becoming a more negotiable instrument in the *bureau de change* of life. Its boundaries are being transformed, tested and trespassed such that, in Garcia Marquez's elegant evocation, we may be 'overwhelmed by the belated suspicion that it is life, more than death, that has no limits'.[180] Sadly, the advance directive may become one more piece in the attrition between true self-determination and the false promise of medical omnipotence. Not a chart to assist in the navigation between Scylla and Charybdis, but a siren to either side of which patients and practitioners are too easily drawn.

176 *Re S* [1992] 4 All ER 671.

177 *Re T* [1992] 4 All ER 649.

178 *Re J* [1992] 4 All ER 614.

179 Ramsey, P, 'Death's pedagogy' (1974) 20 Commonwealth 497.

180 *Op cit*, Garcia Marquez, fn 12, p 348. For an example of what might be meant by this in the current context, see, eg, Cohen, BD, *Karen Ann Quinlan: Dying in an Age of Eternal Life*, 1976, New York: Nash, and Stinson, R and Stinson, P, *The Long Dying of Baby Andrew*, 1983, Boston: Little, Brown.

BIBLIOGRAPHY

Alderson, P, *Choosing for Children: Parents' Consent to Surgery*, 1990, Oxford: OUP

Allison, L (ed), *The Utilitarian Response: The Contemporary Viability of Utilitarian Political Philosophy*, 1993, London: Sage

Almond, B and Hill, D (eds), *Applied Philosophy: Morals and Metaphysics in Contemporary Debate*, 1991, London: Routledge

Andrews, K, 'Managing the persistent vegetative state' (1992) 305 BMJ, 29 August, p 486

Anleu, SR, 'Reproductive autonomy: infertility, deviance and conceptive technology', in Peterson, K (ed), *Law and Medicine*, 1994, Melbourne: La Trobe UP

Annas, G, *Standard of Care*, 1993, New York: OUP

Appelbaum, PS, Lidz, CW and Meisel, A, *Informed Consent: Legal Theory and Clinical Practice*, 1987, New York: OUP

Aries, P, *The Hour of Our Death*, 1982, New York: Vintage

Arthurs, H, 'Globalization of the mind: Canadian elites and the restructuring of legal fields' (1997) 12 Canadian J Law and Society 219

Auden, WH, 'Surgical ward', in *The Penguin Poets: WH Auden*, 1958, Harmondsworth: Penguin

Bankowski, Z and Bryant, J, *Health Policy: Ethics and Human Values: European and North American Perspectives*, 1989, Geneva: CIOMS

Barron, L and Roberts, DF (eds), *Issues in Fetal Medicine: Proceedings of the 1992 Galton Symposium*, 1995, London: Macmillan

Bauby, JD, *The Diving Bell and the Butterfly*, 1997, London: Fourth Estate

Bauer, JC and Ringel, MA, *Telemedicine and the Reinvention of Healthcare*, 1999, New York: McGraw Hill

Bauman, Z, *A Life in Fragments*, 1995, Oxford: Blackwell

Bauman, Z, *Postmodern Ethics*, 1993, Oxford: Blackwell

Beauchamp, T and Bowie, N, 'Corporate social responsibility', in Beauchamp, T and Bowie, N (eds), *Ethical Theory and Business*, 2nd edn, 1983, Englewood Cliffs, NJ: Prentice Hall

Beaumarchais, P-A, *The Barber of Seville*, Wood, J (trans), 1964, Harmondsworth: Penguin

Beck, U and Gernsheim-Beck, E, *The Normal Chaos of Love*, 1995, Cambridge: Polity

Beck, U, *Risk Society: Towards a New Modernity*, Ritter, M (trans), 1992, London: Sage (originally published as *Risikogellschaft. Auf dem Weg in eine andere Moderne*, 1986, Frankfurt: Suhrkamp Verlag)

Beck, U, *What is Globalisation?*, 2000, Cambridge: Polity

Bell, J, 'The Europeanisation of law', in Watkin, T (ed), *The Europeanisation of Law*, 1998, London: UKNCCL

Berlin, I, 'Concepts and categories', in *Four Essays on Liberty*, 1969, Oxford: OUP

Bernat, E, 'Marketing of human organs', in Mazzoni, CM, *A Legal Framework for Bioethics*, 1998, The Hague: Kluwer

Beykveld, D and Haker, H, *The Ethics of Genetics in Human Procreation*, 2000, Aldershot: Ashgate

Black, J, 'Regulation as facilitation; negotiating the genetic revolution', in Brownsword, R, Cornish, WR and Llewelyn, M, *Law and Human Genetics: Regulating a Revolution*, 1998, Oxford: Hart

Bole, TJ and Bondeson, WB (eds), *Rights to Health Care*, 1991, Dordrecht: Kluwer

Boon, A and Levin, J, *The Ethics and Conduct of Lawyers in England and Wales*, 1999, Oxford: Hart

Boorse, C, 'On the distinction between health and disease' (1975) Philosophy and Public Affairs 5

Bottomley, A (ed), *Feminist Perspectives on the Foundational Subjects of Law*, 2nd edn, 2001 (forthcoming), London: Cavendish Publishing

Brahams, D, *Human Genetic Information: Science, Law and Ethics*, 1990, Chichester: John Wiley

Braithwaite, J and Drahos, P, *Global Business Regulation*, 2000, Cambridge: CUP

Brazier, M and Glover, N, 'Does medical law have a future?', in Birks, P (ed), *Law's Future(s)*, 2000, Oxford: Hart

Brazier, M, 'Embryos' "rights": abortion and research', in Freeman, MDA (ed), *Medicine, Ethics and the Law*, London: Stevens

Brazier, M, 'Regulating the reproduction business?' (1999) 7 Med L Rev 166

Brett, P and Fischer, EP, 'Effects on life assurance of genetic testing' (1993) *The Actuary*, July, pp 11–12

British Medical Association, *Euthanasia*, 1988, London: BMA

British Medical Association, *Guidance for Decision Making: Withholding and Withdrawing Life-Prolonging Medical Treatment*, 1999, London: BMA

British Medical Association, *Medical Ethics Today: Its Practice and Philosophy*, 1993, London: BMA

British Medical Association, *Statement About Advance Directives*, 1992, London: BMA

Bryson, B, *Notes From a Small Island*, 1995, London: Doubleday

Buchanan, A, 'Advance directives and the personal identity problem' (1988) 17 Philosophy and Public Affairs 277

Calabresi, G with Bobbitt, P, *Tragic Choices: The Conflicts Society Confronts in the Allocation of Tragically Scarce Resources*, 1978, New York: WW Norton

Carroll, L, 'Alice through the looking-glass', in Gardner, M (ed), *The Annotated Alice*, 1960, Harmondsworth: Penguin

Centre for Medical Law and Ethics, King's College London/Age Concern, *The Living Will*, 1988, London: Edward Arnold

Chadwick, R and Ngwena, C, 'The development of a normative standard in counselling for genetic disease: ethics and law' (1992) J Social Welfare and Fam Law 276

Chadwick, R, *Ethics, Reproduction and Genetic Control*, 1987, London: Routledge

Chapman, A (ed), *Health Care Reform: A Human Rights Approach*, 1994, Washington DC: Georgetown UP

Charlesworth, M, *Bioethics in a Liberal Society*, 1993, Cambridge: CUP

Cheah, P, Fraser, D and Grbich, J (eds), *Thinking Through the Body of Law*, 1996, New York: New York UP

Cohen, BD, *Karen Ann Quinlan: Dying in an Age of Eternal Life*, 1976, New York: Nash

Commission of the European Community, *Adopting a Specific Research and Technological Development Programme in the Field of Health: Predictive Medicine*, 1989, Brussels: CEC

Committee on *In Vitro* Fertilisation, *IVF-Related Research*, 1998, Rijswijk: Health Council of the Netherlands

Cook, RJ, *Women's Health and Human Rights*, 1994, Philadelphia: Philadelphia and Pennsylvania Press

Corea, G and Ince, S, 'Report of a survey of IVF clinics in the USA', in Spallone, P and Steinberg, D (eds), *Made to Order: The Myth of Reproductive and Genetic Progress*, 1987, London: Pergamon

Council of Europe, *Human Artificial Procreation*, 1989, Strasbourg: COE

Cox, A, *The Impact of the Internet on the Doctor-Patient Relationship*, 2000, London: Imperial College Management School

Craig, P, *Public Law and Democracy in the United Kingdom and the United States*, 1990, Oxford: Clarendon

Cronin, A, *Samuel Beckett: The Last Modernist*, 1997, London: Flamingo

Crowe, C, 'Mind over whose matter? Women, in vitro fertilisation and the development of scientific knowledge', in McNeil, M, Varcoe, I and Yearley, S (eds), *The New Reproductive Technologies*, 1990, Basingstoke: Macmillan

Currer, C and Stacey, M, *Concepts of Health and Disease: A Comparative Perspective*, 1986, Leamington Spa: Berg

Cusine, D and Templeton, A (eds), *Reproductive Medicine and Law*, 1990, Edinburgh: Churchill Livingstone

Dahl, TS, *Women's Law: An Introduction to Feminist Jurisprudence*, Craig, RL (trans), 1987, Oslo: Norwegian UP

Dalton, C, 'An essay in the deconstruction of contract doctrine' [1985] Yale LJ 999

Davies, M, *Asking the Law Question*, 1994, Sydney: LBC

Davis, JA, 'Whose life is it anyway?' [1986] BMJ 1128

de Saint-Exupéry, A, *Wind, Sand and Stars*, 1975, London: Pan

de Sousa Santos, B, *Toward a New Common Sense: Law, Science and Politics in the Paradigmatic Transition*, 1995, London: Routledge

Department of Health, *Review of the Common Law Provisions Relating to the Removal of Gametes and of the Consent Provisions in the Human Fertilisation and Embryology Act 1990*, 1998, London: DOH

Descartes, R, 'Meditations on the first philosophy in which the existence of God and the distinction between mind and body are demonstrated', in Haldane, E and Ross, G (eds and trans), *The Philosophical Works of Descartes*, 1967, Cambridge: CUP

Dessaix, R, *Night Letters*, 1996, Sydney: Macmillan

Detmold, M, *The Unity of Law and Morality*, 1984, London: Routledge and Kegan Paul

Devlin, P, *Samples of Lawmaking*, 1962, Oxford: Clarendon

Dewar, J, 'The normal chaos of family law' (1998) 61 MLR 467

Dezalay, Y and Sugarman, D, *Professional Competition and Professional Power: Lawyers, Accountants and the Social Construction of Markets*, 1995, London: Routledge

Dickenson, D, *Property, Women and Politics: Subjects or Objects?*, 1997, Cambridge: Polity

Dolgin, J, *Defining the Family: Law, Technology and Reproduction in an Uneasy Age*, 1997, New York: New York UP

Donson, F, *Legal Intimidations*, 2000, Free Association

Douglas, M, *Purity and Danger: An Analysis of the Concepts of Pollution and Taboo*, 1996, London: Routledge

Doyal, L and Doyal, L, 'Western scientific medicine: a philosophical and political prognosis', in Birke, L and Silvertown, J, *More Than the Parts: Biology and Politics*, 1984, London: Pluto

Doyal, L and Gough, I, *A Theory of Human Need*, 1991, London: Macmillan

Doyal, L, *What Makes Women Sick: Gender and the Political Economy of Health*, 1995, New Brunswick, NJ: Rutgers UP

Dresser, D, 'Life, death and incompetent patients: conceptual infirmities and hidden values in the law' (1986) 28 Arizona L Rev 379

Dworkin, R, *Taking Rights Seriously*, 1977, London: Duckworth

Dworkin, R, *Life's Dominion: An Argument about Abortion and Euthanasia*, 1993, London: HarperCollins

Eekelaar, J, 'Parenthood, social engineering and rights', in Morgan, D and Douglas, G (eds), *Constituting Families: A Study in Governance*, 1994, Stuttgart: Franz Steiner Verlag

Elliott, C, 'Meaning what you say', in Emanuel, L (ed), *Advance Directives: Expectations, Experience and Future Practice* (1993) 4(1) J Clinical Ethics 61

Ely, JH, *Democracy and Distrust*, 1980, Cambridge, Mass: Harvard UP

Ericson, K, *Wayward Puritans*, 1966, Boston: Allyn and Bacon

Evans, HM and Finlay, IG (eds), *Medical Humanities*, 2001 (forthcoming), London: BMJ

Fairbairn, G and Fairbairn, S (eds), *Ethical Issues in Caring*, 1988, Aldershot: Avebury

Felstiner, W, Abel, R and Sarat, A, 'The emergence and transformation of disputes: naming, blaming and claiming' (1980–81) 15 Law and Society Rev 631

Figes, O, *A People's Tragedy: The Russian Revolution 1891–1924*, 1996, London: Pimlico

Finnis, J, '*Bland*: crossing the Rubicon' (1993) 109 LQR 329

Finnis, J, *Natural Law and Natural Rights*, 1985, Oxford: Clarendon

Fish, S, *Doing What Comes Naturally*, 1989, Oxford: Clarendon

Fish, S, *There's No Such Thing as Free Speech (... and it's a good thing too)*, 1994, New York and Oxford: OUP

Fleming, J, *Law of Torts*, 1992, Sydney: LBC

Foucault, M, *The History of Sexuality*, Hurley, R (trans), 1978, Harmondsworth: Penguin

Foucault, M, *The Order of Things*, 1970, London: Tavistock

Fraser, L and Nicholson, A, 'Social criticism without philosophy: an encounter between feminism and postmodernism', in Ross, A (ed), *Universal Abandon? The Politics of Postmodernism*, 1988, Minnesota: Minnesota UP

Frazer, L, Hornsby, J and Lovibond, S, *Ethics: A Feminist Reader*, 1994, Oxford: Basil Blackwell

Freeden, M, *Rights*, 1991, Buckingham: Open UP

Freeman, MDA, 'Death, dying and the Human Rights Act' (1999) 52 Current Legal Problems 218

Fujiki, N and Macer, DRJ (eds), *Bioethics in Asia*, 1998, Tskuba Science City: Eubios Ethics Institute

Fukyama, F, *The End of History*, 1993, Harmondsworth: Penguin

Galanter, M, 'Law abounding: legislation around the North Atlantic' (1992) 55 MLR 1

Garcia Marquez, G, 'Death constant beyond love', in *Innocent Erendira and other Stories*, Rabassa, G (trans), 1981, London: Picador

Garrett, M, *Health Futures Handbook*, 1995, Geneva: WHO

General Medical Council, *Professional Conduct and Discipline: Fitness to Practice*, 1989, London: GMC

Gernsheim-Beck, E, 'Changing duties of parents: from education to bio-engineering' (1990) 42 Int J Social Science 451

Giddens, A, 'Risk and responsibility' (1999) 62 MLR 1

Gilligan, C, *In a Different Voice: Psychological Theory and Women's Development*, 1982, Cambridge, Mass: Harvard UP

Gillon, R and Lloyd, A (eds), *Principles of Health Care Ethics*, 1994, Chichester: Wiley

Glenn, HP, *Legal Traditions of the World*, 2000, Oxford: OUP

Glover, J et al, *Fertility and the Family: The Glover Report on Reproductive Technologies to the European Commission*, 1989, London: Fourth Estate

Glover, J, *Causing Deaths and Saving Lives*, 1977, Harmondsworth: Penguin

Goffman, E, *Stigma: Notes on the Management of Spoiled Identity*, 1964, Harmondsworth: Penguin

Gray, J, *Beyond the New Right: Markets, Government and the Common Environment*, 1993, London: Routledge

Griffith, J, 'Is law important?' (1979) 56 New York UL Rev 339

Griffiths, J, *Euthanasia and the Law in The Netherlands*, 1998, Amsterdam: Amsterdam UP

Grubb, A, 'I, me, mine: bodies, parts and property'(1998) 3 Med Law International 299

Grubb, A (ed), *Challenges in Medical Care*, 1991, Chichester: Wiley

Grubb, A and Pearl, D, *Blood Testing Aids and DNA Profiling: Law and Policy*, 1990, Bristol: Jordan

Gunning, J and English, V, *Human In Vitro Fertilization: A Case Study in Medical Innovation*, 1993, Aldershot: Dartmouth

Hanfling, O, *Life and Meaning: A Reader*, 1987, Oxford: Basil Blackwell

Hansmann, H, 'Markets for human organs', in Mazzoni, CM, *A Legal Framework for Bioethics*, 1998, The Hague: Kluwer

Hargreaves, I and Christie, I (eds), *Tomorrow's Politics: The Third Way and Beyond*, 1998, London: Demos

Harris, J, *The Value of Life: An Introduction to Medical Ethics*, 1985, London: Routledge

Harris, J, *Wonderwoman and Superman: The Ethics of Human Biotechnology*, 1992, Oxford: OUP

Harris, JW, 'Who owns my body?' (1996) 16 OJLS 55

Hill, C, *The Intellectual Origins of the English Revolution*, 1965, Oxford: Clarendon

Hobsbawm, E, *Age of Extremes: The Short History of the Twentieth Century 1914–1991*, 1994, London: Michael Joseph

Holliday, I, *The NHS Transformed*, 1992, Manchester: Baseline

Hollis, M, 'A death of one's own', in Bell, J and Mendus, S (eds), *Philosophy and Medical Welfare*, 1988, London: Sage

Holmes, OW, *The Common Law*, 1881, Cambridge, Mass: Harvard UP

Homans, H, (ed), *The Sexual Politics of Reproduction*, 1985, Aldershot: Gower

Homer, *The Odyssey*, Rieu, EV (trans), Jones, PV (revised), 1991, Harmondsworth: Penguin

Howarth, L, *Autonomy: A Study in Philosophical Psychology and Ethics*, 1986, New Haven, Ct: Yale UP

Hughes, E, *Men and Their Work*, 1958, Chicago, Ill: Free Press of Glencoe

Human Fertilisation and Embryology Authority, *Storage and Use of Ovarian Tissue*, 1990, London: HFEA

Human Genetics Advisory Commission/Human Fertilisation and Embryology Authority, *Cloning Issues in Reproduction, Science and Medicine*, 1998, London: HGAC/HFEA

Hyde, A, *Bodies of Law*, 1997, Princeton, NJ: Princeton UP

Illich, I, *Limits to Medicine: Medical Nemesis: The Expropriation of Health*, 1976, Harmondsworth: Penguin

Inkelfinger, FG, 'Arrogance' (1980) 304 New England J Medicine 1507

Irerson, KV, 'Forgoing hospital care: should ambulance staff always resuscitate? (1991) 17 J Med Ethics 19

Jackson, E, 'Contradictions and coherence in feminist responses to law' (1993) 20 JLS 399

Jacob, J, *Doctors and Rules: A Sociology of Professional Values*, 1988, London: Routledge

Jakobovits, I (Sir), 'The Jewish contribution to medical ethics', in Byrne, P (ed), *Rights and Wrongs in Medicine*, 1986, London: King Edward's Hospital Fund for London

Jecker, N, 'Genetic testing and social responsibility of private health insurance companies' (1993) 21 J Law, Medicine and Ethics 109

Jennings, B, 'Possibilities of consensus: towards democratic moral discourse' (1991) 16 J Medicine and Philosophy 450

Jonas, H, *Philosophical Essays: From Ancient Creed to Technological Man*, 1974, Englewood Cliffs, NJ: Prentice Hall

Jonas, H, *The Imperative of Responsibility: In Search of an Ethics for the Technological Age*, 1984, Chicago, Ill: Chicago UP

Kafka, F, *Metamorphosis and Other Stories*, Muir, W and Muir, E (trans), 1999, London: Vintage

Kant, I, 'Lectures on ethics', in Paton, HJ (ed), 'Groundwork of the metaphysics of morals', 1953, London: Hutchinson

Kass, L, 'Is there a right to die?' (1993) 23(1) Hastings Center Report 34

Kass, L, 'The meaning of life – in the laboratory', in Alpern, KD (ed), *The Ethics of Reproductive Technology*, 1992, New York: OUP

Katz Rothman, B, *The Tentative Pregnancy: Prenatal Diagnosis and the Future of Motherhood*, 1988, London: Pandora

Kennedy, I and Grubb, A, *Medical Law: Text and Materials*, 1989, London: Butterworths

Kennedy, I, 'Agenda for health ethics and law' (1991) 70 Bull Medical Ethics 16

Kennedy, I, *The Unmasking of Medicine*, 1988, London: Allen & Unwin

Kennedy, I, *Treat Me Right: Essays in Medical Law and Ethics*, 1988, Oxford: OUP

Keown, J, 'Beyond *Bland*' (2000) 20 LS 66

Keown, J, *Euthanasia Examined*, 1995, Cambridge: CUP

Kirby, M, *Reform the Law*, 1983, Oxford: OUP

Kirp, D, Yudof, M and Strong Franks, M, *Gender Justice*, 1986, Chicago, Ill: Chicago UP

Klein, D, *The Exploitation of Desire: Women's Experiences with In Vitro Fertilisation*, 1989, Victoria: Deakin UP

Klein, R, *The Politics of the National Health Service*, 1983, London: Longman

Klein, RD, 'What's new about the "new" reproductive technologies?', in Corea, G et al, *Man-Made Women; How New Reproductive Technologies Affect Women*, 1985, London: Hutchinson

Knoppers, B and le Bris, S, 'Recent advances in medically assisted conception: legal, ethical and social issues' (1991) 17 Am J Law and Medicine 329

Koch, L, 'IVF – an irrational choice? (1990) 3(3) Issues in Reproductive and Genetic Engineering 235

Komesaroff, PA (ed), *Troubled Bodies: Critical Perspectives on Postmodernism, Medical Ethics and the Body*, 1995, Melbourne: Melbourne UP

Law Commission, Consultation Paper No 129, *Mentally Incapacitated Adults and Decision Making: Medical Treatment and Research*, 1993, London: HMSO

Lee, RG, 'Legal control of health care allocation', in Ockelton, M (ed), *Medicine, Ethics and Law*, 1987, Stuttgart: ARSP

Lee, RG and Morgan, D (eds), *Birthrights: Law and Ethics at the Beginnings of Life*, 1989, London: Routledge

Lee, RG and Morgan, D, *Human Fertilisation and Embryology: Regulating the Reproduction Revolution*, 2001, London: Blackstone

Lee, RG and Morgan, D, 'In the name of the father: *Ex parte Blood*' (1997) 60 MLR 840

Locke, J, 'An essay concerning the true original extent and end of civil government' (1690), in Laslett, P (ed), *Two Treatises of Government*, 1960, Cambridge: CUP

Lopez, A, 'Lay lawyering' (1984) UCLA L Rev 1

Lynn, J, 'Why I don't have a living will', in Capron, A (ed), 'Medical decision making and the "right to die" after *Cruzan*' (1991) 19 Law, Medicine and Health Care 104

Lyotard, J-F, *The Post-Modern Condition: A Report on Knowledge*, 1979, Manchester: Manchester UP

MacIntyre, A, *After Virtue: A Study in Moral Theory*, 1985, London: Duckworth

Maclean, A, *The Elimination of Morality: Reflections on Utilitarianism and Bioethics*, 1993, London: Routledge

Maddox, I, 'New genetics means no new ethics' (1993) 364 Nature 97

Magnusson, RS, 'The sanctity of life and the right to die: social and jurisprudential aspects of the euthanasia debate in Australia and the United States' (1997) Pacific Rim J Law and Policy 1

Marmor, TR, Smeeding, TM and Greene, V, *Economic Security and Intergenerational Justice*, 1994, Chicago, Ill: Urban Institute

Marquez, GG, *Love in the Time of Cholera*, Grossman, E (trans), 1988, Harmondsworth: Penguin

Marteau, T and Richards, M (eds), *The Troubled Helix: The Benefits and Hazards of the New Human Genetics*, 1996, Cambridge: CUP

Mason, JK and McCall Smith, A, *Law and Medical Ethics*, 5th edn, 1999, London: Butterworths

Mason, K, 'Abortion and the law', in McLean, S, *Legal Issues in Human Reproduction*, 1988, Aldershot: Ashgate

Mason, K, in Dyer, C (ed), *Doctors, Patients and the Law*, 1992, London: Blackwell

Mason, K, *Medico-Legal Aspects of Pregnancy and Parenthood*, 1990, Aldershot: Dartmouth

Matthews, P, 'The man of property' (1995) 3 Med L Rev 251

Matthews, P, 'Whose body? People as property' [1983] Current Legal Problems 193

McHale, J and Fox, M, with Murphy, J, *Health Care Law: Text and Materials*, 1997, London: Sweet & Maxwell

McKeown, T, *The Role of Medicine*, 1979, Oxford: Basil Blackwell

McLean, S (ed), *Contemporary Issues in Medicine*, 1995, Aldershot: Dartmouth

McLean, S and Giesen, D, 'Legal and ethical considerations of the Human Genome Project' (1994) 1 Med Law International 159

Montgomery, J, 'Consent to health care for children' (1993) 5 J Child Law 117

Montgomery, J, 'Rights to health and health care', in Coote, A (ed), *The Welfare of Citizens: Developing New Social Rights*, 1992, London: IPPR

Morgan, D and Lee, RG, 'In the name of the father: *Ex parte Blood*' (1997) 60 MLR 840

Morgan, D and Lee, RG, *Human Fertilisation and Embryology: Regulating the Revolution*, 2001, London: Blackstone

Morgan, D and Lee, RG, *Blackstone's Guide to the Human Fertilisation and Embryology Act 1990: Abortion and Embryo Research – The New Law*, 1990, London: Blackstone

Morgan, D and Nielsen, L, 'Dangerous liaisons; law, technology and European ethics: an Anglo-Danish comparison', in McVeigh, S and Wheeler, S (eds), *Medicine, Law and Regulation*, 1992, Aldershot: Dartmouth

Morgan, D, 'Judges on delivery: change, continuity and challenge in obstetric regulation', in Chard, T and Richards, M (eds), *Obstetrics in the 1990s: Current Controversies*, 1992, Oxford: MacKeith

Mortimer, J, *Murderers and Other Friends*, 1995, Harmondsworth: Penguin

Naffine, N and Owens, RJ (eds), *Sexing the Subject of Law*, 1997, North Ryde, NSW: LBC

Naffine, N, 'The legal structure of self-ownership: or the self-possessed man and the woman possessed' (1998) 25 JLS 193

Nelkin, D, 'Against the tide of technology' (1993) The Higher, 13 August

Nicholson, LJ (ed), *Feminism/Postmodernism*, 1990, London: Routledge

Nietzsche, F, *Beyond Good and Evil*, Hollingdale, RJ (trans), 1973, Harmondsworth: Penguin

Noddings, N, *Caring: A Feminine Approach to Ethics and Education*, 1978, Berkley, Cal: California UP

Noonan, JT (ed), *The Morality of Abortion*, 1970, Cambridge, Mass: Harvard UP

Nordenfelt, C, 'On the relevance and importance of the notion of disease' (1993) 14 Theoretical Medicine 15

Nozick, R, *Anarchy, State and Utopia*, 1974, Oxford: Basil Blackwell

O'Donovan, K, *Sexual Divisions in Law*, 1985, London: Weidenfeld & Nicolson

O'Neill, O, 'Justice, gender and international boundaries', in Nussbaum, M and Sen, A (eds), *The Quality of Life*, 1993, Oxford: Clarendon

Oakley, A, *Essays on Women, Medicine and Health*, 1993, Edinburgh: Edinburgh UP

Otlowski, M, *Voluntary Euthanasia and the Common Law*, 1997, Oxford: Clarendon

Palley, C, *The United Kingdom and Human Rights*, 1991, London: Stevens

Parfitt, D, *Reasons and Persons* 1986, Oxford: OUP

Parker, S and Bottomley, S, *Law in Context*, 1997, Sydney: Federation

Perri 6, *Holistic Government*, 1997, London: Demos

Peters, RS, *Education, Philosophy, Ethics*, 1996, London: Allen & Unwin

Pigou, A, *A Study in Public Finance*, 1928, London: Macmillan

Porter, R, *The Greatest Benefit to Mankind: A Medical History of Humanity from Antiquity to the Present*, 1997, London: HarperCollins

Posner, R, *Sex and Reason*, 1992, Cambridge, Mass: Harvard UP

Privacy Commissioner of Canada, *Genetic Testing and Privacy*, 1992, Ottawa: Ministry of Supply and Services

Pullen, I, 'Family genetics', in Sutherland, E and McCall Smith, A (eds), *Family Rights: Family Law and Medical Advance*, 1990, Edinburgh: Edinburgh UP

Radin, and Shalev, C, *Birth Power: The Case for Surrogacy*, 1989, New Haven, Ct: Yale UP

Radin, MJ, *Contested Commodities: The Trouble with Trade in Sex, Children, Body Parts and Other Things*, 1996, Cambridge, Mass: Harvard UP

Ramsey, P, 'Death's pedagogy' (1974) 20 Commonwealth 497

Ramsey, P, 'The indignity of "Death with Dignity"' (1974) Hastings Center Report 47

Rattray Taylor, G, *The Biological Timebomb*, 1968, New York: World

Raz, J, *The Morality of Freedom*, 1986, Oxford: Clarendon

Richards, S, *Epics of Everyday Life: Encounters in a Changing Russia*, 1991, Harmondsworth: Penguin

Ridley, M, *The Red Queen: Sex and the Evolution of Human Nature*, 1994, Harmondsworth: Penguin

Rix, BA, 'Should ethical concerns regulate science? The European experience with the Human Genome Project' (1991) 5 Bioethics 250

Rose, G, *Mourning Becomes the Law: Philosophy and Representation*, 1996, Cambridge: CUP

Rosser, S, *Teaching Science and Health from a Feminist Perspective*, 1986, New York: Pergamon

Rothman, BK, 'The meaning of choice in reproductive technology', in Arditti, R *et al* (eds), *Test Tube Women: What Future for Motherhood?*, 1984, London: Pandora

Rothman, BK, *The Tentative Pregnancy: Prenatal Diagnosis and the Future of Motherhood*, 1986, New York: Viking

Rowson, R, *An Introduction to Ethics for Nurses*, 1990, Harrow: Scutari

Royal College of Physicians of London, *Prenatal Diagnosis and Prenatal Screening: Community and Service Implications*, 1989, London: RCP

Sapirie, S and Orzeszyna, S, *Health Futures: The Results and Follow-Up of the 1993 Consultation*, 1995, Geneva: WHO

Sarat, A and Felstiner, WF, *Divorce Lawyers and their Clients: Power and Meaning in the Legal Process*, 1995, New York and Oxford: OUP

Saunders, J, 'Medical futility: CPR', in Lee, RG and Morgan, D (eds), *Death Rites: Law and Ethics at the End of Life*, 1994, London: Routledge

Scanlon, T, 'Partisan for life' (1993) *New York Review of Books*, 15 July

Sheldon, S and Thompson, M (eds), *Feminist Perspectives on Health Care Law*, 1998, London: Cavendish Publishing

Silver, L, *Remaking Eden: Cloning, Genetic Engineering and the Future of Humankind?*, 1998, London: Weidenfeld & Nicolson

Singer, P and Cavalieri, P, *The Great Ape Project*, 1995, London: St Martin's

Skene, L, 'Genetics: an Australian report', in Deech, R, Mulders-Klein, T and van Dickerbroeke, P (eds), *Artificial Reproductive Technology and Genetics*, 2001, The Hague: Kluwer

Smart, C, *Feminism and the Power of Law*, 1990, London: Routledge

Smith, GF, 'The *Rios'* *Embryo* case: Australia's frozen "orphan" embryos: a medical, legal and ethical dilemma' (1985–86) 24 J Fam Law 27

Steinbacher, R and Holmes, HB, 'Prenatal and preconception sex choice technologies', in Corea, G et al (eds), *Man Made Woman*, 1985, London: Hutchinson

Stephen, JF, *Digest of Criminal Law*, 5th edn, 1877, London: Macmillan

Stinson, R and Stinson, P, *The Long Dying of Baby Andrew*, 1983, Boston: Little, Brown

Stone, C, 'Do trees have standing?' (1972) So Cal L Rev 450

Stone, C, *Earth and Other Ethics*, 1987, New York: Harper & Row

Strathern, M et al, *Reproducing the Future: Anthropology, Kinship and the New Reproductive Technologies*, 1993, Manchester: Manchester UP

Strathern, M, 'The meaning of assisted kinship', in Stacey, M (ed), *Changing Human Reproduction*, 1992, London: Sage

Sunstien, C, 'The right to die' (1997) 106 Yale LJ 1123

Susskind, R, *The Future of Law*, 1998, Oxford: OUP

Suzuki, D and Knudtson, R, *Genetics: The Ethics of Engineering Life*, 1988, London: Unwin Hyman

Tarantino, Q, *Reservoir Dogs*, 1994, London: Faber & Faber

Teff, H, 'Consent to medical procedures' (1985) 101 LQR 432

Teubner, G (ed), *Juridification of Social Spheres*, 1987, Berlin and New York: Walter de Gruyter

Thomas, K, *Man and the Natural World*, 1983, Harmondsworth: Penguin

Thomas, K, *Religion and the Decline of Magic: Studies in Popular Beliefs in Sixteenth and Seventeenth-Century England*, 1973, Harmondsworth: Penguin

Thubron, C, *Behind the Wall*, 1988, Harmondsworth: Penguin

Townsend, P and Davidson, N (eds), *Inequalities in Health*, 1982, Harmondsworth: Penguin

Trombley, S, *The Right to Reproduce: A History of Coercive Sterilisation*, 1988, London: Weidenfeld & Nicolson

Unger, S, *Controlling Technology: Ethics and the Responsible Engineer*, 1994, Chichester: John Wiley

Velasquez, M, *Business Ethics*, 1982, Englewood Cliffs, NJ: Prentice Hall

Vitelli, KD (ed), *Archaeological Ethics*, 1996, London: Alta Mira

Waller, L, 'Controlling genetic research', in Smith, RG, *Health Care, Crime and Regulatory Control*, 1998, Sydney: Hawkins

Watkin, D, *Morality and Architecture*, 1977, Chicago, Ill: Chicago UP

Weatherill, S, *Law and Integration in the European Union*, 1995, Oxford: Clarendon

Wells, C and Morgan, D, 'Whose fetus is it?' (1991) 18 JLS 431

Wells, C, 'I blame the parents', in Brownsword, R, Cornish, WR and Llewelyn, M, *Law and Human Genetics: Regulating a Revolution*, 1998, Oxford: Hart

Wells, C, 'Medicine, morals, money and the newborn' (1989) J Social Welfare Law 57

Wertheimer, A, 'Two questions about surrogacy and exploitation' (1991) 21 Philosophy and Public Affairs 237

Williams, B, 'The idea of equality', in Laslett, P and Runciman, WG (eds), *Philosophy, Politics and Society*, 1962, Oxford: Clarendon

Williams, B, *Problems of the Self*, 1973, Cambridge: CUP

Williams, G, *Textbook of Criminal Law*, 2nd edn, 1983, London: Stevens

Williams, N, *The Right to Life in Japan*, 1997, London: Routledge

Williams, P, *The Alchemy of Race and Rights*, 1991, Cambridge, Mass: Harvard UP

Wilmut, I, Campbell, K and Tudge, C, *The Second Creation: The Age of Biological Control by the Scientists who Cloned Dolly*, 2000, London: Headline

Wisdom, J, 'What is there in horse racing?', in Hanfling, O (ed), *Life and Meaning: A Reader*, 1987, Oxford: Basil Blackwell

Wittgenstein, L, *Tractatus Logico-Philosophicus*, Ogden, CK (trans), 1922 (reprinted 1992), London and New York: Routledge

Wolf, SM, *Feminism and Bioethics*, 1996, New York: OUP

Wolf, SM, 'New pragmatism', (1994) 20(4) Am J Law and Medicine 395

Wynne, B, 'Technology, risk and participation: the social treatment of uncertainty', in Conrad, J (ed), *Society, Technology and Risk Assessment*, 1982, London: Academic

Yoxen, E, *Unnatural Selection? Coming to Terms with the New Genetics*, 1986, London: Heinemann

Zamyatin, Y, *We*, 1972, Harmondsworth: Penguin

INDEX

Abortion,
  genetics 169–73
  prevention by
    husband/partner 115–16
  sex identification 144–51
    ambit of Abortion
      Act 1967 147–49
    male children,
      mania for 146–47
    prevalence of
      sex selection 144–47
    reproductive ethics 149–51
  time limits 169–70
Advance directives 223–58
  arguments for 224–25
  autonomy 223–25
  competence 241–42,
                        248–51
  conclusions 256–58
  English law 234–48
    background 234–38
    case law 238–41
    committed directive 243–48
    competence 241–42
    next of kin 243
  experience of dying 225–27
  generally 223–24
  identity 251–54
  kinds 228–31
  management of
    deteriorating
      conditions 228–31
  meaning 228
  refusal of treatment 228
  United States 231–34
Annas, G 157
Arditti, R 70
Australia,
  right to die 214–15

Beck, U 17, 18, 33,
                    34, 35, 41,
                    81, 103, 176,
                    179, 207
Bell, J 29
Berlin, I 6
Beykveld, D 191, 192
Biomedical diplomacy 29, 31,
                        37–43
  conceptual level 39
  development 38
  descriptive level 38
  evaluative level 38–39
  generally 37–38
  legitimation question 39–40
  normative level 38–39
  reflexive
    modernisation 41
  risk society 41
  tasks 38
  tragic choices 38–40
Bland, T 217–18,
                    220, 221,
                    222, 231
Blood, D 220,
                    221, 222
Body,
  knowledge of
    the body 3, 206
  ownership
    See Ownership of the body
  uses of the body 3
Bottomley, A 66, 67
  legal responses 67
Brazier, M 6, 21, 22,
                    24, 27, 189,
                    190, 191, 192
Buchanan, A 224, 250, 254

Calabresi, G 203, 220

Canada,
  right to die 213–14

Chadwick, R 143, 149,
                        168, 169

Charlesworth, M 205,
                     206, 207

Children,
  consent 173–76

Chronic illness,
  ethical issues 5
  treatment 5

Cloning .187–93
  See, also, Nucleus substitution

Confidentiality,
  genetics 166–68

Congenital disabilities 116–18,
                    124–26

Consent,
  children 173–76
  Gillick test 174

Constitution 24–32
  Europeanisation
    of law 27–29
  globalisation 29–32
  holistic government 26–27
  knowledge economy 25–26
  problem solving 26–27
  social investment State 25–26

Corea, G 70

Cox, B 21

Craig, P 51

Dalton, C 35

Davies, M 67

de Saint-Exupèry, A 37

de Sousa Santos, B 19, 79,
                86, 103

Death,
  advance directives
    See Advance directives
  awareness of 226
  biomedical model 207
  brain stem 208
  euthanasia
    See Euthanasia
  living wills
    See Advance directives
  locked in syndrome 206
  medicalisation 205
  metamorphoses of 208
  modern shifts 206–07
  negotiating 219–22
  public health 207
  refusal of
    medical treatment 208–09
  right to die 205,
                210–17
    Australia 214–15
    Bland, T 217–18
    Canada 213–14
    England and Wales 215–17
    food and water,
      refusal of 210–11
    liberty interest
      argument 210, 211
    refusal of
      medical treatment 212–13
    United States 210–13
  rights 209–10
  significance 227
  tragic choices 203–22

Devlin, P 32, 52,
                257

Dewar, J 35

Distributive justice 8–9

Doyal, L 49, 72,
               74, 75

Dworkin, R 231, 233,
              254, 255

Ely, JH 204

Embryo,
  common law 114–18
  consent to use 121–23
  conundrums 109–14
  destruction 109–14
  generally 107
  hospitals and 206
  Human Fertilisation and
  Embryology Act 1990 118–27
    consent requirements 121–23
    general prohibitions 119–20
    generally 118–19
    posthumous
      treatments 123
    research, embryo 120–21
  legal status 107–23
  ownership of
    the body 99–101
  posthumous
    treatments 123
  research 120–21
  Warnock
    Committee 108–09, 114

Epistemology,
  metamorphoses
    in medical law 18–20

Eser, A 28

Ethics,
  focus on 5
  meaning 5
  medical 7
  metamorphoses
    in medical law 18–20
  re-emergence 7

Euthanasia,
  See, also, Advance
    directives; Death
  generally 203
  meaning 205
  medicalisation of death 205
  rights 209–10

Evans, M 5

Feminism,
  categories 67
  reproductive
    technology 63–81
    See, also, Reproductive
      technology

Fetus,
  congenital disabilities 116–18,
                                124–26
  contingent rights 117
  crystallisation of
    rights on birth 116
  early attitudes 107–18
  legal status 107–23
  Scotland 116
  sex identification
    See Sex identification
  ward of court 115
  Warnock Committee 108–09,
                                114

Finnis, J 205

Foucault, M 206

Freeden, M 8

Galanter, M 33, 34, 103

Genetics 16–17, 18,
                                155–78
  abortion 168–73
  children and consent 173–76
  cloning 187–93
    See, also, Nucleus substitution
  conclusions on 176–78
  confidentiality 166–68
  developments 155
  epistemology 155–58
  ethics 155–58
  genome project 155–57
  historical
    development
    of law 179–200
    committees 180–81
    generally 179–80

nucleus
    substitution 187–88
    public policy 199–200
    regulation 180–200
    scientific
        developments 199–200
Human Tissue Act 1961 196–99
information 159–78
intellectual property 157
nucleus substitution 187–93
    See, also, Nucleus substitution
oocyte preservation
    and ovarian
        tissue storage 194–99
ovarian tissue and
    gametes, legality of
        taking and storing 194–99
patents 157
privacy 159–78
public interest 166–68
public policy 199–200
regulation 180–200
screening 160–61
Gernsheim-Beck, E 35, 173, 177
Giddens, A 10–11,
                                41, 200
Gillick test 174
Glenn, P 27
Glover, J 13, 111,
                                136, 142,
                                151
Glover, N 21, 22,
                                24, 27
Goffman, E 159
Gostin, L 232, 233
Gough, I 49
Gray, J 17, 18, 50,
                                227, 255–56
Griffith, J 33
Grubb, A 97–98, 100,
                                108, 109,
                                113, 243

Hansmann, H 99
Harris, J 149
Healthcare 227
Health, right to 47–61
allocation 48–50
generally 47–48
health care, rights to 53–54
    opportunity costs
        of rhetoric 54–61
human rights 51
rights 50–53
Hill, C 81, 179
Hobsbawm, E 10, 11, 34,
                                37, 179
Hollis, M 257
Holmes, OW 107–08
Homans, H 63
Human Tissue Act 1961 196–99
Hyper-regulation 33

Illich, I 50, 205,
                                207, 225
Inkelfinger, F 22
Intellectual property,
    genetics 157
IVF
    See Reproductive technology

Jennings, B 19, 34
Jonas, H 39, 42, 173
Justice 7
distributive 8–9
types 7

Kass, L 205, 254
Kennedy, I 100, 109,
                                209
Klein, D 70
Koch, L 64, 73, 74

Living wills
  See Advance directives
Locke, J 86, 91
Locked in syndrome 206
Lynn, J 224, 235, 256

McKeown, T 17, 50, 207
Maclean, A 65, 79, 169
Mclean Report 198
Maddox, J 156, 158
Market in organs 99
Mason, K 99, 142
Matthews, P 93, 94, 97
Medical jurisprudence,
  vocabulary 7–11
    constituting
      medical law 9–11
    treat me gentle 7–9
Medical law,
  amalgam of
    legal categories 3, 4
  blaming in 4
  claiming in 4, 5
  construction 9–11
  context 3–4
  declaiming in 4, 5
  developments 4
  dynamic 3, 4
  elements 4
  human values 6
  jurisprudence 6
  meaning 3–11
    conceptual questions 5–6
  metamorphoses
    See Metamorphoses in
      medical law
  naming 4
  philosophy 6
  responsibility, as 3
  subject, as 3

traditional areas 4
unplugged 3–6
Metamorphoses
  in medical law 13–36
  constitution, changing 24–32
    See, also, Constitution
  epistemology 18–20
  ethics 18–20
  generally 11, 13
  nature of law's responses 32–36
  patient, nature of 20–24
  scientific medicine 13–18
Montgomery, J 47, 175, 176, 234

Naffine, N 90, 91
Nelkin, D 159
Nozick, R 48–49, 50
Nucleus substitution 187–93
  Dolly technique 187–88, 190, 191
  identity issues 187–88
  legal argument 190–93
  licences 187
  moral argument 188–90
  techniques 190
  Warnock Committee 188, 189
Nuffield Council
  on Bioethics 92

Oakley, A 146
Oncomice 101
Oocyte preservation
  and ovarian
    tissue storage 194–99
Ovarian tissue and gametes,
  legality of taking
    and storing 194–99
Ownership of the body 83–104
  autonomy and 83–91
  body shopping 97–104

common law 92–97
DNA 102–03
domination, human 85–86
embryo 99–101
generally 83
genetic information 102–03
individuation of
  the body 84
Kant, I 85,
  87–88, 91
Locke, J 86
Mill, JS 85
Nuffield Council
  on Bioethics 92
oncomice 101
ownership 84–87
patient, nature of 84
philosophy 85–86
property 85–86
shopping, body 97–104
theft 96–97
who owns the body 90–91

Patents,
  genetics .157
Patient,
  identity 19
  nature of 20–24
Pattinson, S 191
Pearlman, R 226
Pharmacogenetics 16, 17
Physician assisted
  suicide 203, 204
Porter, R 13, 18
Posthumous
  treatments 123
Privacy,
  genetics 159–78

Public interest,
  genetics 166–68
Pullen, I 164

Ramsey, P 226
Reproductive
  technology 63–81
  assisted reproduction 64
  biomedical model 69–81
  choice, reproductive 75–76
  complexity 65
  constitutive aspect
    of law .66
  contextualist
    approach 71–75
  ethics .76–81
  feminist account 63–81
    assisted
      reproduction 64
    biomedical model 69–81
    categories
      of feminism 67–68
    choice, reproductive 75–76
    contextualist
      approach 71–75
    different approaches 64
    ethics 76–81
    regulation, response to 68–69
  globalisation 64–65
  reasons for examining 63–66
  scope 63
  surrogacy 65–66
Rights 8, 9
Risk society 10, 33
Rose, G .19, 78
Rothman, BK 147, 151

Samsa, G 32
Saunders, J 226

Scientific medicine,
metamorphoses
in medical law 13–18
Scientific progress 10
Sex identification 129–51
abortion 144–51
ambit of Abortion
Act 1967 147–49
male children,
mania for 146–47
prevalence of
sex selection 144–47
reproductive ethics 149–51
appeal of 129
congenital
malformations,
screening for 134
diagnostic issues 129–31
ethical dilemma,
external 141–44
internal 140–41
inherited diseases,
screening for 135–36
issues 129
methods 131–33
perfect body,
search for the 136–40
screening,
congenital
malformations 134
inherited diseases 135–36
techniques 129, 131–33
uses of selection 133

Silver, L 186, 188–89
Skene, L 181–82
Smart, C 64
Spallone, P 70
Stephens, RL 250
Strathern, M 80, 158
Surrogacy 65–66
Susskind, R 33

Teubner, G.....................103
Transplants 42, 99
See, also, Ownership
of the body

United States,
right to die 210–13

Ward of court,
fetus 115
Warnock Committee 108–09,
114, 149,
188, 189
Watson, J 155
Williams, B 48
Williams, P 78
Wittgenstein, L 226
Wolf, S 23
Wynne, B 156